MW01155732

Fiesta, Harlequin, & Kitchen Kraft Dinnerwares

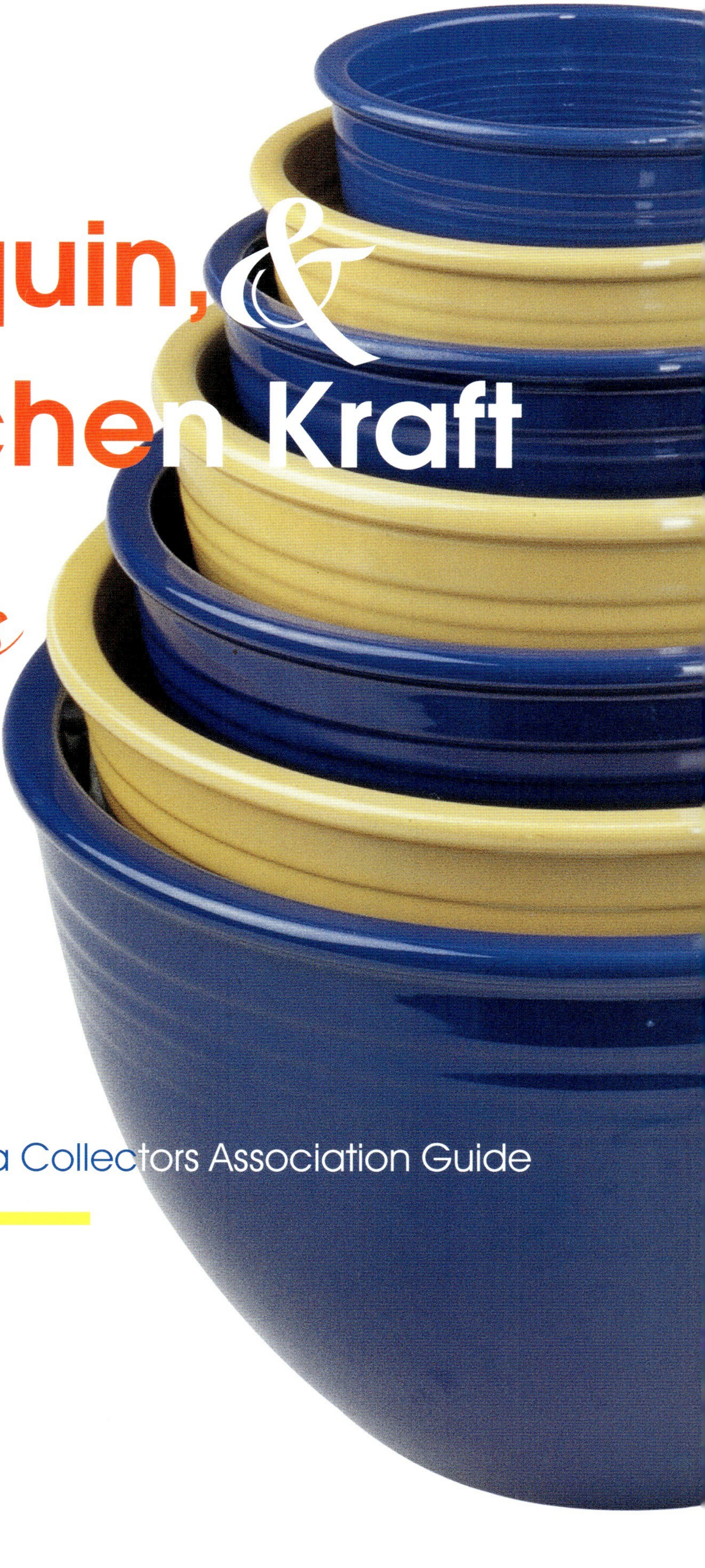

The Homer Laughlin China Collectors Association Guide

4880 Lower Valley Road, Atglen, PA 19310 USA

Library of Congress Cataloging-in-Publication Data

Fiesta, Harlequin, & Kitchen Kraft dinnerwares : the Homer Laughlin China Collectors Association guide.
p. cm.
ISBN 0-7643-1148-4 (hardcover)
1. Homer Laughlin China Company--Catalogs. 2. Ceramic tableware--Ohio--Catalogs. 3. Ceramic tableware--Collectors and collecting--United States--Catalogs. 4. Pottery--Marks--Catalogs. I. Title: Fiesta, Harlequin, and Kitchen Kraft dinnerwares. II. Homer Laughlin China Collectors Association.
NK4210.H65 A4 2000
738'.09754'12075--dc21
00-008593

Designed by Bonnie M. Hensley
Type set in Avantgarde Bk BT/ZapfHumnst BT

ISBN: 0-7643-1148-4
Printed in China
1 2 3 4

Published by Schiffer Publishing Ltd.
4880 Lower Valley Road
Atglen, PA 19310
Phone: (610) 593-1777; Fax: (610) 593-2002
E-mail: Schifferbk@aol.com
Please visit our web site catalog at
www.schifferbooks.com

This book may be purchased from the publisher.
Include $3.95 for shipping. Please try your bookstore first.
We are always looking for authors to write books on new and related subjects. If you have an idea for a book please contact us at the address above.
You may write for a free printed catalog.

In Europe, Schiffer books are distributed by
Bushwood Books
6 Marksbury Avenue
Kew Gardens
Surrey TW9 4JF England
Phone: 44 (0)208-392-8585; Fax: 44 (0)208-392-9876
E-mail: Bushwd@aol.com
Free postage in the UK., Europe; air mail at cost.

Contents

Chapter 3. Fiesta Evolves

Chapter 4. Fiesta Ironstone

Chapter 5. Post-1986 Fiesta

Chapter 6. Kitchen Kraft

Acknowledgments

This book is the result of a collaborative effort by dedicated members of the Homer Laughlin China Collectors Association. Specialists on individual topics have combined their knowledge to create this magnificent study. In alphabetical order, the book committee members are:

Steven Beals – Principal author of Vintage Fiesta and Kitchen Kraft sections. Steve has been collecting Fiesta for a number of years and had amassed tremendous knowledge on the history of Fiesta, its production, variations, and marketing. Steve was an indispensable resource for this project with contributions to research, photography, drawing, and writing.

Deane Bergsrud – Deane has been collecting Fiesta and Harlequin for over 20 years and is one of the leading authorities on Fiesta and Harlequin based on his collecting experience.

Ben Bright – Treasurer HLCCA 1998-1999. Ben also spent a number of hours for the HLCCA driving to and from the HLC factory and libraries to copy research material.

Cinda Gambill – Secretary HLCCA 1998-2000.

Joseph Jordan – A noted collector, Joe spent countless hours in libraries from Pittsburgh to Newell and East Liverpool.

Fred Mutchler – Editor of the entire project. Fred spent countless hours and sleepless nights editing and assembling the text for this project. Fred is a noted collector of many patterns of Homer Laughlin China and related paper and ephemera amassed over the last 20 years. Fred was also the first Grand Award Winner in the 1999 HLCCA conference exhibition category.

Terri Polick – Principal author of the sections related to Post-1986 Fiesta. Terri has been an unbelievable asset to this project. In preparation for writing her text, Terri spent many days interviewing HLC employees in the fall of 1999 regarding their work. Terri also is a frequent contributor of *The Dish*, the HLCCA magazine. When not writing, Terri collects Post-1986 Fiesta.

David Schaefer – Editor, HLCCA. During David's 15 years of collecting Fiesta, Harlequin, HLC art pottery, and paper ephemera, his collections have been featured on television and in various magazine publications. David is editor and production director for *The Dish* and edited text with Fred and consulted on the project.

Saarin Schwartz – Vice President HLCCA 1999-2001.

Sam Skillern – Contributor to sections related to ephemera. Sam is a noted ephemera collector, specializing in paper items related to Homer Laughlin China.

Vince Varia – Vice President HLCCA 1998-1999, Principal author of the sections on Harlequin. Vince has been an avid Harlequin collector for many years and jumped at the opportunity to share his knowledge with fellow enthusiasts of Fiesta's colorful cousin. Vince is also the author of a regular column in *The Dish*, the HLCCA publication.

Jake Wesner – Treasurer HLCCA 1999-2001.

Matthew Whalen – President HLCCA 1998-2000. Matthew Whalen was the chairperson of the committee, arranged for the photographs appearing in this book, and analyzed the price data submitted by the HLCCA membership. Matthew also served as the liaison between the book committee and our editor at Schiffer Publishing, Nancy Schiffer.

This book could never have been written without the support of a very large number of people. It is impossible to list them all in this brief space, however, there are several that we must thank and show our sincere gratitude for their help.

Terral Rich and Gregory Schmuker were gracious enough to allow us disrupt their home and business to photograph their collection. The majority of the photos in this book were taken in their home over several days in April, 1999. Thank you very much for all your help and support.

Thank you, Jonathan O. Parry and the staff of the Art Department at the Homer Laughlin

China Company. Mr. Parry literally opened the doors to the past and allowed our researchers to examine and photocopy pages from Frederick Hurten Rhead's personal journals. He also provided copies of the "Modeling Log Book" kept by Rhead and his modelers over an eleven-year period from 1933 to 1944. These two very informative documents provided the basis for our in-depth study of Fiesta, Harlequin, and Fiesta Kitchen Kraft. Without access to the information contained within them, our book would not exist. He also provided invaluable insight during our research and questioning on the "new" Fiesta line that likewise will assist many collectors in their understanding of the ongoing tradition.

The members of the HLCCA completed two surveys for this book. The second was very large and provided the majority of the pricing information. Thank you to everyone that took the time to complete the survey. We know it was difficult to complete, and we appreciate your dedication. Thank you to Jill Popowich for all the help working on the drawings with us and Darrell Ertzberger for editing assistance.

Also, we wish to extend a special thank you to Sharon Dale, Ph.D. of the University of Pennsylvania, Erie and to the Erie Art Museum for photographs and text on the history of Frederick Rhead. Sharon Dale is the author of "Frederick Hurten Rhead: An English Potter in America." Ellen Hochheiser, Ph.D. provided the information on glaze safety, lead hazards, and radiation risks. Ellen.Hocheiser is Manager of Operational Health Physics at the University of Arizona. Marcia Kinnear and Joel Wilson (*Fiesta Collector's Quarterly*) gave permission to adapt Marcia's excellent analysis on color trends.

We also want to recognize the encouragement, assistance, and dedication of the dozens of individuals who felt this project was worthwhile. Their contributions included everything from the confirmation of glaze colors on certain items to the lending of expensive pieces for photographs. Our friends and families certainly played a major role in finishing the book. With their support, we were able to focus on the project and accomplish our goal of producing the most comprehensive book on the subject to date.

Finally, we need to thank our readers. By purchasing this book, you are supporting the principal cause of the Homer Laughlin China Collectors Association: education. Revenue from this work will enable us to produce more books on Homer Laughlin china in the future.

The following people gave much needed support and help:

Buck Barnes
Steven Beals
Bill Beck
Deane Bergsrud
Joe and Michele Boeckholt
Ben Bright
Ken Brown
Daniel J Carter, Ph.D.
Angel and Tim Cogan
David Conley
Brian Cover
Gary Crabtree
Pat Crowley and Jan Tuckwood
Ann Culler
Tim and Karen Cunningham
Sharon Dale, Ph.D.
Jean Danko
Jeff Daugherty
Chuck and Margaret Denlinger
Darrell Ertzberger
Candy Fagerlin
Brian and Stephanie Fischer
Andy and Jane Flachs
Brian and Judy Franks
Keith Fred
Cinda Gambill
Joseph Geisse
Mark Gonzalez
Ellen Hochheiser, Ph.D.
Anthony Jones
Joseph Jordan
Gordon Kiger
Marcia Kinnear
Jennifer Lange
Harvey C. Linn, Jr.
Ronald Lombardi
Bill Mackall
Kevin McCarty
Marvin McNuss
Fred Mutchler
Bob Niemi
Judi Noble
Paul Nowack
Jonathan O. Parry
Bradley Payne and Sarah Gatza
Diane Petipas
Terri Polick
Jill Popowich
Terral Rich
Mark Rumbolo
David Schaefer
Nancy Schiffer
Gregory Schmuker
Saarin Schwartz
Ralph Sheets, Ph.D.
Pat Shreve
Sam Skillern
Therese Smith
Randy and Becky Stephens
John Stokes
Vince Varia
George Vincel
John Waugh
Jake Wesner
Matthew Whalen
Nancy Williams
Joel Wilson
Lucille Wilson
Rod Wilson

Chapter 1

The Homer Laughlin China Company and its Markings

Introduction

The year was 1872. The location - East Liverpool, Ohio. The parties involved - the city council and two brothers, Homer and Shakespeare Laughlin. Anticipating an end to the appeal of the yellow ware of the day, the city council offered $5,000 to anyone that would agree to build a 4-kiln pottery to produce white ware. The Laughlin brothers entered and won the ensuing competition and proceeded to build a pottery in East Liverpool. Although Homer and his brother had worked in the pottery industry prior to this point, it had been primarily in sales and production. They were not technical experts when it came to making the ware.

In spite of their inexperience, they accepted the assembly's bonus on September 1, 1873 and proceeded to break ground for the new plant a month later on October 1. They opened for production the following year on September 1, 1874. The advance into the history books begins there and continues to today.

The original plant struggled due to lack of experience and little capital. White ware had not been produced in the area before this time and the Laughlin's had had no previous exposure to it as well. It has been told that the first batch of ware out of the kilns was cups and that when this new white ware cooled all the handles promptly fell off. Unyielding to a few early setbacks, they pressed on. Originally named "The Ohio Valley Pottery" and then "Laughlin Bros. Pottery," by 1874 they had enough success to grow to one hundred employees. A short two years later, in 1876, they were awarded a medal for best white ware at the Centennial Exposition in Philadelphia, Pennsylvania and they were on their way to being regarded as a quality white ware producer in the market of the day.

In 1880 Homer hired W.E. Wells as bookkeeper. Wells would eventually become the general manager and today his descendants still run the company. Throughout the late 1800s Homer Laughlin produced a variety of ware. Primarily a basic white ware that could be used in hotels and other public institutions, the plant also turned out what truly could be deemed genuine American china. Following a demonstration of its translucence and vitreous qualities J. Simms, editor of the local newspaper, wrote "It is no longer a question of doubt that the finest, thinnest and most translucent of china can be produced in America."

Homer Laughlin retired from the business to pursue business interests in California in 1897. Wells and the Aarons - Louis, Marcus and Charles - purchased interests in the company with Louis Aaron as president and Wells as secretary and general manager and it was decided that they needed to expand.

In 1899 they built a new plant east of the original pottery known as plant #2. Just two years later they built plant #3 along side plant #2. After this expansion and with thirty-two kilns, they were still unsatisfied. Motivated by the demand for their wares the owners wished to expand further, however there was no suitable land in the east end of East Liverpool near their existing plants. They turned their vision across the Ohio River in West Virginia and there pursued the purchase of a three-mile tract of land in a small community that would become known as Newell. The location had the elements to remain successful in the highly competitive pottery industry - access to fuel, an existing railroad, and river transportation. After creating the North American Manufacturing Company to develop the property into a viable industrial location, the Homer Laughlin Company set about developing this relatively inaccessible parcel of West Virginia. At the time, the only way to get to the property from Ohio was by ferry. By 1904 they had begun construction of a metal suspension bridge. Called the Newell Bridge today, it is still in operation as a toll bridge across the river. The first traffic moved across on July 4, 1905. The little town of Newell grew to a prospering community with one hundred thirty additional homes in 1907.

The plant expanded with the same fervor as well. Considered the largest in the world at that time and covering ten acres, it extended 700 feet along the Ohio riverbank. This large plant stood five stories tall and had fifteen acres of total floor space. With the addition of this new plant in January 1907, there were sixty-two firing kilns and forty-eight decorating kilns capable of producing approximately 300,000 pieces of ware each day. In 1914 they added plant #5, with sixteen additional kilns, just to the north of plant #4 and by 1919-1920 they were ready to expand once again.

The pottery industry was changing extensively at this time with new technologies for better and more efficient production. These changes required the introduction of science and scientists into the business and Homer Laughlin was once again an industry leader. HLC hired Albert Victor Bleininger, a scientist in ceramics, and he would remain with the company until his death in 1946. His first task was to build a new plant - plant #6. This plant was built across from and to the south of plant #4 and was the largest pottery ever constructed in the world. The plant was 290 feet wide by 800 feet long. In the extensive basement, HLC mixed the clay, flint, and feldspar.

Under Bleininger's tutelage, the new plant was to be a leader in the worldwide manufacturing of ceramics. It was state-of-the-art with a major innovation being the construction of tunnel kilns. These tunnel kilns were of continuous operation unlike their predecessor bottle kilns. The plant also had other technological advantages that allowed for further streamlining the entire process.

Following the success of plant #6, in 1927 they built plant #7 as well as replacing the bottle kilns in plants #4 and #5 with more tunnel kilns. Because the three oldest plants in East Liverpool were soon obsolete, HLC abandoned them and in 1928, Laughlin built plant #8 just south of plant #6. This new and final plant replaced all the old plants in Ohio and the company was now firmly entrenched in West Virginia. Plant #8 was 1,200 feet long and 300 feet wide and employed 900 people, equal to numbers at plants #6 and #7 combined. The Homer Laughlin China Company employed 3,500 people at peak employment.

Frederick Hurten Rhead, one of the world's foremost ceramists of the day, was hired by HLC in 1927 and stayed with the company until his death in 1942. Rhead's first job was to update the company's pottery selection, most of which had been in production for decades. He slowly changed the product over a period of several years and in 1935 he created Fiesta ware. As shown in this publication, Fiesta would become HLC's most popular and most collected line of Homer Laughlin China. Rhead also created Kitchen Kraft, Riviera (from the Century line), and Harlequin that was the Woolworth Companies biggest seller.

Peak production for the company was in 1948 when they produced 10,129,449 dishes. The year 1959 saw the adaptation of plant #6 to produce heavy vitreous ware for restaurants. Hundreds of hotels and restaurants across the country continue to use Laughlin restaurant ware today.

W.E. Wells retired from the company in 1930 and his son, Joseph Wells, succeeded him. Following in the family's history, his son Joseph Wells Jr. became general manager in 1960. His son, Joseph Wells III, also became executive vice-president. In 1986, Joseph Wells III would become general manager. In like manner, the Aaron family had deep ties to the company. Louis Aaron passed the duties of president of the board to his son, Marcus Aaron, in 1911. In 1940, Marcus Lester Aaron became president eventually retiring in 1989 after 65 years of service. His son Marcus Aaron II would succeed him.

The Homer Laughlin China Company is still America's largest producer of china and the company still operates at the Newell, West Virginia site.

Frederick Hurten Rhead

The following text is adopted from "Frederick Hurten Rhead: An English Potter in America" by Sharon Dale, Ph.D. and is used with permission of the author and the Erie Art Museum.

Like his subject, Frederick Hurten Rhead was a distinctive blend of the old and the new. Steeped by patrimony and taste in the pottery of Staffordshire, Rhead's work executed in the United States were the syntheses of British commercial designs, contemporary art styles and American conceptual clarity. Rhead was not a singular genius, but a talented and prolific designer who significantly improved the quality of mass-produced ceramics in the United States and subtly, yet insistently, altered the pottery esthetic of his adopted country.

A study of Rhead's design process reveals several important features. First and foremost, Rhead was not an especially original designer. Despite his oft-voiced contempt for lack of originality in art, Rhead's best designs are usually brilliant adaptations from other sources.

After working for the Vance/Avon pottery and the S. A. Weller pottery, Rhead was named Art Director of Roseville in 1904. Although Rhead had substantially altered the Roseville product within two years of his arrival, his particular inventiveness was not fully apparent until the design of "Della Robbia." This line, developed in 1905 and produced in 1906, established Rhead as a major figure in American art pottery.

After periods at other potteries such as Arequipa, his own studio, Rhead Pottery, and American Encaustic Tiling Company, Rhead accepted the position of Art Director at the Homer Laughlin China Company in 1927.

Rhead developed scores of designs for Homer Laughlin, which supplied dinnerware for mass merchandisers. Rhead was particularly pleased with the design of and commercial response to a

Frederick H. Rhead

Roseville Della Robbia vase, designed by Rhead. Collection of the Erie Art Museum. Photograph by Mark Fainstein.

dinnerware line combining the rectilinear shape of "Century" with a "Vellum" glaze, originally developed as part of the "Wells Art" line.

One group of "Well Art" dinnerware was especially noteworthy in Rhead's stylistic development. Rhead and Dr. Albert Bleininger developed a line featuring matte luster glazes that are stark and somewhat somber. The "Wells Art" glazes are noteworthy not only as they look backward in Rhead's career, but more importantly, for their roles as precursors to Rhead's most impressive and significant contribution at Homer Laughlin, "Fiesta," the brightly colored dinnerware that changed the look of millions of tables in America.

"Fiesta" was an industrial design revolution. Rhead took unabashed pride in the wares that featured brightly colored monochromatic glazed on sculptural, yet simple shapes. "Fiesta" made Rhead's reputation. After over thirty years in America, he had finally attained widespread recognition.

Following the success of "Fiesta," Rhead introduced variants on the theme, "Harlequin," which was sold exclusively at Woolworth's, and "Riviera," which combined the rectilinear "Century" shape with the "Fiesta" colored glazes.

Rhead's career at Homer Laughlin was cut short in 1942 by a diagnosis of cancer. By September of that year, Rhead has moved to New York and by October, he had entered Memorial Hospital where he died on November 2, 1942.

Identification

From its founding in 1873, the Homer Laughlin China Company has had a policy of marking its products. That's good news for today's collectors because it usually makes identification of the ware easier. Hundreds of dinnerware lines in solid colors were made between 1930 and 1960. Telling them apart can be difficult and frustrating for collectors and dealers. Many potteries did not mark their ware at all and others marked only some pieces. People not familiar with these lines often use "Fiesta" as a generic term for all colored ware. Knowing what marks to look for and which type of mark was used on the various HLC shapes will make it easier to tell the difference between Fiesta and the other lines. This section will provide examples of most of the marks used on Fiesta, Harlequin, and Fiesta Kitchen Kraft as well as explain how and why they were applied.

In general, there are three ways for pottery to be marked. The logo or name of the ware can be applied with a rubber stamp, either by hand or by machine. The name can be impressed into the clay when the piece is formed. This can be accomplished by actually stamping the ware with an iron or steel device, or the mark can be formed as part of a mold. Using a paper label is the third method. All three types of marks were used for the HLC colored ware being discussed in this book.

The type of mark made with a rubber stamp is called a backstamp. The "ink" used was actually a form of glaze, a ceramic color, that would not burn off in the kiln. It was applied by hand to the ware in the bisque stage (see below) before the colored glaze was applied.

The impressed mark can also be called "in-mold", "inscribed", or "indented" because of the way the design appears to have been pressed into wet clay. This type of mark on HLC pottery was created as part of a mold and was not actually engraved in the clay.

There is no documented use of paper labels on Fiesta or Harlequin, but they were applied to most Kitchen Kraft items.

Pottery Shapes and Production Methods

In order to understand pottery marks one must have some knowledge of how pottery is made. It is beyond the scope of this book to explain every step of the process in detail. Only the basic methods are presented. A distinction must first be made between flatware and hollowware because they tend to be marked differently. In general, flatware refers to plates, platters, and some low, open bowls. These items are usually marked with a rubber stamp, although some flatware can have an in-mold mark. Hollowware consists of vessels such as teapots, sauceboats, and carafes. Hollowware is made by slip casting and usually has an impressed mark.

Jigger and Jolly

To create a piece of pottery by jiggering means one side of the piece is formed in a plaster mold and the other side by scraping with a metal blade, called the "tool", as the mold (or the blade) rotates. Technically, when the inside or top of a piece is formed by a mold and the back or bottom by the tool it is said to be jiggered. When the outside of an item is shaped by a mold and the inside by the tool it is called jollying. In the ceramic industry today "jiggered" is commonly used for both jiggered and jollied ware.

For example, the face of a Fiesta plate, with its intricately carved concentric rings, was created by a plaster mold. Plates were made upside down. A piece of clay was placed in the center of the mold, the mold was rapidly rotated, and the back of the plate was shaped by the jigger "tool" as it was lowered manually to spread out and shape the clay. At HLC this was done by hand until the 1940s when an automatic jigger was installed and many items were switched to the new machine. Cups and cup shaped objects are also made by jiggering. The outside of the cup is formed by a mold, the inside by a spinning tool.

A manual jigger machine.

Ram Press

Some flatware is made on a ram press. Items that are flat, but not round, cannot be jiggered since they cannot be rotated evenly on a central axis. Ram press items are made by hydraulically squeezing two molds together after a piece of clay is placed between them. Ram press molds are called "dies." Ware made by the ram press method may have an impressed mark as part of the die or a backstamp can be applied later. Fiesta's oval platter, early utility trays, and some relish tray parts were made this way.

Slip Casting

Hollow pieces are cast from liquid clay, called slip, by pouring it into a plaster mold. The mold absorbs water from the slip leaving a deposit of clay on the inner surface of the mold. After a certain amount of time, the remaining slip is poured out and the mold is set aside. When the clay layer is hard enough, the mold is opened and the seam lines are removed, or "finished", by hand.

Slip cast ware is marked in the mold. That is, the mark is part of the mold and as water is absorbed, the clay forms around the mark. This leaves an impression of the mark in the clay body of the item. This type of mark looks engraved or impressed, but it is formed as the item itself is formed from the liquid slip.

Bisque Firing and Glazing

Until the 1980s, most of HLC's products were made in a two-fire process. The ware was fired in two kilns, a bisque kiln and a glost kiln. Bisque comes from "biscuit" meaning hard and dry, like baked goods such as crackers or cookies. The first firing changes the soft clay into hard ceramic. The ware was then allowed to cool, usually for days or weeks, before glaze was applied. The glost kiln was used for the second firing, which solidified the glaze into a hard covering on the ceramic piece. Backstamps were applied to ware in the bisque stage before the glaze was applied.

All ware created at HLC today is made using a one-fire process. The same methods are used to form the clay into shapes, but a different clay formula is used. This clay can be glazed after drying and sent through only one kiln that hardens the clay and the glaze at the same time. Once fired ware tends to have a better bond between the glaze and the ceramic body that makes it stronger and more resistant to chipping and cracking.

Markings

Marks on Fiesta

There is one fact about Fiesta that makes it much easier to tell the real thing from other colored ware: it was usually marked. Some items may have missed being marked due to human error, but nearly every item in the line was marked or was supposed to be marked. As stated previously, flatware, such as plates and platters, generally received the "Genuine Fiesta" backstamp. Hollowware, such as teapots and carafes, and most open bowls had an impressed mark. There are a few exceptions, but knowing these basics can save a novice collector from inadvertently buying a Fiesta "look alike."

The manner in which each item in the Fiesta line was marked, as well as the method used for its production, is covered in the main Fiesta section of the book. Over the years, the way some Fiesta items were made was changed. Sometimes the method of marking the piece changed as well. Collectors may find the same item marked in two different ways. Any differences like this are explained in the main Fiesta section.

A few items in the Fiesta line were not marked. The usual reason for not marking something was because there was no space for a mark due to the size or shape of the piece. The following items were not intended to have marks: teacups, A.D. coffee cups, salt and pepper shakers, mustards, sweets comports, and juice tumblers. Of course, there are always exceptions. Some examples of these six items have been found with a rubber stamped "HLCo USA". It is generally believed that this mark was used on ware exported to other countries. Most of these marked pieces have been reported by collectors in Canada, which supports the export theory.

Some collectors feel that none of the early Fiesta flatware was marked, or that only certain pieces were marked. This is the reason, they say, that so many plates are found without a backstamp. We were not able to find anything to confirm this. However, there are three early items, all discontinued before 1938, which were never marked: flat cake plates, 12" compartment plates, and mixing bowl lids. The cake plate may have been made for another company and not marked for that reason.

See the main Fiesta section for detailed information on each of these nine unmarked items.

Fiesta mixing bowl with impressed mark and ink stamp

Rhead's Notes On Fiesta Marks

Frederick Rhead's journal mentions specific marks, or items used in marking the ware, several times. Some insight into the process of the tools needed to mark ware can be gained by reading the relevant entries.

May 14, 1935: "[From] J.M.W.-to work on a mark 'Fiesta' for molds of colored wares."

May 16, 1935: "Sketches of mark for Fiesta ware. Drawings for clay stamp and for cutting in cases."

May 18, 1935: "Made... drawings of 'Fiesta' stamp for molds and clay stamp."

These passages seem to indicate that HLC intended to mark all items from the beginning. The "clay stamp" would be used for placing a backstamp on flatware.

May 20, 1935: "Fiesta stamp inquiry to Matthews. Also, commenced the incise mark on moulds. June 26, 1935: Fiesta stamp here from Matthews. Gave this to Al Croft [Kraft?]—asked him to advise me with regard to satisfactory operation."

Two companies made rubber stamps for use by HLC on Fiesta. James Matthews owned a rubber stamp company in Pittsburgh. That company produced the first rubber stamps used for Fiesta. Relevant records were not available for our researchers, so we were unable to determine what the original backstamp looked like. Evidence exists that identifies Quality Stamp Company of East Liverpool, Ohio as the maker of the later "Genuine" Fiesta backstamps.

In the "Record of Sketches and Drawings" Rhead recorded: "May 19 [1935], #411, mark for molds, Fiesta line and #412, mark for clay stamp, Fiesta line." In March 1937 he created drawings of the Fiesta logo for the U.S. Patent Office when HLC officially registered it as a trademark. The Patent Office drawing can be seen in the Modeling Log Information section of the appendix.

The "Genuine Fiesta" Backstamp

On January 23, 1939 Rhead wrote in his journal: "A.A.W. [Arthur A. Wells, in charge of production at plant #4] Genuine Fiesta stamp. (Gave sample above to A.A.W.)" This is the only reference we could find to the use of the word "genuine" on the Fiesta backstamp.

It has been suggested that "genuine" was added to the backstamp as a result of a lawsuit by HLC against a competitor for copying the look of Fiesta. We found very little about the lawsuit in Rhead's journals. A June 10, 1938 note says, "Named by Campbell for lawsuit in Dayton." Then, at the bottom of the page, "Case postponed until Tuesday or Wednesday." Rhead did refer to one company copying the designs of another in his January 1939 report as chairman of the Art and Design Committee of the United States Potters' Association. His report was presented at the annual meeting in Washington, D.C. While discussing "Colored Glazes" he said:

> In last year's report we commented upon the possibilities in connection with this type of tableware, provided that each manufacturer interested in such a product created and developed a distinctive and non-imitative type. We enlarged upon the fact that a competent art organization could create and develop distinctive wares of this character which would in no way conflict with types already developed.
>
> What happened? One organization, via the usual town-pump channels, plus a complete lack of business and developmental imagination, not only deliberately copied a successful and already established colored-glaze ware, but in addition it appropriated and adopted the sales and merchandizing set-up of the successful product. Even the name of the successful product was pirated so closely that there was no doubt in the mind of anyone in the business that such was the case.
>
> The result was disastrous. Commercially and artistically the line was a complete and expensive flop and deservedly so. We hope that this venture will be a lesson to that type of organization whose creative and developmental program such as it is, has been dominated by the influence of the town-pump salesmen.

Fiesta 2 pint jug with impressed mark and "5" size marking

While a couple companies come to mind, we cannot say for sure which was the target of the suit. Regardless, the story about how the Fiesta backstamp came to include "genuine" is an interesting one.

The question still remains whether it was used from the beginning or not until 1939. For now, we support the theory that early flatware was not marked at all and items that did receive a backstamp were marked with one that had the word "genuine" as part of it.

One variety of impressed mark

"Made in USA" Impressed Marks

When Frederick Rhead created the incised mark to be used on Fiesta items it was a simple script "Fiesta" with "H.L.C. U.S.A." below it. Molds for jiggering or slip casting were made from a master mold. The master was, in turn, made from the original model. Any writing or lettering on the model was created manually by the modeler. One would expect hand-made letters, especially the script "Fiesta," to be different on each model made. Yet they are surprisingly consistent. This logo is so carefully repeated on several different shapes that it might indicate that a pattern or metal stamp of some sort was used to create it. However, we were unable to verify this.

The early "Fiesta HLC USA" mark was unadorned. It was the only thing present on the bottom of items such as the stick-handled creamer or marmalade and was usually surrounded by a significant amount of empty space. Three rings encircled later versions of this mark and on some items the whole mark was also made larger. It cannot be reliably determined when this revised mark was used, but it had to be between the end of 1936 and the end of 1937.

Toward the end of 1937 HLC changed the impressed mark on Fiesta items. The words "MADE IN USA" replaced "HLC USA". The "HLC" was retained, but would appear above or below the new logo depending upon the item being marked. A stylized monogram of the HLC initials frequently accompanied this revised mark.

Most collectors are not concerned with exactly dating the Fiesta that is in their collections. Glaze colors, obviously, are a way to do that, but the different versions of the impressed mark can also be used. Items added to the line after late 1937 will generally be found with only the "MADE IN USA" version of the mark. Items in production before the new logo was adopted had their marks changed to include it as new molds were needed. The changeover to the new mark on all items in production probably took several years, with some items not being revised until the 1940s.

Another variation on the "Made in U.S.A." Fiesta mark.

Fiesta Made Since 1986

Several slip cast and jiggered items in the contemporary Fiesta line are made from the original Fiesta molds. Therefore, they carry the same inscribed marks as the vintage ware and the marks cannot be used to tell the difference between the two lines. Shapes newly created for today's Fiesta have markings designed by the current modelers at HLC and are distinctly different from the vintage marks.

Glaze colors are the best way to tell old from new. However, some new glazes, such as Pearl Gray, look very much like the vintage colors and can fool even veteran collectors. Homer Laughlin has attempted to alleviate some of the confusion by adding a small "H" to items bearing older impressed marks. The letter H was chosen because it is easy to add to existing molds. Markings in a mold appear as mirror images when one views the mold directly. Unlike most other letters, an H can easily be written "backwards" in the mold to produce the letter correctly when the piece is made. HLC started using the H with the introduction of the new chartreuse glaze in early 1998.

Additional marks may be found on new Fiesta items made with the ram press. Generally this will be oval platters and relish/utility trays. The plaster molds for the ram press are called dies. A raised "ZZ" or "GG" indicate the die maker.

A rubber backstamp is used on contemporary Fiesta, mainly on plates and some bowls. It is applied to jiggered items that cannot have an in-mold mark due to the manufacturing process. The earliest version of the backstamp has basically the same information as the vintage mark, including "genuine" and "HLC USA", but does not look the same. This mark was not used on cups or items with an inscribed mark. Starting in 1991 or 1992 "lead free" was added and shortly after that a new stamp was designed that included a date code. Around 1995 HLC began marking cups, mugs, and tumblers, in addition to the plates and bowls, with this newest stamp.

The date coding system in use at HLC today had its beginnings in the 1960s when a single letter of the alphabet represented the year. Current backstamps have two letters for the year with a third letter indicating the yearly quarter. The pair "JJ" is 1995, "KK" is 1996, "LL" is 1997, and so on. An "A" after the year code indicates the first quarter of the year, "B" is the second quarter, "C" is the third, and "D" is the fourth. Thus a piece marked "LLC" was made during July, August, or September of 1997. This does not mean that glaze was applied and the piece was shipped in those months. It only means that the clay shape was made during that quarter.

Backstamps are applied by machine now and are placed on the item as soon as it is created. The ware can sit in racks for weeks before being glazed and fired, then for months before being shipped. The date codes should be viewed as only an approximation when trying to determine when an item was made.

According to HLC officials all contemporary Fiesta items will eventually have a backstamp, even pieces that have an impressed mark. This will provide the "lead free" designation and a date code for every item in the line.

A style of the Fiesta impressed marking

Marks on Harlequin

Because it was intended for sale by only one retailer, Harlequin was not marked with the name of the line or manufacturer. However, many Harlequin (and some Fiesta and Kitchen Kraft) items will have small impressed letters or numbers that identify the worker who created or finished the piece. They were used for quality control and perhaps for determining the salary of workers who were paid by the number of pieces made during a shift.

One style of Fiesta mark not utilizing the HLC logo.

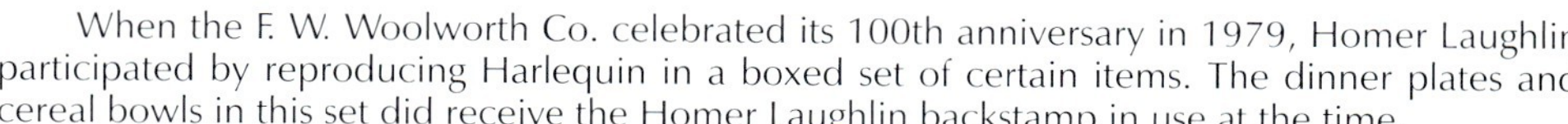

When the F. W. Woolworth Co. celebrated its 100th anniversary in 1979, Homer Laughlin participated by reproducing Harlequin in a boxed set of certain items. The dinner plates and cereal bowls in this set did receive the Homer Laughlin backstamp in use at the time.

Harlequin did not have a standardized typeface for its name on brochures and there was no mention by Rhead in his journal about markings for the line. Advertisements and flyers prepared for Woolworth's featured a Harlequin clown, which was consistently used throughout the time the ware was sold, including the 1978 reissue line.

Because it was not marked, Harlequin is frequently mistaken for Fiesta by non-collectors. The presence of a pattern made of rings or lines and the bright glazes can be confusing to those not familiar with HLC colored ware.

Marks on Fiesta Kitchen Kraft

Using existing Kitchen Kraft shapes, HLC created Fiesta Kitchen Kraft in December 1937. The HLC modeling log contains an entry labeled "KK casserole, Fiesta writing." This entry represents the original model for a new incised mark to be used on the new line. The items selected from the Kitchen Kraft line were glazed in Fiesta's red, green, yellow and blue glazes and received the new mark designating the ware as "Fiesta Kitchen Kraft." There were several sizes of the mark used, but they all look the same.

Most of the items in the Fiesta Kitchen Kraft line had impressed marks. Some items had only paper labels although the labels were also used on items with the in-mold mark.

Another form of vintage Fiesta markings.

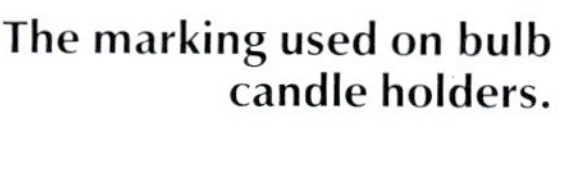

The marking used on bulb candle holders.

A clear example of the vintage ink stamp.

Mark used on Fiesta.

Chapter 2

Fiesta

Vintage Fiesta

In the late 1920s a small island pottery off the coast of Southern California began a trend in dinnerware styling that would spread across the country and last for more than two decades. The pottery started by William Wrigley on Catalina Island, twenty-two miles from Los Angeles, was the first American pottery to use glazes in bright, primary colors as the main decoration on simple dinnerware shapes. Sold on the island and distributed nationwide, the new style soon had dozens of imitators. First in and around Los Angeles, then by dinnerware manufacturers on the East Coast, including one in Newell, West Virginia.

The Homer Laughlin China Company's "Fiesta" was no mere imitation, however. It was the result of a bold marketing plan married to the designs of one of America's foremost ceramic artists. A full year was devoted to creating the shapes, testing the glazes, preparing the plant, and beginning the marketing effort that resulted in 37 years of production for Fiesta.

The success of J. A. Bauer's "California Colored Pottery" must have been a stimulus for the executives at Homer Laughlin. By 1934, Bauer had been successfully producing that line for several years. Other Los Angeles potteries, including Pacific Clay Products, Gladding-McBean, and Metlox, were also experiencing increased sales from their solid color dinnerware lines. It was time for Homer Laughlin to enjoy the benefits of the public's interest in this new trend. In the closing months of 1934, Frederick Hurten Rhead, artistic director for the company, was asked to develop a new line of colored ware for HLC.

Glaze and Clay Body Formulas

The colored glazes were the first priority. Before the end of January 1935, Rhead, along with Dr. Albert Bleininger and the staff of HLC's ceramics laboratory, began to look at dozens of colors and combinations of them. On January 25, he made a note in his daily journal, *Confab with [Harry] Thiemecke and A.V. [Bleininger] Getting plates dipped for glaze treatments to go in this kiln. Picked out upright pieces for glaze tests.* Fiesta's shapes had not yet been created, but Rhead must have had an idea in mind for them. He was selecting items from existing lines that would stand in for the new ware during these early glaze trials.

In order to obtain a broader range of colors, Dr. Bleininger ran tests with glazes that would be fired at lower temperatures than those previously used at HLC. On March 12, Rhead listed several undergoing a test run on the new shapes. Colors included were two blues, red, turquoise, two yellows, rose ebony, black, and green.

By April they had a good idea of where they were going with the colors and Rhead's journal listed the glazes under consideration: turquoise, yellow, bright red, lava red, blue, ochre, rose ebony, white, green, and buff. Soon after, Joseph M. Wells, HLC's General Manager, selected six of them for production. These colors were put into limited production on the first thirteen shapes in mid-April. The shapes were basic table setting items including plates, cups and saucers, sugar, cream, nappies, and a chop plate. Samples were sent to HLC's advertising agency and were shown to buyers from the major department stores as they visited the HLC showroom. The six colors were mandarin red, deep blue, rose ebony, white, turquoise, and yellow.

Dr. Bleininger was also working on a clay "body" for the new ware that would be compatible with the low-temperature glazes. In late July 1935, Rhead wrote, "Fiesta kiln out, A.V. states that new body is closer to solution. Less dunting. See 'dandruff' on many samples." Dunting occurs when the clay cracks due to the contraction of the glaze as it forms in the kiln. Crazing refers to cracks in the glaze which form due to contraction or expansion of the clay body. If the glaze and body do not have compatible rates of shrinkage, one or the other will break.

By mid-October Bleininger had perfected the new talc body for Fiesta and submitted a report to Rhead and HLC management about his tests of it in comparison to HLC's "regular" body and some California ware.

> A number of samples representing the California ware, our regular body and the latest talc body were subjected to oven tests in which the temperature was maintained at 395° F and five quenchings [in water] were made...
>
> A. California ware.
>
> It was found that most of the bright glazes crazed in a rather characteristic manner... However, most of the matte glazes were craze resistant though there were exceptions. The

non-crazing pieces had a tendency to dunt. As a whole we can say that each glaze has its individual characteristics from this standpoint… It might be said that from our tests it seems that the non-crazing character of the California ware has been exaggerated and that the bodies in question are not as sound as was expected.

B. Our regular body to which colored glazes maturing at our standard glost heat have been applied.

As was to be expected all of these showed a greatly superior resistance to the California ware.

C. Our regular body to which cone 03 [2014° F] glazes were applied.

Practically all of these showed a low crazing resistance and crazed in a typically open pattern of lines…

D. Low talc body No. 816, fired at cone 5 [2185° F] and with glaze fired at cone 03.

Here, as in the California ware, each glaze behaved in a manner peculiar to itself… The type of crazing observed is quite different from that of the California glazes inasmuch as the lines cannot be seen even with the magnifying glass and only immediately after the quenching is it possible to detect dark shadows apparently below the glaze surface. No permanent craze lines appear later. Three of the glazes neither dunt nor craze, tending to show that the body itself is sound… From the evidence so far collected we believe that the crazing resistance of the No. 816 body type is superior or at least the equal of the California ware… Hence we can see no objection to its commercial production as far as this quality is concerned.

With the glaze fit to the new body confirmed, the final selection of colors was made. We were not able to locate an entry in Rhead's journal that would provide the exact date, but rose ebony, white, and turquoise were eliminated and green and ivory were added. Full production probably began soon after Dr. Bleininger's report.

Frederick Rhead would later describe the hues of the final glaze colors in an article for Crockery and Glass Journal. He said, "As you know, we make five colors. An orange red, deep blue, cucumber green, egg yellow and a vellum ivory." A more detailed account of the selection process is presented in the section on Fiesta Colors later in this book.

Shape Designs

Even though Frederick Rhead is credited with designing the shapes of the new ware, it was the modelers who brought Rhead's ideas to life. Al Kraft, Bill Berrisford, and a man named Watkin were the modelers at HLC most involved with the creation of the distinctive Fiesta shapes. They could take a pen and ink or watercolor drawing and turn it into physical reality in plaster.

Using metal sculpting tools, some of which were of their own design, they carved the soft plaster into the final shape. Bowls, plates, and other round objects were formed on a rotating platform like a potter's wheel. Handles, knobs, and small decorative items were shaped and smoothed by hand from a plaster block. Because clay shrinks as it hardens in the kiln, everything had to be made approximately 10% larger than the required final size. Special "shrinkage rulers" were used to measure the models progress. This insured that the piece that came out of the kiln would be the exact size it was supposed to be.

When the model was finished, a form was placed around it and plaster poured in. This created the "block mold." From the block mold, the "master shape" mold was made. This mold, called the "case," was the basis for all the molds used on the production line for that shape.

Rhead's first journal note about the new shapes was on January 27, a Sunday. He wrote, *All day at plant. Made sketches of glazed plate, sketch 335.* In addition to a daily journal, Frederick Rhead maintained a log of the sketches and drawings he made. Unfortunately, the actual drawings no longer exist. Sketch 335 is recorded simply as, *glazed plate.* It was probably an early idea and was not even modeled in plaster. Soon, however, both the "Record of Sketches and Drawings" and the "Modeling Log Book" were full of items for the new line.

On January 30 he wrote, *Working on new shape for colored glazes. Idea to develop curve shape based upon concentric fluted circles.* Work on the shapes and the actual modeling of items began in earnest in February. Throughout that month, and the one following, Rhead made many entries in his journal related to his work on the shapes.

Rhead's desire was to create shapes that were easy to mass-produce. Intended for informal, mix-and-match use, the ware would have the glaze color as the primary decoration. He was simply following current styling trends. In an interview with the Pittsburgh editor of Ceramic Industry magazine later that year, Rhead discussed the direction pottery design was taking. He said, "…kitchenwares are becoming more ornamental and decorative… while we are still manufacturing ten Victorian styles to one of the modernistic, the trend is unmistakably toward the latter because of the effects of the new housing [design] influence." Modernism was sweeping the country and everything from automobiles to refrigerators was being influenced.

A few years later he wrote an article for *Crockery and Glass Journal* in which he explained the design process for Fiesta.

We wanted a suggestion of a stream line shape, but one which would be subordinate to texture and color. Then the shape must be jolly and pleasant, that is, convex and curving rather than concave or angular. There was to be no relief ornamentation. The color must be the chief decorative note, but in order that the shape be not too severely plain we broke the edges with varying concentric bands.

Most of his drawings for the new line were finished by April or May. A few items were added during the remainder of the year, but principal modeling was completed by September. Throughout the year, and particularly after May, the new line was shown to prospective buyers from department stores and pottery wholesalers. Rhead often took their suggestions for new items directly to the drawing board. He noted in his journal where a suggestion had originated: "Maxwell [of] Bullock's Los Angeles here. Notes on colored glaze ware – red too bright, shapes O.K. Many suggestions for shapes, noted on chart. Also noted: Meyer from Seller... [of] Los Angeles here. Likes colored glaze line. Recommended bowls – made sketch for 10" bowl – deep. Started Berrisford [on it]."

By the end of 1935 forty-two items were in production. The last one of them to be modeled, on December 27, was the ashtray. At that point, 66 models and at least 70 drawings had been created for Fiesta. Suggestions continued to come in, including one from George Fowler, head of HLC's sales department, for a mustard. The next year would see more than a dozen new shapes added to the line.

The Name

"Faience" (pronounced *feye-ahns'*) is a French term originally referring to earthenware decorated with colorful, opaque glazes first made in Faenza, Italy. It eventually came to mean any solid-color glazed earthenware. Rhead and others at HLC liked this term and used it in several combinations while trying to decide on a name for the new line. He recorded quite a few interesting suggestions in his journal:

April 1	Rhumba ware
April 5	Park Lane
	Rhapsody
	Plaza
	Faience
	Tazza
	Tazza Faience
	Chalet Faience
April 12	Dashe Faience
April 15	Flamingo

Collectors would search for it just as diligently, but what images would come to mind with a name like "Flamingo?" This name seems to have been accepted by Rhead, at least temporarily, because on April 26 he wrote, "J.M.W. up. Went over shape program for Flamingo line." However, by May 8 he was again referring to the new shapes as "colored ware."

Sometime before May 14, 1935 another name was suggested and chosen as the one to use. On that day, Rhead wrote, "To work on a mark, 'Fiesta,' for molds of colored wares." Thereafter, he used the new name whenever writing about the line. Clearly based on the Mexican/California influence, "fiesta" is a Spanish word that is based on the Latin festa (feast) and means "a festival, carnival, a religious holiday, or the celebration of a saint's day."

The bright, colored glazes must have been the stimulus for a name that suggests a party. Perhaps there was also some attempt to use a name that would bring to mind happier times for families struggling through the depressed economy of the mid-1930s. Whatever its origins, the name would become synonymous with high-quality, solid color dinnerware. As early as the last years of the 1930s consumers were using "Fiesta" as a generic term for solid color dishes, especially if Homer Laughlin made the ware. For example, Harlequin and Riviera are called "Fiesta" to this day by those who don't collect them.

There is no record of when the "dancing lady" was adopted as the human embodiment of the name, but she appears on the first price lists and in advertising to the trade in February 1936. She is, of course, a flamenco dancer and represents the spirit of the festival for which the dishes were named.

Production

During March and April 1935, Rhead's journal contains many entries related to "colored glaze kilns." Once the decision was made to use the low temperature glazes modifications had to be made to existing kilns in order to use them for production of the new ware. It was decided to use plant number four for Fiesta production. Plant #4 also contained (and still does) the main offices of the company.

This building was the first of HLC's five Newell, West Virginia plants and was built in 1907. It originally contained 32 "bottle" kilns. These were periodic, meaning that they were loaded with ware, then fired for a period of about twenty hours, then allowed to cool before being unloaded. The loading and unloading was done manually. In 1927, the periodic kilns were replaced with continuous fire "tunnel" kilns designed by Dr. Albert Bleininger. Ware was loaded on carts that ran on a track through the kiln continuously. Production was vastly improved using the new kilns. Plant four is still used for Fiesta production today.

Uranium oxide gave Fiesta red its bright orange color. The temperature at which this color developed, less than 1700° F, was lower than the usual glost kiln temperature. Depending on the other minerals in the glaze, uranium oxide could turn yellow if fired at a higher temperature. It was apparently used for that purpose in Fiesta's ivory glaze. However, for the lower temperature requirements of the red glaze, a separate kiln had to be constructed in order for HLC to produce the ware in that color. There was also a problem of color contamination to be dealt with when the red glaze was fired with other glaze colors in the same kiln. This was another reason to have a separate kiln for this color only. The "little red kiln" still exists at HLC, but has not been fired since the early 1970s.

On April 20, 1935, J.M. Wells told Rhead he wanted the new colored glaze line ready for the July 1935 housewares shows. This was an impossible assignment. Only half of the designs had been modeled and work on the kilns had just begun. Still, four days later Mr. Wells released to production the first Fiesta items: 10", 9" and 7" plates, teacup and saucer, A.D. cup and saucer, 15" chop plate, sugar, cream, 6" dessert bowl, 8-1/2" nappie, and 9-1/2" nappie. The ware produced at this time was still in "experimental" glazes and the line had not yet been named. Samples from this limited production run were sent to buyers and HLC's advertising agency.

Throughout June Rhead was kept busy working on ceramic jars for the Kraft cheese company. His journal records the many attempts to get things right for this demanding buyer. Work continued in the modeling shop on the designs Rhead had already made, but full production would not occur in July.

On July 22 Rhead wrote, "Three buyers here to see colored line. Same reaction. A.V. states that experimental work will be over this week. To start in small production next week." But that did not happen. New glaze trials and new shape designs delayed production for several more months. In August, Rhead was designing ovenware for the new line. He wrote, "Modeling program: 'Fiesta' casseroles with turned knobs, pie plates, baking dishes, coaster, tankard." However, in the end, none of those items were produced.

It wasn't until late September that Rhead completed the "chart" which specified the shapes and sizes of all items in the line with approximate sagger counts, etc. In mid-October, he noted meetings being held with the modelers, Bleininger, and managers of plant #4 at which plans were laid down for full Fiesta production. We found no record of when it began, but it must have been sometime in November 1935. In order to be ready for a January introduction, items continued to be added to the line even after production started. Included in this small group were the large teapot, a revised 5-1/2" fruit bowl, and the ashtray.

Marketing

The usual way dinnerware was sold to American consumers before the 1930s was in sets. Most of it consisted of white or ivory glazed pottery or china with decals or hand painted decoration. Patterns copied from old European designs predominated. The contents of the sets had decreased dramatically in number from the huge assortment of dishes required for late Nineteenth Century meals, but it was still the primary way to buy dinnerware.

Frederick Rhead had studied the market and talked with the buyers about which items were popular with the public. He explained his reasoning for creating a line of items that could be purchased individually, rather than in formal sets, in an article for *Crockery and Glass Journal* in June 1937.

> We were not interested in confining our program to the conventional tableware items because we felt that the formal service for six, eight or twelve would not have the appeal that could be aroused by means of a well planned series of articles which could be assembled for many uses, and better still, be used in conjunction with existing wares... It was our feeling that while a modernistic interpretation of a formal table service—however attractive—might be met with some reservation by the every day housewife, an easy going informal series of articles, smart enough to fit in any house and obvious enough to furnish spots of emphasis, might get by.

There were major glass and pottery shows held in both Chicago and Pittsburgh during January and July each year. The Associated Glass and Pottery Manufacturers sponsored the Pittsburgh exhibit. In 1936, the fifty-sixth year of the event, it was held at the Hotel William Penn and required five floors of rooms to house the more than 100 exhibitors. The following month, *Ceramic Industry* heralded it as "the biggest and most widely attended display in a decade." It was said that orders from the 1,200 buyers ran "well up into the millions of dollars" and was certainly a needed stimulus to the ceramics industry.

It was at this well-attended and profitable show that Homer Laughlin introduced Fiesta to the public. The next month every major trade journal featured HLC ads promoting the new line: "Fiesta captured the imagination of the trade... instantly... at first sight... a forecast of the success that Fiesta is destined to achieve with the women of America." Fiesta continued to be featured in HLC ads to the trade over the next ten years and eventually proved to be one of the company's best selling lines.

Continued Development

Soon after Fiesta was in stores, Rhead began working on new additions to the line. Suggestions continued to come in from buyers and he no doubt had some of his own. In the August 1936 trade journals, this announcement was made: "New items in the famous 'Fiesta' line of solid-color tableware include egg cups, deep eight-inch plates, Tom and Jerry mugs, covered mustards, covered marmalade jars, quart jugs, utility trays, flower vases in eight, 10 and 12-inch sizes, and bowl covers in five, six, seven and eight-inch sizes."

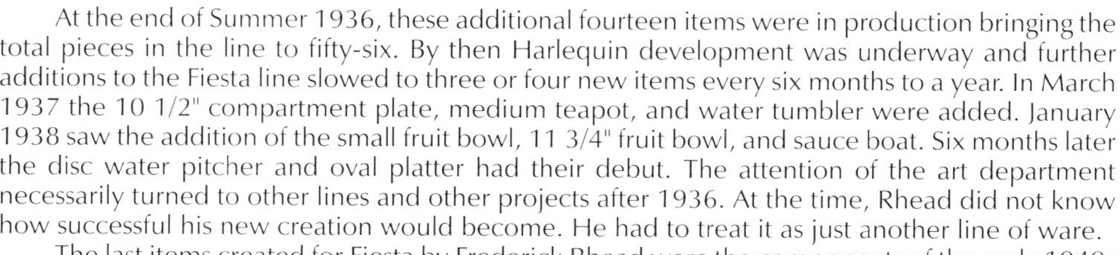

At the end of Summer 1936, these additional fourteen items were in production bringing the total pieces in the line to fifty-six. By then Harlequin development was underway and further additions to the Fiesta line slowed to three or four new items every six months to a year. In March 1937 the 10 1/2" compartment plate, medium teapot, and water tumbler were added. January 1938 saw the addition of the small fruit bowl, 11 3/4" fruit bowl, and sauce boat. Six months later the disc water pitcher and oval platter had their debut. The attention of the art department necessarily turned to other lines and other projects after 1936. At the time, Rhead did not know how successful his new creation would become. He had to treat it as just another line of ware.

The last items created for Fiesta by Frederick Rhead were the components of the early 1940s promotional campaign. This brought the total pieces of Fiesta in production to sixty-one. It was the largest number of items being made for the line at one time during it's entire 37-year run.

A complete list of additions and deletions can be found at the end of this introductory section under "Fiesta Timeline." Additional production information is provided with the review of each item later in the book.

Harmony Dinner Sets

One way the company could broaden the appeal of Fiesta was to sell it in combination with decaled ware from another HLC line in coordinated sets. On May 25, 1936, the Fiesta Harmony dinner sets were introduced at Kaufmann's department store in Pittsburgh. The trade press soon carried full-page advertisements from HLC promoting the new concept. For the Harmony service, HLC's Nautilus shape was used as the coordinating line. Nautilus was developed immediately after Fiesta in 1935 and was itself a relatively new shape. The Harmony concept helped promote both lines to the buying public.

The basic concept was to sell a dinnerware service for eight that consisted of items from both lines. The solid color Fiesta was to compliment the white glazed Nautilus that featured color-coordinated decals in four Fiesta colors: yellow, green, red, and blue. The decals may have already been in use on the Nautilus shape. Hand-applied accent stripes were added to the Nautilus pieces in the same color as the decal. The retail price for the yellow, green, and blue sets was around $20, the red sets sold for about $3.50 more.

Over the years Homer Laughlin had used thousands of different decal designs. They were almost never identified by name, but were instead given a reference number such as "R2140". The letter indicated which decalcomania company had produced the transfer. (HLC worked with three different decal makers.) Once a decal was applied to a dinnerware shape, the product it created was a unique combination of the two. The buyers for department stores would order ware based on a "treatment" or "decoration" code that contained a letter (or letters) and a number. The letter indicated the dinnerware line. The four used for the Harmony service had an "N" prefix to identify them as Nautilus decals. N258 was yellow, N259 was green, N260 was red, and N261 was blue.

The retailer was usually the originator of a treatment name. We could not find any official references that gave names to the decals used for the Harmony service. Over the years, collectors have created their own names for them. The "yellow" decal features colorful flowers and leaves. Yellows and golds are the predominant hues. Because of the shape of the blossoms, collectors call this decal "shaggy flower." The "green" decal is a bunch of pastel-colored tulips with bright green stems and highlights. No collector name is known for this one. The "red" decal is an abstract leaf design in black and red-orange which collectors now call "art deco leaf." The "blue" decal, which is apparently very difficult to find, consists of a blue basket full of flowers and trailing vines. No collector name is known here either, but the decal suggests "blue basket."

The sets consisted of 76 items in the following combination:

Fiesta	Nautilus
Eight 10-inch plates	Eight 9-inch plates
Eight 7-inch plates	Eight 6-inch plates
Eight 6-inch dessert bowls	Eight teacups and saucers
One 15-inch chop plate	Eight 6-inch fruit bowls
One 12-inch comport	One 13-inch oval platter
Two bulb candleholders	One 9-inch oval baker
One each salt and pepper	One 9-inch nappie

Our sources conflicted on the sugar and cream offered in the sets. HLC's advertisements in August 1936 trade journals say they were Fiesta. However, an article in the June 1936 issue of *China, Glass and Lamps,* as well as a May 1936 newspaper advertisement from Kaufmann's, indicate the sugar and creamer were from the Nautilus line. The constitution of the Harmony sets may have changed after the initial introduction at the department store. However, the sugar and cream set have been found in the Nautilus shape bearing the Harmony decals.

Collectors attempting to recreate a Harmony set will have a difficult time. The Nautilus Harmony pieces are generally not easy to find, especially the tulip and "blue basket" designs. And it would be rather expensive. Some of the Fiesta pieces from the sets (15" chop plate, comport, and pair of bulb candleholders) are now some of the more highly valued items in the line.

Ensembles

Another popular marketing strategy, used by many pottery manufacturers and department stores, was the Ensemble. The ensemble consisted of a complete table service for 8 or 12 people and included the dinnerware, serving pieces, glassware with coordinated stripes or decals, colorful Catalin-handled eating utensils, and miscellaneous glass items like ashtrays and swizzle sticks. Newspaper advertisements for ensembles by many of the major dinnerware makers have been found. Fiesta was offered first in one that was a combination of Fiesta and HLC's "Riviera" and later in an ensemble using only Fiesta.

This method of purchasing dinnerware was popular and reasonably priced. In the late 1930s, a Fiesta ensemble for eight sold for less than $15.00 ($175 in today's dollars). This included over 100 individual items. Ensemble sales generally took place before 1941.

Later in this book is a section devoted to Paper and Emphemera that includes some ensemble advertising. More information about this marketing technique can be found there.

Vintage Seconds

First time visitors to the Homer Laughlin factory outlet store today are amazed at the large room of second quality ware for sale. It apparently isn't well understood that thousands of pieces of Fiesta are made each day and that some of it is graded less than first quality. There always have been seconds (and thirds) at HLC. These were sold, usually by the pound, to other businesses for sale. Sometimes the ware would receive decals to hide the defects. At other times it was sold "as is" and labeled as second quality. Collectors should be aware that Fiesta seconds were sold in the past and that not every piece of vintage ware for sale today was at one time first quality.

An example: In late 1938, The Famous department store of Long Beach, California purchased 15,000 pieces of second quality Fiesta and offered it for sale at "give-away" prices. A three-quarter-page ad in the Long Beach *Press-Telegram*, featuring drawings of every item in the Fiesta line, promoted "a merchandising achievement seldom equaled in retail annals." There were four price groups (5¢, 9¢, 19¢, and 29¢ per item) with the price depending on the defects present. All pieces were sold "as is—no refunds" and no telephone, mail order, or C.O.D. orders were taken.

In the five cent per piece category were deep plates, sauceboats, disc pitchers, cream and sugar sets, and various plates and bowls. For nine cents, the customer could have a coffeepot, a teapot, a utility tray, or a nappie among other things. Nineteen cents would buy a 13" or 15" chop plate, a better quality teapot, mixing bowls, cups, plates, or an oval platter. The smallest group, at 29¢ per piece, included better disc pitchers, carafes, chop plates, coffee pots, platters, and nappies. Some pieces were present in more than one category; deep plates, for instance, were in the 5¢, 9¢, and 19¢ groups. All together, 51 items were offered in the four price groups.

Opposite page:
Famous Store ad. 1938.

Changing Times

Significant changes to Fiesta occurred in the 1940s. The decade started with the introduction of new items for a special promotional campaign. Several innovative pieces were designed, including a sugar and cream on a special tray and a French casserole with lid. Rhead had ideas for other pieces that were never more than notebook sketches. The campaign lasted several years.

Frederick Hurten Rhead would not see the end of it. After more than a year of undergoing a debilitating series of x-ray treatments for his mouth cancer, he died in 1942. He had enjoyed an illustrious 50-year career, most of it in this country. America lost one of its most well known, respected, and influential ceramic artists that year.

As the World War progressed and the United States became more involved, many changes in American life occurred. It affected everyone and every business. For Homer Laughlin, these changes were both positive and negative. Production of domestic dinnerware had to take a back seat to war related activities. Restaurant and hotel ware began to be designed and produced in greater and greater quantities. A contract was awarded by the U.S. Navy for tableware to be used in the Officer's Mess. While still a popular line, Fiesta production changed as well.

As the war progressed, items began to be eliminated. In 1942, the two large flower vases, A.D. coffeepot, and tripod candleholders became the first deletions from the line since the covered onion soup bowl in late 1937. A year later the promotional campaign ended and five more items were dropped. HLC stopped making Fiesta mixing bowls in the Spring of 1944.

It was about that time that production of Fiesta's red glaze ceased. This is discussed in greater detail in the book section on colors. Uranium oxide, the main colorant for this glaze, became unavailable as the U.S. government began work on the Manhattan Project. The exact end of red production is not known, but we calculate it was late 1943 or, more likely, early 1944.

Below:
"Possible Fiesta item night set. $1.00 retail."
Even in the 1940s, Rhead was contemplating adding items to the Fiesta line.

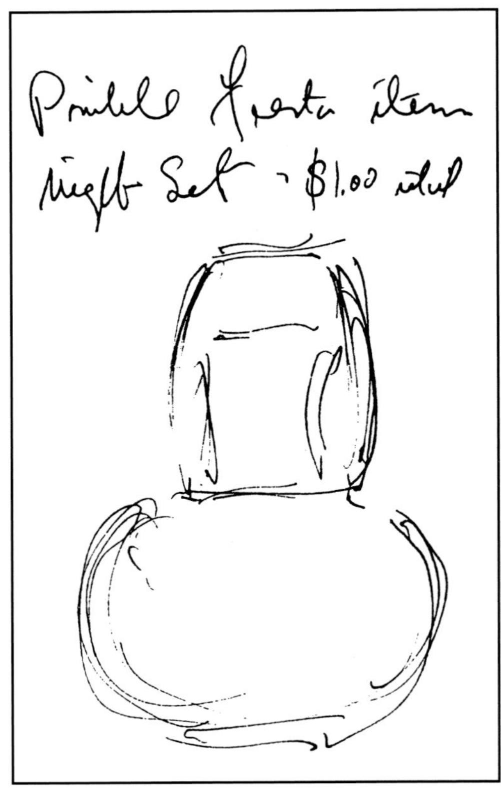

The FAMOUS
6th and PINE AVE.
Department Store
LONG BEACH
Open Friday and Saturday Nights Till 9. Free Parking for Customers.
A Merchandising Achievement Seldom Equaled in Retail Annals
Gigantic Purchase SALE
15,000 Pieces (We bought all we could get)
FIESTA POTTERY
Imperfects and Seconds
EXTRA FLOOR SPACE
EXTRA SALES HELP
Give-Away Priced in 4 Sensational Groups
Pieces if Perfect Would Sell From 20c to $2.00

QUANTITY	ITEM	Reg. Price If Perfect
9	Soup Plates	35c
29	Cream Soups	60c
684	Fruit Dishes	20c
9	Ash Trays	20c
6	Ash Trays	50c
29	Gravy Boats	$1.00
89	Pitchers	$1.00
45	Dinner Plates	35c
104	Fruit Dishes	20c
323	Saucers	20c
28	Bread & Butters	25c
64	Bowls	35c
19	Cream & Sugar	55c
436	Cups	30c
508	Small Fruit	20c

YOUR CHOICE 5¢

QUANTITY	ITEM	Reg. Price If Perfect
28	Coffee Jugs	$2.00
289	Celery Dishes	50c
42	Soup Plates	35c
696	Salad Plates	35c
429	Bread & Butters	25c
284	Saucers	20c
300	Cups	30c
1488	Sauce Dishes	20c
80	Tea Pots	$1.60
99	Coffee Pots	$1.75
25	Vegetable Dishes	70c
400	Dinner Plates	35c

YOUR CHOICE 9¢
Early Shoppers Have Best Choice—Be Here at 9 a. m.

QUANTITY	ITEM	Reg. Price If Perfect
1006	Dinner Plates	45c
37	Large Chop Plates	$1.50
191	Small Chop Plates	$1.00
166	Platters	$1.00
39	Lrg. Vegetable Bowls	70c
180	Med. Veget. Bowls	55c
19	Salad Plates	35c
64	Cream Soups	60c
98	Gravy Boats	$1.00
97	Pitchers	$1.00
706	Cups	30c
31	Soup Plates	35c
29	Tea Pots	$1.75
47	Pitchers	$1.00
61	Mixing Bowls	75c
242	Celery Dishes	50c

YOUR CHOICE 19¢

QUANTITY	ITEM	Reg. Price If Perfect
40	Coffee Pots	$1.75
26	Coffee Jugs	$1.60
22	Water Jugs	$1.00
367	12½" Chop Plates	$1.00
88	14½" Chop Plates	$1.50
282	Platters	$1.00
39	9½" Veget. Bowls	79c
240	8½" Veget. Bowls	55c

CHOICE 29¢
All Pieces Sold As Is—No Refunds
On Sale, L.B. Store Only!
No Phone, Mail Orders or C. O. D.'s

After the war, American lifestyles changed dramatically. People were more mobile, suburban living was becoming the norm, and dining was less formal. There seemed to be less need for some "specialty" pieces available in the Fiesta line. In November 1946, the largest wholesale reduction of items occurred with fifteen pieces being eliminated. Among them were the carafe, mustard, marmalade, relish tray, and large teapot. A complete list is provided below. Paradoxically, 1948 is reported as Fiesta's best year. Even after the removal of 1/3 of the items in the line, it was selling better than ever.

The Fifties

Nearly three years passed after Rhead's death before Don Schreckengost was hired as artistic director at HLC in late 1945. He had been a friend of Rhead and succeeded him as chairman of the Art and Design Committee of the United States Potters Association. He well understood Rhead's design philosophy for Fiesta, Harlequin, and Riviera. Unfortunately, by the time he was in charge of the art department, Fiesta was nearly ten years old. As noted above, pieces had already been dropped from the line. Schreckengost made few changes to Fiesta. There were even a considerable number of additional items in the Fiesta line discontinued during his time at HLC, but the decision to do that came from HLC management and sales.

He is much better known for his designs of several other popular solid-color dinnerware lines at HLC, including Jubilee, Rhythm, and Epicure. In a recent interview, Mr. Schreckengost could not recall creating any new shapes for Fiesta, including the individual salad bowl of 1959. He apparently approved the design, which likely had been done by someone else in the art department. Schreckengost did keep a journal of his activities at HLC as well as a modeling log. Unfortunately, his personal documents were unavailable to us for this book and information from the interview was our only source.

The one significant thing Don Schreckengost did do with Fiesta was to change the colors. After the Second World War, popular tastes changed from the bright California colors to those more subdued in nature. These first revolved around New England, then ones with a New York influence. Following these popular trends, Schreckengost and HLC began producing Fiesta in chartreuse, gray, forest green, and rose. The four replacement colors are now called Fiesta's "Fifties colors" by collectors, even though that term should also include yellow and turquoise, which continued in production. Old ivory, light green, and cobalt blue were discontinued.

The only documentation we could find for the color changes was vintage price lists. The list dated October 1, 1951 is the earliest to have the new colors. It is unlikely that the colors were designed specifically for Fiesta. The line was certainly not as popular as it had been in the Thirties and Forties, and it is fairly well documented that all of these "new" colors were already in use at HLC on other lines. The rose glaze had been a Harlequin color since the 1940s. Chartreuse, dark green, and gray were standard colors for Rhythm and Charm House, another Schreckengost design. Both of these lines had been introduced a few years earlier. It isn't known exactly when these three glazes were first used at HLC, but is seems likely that it was before the Fall of 1951.

During almost the entire decade, the Fiesta line remained stable. There were no items discontinued and the color selection remained the same until June 1959. It was at that time that price lists indicate changes in both the contents of the line and the colors available.

Fiesta price lists remain the sole source of information for this period. Of the price lists known to exist, the latest one to contain 15" chop plates, A.D. coffee cups and saucers, coffeepots, compartment plates, cream soup cups, egg cups, small fruit bowls, and 2 pint jugs is dated October 1, 1957. The June 1, 1959 price list has the same prices as the 1957 list, but on a reduced inventory and with new colors. We have found that HLC usually released a new price list only when colors changed, items in the line changed, or prices changed. If these nine items had been discontinued soon after the October 1957 price list, another list would have been printed. So far, a 1958 or early 1959 list has not been found. The logical assumption follows that the colors and items in production during the 1950s likely continued until mid-1959.

The Sixties

Fiesta in the Sixties really began in June 1959. The line was revamped with new colors and slimmed down with the loss of nine items. Color trends had changed again and apparently HLC felt something brighter would help keep sales up. The Fifties colors were discontinued, while yellow and turquoise continued to be made. Fiesta red was reintroduced (in May according to information provided by HLC in Lois Lehner's *American Kitchen and Dinner Wares*) along with a new shade of green. The items removed from production were things that modern Americans no longer used for dinner service: egg cups, ceramic coffee servers, demitasse cups and saucers, etc.

The items left would remain essentially unchanged for ten years. One new item was added—an individual salad bowl—which was the first new addition to the line since 1940. The 6" dessert bowl was discontinued in late 1960. Exact production figures were not available to our researchers, but it is estimated that sales did decline during the decade. One thing that some use as an indicator of factory volume is the relatively decreased number of items in the medium green glaze. That color is used because it was only produced during the Sixties, unlike the other three, which had previously been available. However, the low number of medium green items (which translates into higher prices for collectors) may simply be due to the fact that the color itself was not popular and may have nothing to do with Fiesta sales figures overall. Regardless of the reason, medium green is a highly sought color within the collecting community.

Toward the end of the 1960s, HLC began to be involved in supermarket promotions. The Fiesta shape was used for one of the early attempts in this marketing genre. Amberstone, the "brown Fiesta," is fully discussed in our section on Fiesta with decals and decoration later in the book. Some of the bowl shapes were changed for Amberstone and those shapes formed the basis for yet another Fiesta incarnation, Fiesta Ironstone, which was to be HLC's final attempt to keep the old line alive.

Fiesta Ironstone

In the early part of 1969 revisions were made to some of the Fiesta shapes that had been changed for Amberstone, signaling that a change was coming. By July, a new product was on the market - Fiesta Ironstone. The "Ironstone" part of the name was apparently only for marketing purposes since the composition of the ware had not changed. It was produced in three colors, Mango Red, Turf Green, and Antique Gold. These corresponded with popular hues in the kitchenware industry: burnt orange, avocado green, and harvest gold.

The changes are said to have been due to the need for HLC to consolidate production activities. The green and gold glazes, or slight variants of them, were already in use on other lines. Hand marking of the ware was discontinued and the serving pieces were offered in only one color. These changes helped make production less expensive.

Production of the red glaze ended in November 1972. According to information provided by HLC for *American Kitchen and Dinner Wares*, the kiln operators and glaze technicians who had "maintained control over the complicated manufacturing and firing" processes had retired. Discontinuing the color was more in line with modern manufacturing techniques. Additional information about this line can be found in the section on Fiesta Ironstone later in the book.

The End

When Ironstone production began in 1969, Fiesta was 33 years old. Quite an age for most dinnerware lines and it wasn't about to last much longer. The end came on the line's 37th birthday, January 1, 1973. The new ware was produced for about three and a half years.

Almost immediately, the older, brighter Fiesta became a collectible. Slowly at first, but within a year several people had written collector books about it. Its popularity continues strongly today.

Now Fiesta is again in production at Homer Laughlin. The new ware, too, is extremely popular, both as tableware and as a collectible. Because of this, we've included a section on the new ware later in the book.

Fiesta Timeline

January 1936, Original Line
(red, blue, green, yellow, ivory)
Ashtray
Bowl, mixing 11.5"
Bowl, mixing 10"
Bowl, mixing 9"
Bowl, mixing 8"
Bowl, mixing 7"
Bowl, mixing 6"
Bowl, mixing 5"
Candle holder, bulb
Candle holder, tripod
Carafe, 3 pints
Casserole, covered
Chop plate 15"
Chop plate 13"
Coffee cup, A.D.
Coffee saucer, A.D.
Coffeepot, A.D.
Coffeepot, regular
Compartment plate 12"
Comport 12"
Comport, sweets
Covered onion soup
Cream soup cup
Creamer (stick handle)
Dessert bowl 6"
Fruit bowl 5 1/2"
Ice pitcher
Nappie 9 1/2"
Nappie 8 1/2"
Plate, 10"
Plate, 9"
Plate, 7"
Plate, 6"
Relish tray
Salad bowl, footed
Shaker, pepper
Shaker, salt
Sugar, covered
Teacup (ring handle)
Tea saucer
Teapot, large, 8 cup
Vase, bud

August 1936, Additions
Cover, mixing bowl 8"
Cover, mixing bowl 7"

Cover, mixing bowl 6"
Cover, mixing bowl 5"
Deep plate
Egg cup
Jug, 2 pint
Marmalade jar
Mustard jar
Tom & Jerry mug
Utility tray
Vase, flower 12"
Vase, flower 10"
Vase, flower 8"

March 1937, Deletions
Cover, mixing bowl 8"
Cover, mixing bowl 7"
Cover, mixing bowl 6"
Cover, mixing bowl 5"
Compartment plate 12"

March 1937, Additions
Compartment plate 10 1/2"
Teapot, medium, 6 cup
Water tumbler

January 1938, Deletions
Covered onion soup

January 1938, Additions
(turquoise)
Fruit bowl 4 3/4"
Fruit bowl 11 3/4"
Sauce boat

July 1938, Deletions
Creamer (stick handle)

July 1938, Additions
Creamer (ring handle)
Disc water jug
Platter, 12" oval

October 1942, Deletions
Candle holder, tripod
Coffeepot, A.D.
Vase, flower 12"
Vase, flower 10"

May 1939, Additions
Disc juice jug
Juice tumbler
Syrup

February 1940, Additions
French casserole
Promotional salad bowl
Sugar, cream & tray set

October 1942, Deletions
Candle holder, tripod
Coffeepot, A.D.
Syrup
Vase, flower 12"
Vase, flower 10"

Late 1943, Deletions
Disc juice jug
French casserole
Juice tumbler
Promotional salad bowl
Sugar, cream & tray set

May 1944, Deletions
(red)
Bowl, mixing 11 1/2"
Bowl, mixing 10"
Bowl, mixing 9"
Bowl, mixing 8"
Bowl, mixing 7"
Bowl, mixing 6"
Bowl, mixing 5"

August 1946, Deletions
Vase, flower 8"

November 1946, Deletions
Candle holder, bulb
Carafe, 3 pints
Comport 12"
Comport, sweets
Ice pitcher
Marmalade jar
Mustard jar
Nappie 9 1/2"
Relish tray
Salad bowl, footed
Teapot, large, 8 cup
Water tumbler
Utility tray
Vase, bud

October 1951, Deletions
(blue, green, ivory)

October 1951, Additions
(rose, gray, chartreuse, forest)

June 1959, Deletions
(rose, gray, chartreuse, forest)
Chop plate 15"
Coffee cup, A.D.
Coffee saucer, A.D.
Coffeepot, regular
Compartment plate 10 1/2"
Cream soup cup
Fruit bowl 4 3/4"
Jug, 2 pint

June 1959, Additions
(red, medium green)
Salad bowl, individual
Egg cup

January 1961, Deletions
Dessert bowl 6"

July 1969, Deletions
(red, yellow, turquoise, medium green)
Ashtray
Casserole, covered
Chop plate 13"
Creamer (ring handle)
Deep plate
Fruit bowl 5 1/2"
Nappie 8 1/2"
Plate, 9"
Plate, 6"
Salad bowl, individual
Sugar, covered
Teacup (ring handle)
Tom & Jerry mug

July 1969, Additions
(mango red, antique gold, turf green)
Bowl, dessert/fruit
Bowl, soup/cereal
Bowl, salad 10.25"
Bowl, vegetable
Casserole (restyled)
Coffee mug
Coffeepot, regular
Creamer ("c" handle)
Sauce boat stand
Sugar, covered (restyled)
Teacup ("c" handle)

December 1972, Deletions
(mango red, antique gold, turf green)
Bowl, dessert/fruit
Bowl, soup/cereal
Bowl, salad 10 1/4"
Bowl, vegetable
Casserole (restyled)
Coffee mug
Coffeepot, regular
Creamer ("c" handle)
Disc water jug
Plate, 10"
Plate, 7"
Platter, 12" oval
Sauce boat
Sauce boat stand
Shaker, salt
Shaker, pepper
Sugar, covered (restyled)
Teacup ("c" handle)
Tea saucer
Teapot, medium, 6 cup

Vintage Fiesta Colors

Fiesta Color Trends

The following text has been adopted from two articles by Marcia Kinnear, an interior designer, which first appeared in the Fiesta Collector's Quarterly, *(Summer 1995 and Fall 1999). Reprinted with permission from Ms. Kinnear and the* Fiesta Collector's Quarterly.

In the 1930s, there was an intense interest in Southern California lifestyle. It was a period that was dominated by the glamour of movies and movie stars as well as the glamour of where they lived. Southern California with the Spanish style architecture, lush vegetation and heavy Mexican influences appeared very glamorous and appealing to depression weary Americans.

The concept of the "Patio" became known to the average American. The Mexican/Californian colors of Orange, Cobalt Blue, Sunflower Yellow, and Turquoise were new and fresh to the housewife of the early 1930s and were brought to the mass market by Homer Laughlin in the form of Fiesta in 1936. Homer Laughlin did not innovate here, but was merely following the lead of other, more cutting edge California potteries that had introduced very successful mix and match dinnerware services for casual "Patio" dining in the early 1930s.

The light green was not so much a part of this Mexican/Californian trend as a holdover from the dominant early 1930s kitchen colors of green and ivory (the combination of green and ivory was available in everything from enamelware and wood stoves to kitchen hoosier cabinets).

Manufactures of all sorts of items used these color combinations of orange, cobalt, turquoise, yellow, and green... everyone from Griswald, who offered enameled cast iron cookware, to Hazel Atlas Glass, who offered their "HEAT TEMPERED" platonite glass dinnerware in a near duplicate of Fiesta's colors. The bright colors offered some gaiety and California Glamour to middle America.

By the end of the war however, these colors were passé. There was a focus on New England and Early American traditional, more muted colors of a softer cobalt blue, creamy yellow, barn red and pine green. Fiesta was starting to look dated and garish.

Still, in 1948, Fiesta sales peaked at 30 million pieces according to Forbes magazine. This was due more to post war household formation and scarcity of other dinnerware lines rather than Fiesta's trendiness, however. Soldiers back from the war were moving into Levitown-type developments and buying whatever dishes and household goods could be found. The discontinuation of many accessory pieces of Fiesta in 1946 may have had more to do with the need to turn production to more plates, cups, and bowls of all types to fulfill pent up demand than a sudden disaffection for big vases and pottery tumblers.

In the very late 1940s, American color tastes became much more subdued and subtle... California was now not quite as glamorous as New York City. Gray and grayed, muted, complex, "sooty" colors like ashes of roses were considered much more sophisticated. Among stylish war brides, those who could afford it and (more importantly) those who could find it, were purchasing Heywood-Wakefield blond or limed furniture and Russel Wright dinnerware in gray, seafoam, coral, and chartreuse.

Fiesta with its garish, simple colors was regulated to the weekend cabin or to less advantaged, less stylish relatives. Fiesta was no longer a market leader, but now a secondary dinnerware with out of date colors more likely to be found in stamp catalog showrooms and small town hardware stores than in stylish department stores.

Homer Laughlin revamped the color line-up in 1951 to include gray, rose, chartreuse, and forest green in addition to the yellow and turquoise.

How did these four new colors relate to the times? America's design eye was on New York City, and where did upscale New Yorkers vacation in the late 1940s? Florida of course, and we see a great influx of "tropical" print textiles being used in design catalogs in the early 1950s. Giant tropical leaf designs on cotton barkcloth in shades of chartreuse and forest green, with gray and muted rose flowers were prominent in the early 1950s... and while Fiesta colors had caught up with the times, its streamlined design was dated and at odds with the new "form follows function" design stylemakers were pushing.

As the fifties progressed, colors became less somber, and at the same time more pastel... turquoise, peachy pink, butter yellow and deep beige were used in various combinations, but dinnerware shapes became more and more exotic, becoming squared, then free-form.

The war time shortages were gone and American consumers were moving through a vast array of consumer choices. Dinnerware was no longer seen as something that was kept until

the last piece was broken. Fiesta was now dated not only in design and in color selection but material.. American Housewives had discovered that wonder dinnerware Melamine!

In an attempt to resurrect the line, HLC revamped the colors once again in 1959. Note that the first color change had come 15 years after the introduction, the second color change only nine years after that. The velocity of taste change was picking up speed, as the average American housewife could now afford to redecorate, even if it meant just painting the room and buying new slipcovers and rugs, she began to discard things well before they were worn out.. the modern American consumer came of age in this era. Fiesta was apparently just limping along in the sixties based on the scarcity of medium green in the marketplace at this time.

By 1968, like some grand old dowager down on her luck and forced to scrub floors to earn her keep in her old age, Fiesta was being dipped in brown, called Sheffield Amberstone and given away as grocery store premiums. Fiesta just sputtered out altogether soon after that.

When Fiesta was given a face lift and brought out again in 1986, all things were right for its reintroduction. Art Deco was an important interior design trend in the mid-1980s, and more importantly, the color assortment fit the American Southwest look that American housewives considered every bit as glamorous as the 1930s housewife considered the Southern California look.

In the late 1990s, there was a move toward more subtlety and more complex color palettes in home decoration, but more importantly, the period of "mass customization" was upon us. For at least the last decade, the American consumer no longer follows the dictates of fashion designers. The consumer has become more comfortable with themselves and more confident in their own style (or lack thereof). They stress utility and personal comfort over appearance and stylishness. Gone are the dramatic shifts in fashion based entirely upon appearance.

Home decoration has become more individualized. The last actual pervasive home decoration trend was American Southwest of the mid-1980s, which was what Post 86 Fiesta's color palette was based upon in the early years – Apricot, Rose, Turquoise, Pale Yellow, Seamist Green, and Periwinkle Blue. A full 75% of the United States would now answer "Country" as the style they prefer in home decoration, but because it is a catch all, it really has no meaning. Consumers have come to use the word "Country" in decoration to simply mean their own personal style, whatever it may be.

As mentioned earlier, the concept of "Mass Customization," especially in home furnishings, is upon us. Made possible by computers which can accumulate, sort, and streamline orders for efficient production, goods are still being produced in large factories but are customized in some way to reflect a customers specific desires or needs. More consumers than ever are ordering their furniture with not just custom coverings, but are combining the desired frame style with this leg and that arm in a desired wood finish, while fewer are buying standard furniture off the showroom floor. Modular wall units and entertainment centers allow the consumer to combine standard units from a series into a custom configuration to fit their room and needs.

The use of quality materials has overtaken having the "in" color as the mark of the fashionable kitchen. The upper end kitchen of today is light and neutral in coloration, with high quality, natural materials such as real marble, real granite and natural woods (rather than an applied pattern or colors) making their own statement. Today's upscale kitchen depends on accessories such as the dinnerware to provide color. Fiesta currently fits right in with this trend. It is also the original "mass customization" dinnerware... each consumer picking only the colors they want to combine in a set of their own making. It is interesting to note that never before has Fiesta been offered in such a wide range of colors at one time, yet consumers are continually demanding even more colors. Most people do not use all the colors together, as they did in the days of the "Original Six," but mix two, three or four colors together in their own individual color combinations. Pearl gray has been well received and in an excellent color to tone down an assortment and keep it from being too garish. This demand for new colors will only accelerate as consumers look at the Fiesta color assortment as they did a box of crayons when they were children.. they may not use or buy all the colors, but they want the biggest assortment of choices possible.

The trend is clearly toward textures and natural colored materials in home (and particularly the kitchen décor). Fiesta's ability to provide the color accent in a neutral colored kitchen will assure many years of continued popularity, especially with Homer Laughlin China's present commitment to keeping the palette of colors fresh and current.

Vintage Fiesta Glaze Colors

Although Frederick Hurten Rhead had created many glazes during his career as a ceramic artist, that was not his function at Homer Laughlin. The distinguished chemist Albert Victor Bleininger filled that role and also devised the clay formula, or body, for Fiesta that proved to be the perfect match for his glazes. Harry W. Thiemecke, a chemical engineer who became technical director of the HLC lab upon Bleininger's retirement, assisted Dr. Bleininger in the HLC laboratory.

Albert Bleininger was born in Germany in 1873 and moved to the United States with his parents at the age of fourteen. He eventually attended the Ohio State University and graduated with a degree in chemistry in 1901. After serving as an instructor and associate professor at that university, he held positions with the University of Illinois, the U.S. Geological Survey, and the Division of Ceramics at the U.S. Bureau of Standards. He became the head of the Ceramic Research Department at Homer Laughlin in 1920.

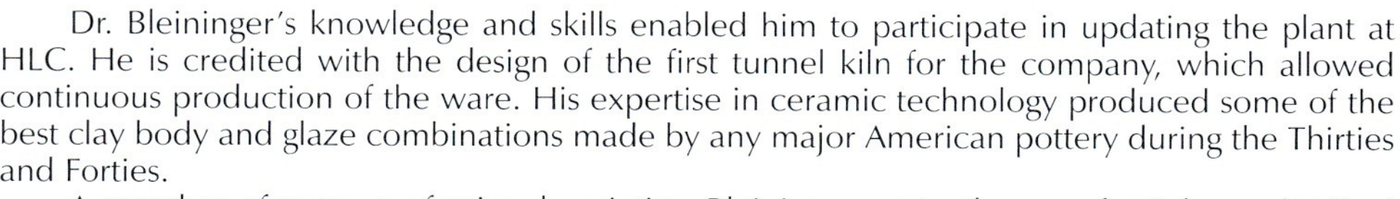

Dr. Bleininger's knowledge and skills enabled him to participate in updating the plant at HLC. He is credited with the design of the first tunnel kiln for the company, which allowed continuous production of the ware. His expertise in ceramic technology produced some of the best clay body and glaze combinations made by any major American pottery during the Thirties and Forties.

A member of many professional societies, Bleininger wrote dozens of articles and edited several books on the subject of ceramics. In 1933, he received an honorary Doctor of Science degree from New York's Alfred University. After his death, he was honored by the American Ceramics Society with the creation of the Albert Victor Bleininger Memorial Award. The award is still given by the society to individuals for "distinguished achievement in the field of ceramics." Dr. Bleininger retired from Homer Laughlin in 1945 after 25 years of service to the company. He died on May 19, 1946.

Early Glaze Trials

The most detailed accounts available today documenting the glaze trials for Fiesta are in the daily journals kept by Frederick Rhead. Only three weeks into the new year of 1935, on January 21, he recorded his first observations: "Colored glazes from kiln, selected group and classified according to color." He would continue to note the numerous attempts to refine the selection until five glazes were chosen and put into full production near the end of the year.

By the end of the month he had conferred with Dr. Bleininger (always referred to as "A.V." in the journals) and Harry Thiemecke several times. They must have already had quite a few colors in the works because he recorded these comments made by HLC's general manager, Joseph M. Wells: "J.M.W. spoke to A.V. on color program. Doesn't want many colored glazes. Saw me yesterday about this. I explained that we were only developing a normal line from which we could make proper selections."

The first mention of specific colors in Rhead's notes occur on March 12: "Low temperature glazes selected for test run on new shape: Blues H103 & 1972, red H23, turquoise 1943, yellows H31D & 1974, rose ebony 1936, black H36, [and] green H10." By this time only a plate, the teacup, and saucer had actually been modeled, so all the trial colors were being done on other shapes or test forms. Less than a week later they must have decided that the low temperature glazes were the way to go because Rhead recorded that plans were made for a special kiln in which to make the colored glazes.

HLC management was deeply involved with the new line throughout this year of trials. On March 23 Rhead wrote, "J.M.W. up on colored glaze development. I [suggested] that we get equivalent glazes to California development. To spare no expense for stains, etc. Advised the use of higher tin content and frits for turquoise."

The next week glazes were being applied to the actual shapes designed for the new line. It is clear that the final selection of colors was a long way off when examining this log entry: "New shapes out of glost kiln. Glazes mostly dipped too lightly. Three glazes too light to include in skeleton setup. We need color types not in present line. Good yellows, a clear rich turquoise, rose or crimson, clear green and cream enamel." Later that week Rhead went to Pittsburgh and evaluated the competition for sale at Kaufmann's and other department stores. He found the best selling items were short sets and that larger pieces were only occasionally purchased. He noted that ovenware was also selling well.

On the first of April, Rhead recorded the full formulas of the glazes under consideration: turquoise, yellow, bright red (also called mandarin), lava red (bright red fired in an open sagger), a dark blue, ochre, rose ebony, white, green, and buff. Ten days later there's a note recording which of the glazes had been approved by Mr. Wells: "J.M.W. up. Looked at colored glaze development. Approves turquoise, dk. blue, rose ebony, bright yellow, bright red, white, and should try for a rose." Toward the end of April the first shapes of the as yet unnamed line were released to production: the three larger plates, teacup and saucer, 15" chop plate, cream and sugar, desert bowl, and both sizes of nappie. A few days later Rhead sent a large group of colored ware to HLC's advertising agency in New York. Place settings and serving pieces were included in the colors under consideration: red, blue, rose ebony, white, turquoise, and yellow.

During the second week of May more color trials were done and Rhead noted, "Colored kiln out – new green. J.M.W. etc. like this color. Must blue up turquoise because this may be eliminated from series." The next week the name "Fiesta" began appearing in his journal and Rhead's prediction came true; turquoise was not mentioned again.

For the next few months Mr. Rhead was kept busy working with the Kraft-Phenix Cheese Corporation, which had asked HLC to make crocks for their cheese products. It wasn't until August that another note regarding Fiesta glazes appeared in his journal. "Long conference between A.V., G.F., L.F., and self on possibilities in Fiesta of glazes of the vellum type for cone 4-5. If present development does not go through we can make: deep blue, yellows, vellum ivory, green, white, crimson, etc. Suggested a program for A.V. for glazes while I am continuing to plan decal and other decorations. My original idea expressed to L.F. is that even with the low temperature glaze development, which will not be suitable for cooking, we can add certain casserole items in the vellum or cone 4-5 glaze. Then future development or production plans may go in either direction."

An October 19 report by Dr. Bleininger regarding his tests on HLC and California ware for craze resistance indicated that the low temperature glazes were approved. On October 28, Rhead noted the lowest costs for production, by color, of Fiesta 7" plates and teacups. The colors listed were - vellum, white, green, blue, and red. The next day was filled with meetings to finalize Fiesta production. "Meeting in morning and afternoon on Fiesta. Selected shapes in morning and settled prices in afternoon. Two prices, one for red and one for other colors. Price seems very low."

In a November 12 note about a meeting with the buyer from Macy's, Rhead mentions yellow Fiesta. Although our researchers did not find a journal entry documenting the final decision on Fiesta glazes, it seems to have been made by this date. The low temperature glazes combined with the "Fiesta" clay body, both created by Dr. Bleininger, proved to be an excellent combination that would sell well for the next thirty years.

Fiesta tripod candle holders in trial rose-ebony color. No established value.

Collector's Finds

Items from Fiesta glaze trials are still found by collectors today. Most of the time it is a plate or a cup, often with a hand-written four or five-digit number under the glaze. Sometimes it is something more unusual like a pair of tripod candleholders or a cream and sugar set. There seem to be two types of trial pieces. One is the initial trial for the color. Six-inch and nine-inch plates seem to have been the favorite medium on which to test glazes. These items will have an identification number on them and groups of items have been found with consecutive numbers. The numbers apparently corresponded with entries in a log that documented the glaze formula used. Our researchers were unable to locate such a log, which may still exist in the HLC lab.

The second type of trial piece was one used to show how the glaze looked on various items. Place setting items and serving pieces were glazed in the same color and used with items in other colors to see how they "worked together" on the table top. Rhead's journal contains several entries where he discusses these groupings. Items from this type of trial will not be numbered.

While most things like this are discovered near the HLC plant in eastern Ohio or western Pennsylvania, they can be found anywhere. In 1998, a group of 15 items, all in the red glaze and all numbered, were found in Knoxville, Tennessee. A few months later, a 16th numbered piece to this group was found in Dallas, Texas. The shape of the teacups in the group indicates that the pieces were probably color trials for the reintroduction of red in 1959. The numbers in that group were in the range of 18XXX to 21XXX. Earlier trial items, with numbers in the 3000 range, have been discovered in Ohio. Two collectors have plates in early turquoise and maroon, the latter is probably a variant of the rose ebony glaze.

Recently a Fiesta cream and sugar were found with a brownish maroon glaze. They were discovered in a box of pottery at an auction in eastern Ohio. The shapes are the earliest production versions, a stick-handled cream and a flat-bottomed sugar. The glaze may be rose ebony or another unnamed glaze. These pieces, and the tripod candleholders shown nearby, were most likely items from Rhead's test table settings. The biggest clues are the fact that they are different shapes in the same glaze and do not have identification numbers.

The Production Colors

The Original Five

It has been stated fairly often that Fiesta was first produced in only four colors and that ivory was added later in 1936. This belief probably stems from information provided by the Homer Laughlin China Company itself in response to a query by Lois Lehner for her book *American Kitchen and Dinner Wares*. In the material sent to Lehner it says, more than once, that Fiesta was "produced in green, blue, yellow and red." Later in the document it says, "Ivory was added in 1936, turquoise in 1938, blue, rose, gray, chartreuse and olive green in 1943 to be followed by several other distinct colors over the years."

Our research indicates that Frederick Rhead himself stated more than once in print that there were five original colors and that ivory was one of them. We also know, from price list data, that rose, gray, chartreuse, and dark green were used after 1950, not 1943. The material submitted for Lehner's book appears to have been constructed from the recollections of plant workers and not from official records.

In the trade magazine *Ceramic Industry*, a February 1936 article discussed the pottery and glass show held in Pittsburgh the month before. Frederick Rhead was quoted and had this to say about Fiesta: "It is a modern shape with brilliantly colored glazes in red, yellow, green, blue and ivory sets for informal use."

Homer Laughlin prepared ads for the trade journals promoting the new ware. The February 1936 issue of *China, Glass and Lamps* carried one of them which said, "Fiesta is available in five lovely colors... Green, Yellow, Blue, Ivory and Red... all brilliant, all eye-catching, all modern." The earliest Fiesta price lists used essentially the same words to explain the available colors.

In 1937 Rhead wrote two articles for *Crockery and Glass Journal* discussing color and design. In the June issue, his piece "More About Color" recounted the story of how the Fiesta glazes were developed:

> The final selection of five colors was a more difficult job because we had developed hundreds of tone values and hues and there were scores which were difficult to reject. Then, there were textures ranging from dull mattes to highly reflecting surfaces. We tackled the texture problem first. (Incidentally, we had made fair sized skeletons in each of the desirable glazes in order to be better able to arrive at the final selection.)
>
> We eliminated the dull mattes and the more highly reflecting glazes. First because in mass production practice, undue variation would result in unpleasant effects. The dull sur-

faces are not easy to clean and the too highly reflecting surfaces show "curtains" or variation in thickness of application. We decided upon a semi-reflecting surface of about the texture of a billiard ball. The surface was soft and pleasant to the touch and in average light there was no disturbing reflections to distract from the color and shape.

We had one lead with regard to color. There seemed to be a trade preference for a brilliant orange-red. With this color as a key note and with the knowledge that we were to have five colors, the problem resolved to one where the remainder would "tune in" or form appropriate contrasts.

The obvious reaction to red, we thought, would be toward a fairly deep blue. We had blues ranging from pale turquoises to deep violet blues. The tests were made by arranging a table for four people and as the plate is an important item in the set, we placed four plates on various colored cloths and then arranged the different blues around the table. It seemed that the deeper blues reacted better than the lighter tones and also blues which were slightly violet or purple. We also found that we had to do considerable switching before we could decide upon the right red. Some were too harsh and deep, others too yellow.

With the red and blue apparently settled, we decided that a green must be one of the five colors. We speedily discovered that the correct balance between the blue and red was a green possessing a minimum of blue. We had to hit halfway between the red and the blue. We had some lovely subtle greens when they were not placed in juxtaposition with the other two colors, but they would not play in combination.

The next obvious color was yellow and this had to be toned half way between the red and the green. Only the most brilliant yellow we could make would talk in company with the other three.

The fifth color was the hardest nut to crack. Black was too heavy, although this may have been used if we could have had six or more colors. We had no browns, purples or grays which would tune in. We eliminated all except two colors; a rich turquoise and a lovely color, we called rose ebony. But there seemed to be too much color when any fifth was introduced in any table arrangement. The quartette seemed to demand a quieting influence, so we tried an ivory vellum textured glaze which seemed to fit half way between the yellow and the regular semi-vitreous wares and which cliqued when placed against any one of the four colors selected. It took a little time to sell the ivory to our sales organization but when they saw the table arrangements they accepted the idea.

Turquoise Is Added

One question about vintage Fiesta colors that is difficult to answer concerns when the turquoise glaze was first put into production. The best place to look for the answer would be in Rhead's journal. Unfortunately, the volume for 1937 is missing. Other methods were used to arrive at our best guess. Using information from HLC's modeling log and by examining turquoise items in several large collections, the date range can be narrowed only to "sometime in June, July, or August 1937."

In the sixth edition of *The Collectors Encyclopedia of Fiesta* (1987) the authors claim to have a "mid-1937" Fiesta price list which pinpoints the date of the introduction of the turquoise glaze. They also say that same price list includes the 4-3/4" fruit bowl. Our researchers have not been able to locate a Fiesta price list between those dated May 15, 1937 and January 1, 1938. We do know, however, that the small fruit bowl was not modeled until October 1937. It had a major revision in mid-November and was released to production on November 26. This bowl is unlikely to have appeared on any 1937 price list.

One good source for information like this is the trade journals of the time. We were not able to find an article or press release in the 1937 journals available to us that referred to the adding of a new color for Fiesta. Perhaps future researchers will locate something more definitive.

There are, however, a few clues to the date turquoise was added to the Fiesta glaze palette. One is the restyling of the teacup. As noted in the *Fiesta* section later in this book, the original teacup features a flat bottom inside the cup, like the flat bottom of the Fiesta creamer. This was changed in mid-August 1937 when the cup was restyled. Later cups have a rounded bottom inside the cup. Flat bottom teacups in the turquoise glaze are very rare. Our authors and editors know of less than half a dozen. The change in teacup shape must have occurred shortly after the introduction of that color or there would likely be more early style cups in turquoise.

The mixing bowl lids and 12" compartment plate were not made in turquoise, but the discontinuation of those items was too early to be helpful in determining the date of introduction for turquoise. The color was not listed on the May 15, 1937 price list, so the decision to add it to the line must not have been made until mid-May at the earliest. Turquoise had been "in the running" as one of the original colors, so lengthy tests were not needed when it came time to put it into production.

The Royal Metal/Fiesta flat cake plate was put into production the first week of March 1937, but the length of time it was made is not known. Due to their scarcity, an estimate of only four or five months seems likely. They may have been made only until July. If they exist in turquoise, which we have not been able to verify, they are extremely hard to find in that color. That would indicate the color was introduced late in the production run of the cake plate, probably in June or July 1937.

For now, there are too many unknowns to pinpoint a date with more precision than a two and a half month spread from early June to mid-August 1937. Common sense and the evidence provided by the ware in collections seem to point to a date toward the end of that period.

A New Green

Were there two shades of light green used for Fiesta? Some collectors believe there are two subtly different greens, one being lighter or paler than the other. Rhead's journal seems to indicate that a new shade was indeed substituted for the original green in mid-1938.

A journal entry on May 19 reads: "J.M.W. wants A.V. [Bleininger] to further adjust new Fiesta green before changing." The next day Rhead wrote, "Arranged Fiesta green in showroom, placing new with regular. L.F., J.D.T. and G.F. [senior members of HLC's sales staff] could not distinguish one from the other."

Early Fiesta items can be found in a light green that is pale and shallow compared to the color on later pieces. It can only be assumed that the change was actually made, but the reasons for it and exactly when it occurred cannot be determined from the available records. It can be noted from the comment above that the two shades are apparently so close in hue that they're perhaps indistinguishable side by side in collections.

Pre-1938 teacup and saucer in light green glaze compared to a set made after the color change.

Red Eliminated

At the suggestion of Albert Einstein in 1939, President Roosevelt encouraged the investigation of nuclear fission by scientists in the United States. There was concern that the Germans, who had discovered nuclear fission, might be working on an atomic bomb. The Manhattan Project was started in August 1942 and was the means by which the United States became the world's first nuclear power.

Uranium 235 was one of the principal materials needed for making fission bombs and it was difficult to extract from uranium ore, let alone uranium compounds such as the oxide used by Homer Laughlin, and others, to make red orange glazes. It seems improbable that the sale of the oxide to civilian companies was halted so the U.S. government could use it as a source of U-235. More likely the restriction was to prevent foreign governments from attempting to do so.

Research sources give various dates, none specific, for when the sale of uranium oxide was curtailed. The most accepted is sometime during 1943. We were unable to determine a more exact date. It seems reasonable to assume that HLC had some of this material on hand when the restrictions were imposed and that production of the popular red glaze was continued for as long as possible.

Much of the information about vintage Fiesta production comes from HLC-created price lists. One would expect them to fairly accurately reflect what the company was making when the lists were printed. A new price list was usually printed when items were added or removed from the line or when significant things, like glaze colors, changed. The only Fiesta price lists that our researchers were able to locate for the time around 1943 were those dated October 1, 1942 and May 1, 1944. The red glaze was included on the first one, but not the second.

If production of the red glaze had actually stopped in 1943, it seems that HLC would have printed a new price list to reflect it. Perhaps they did, but we were not able to locate a copy. Based on the price lists we do have, it appears that a new list was not needed until May 1944. Therefore, we are using "early 1944" as the time when the red glaze was discontinued.

The remaining colors—blue, green, yellow, ivory, and turquoise—continued in production until late 1951 or longer. While some shapes in the line were discontinued shortly after the red glaze was, others continued in production. Those that did are more readily found today than the same item in red since the other colors were produced for a longer period.

Backstamps on Ivory

Collectors may notice that the color of the "Genuine Fiesta" backstamp on pieces with the ivory glaze is not always the same. Some items have a blue-black mark, others a soft yellowish brown one. Why? The difference may be due to a change in the ivory glaze formula, the backstamp color itself, or both. Our research was not able to give a definite answer.

Backstamp "ink" is not ink at all, but a ceramic color, much like a concentrated glaze. Ivory was not the only glaze that reacted with the backstamp color, but it did so with the most dramatic results. The same stamp could appear very blue with turquoise, black under the red glaze, and brown under ivory.

Only one color was used for marking Fiesta at a given time. Theories that a different backstamp color was applied to the ivory pieces are unfounded. The marks were put on the ware in the bisque stage before a colored glaze was applied. It was not known what color glaze would be used on a given item at the time it was stamped.

There does seem to have been a need to change the ivory glaze formula. Fiesta's red glaze was not the only one that contained uranium. The oxide was used in ivory to give it a warm, yellowish hue. When the sale of uranium oxide to private companies was stopped in 1943, it affected the glaze formula for ivory as well. However, our tests on two saucers, one with a brown mark and one with a black mark, showed that both saucers were radioactive. In this case, the brown mark must be due to something other than the glaze formula.

Perhaps the marking color was itself changed during the time ivory was in production. This, too, could account for the different colors found today. Whatever the cause, it should be considered normal for ivory Fiesta to have two colors of backstamps.

New Colors For The Fifties

Just as they had in the mid-1930s, national color trends influenced the glazes used on Fiesta in the Fifties. In the Thirties, it had been the "California" influence of bright colors and mix and match patio dining. In the 1950s, it was the cool sophistication of New York as well as the use of "tropical" styling in home design. In her excellent article on color trends for the Summer 1995 issue of the *Fiesta Collectors' Quarterly*, interior designer Marcia Kinnear noted [see section on color trends], "Giant tropical leaf designs on cotton barkcloth in shades of chartreuse and forest green, with grey and muted rose flowers were prominent in the early 1950s."

There are no records at HLC for this period that can compare to the wealth of information left by Frederick Rhead. Daily activities and important decisions about the line come only from interviews with those involved. Don Schreckengost, who followed Rhead as head of the HLC Art Department, made the decision to change Fiesta's colors. Mr. Schreckengost was very accommodating and responded to our requests for discussions several times. He is still active in the pottery business at the Hall China Company of East Liverpool, Ohio.

The choice of new colors was relatively simple since he was following the trend of the day. Many other dinnerware manufacturers did the same thing and chartreuse, gray, and dark green are common colors on Fifties dishes. Universal Pottery's "Ballerina", Steubenville's "Woodfield" and "American Modern", as well as Bauer Brusché's "Al Fresco" and HLC's own "Rhythm" are only a few of the many lines of that decade glazed in these familiar colors.

Bright colors were not entirely forgotten. In addition to the new, somewhat muted colors, the popular yellow and turquoise glazes continued in production. Collectors sometimes forget that there were six "Fifties colors", not just the four new ones. The golden yellow and sky-blue turquoise complimented the other colors and provided the American housewife with the ability to mix and match a wider variety of colors on her dinner table. Lasting only as long as the decade, the once trendy colors soon gave way to others; perhaps a last ditch effort by HLC to keep Fiesta popular with the buying public.

Even though production continued at a strong pace during the Fifties, ware in the new colors was made for less than nine years. That makes many items in the "Fifties colors," especially serving pieces, harder to find and correspondingly more expensive for today's collectors.

Old And New In The Sixties

It isn't known why the Atomic Energy Commission took so long to release restrictions on the sale of uranium oxide. When the commission did so in the late 1950s, Homer Laughlin was again allowed to buy it and production of Fiesta's red glaze was resumed. There were changes in the isotopes, but it was still radioactive and continued to give Fiesta a deep red orange color that had once been so popular. By this time, the shapes were very dated. Perhaps the return of a well-liked color would boost sales. The inactive "little red kiln" was put back into service in mid-1959 and continued to turn out red Fiesta for another thirteen years.

The "old standbys" yellow and turquoise were still being made, but a fourth color was needed to round out the line. Color trends had changed again and HLC felt a bright, Kelly green would complete the palette. Simply referred to as "green" on price lists, collectors use the term "medium green" to differentiate it from previous shades of that color.

Nascent collectors often ask why medium green Fiesta is so expensive. The answer, basically, is that less of it was made than any other color. During the 1960s the popularity of Fiesta was waning. Even the new colors were not enough to make the line as profitable as it had been. Because of a reduction in sales, there was a decrease in production of the ware. Theoretically that means that all Fiesta items produced during the Sixties should be harder to find today. In spite of the fact that ware in the new colors was made for ten years, there was less of it.

For collectors, the impact is felt mainly in prices for items in medium green. In the end, yellow and turquoise had been in continuous production for more than 30 years. Most of the items available in those colors during the 1960s had been made for a long time. Red pieces, too, had been made before. Certainly not for the same length of time as yellow, but enough that common items can still be easily found. Medium green, on the other hand, was made for only that ten year period and not in great quantities. Because of that, a common tea saucer in medium green can be two to four times the value of the same item in yellow or turquoise.

Common Names

The terms collectors use for glaze colors are not always the ones that were used by Homer Laughlin in Fiesta advertisements or on price lists. The official names for vintage Fiesta's eleven colors and the names used by collectors are:

Fiesta Price Lists	Fiesta Collectors
green	light green, original green
yellow	yellow, Fiesta yellow
blue	cobalt, cobalt blue, dark blue
red	red
old ivory	ivory
turquoise	turquoise
forest	forest green, dark green
chartreuse	chartreuse
gray	gray
rose	rose
green	medium green

Authors of early books about Fiesta are partly responsible for the terms we collectors use today. For example, the terms "light green" and "medium green" were first used in January 1974 by LaHoma Reiderer and Cynthia & Charles Bettinger in one of the first Fiesta books, *A Collector's Guide to Fiesta Dinnerware.* See the appendix for a complete list of previously published books on HLC's colored wares.

Color Errors and Oddities

For most of 1935, Dr. Albert Bleininger, HLC's distinguished chemist in charge of glaze development, made dozens of formulations in a wide variety of colors. Most of the trial run pieces were discarded, but a few survived and have made their way into Fiesta collections. As previously noted, items used for HLC glaze experiments will usually have a four or five digit number on the back or bottom. The numbers are handwritten under the glaze and were used to identify the glaze formula. Occasionally Fiesta items in odd colors will turn up which may or may not be a trial glaze piece. This section will list some of the more frequently found colors and attempt to explain their probable origins.

Mottled Fiesta Red

From time to time an unusual piece of red Fiesta will turn up that exhibits a strange brown mottling. These items appear to be nothing more than rejects from kiln runs with temperature control problems. The temperature at which the original red glaze was fired had a very narrow range. If it was too high, the glaze simply burned off. If it was moderately high, the glaze began to turn brown, usually on the edges or thin parts of the ware. The resulting mottled pieces were considered kiln temperature failures and thrown out.

During the early part of April 1935, when Dr. Bleininger was making several tests trying to obtain the right kiln temperature for the red glaze, Frederick Rhead noted in his journal, "Red kiln out. Too much reduction and firing too quick... majority of ware brown and burnt out."

Reduction occurs when there is decreased oxygen available for the kiln's fuel to burn correctly. Radical chemical changes can take place with reduction. Metallic luster glazes are made this way. The occurrence of a reducing atmosphere in HLC's Fiesta kilns was never intentional.

Even after production began there were kiln mishaps and these brown mottled pieces are the likely result. Collectors should understand that such items are not trials or experiments, but only rejected pieces of ware that made their way out of the HLC trash bin.

Cream of Tomato Red

Another odd color sometimes found has been referred to as "cream of tomato soup" red because it is a pale, creamy orange. This color is known on early Fiesta pieces (a mixing bowl) and Sixties pieces (5 1/2" fruit bowls with a wiped foot). Could this have been an experiment that spanned twenty years? Not likely. The items found to date are not typical items chosen for glaze trials (usually plates and cups) nor do any of them have identification numbers. This color is probably another that resulted from temperature fluctuations or kiln atmosphere problems during production. While they are interesting additions to a Fiesta collection, they should be viewed as oddities rather than as a specific color that HLC was considering for use on Fiesta.

Harlequin Colors on Fiesta

There are several pieces of Fiesta known in Harlequin colors. Yellow is the color most often reported, especially on Fiesta juice pitchers. In that case, it seems to have been intentional. Perhaps they were made for a specific retailer since so many of them are available or possibly to provide seven distinct colors in the promotional juice set. No records have been found to indicate a definitive answer. Other items are best described as "employee inventions" or were probably created in error by the application of the wrong glaze. One collector reports a Fiesta plate in spruce green. Another has a Fiesta individual sugar in Harlequin yellow. A 4 3/4" Fiesta fruit bowl is also known in this color. There are likely to be other Fiesta pieces in glazes of other lines.

Fiesta 5 1/2" fruit bowl in cream of tomato red color compared with traditional Fiesta red.

Fiesta ice pitcher in Harlequin yellow. The tumbler is Fiesta yellow. No established value.

Fiesta after dinner coffee pots in unusual medium green and Harlequin yellow. No established value.

Fiesta 5 1/2" fruit bowl in Skytone blue. No established value.

Fiesta 10" vase in marron. No established value.

Employee Inventions

Over the years HLC had a large and varied group of people making dinnerware. At the most busy time there were more than 3,000 employees working three shifts a day to keep up with demand. It is not unknown in the pottery industry for "lunchtime" projects to be made by artistically inclined employees during breaks or meal periods. Those who worked in Plant #4 making Fiesta were no different.

Another reason that Fiesta items in unusual clays or glazes exist was to satisfy the desires of HLC's senior management for special items. Because it is a privately held company, officials have much greater freedom in the way they utilize company resources. This includes having out of the ordinary pieces made for their own use. Quite a few of these have turned up in the estates of HLC's owners. Kitchen Kraft items in turquoise, Fiesta in unusual colors, and whole sets of dinnerware with special decals or glaze treatments are known. Some of these items are even displayed in HLC's own museum located within the factory outlet store.

Maroon Vase. Timing is what prevents the maroon Fiesta vase shown nearby from being a glaze trial piece. The shapes of the Fiesta vases were not modeled until very late December 1935 and early January 1936 and they were not put into production until the following July. The color trials for Fiesta's original glazes were completed by mid-November. This 10" vase, one of a pair, was likely made for HLC management using Harlequin's maroon glaze.

Kraft Blue Bowl. Kraft Blue and Kraft Pink were HLC lines that began production in mid-1937. The clay body was colored and the pieces received a clear glaze. Fiesta bowls like this were made by hand at that time and it would have been relatively easy for a jiggerman to substitute the blue clay for the clay normally used for Fiesta.

Blue and Pink "Swirl" Ashtray. Recently an unusual Fiesta ashtray sold on an Internet auction site. It was covered in pink and blue glazes that had been swirled together. Although it did have the "Genuine Fiesta" backstamp, the bottom of the ashtray was not glazed indicating that the two colors had been applied by hand. The shape was the one used after 1940.

Items Available in Vintage Fiesta

In this section every item in the vintage Fiesta line will be reviewed. The information given will include a complete history of the piece from the initial model to the last month of production. Every item is shown in every color produced. Every item includes a drawing giving accurate dimensions. Variations that might be found are discussed along with the reason for them, if known. An estimation of the availability of the item to today's collector is also provided for most items.

In the listings that follow a summary of each item's production history is presented. The information contained requires some explanation.

The modeling date and number are taken directly from HLC documents. Production start and end dates are estimates based on information provided in the modeling log, Frederick Rhead's journals, and known Fiesta price lists. Except in the case of items not found on price lists, these dates are felt to be fairly representative of actual production dates. The "length of production" figures were calculated from the production date estimates and are themselves only estimates.

The years that certain colors were in production, especially red, are difficult to determine. There were no company records available to our researchers that specified anything about when colors were changed. The dates given here are best estimates based on price list data and comparison of known pieces to dates in the HLC modeling log.

For example, the production dates of the original red glaze are given in this book as November 1935 to early 1944. It has been well documented that in 1943, to support the war effort, the United States government restricted the sale of uranium oxide. This material was used in the production of red orange glazes at Homer Laughlin and other potteries. HLC must have had some amount of it in stock in 1943 because a new price list, with red eliminated, was not published until May 1944. Based on the fact that the prices on that list are the same as the October 1942 price list and the only items eliminated were the nested mixing bowls, we reasoned that the new price list in May 1944 was printed because red was no longer being made. If red had been discontinued a year earlier, why delay in creating a new price list? The new list must have been created shortly after production of red stopped, thus the "early 1944" date used in this book.

In the introduction of the Fiesta section we explained how glaze trials were conducted until late October 1935. Because of the continuing trials, normal production could not have started earlier than November of that year and may have started later. Therefore, based on information in Rhead's journals and other HLC documents, the November 1935 date is being used as the start of production for all original Fiesta items and glaze colors although the actual start of production may have been as late as January 1936.

This section contains items made for the vintage, original Fiesta line only. Separate sections follow for Fiesta Ironstone, Fiesta shapes with decals and applied decoration, and for the currently produced Fiesta line. Some shapes, such as the sauce boat, were used in those other lines. However, this section will cover their use in the original line only. Thus the Statistics for the sauce boat show its production ended in "early 1969" even though it was actually made (without the impressed mark) until Fiesta Ironstone was discontinued three years later. See the Fiesta Ironstone section for production dates for that line.

Ash Tray

The inclusion of an ash tray in a dinnerware line may seem odd to today's collectors, but at the time Fiesta was introduced smoking was a socially acceptable practice. Rhead intended Fiesta to be purchased by the masses and included items that could be used in everyday life. The utilitarian design of the Fiesta ash tray is not unlike others made by HLC, but the distinctive Fiesta ring pattern and glaze colors set it apart.

There are two varieties of the ash tray, the difference involves the bottom of the piece. In early 1940 an automatic jiggering machine was installed at HLC. This required new molds and tools for many items. The result most often seen is a change in the design of the bottom or back of the item being made. Changes seen on the bottom of the Fiesta ash tray may have been a result of that item being moved to production on the auto jigger.

Older models of the ash tray have seven concentric rings in the center of the foot. They are generally unmarked for there was no place to apply the backstamp. This version of the ash tray can be found in the first six vintage colors and probably was made from late 1935 until early 1940.

The newer model has only two rings on the foot leaving a large center space for the normal "Genuine Fiesta" backstamp. These are almost always marked and can be found in all eleven vintage colors.

Fiesta ash trays are not difficult to find, however those in medium green are valued significantly more reflecting their relative scarcity.

Fiesta ash trays in colors available at shape introduction. Cobalt, $56-58; Green, $51-53; Red, $60-61; Ivory, $55-57; Yellow, $47-49.

Fiesta ash trays in colors added after introduction. Forest, $82-86; Gray, $85-88; Rose, $83-85; Chartreuse, $86-88; Turquoise, $50-52.

Fiesta ash tray in Medium Green. Medium Green, $180-190.

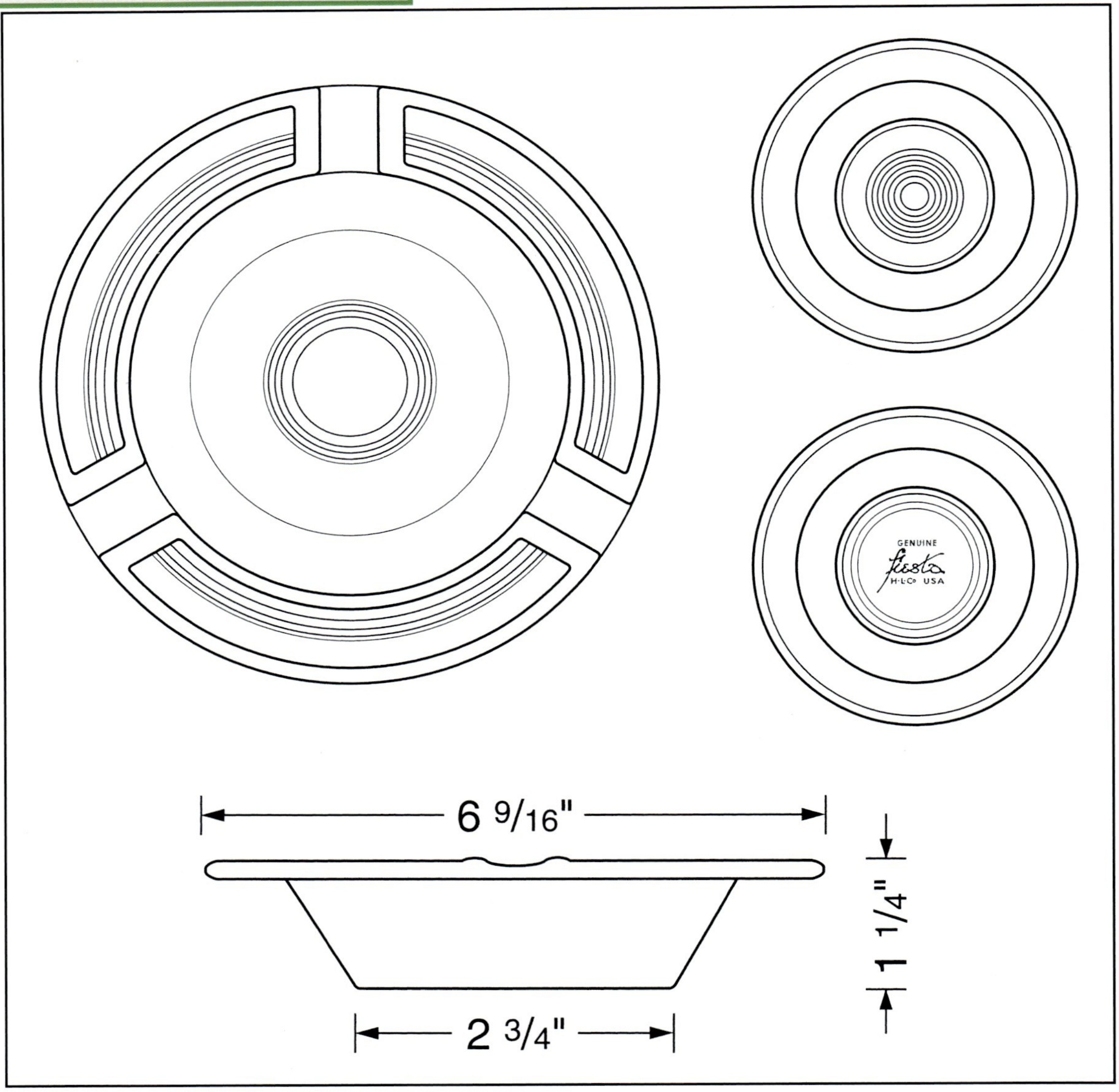

GENUINE Fiesta H.L.Co USA

6 9/16"

1 1/4"

2 3/4"

Fiesta Ash Tray

Modeling Date .... December 1935
Model Number 512
Revisions .... None
Production Began .... December 1935*
First Price List .... Early 1936 (undated)
Last Price List .... January 1, 1968
Discontinued .... Early 1969*
Length of Production .... 33.2 Years*
Colors: Red†, Cobalt, Green, Yellow, Ivory, Turquoise, Rose, Gray, Chartreuse, Forest, Medium Green
*Estimate
†Red discontinued in early 1944, reintroduced mid-1959

Covered Onion Soup

Covered onion soup bowls were a common item in many dinnerware lines of the 1930s, but the market at which Fiesta was targeted apparently didn't appreciate them. These bowls were in production for about two years, being discontinued around the time of the introduction of Fiesta's turquoise glaze. HLC seems to have stopped production because of a lack of sales. In Rhead's personal journal, a December 1935 entry indicates that HLC's salesmen were having problems with it even as production began. "Letter from G.F. [George Fowler, HLC's marketing director] stating that onion soup not liked; that regular cream soup with cover would be better." There were a couple attempts at creating a cream soup bowl with a lid (see reference in the cream soup listing), but they were never produced. In the end, as it always did, HLC bowed to the wishes of its clients and stopped making the bowl.

In spite of its short production time, the Fiesta onion soup had at least two revisions after the first model. Onion soup production is dated by the colors available. Almost all of them are in red, yellow, green, cobalt or ivory. Not many have been found in turquoise. Price lists suggest that onion soups were discontinued in the fall of 1937.

The HLC modeling log indicates the first model of this bowl was created in March 1935. It was a shorter bowl than the final model, with tab handles, a flared rim, a wider foot, and flattened lid. A few of the scarce trial run pieces of this shape have made it into collector hands. It was not put into production.

A second version was created in August 1935 and Rhead had it modeled with both ring handles and scroll handles. The scroll handle was chosen as more practical and this bowl is one of the two types that can be found today. Like the early tea cup and after dinner coffee cup, a flat bottom inside the bowl is a prominent feature. This bowl is marked on the base with a cast-in mark showing "Fiesta" in script with "HLC USA" in capital letters below. This mark was used on most of the slip cast pieces during early production. The lid appears to have been slip cast as well. It features a deep flange compared to later models, extending 5/16 inch below the lid rim.

A February 1936 entry in the log is the last one for Fiesta onion soups and represents the type most often found. The changes from the August 1935 version include a rounded bottom inside of

Fiesta covered onion soups in colors available at shape introduction. Yellow, $515-570; Red, $670-715; Cobalt, $710-755; Ivory, $710-735; Green, $575-630.

The original design for the vintage Fiesta covered onion soup never went to production. This example is missing its lid. No established value.

Fiesta covered onion soup in turquoise. Turquoise, $6870-7970.

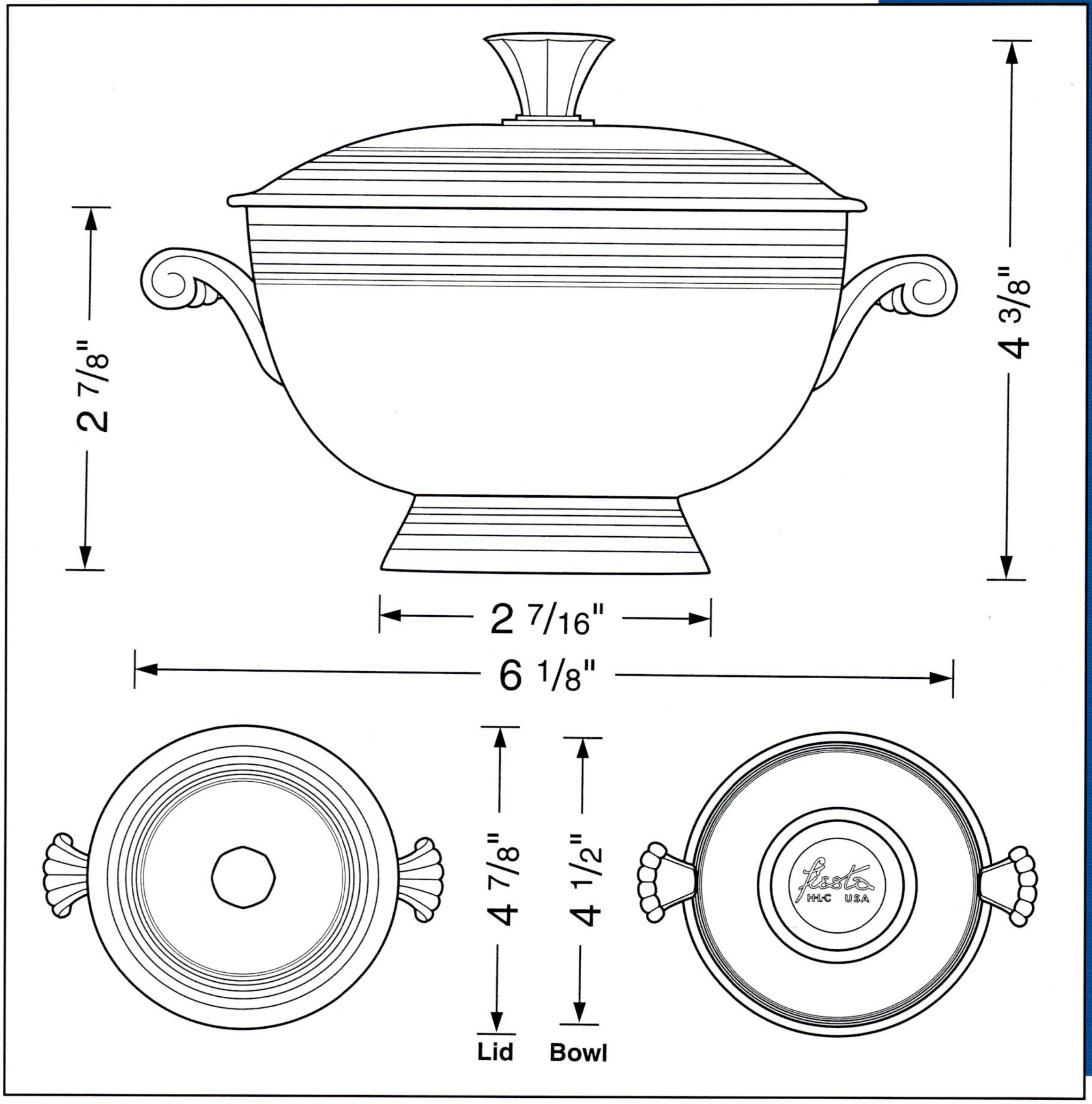

2 7/8"
4 3/8"
2 7/16"
6 1/8"
4 7/8"
4 1/2"
fiesta
H-L-C USA
Lid
Bowl

the bowl; a hand turned foot, the absence of any mark, and a lid with a different flange design (extending only 1/8 inch below the rim). This model and its lid were made on a jigger. Both types of onion soup bowls feature hand-applied scroll handles. The knob, or finial, on the lid was also individually attached by hand.

Because they were made for such a short period of time onion soups are quite expensive. Those found in turquoise commanding a price that can be ten to fifteen times the price of bowls in the other colors.

Fiesta Covered Onion Soup

Modeling Date	March 1935
Model Number	355[1]
First Revision	August 1935, 422[2]
Second Revision	February 1936, 537[3]
Production Began	November 1935*
First Price List	Early 1936 (undated)
Last Price List	May 15, 1937
Discontinued	Late 1937*
Length of Production	2 Years*

Colors: Red, Cobalt, Green, Yellow, Ivory, Turquoise

*Estimate

[1]First model not produced

[2]Slip cast, marked

[3]Revised for jiggering, not marked

Cream Soup Cup

After plates, the cream soup cup was probably the piece of Fiesta most often used in magazine advertising of the late 1930s and throughout the 1940s. Soup companies, cereal makers, and several other food advertisers featured this bowl in their ads in a wide variety of magazines. Today it is a favorite of collectors and is one vintage shape that some wish HLC would add to the new Fiesta line.

Although there were two lidded versions modeled as replacements for the covered onion soup, the cream soup cup was produced in only one shape. It has a similarity to several other items in the Fiesta line in that there are variations in the slogan impressed into the bottom of the bowl, but the overall shape never changed.

Like tea cups and sugar bowls, the cream soup was made by jiggering. The inside was formed by a metal tool and the outside by a plaster mold. Due to the use of different tools over the years, the ring pattern in the center of the bowl can vary in size, but it is always four concentric rings. This bowl has a hand-turned foot that will show some variation based on the skill of the worker. The lug handles were added by hand and may not be directly opposite each other and may even be slightly crooked.

While the cream soup remained popular through the 1950s, it apparently had a decline in sales by the end of the decade. It remains difficult to accurately date when it was discontinued, but the time was clearly just after the introduction of the medium green glaze in mid-1959. Enough medium green cream soups have been found to indicate it was probably produced for a few months even though it did not appear on the June 1959 Fiesta price list. After the turquoise onion soup, a medium green cream soup cup is the most expensive regularly produced Fiesta item that one can add to a collection today.

Fiesta cream soup cup in colors available at shape introduction. Yellow, $43-44; Cobalt, $62-64; Green, $46-48; Red, $66-68; Ivory, $55-57.

Fiesta cream soup cup in colors added after introduction. Turquoise, $47-48; Forest, $70-73; Gray, $66-70; Rose, $70-72; Chartreuse, $64-66.

Fiesta cream soup cup in medium green. Medium Green, $4580-4970.

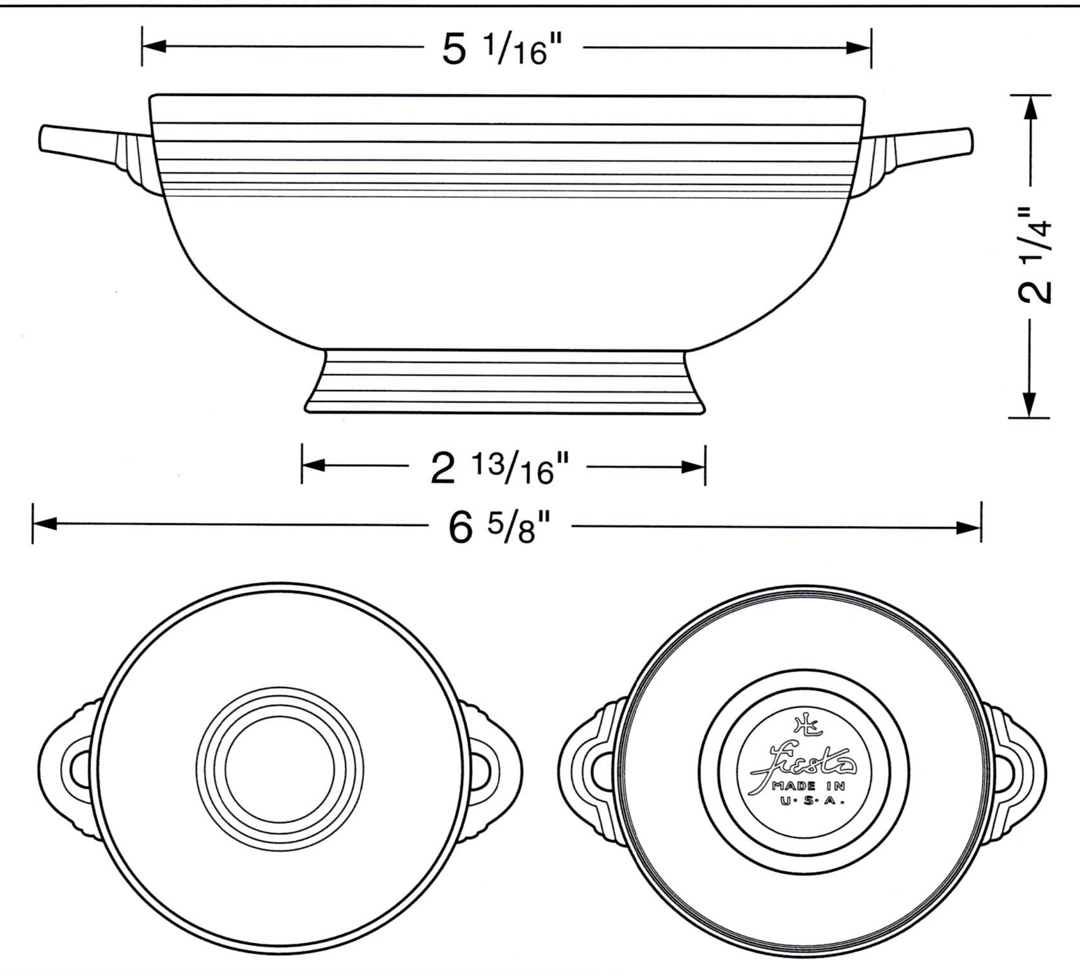

Fiesta Cream Soup Cup	
Modeling Date	May 1935
Model Number	372
First Revision	505[1]
Second Revision	597[2]
Production Began	November 1935*
First Price List	Early 1936 (undated)
Last Price List	October 1, 1957
Discontinued	Mid 1959*
Length of Production	23.6 Years*

Colors: Red†, Cobalt, Green, Yellow, Ivory, Turquoise, Rose, Gray, Chartreuse, Forest, Medium Green

*Estimate

†Red discontinued in early 1944, reintroduced mid-1959

[1] Cover and knob for cream soup, not produced

[2] Cream soup, covered, not produced

Dessert Bowl

Frederick Rhead first envisioned this bowl as the Fiesta fruit bowl and named it as such in the modeling log. The name was changed to dessert bowl when the Fiesta "oatmeal" became the five inch fruit bowl. The dessert bowl was in continuous production from Fiesta's introduction in 1936 until sometime in late 1960.

Like many Fiesta bowls, this one was made on a jiggering machine and thus has some variation inside the bowl from the jigger tool. The center ring pattern can vary in size from 2 1/4" to 2 3/8" and contain four or five rings. Most of these bowls will be found with "wet" feet and will have three glaze imperfections in a triangular pattern on the bottom left by the tripod kiln stilt. There are some, however, with an unglazed foot. This type is most often seen in the colors of the 1960s, but a few have been found in the 1950s glazes.

Like the cream soup cup and 4-3/4" fruit bowl, HLC ceased production of this piece shortly after the medium green glaze was introduced. It is very hard to find in that color and has a correspondingly higher price than dessert bowls in other colors.

Fiesta dessert bowls in colors available at shape introduction. Yellow, $37-39; Cobalt, $47-51; Green, $42-43; Red, $53-56; Ivory, $49-51.

Fiesta dessert bowls in colors added after introduction. Turquoise, $39-41; Forest, $49-52; Gray, $51-54; Rose, $55-58; Chartreuse, $51-55.

Fiesta dessert bowl in medium green. Medium Green, $610-645.

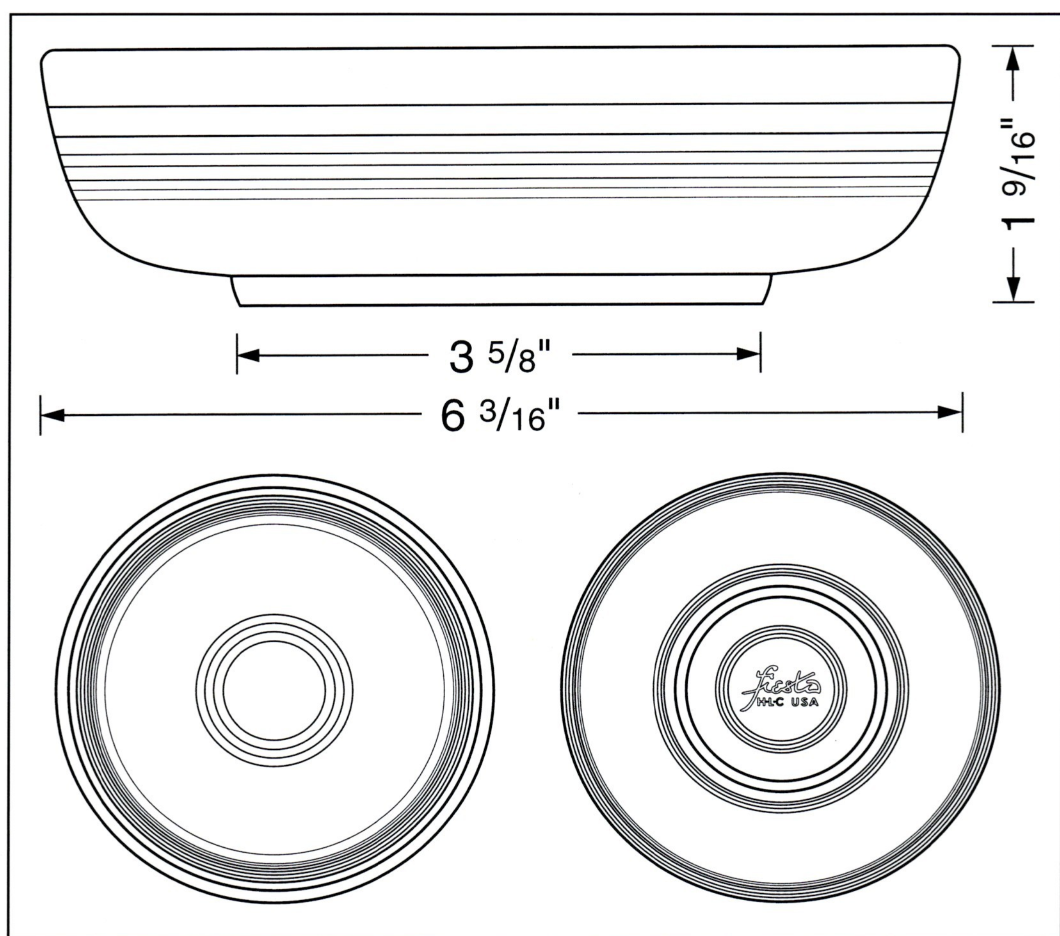

Fiesta Dessert Bowl

Modeling Date	March 1935
Model Number	348
Revisions	None
Production Began	November 1935*
First Price List	Early 1936 (undated)
Last Price List	June 1, 1959
Discontinued	Late 1960*
Length of Production	25 Years*

Colors: Red[†], Cobalt, Green, Yellow, Ivory, Turquoise, Rose, Gray, Chartreuse, Forest, Medium Green

*Estimate

[†]Red discontinued in early 1944, reintroduced mid-1959

Fiesta 4 3/4" Fruit Bowl

Interior volume must have been the reason for the creation of the 4 3/4" fruit bowl. The first Fiesta fruit held ten ounces and no doubt there was demand from retailers for a smaller one. The bowl Rhead designed in the Fall of 1937 held seven ounces and proved to be just what was needed. The first model of this bowl was actually 1/4 inch larger, but was resized a few weeks later. It was added to the line in January 1938 and was produced until mid-1959.

There are only two variations of this piece. Like the other bowls, it was jiggered and will show some variety in the size and number of rings inside the bowl based on the jiggering tool used. The other difference involves the foot. Beginning in the early 1950s HLC started wiping the glaze from the foot of bowls with this shape (fruits and nappies) and running them through the kiln on shelves rather than in saggers. This was a labor saving method and one already in use on items like tea pots and sugar bowls. Small fruit bowls in the glazes of the 1950s and 1960s will almost always have wiped feet.

Unlike the larger fruit, this bowl is invariably found with the impressed mark that includes "MADE IN USA." The date and reason for the change in this mark from "HLC USA" is unknown, but appears to have occurred in late 1937 for this bowl. Over a period of time nearly all items in the line had new molds that included the "MADE IN USA" slogan.

This bowl and its larger sibling have a flat lip on the rim that makes them resemble small nappies. Dealers or collectors not familiar with the term "nappie" may use it when describing these fruit bowls. Fiesta fruits must have been sold in large numbers as they are not difficult to find, except in medium green. Like the cream soup cup, this item was discontinued as that glaze was being introduced and therefore is relatively scarce in that color.

Fiesta 4.75" fruit bowl in colors available at shape introduction. Turquoise, $26-27; Cobalt, $34-35; Green, $26-27; Red, $34-35; Ivory, $32-33; Yellow, $25-26.

Fiesta 4.75″ fruit bowl in colors added after introduction. Chartreuse, $33-35; Forest, $36-37; Gray, $33-35; Rose, $33-34.

Fiesta 4.75″ fruit bowl in medium green. Medium Green, $510-535.

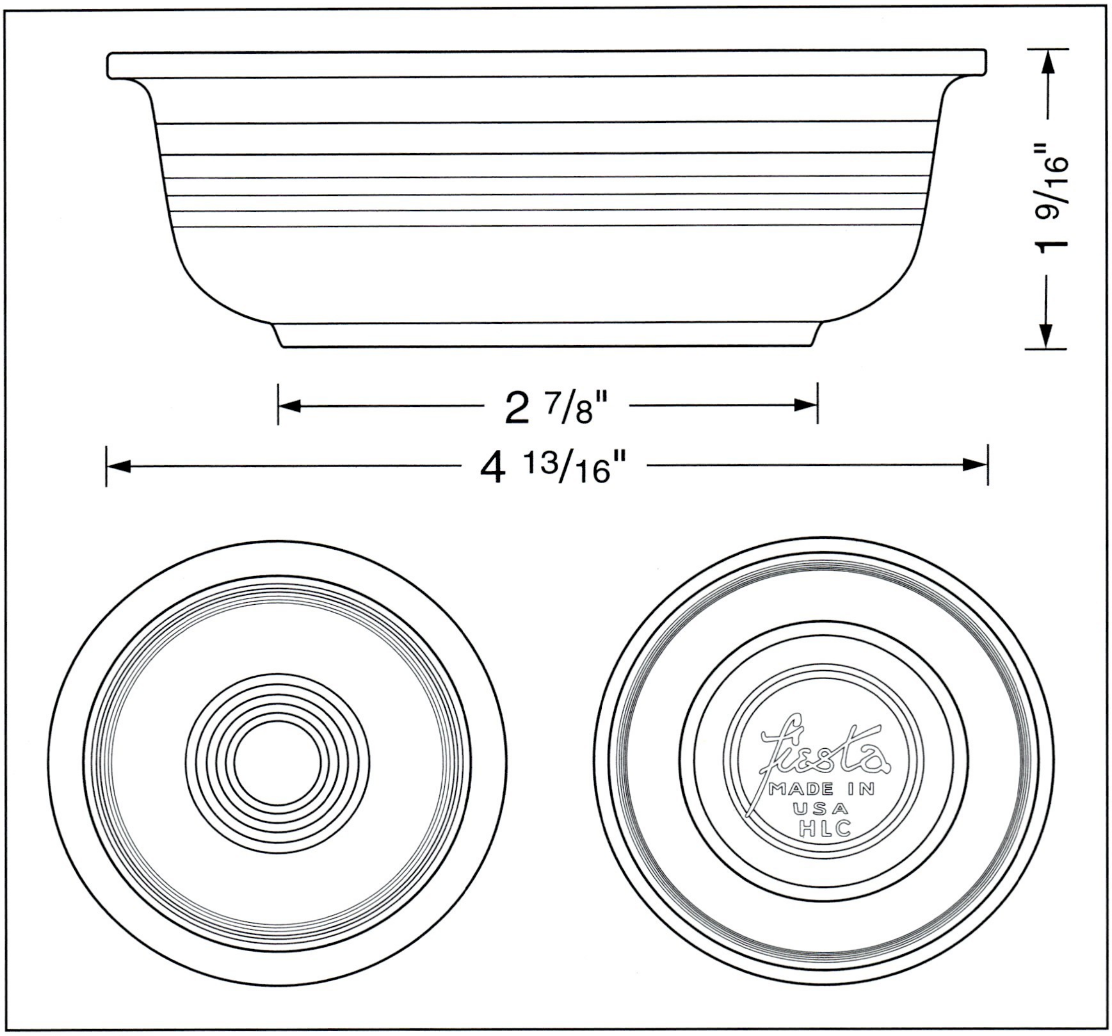

Fiesta 4 3/4" Fruit Bowl

Modeling Date .... October 1937
Model Number .... 964[1]
Revision .... November 1937, 986
Production Began .... December 1937*
First Price List .... January 1, 1938
Last Price List .... October 1, 1957
Discontinued .... Mid 1959*
Length of Production .... 21.6 Years*
Colors: Red[†], Cobalt, Green, Yellow, Ivory, Turquoise, Rose, Gray, Chartreuse, Forest, Medium Green
*Estimate
[†]Red discontinued in early 1944, reintroduced mid-1959
[1]First model not produced

Fiesta 5 1/2" Fruit Bowl

The HLC modeling log indicates that this bowl, modeled in April 1935, was originally called the Fiesta "oatmeal." The name was changed at some time before the first revision. Frederick Rhead's journal indicates that the original six-inch model was revised to a smaller size on the order of a company official while Rhead was out of town (model 492, November 1935). It was ordered "over 1/4 larger" by the same official after Rhead's return. This last revision was the one produced for more than 30 years.

Early price lists did not have a 5 1/2" fruit bowl, but one that was listed as five inches. This is merely semantics and not an indication that there was another separate five inch fruit. When the 4 3/4" bowl was introduced, an accurately measured 5 1/2" bowl was placed on the price lists.

Produced on a jigger machine, with its attendant variations in center rings, this bowl was placed in saggers in the glost kilns until the early 1950s. At that time, like nappies and the small fruit, HLC began wiping the glaze from the foot. Thus bowls in the 50s colors and later will have a white ring of clay showing on the bottom. Those made before 1951 will have sagger pin marks in the glaze under the rim.

Fiesta 5 1/2" fruit bowl in colors available at shape introduction. Yellow, $24-25; Cobalt, $31-32; Green, $28-29; Red, $31-32; Ivory, $32-33.

Fiesta 5 1/2" fruit bowl in colors added after introduction. Turquoise, $25-26; Forest, $37-38; Gray, $35-36; Rose, $37-38; Chartreuse, $37-38.

Early bowls, made before the end of 1937, have an impressed mark containing "HLC USA" along with the script Fiesta logo. Those made after that year, including probably all the bowls in turquoise, will have the mark with "MADE IN USA" as part of its design. A decorative band of graduated rings around the foot of the bowl was removed when the master mold with the new mark was made.

As with the smaller fruit bowl, these are not hard to find. They were produced in all eleven vintage colors and made until the restyling of the line for Fiesta Ironstone in 1969.

Fiesta 5 1/2" fruit bowl in medium green. Medium Green, $65-67.

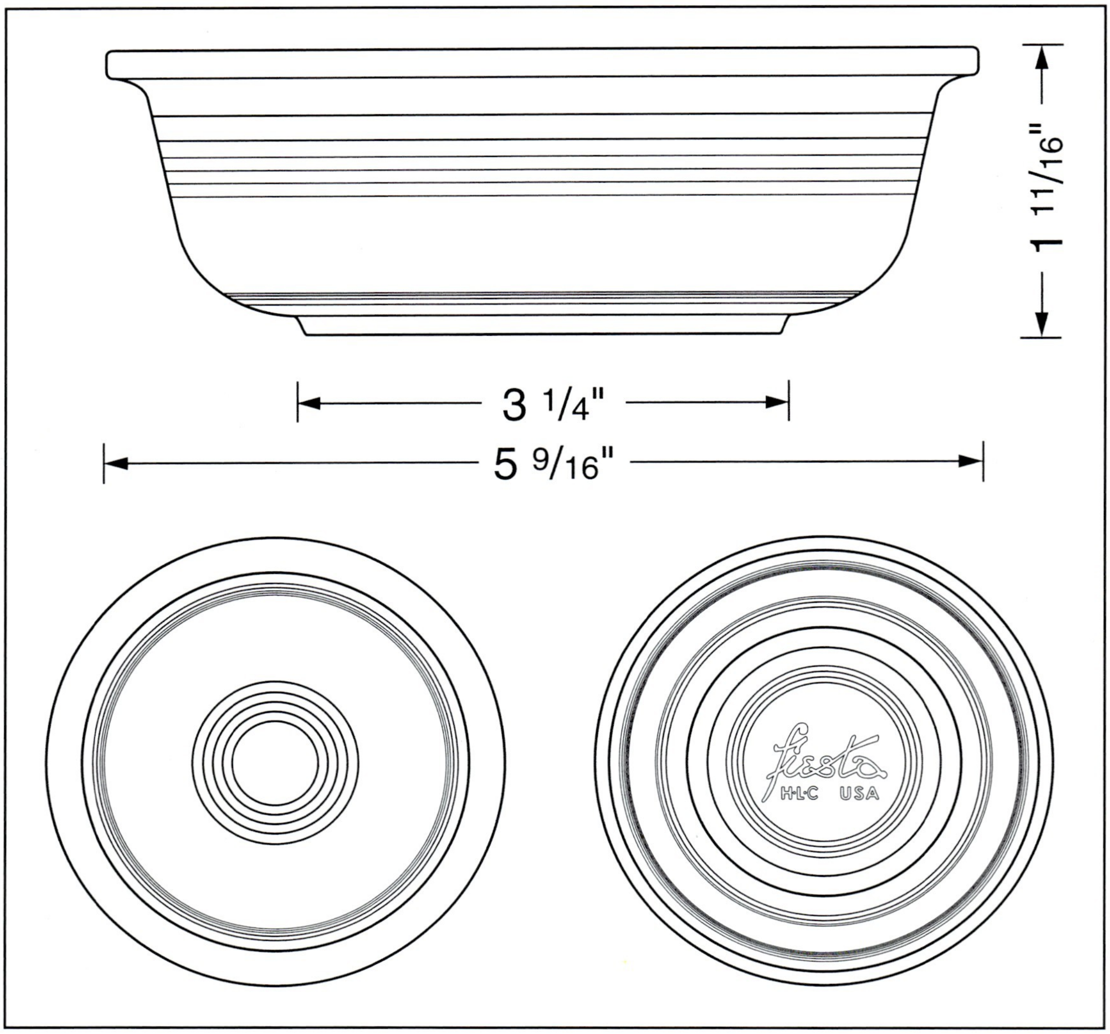

1 11/16"

3 1/4"

5 9/16"

fiesta
H·L·C USA

Fiesta 5 1/2" Fruit Bowl

Modeling Date	April 1935
Model Number	358[1]
First Revision	November 1935, 492[2]
Second Revision	December 1935, 495[3]
Production Began	December 1935*
First Price List	Early 1936 (undated)
Last Price List	January 1, 1968
Discontinued	Early 1969
Length of Production	33.2 Years*

Colors: Red[†], Cobalt, Green, Yellow, Ivory, Turquoise, Rose, Gray, Chartreuse, Forest, Medium Green

*Estimate

[†]Red discontinued in early 1944, reintroduced mid-1959

[1]First model, 6" diameter, not produced

[2]Revised slightly smaller, apparently not produced

[3]Same size as 492, final model

Fiesta 11 3/4" Fruit Bowl

The name for this item comes from Fiesta price lists, which incorrectly gave the size as 11 3/4 inches. The bowl's actual diameter is 11 3/8 inches. Frederick Rhead designed it in the Spring of 1937 as part of the Kitchen Kraft line. He called it a "salad nappie." At that time he also added a fork to the OvenServe line to be used with the existing spoon as part of a salad set with this bowl. Even though the fork and spoon became part of Kitchen Kraft, the bowl did not.

A note in company records, dated Wednesday, June 9, 1937, says, *"J. M. Wells released the large salad nappie. This to be made in Fiesta colors including the ivory (not OvenServe)."* Joseph M. Wells, Sr. had total control over what was produced by Homer Laughlin. His name is mentioned frequently in Rhead's journal.

One telltale sign of the bowl's origin are the two "stair step" rings just under the rim on the outside of the bowl. All Kitchen Kraft bowls and large casseroles have these rings. It was easy for HLC to change the inside from plain to having a ring pattern by simply making a new jiggering tool. The outside only needed the Fiesta mark.

As implied, this bowl was jiggered. There are two varieties and the difference involves the inside of the bowl. One has the familiar graduated rings descending the side and getting closer together toward the bottom. The other type has an inch wide band of closely and evenly spaced rings that begin approximately 1/2" down from the rim. Each

Fiesta 11 3/4" fruit bowl in all available colors. Yellow, $305-320; Cobalt, $330-365; Green, $315-330; Red, $340-360; Turquoise, $305-325; Ivory, $325-340.

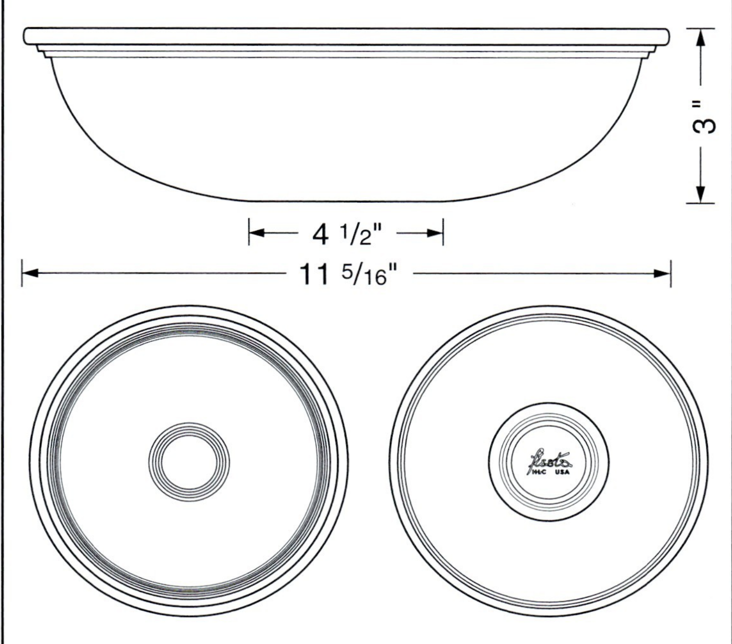

type also has a different pattern of rings in the center. The bottom of all bowls are the same and are marked in the mold with the "Fiesta/HLC USA" mark.

Even though they were available for nearly ten years, these bowls are very hard to find. No color seems more elusive than any other does, but those in red and cobalt seem to command higher prices.

Fiesta 11 3/4" Fruit Bowl	
Modeling Date	May 1937
Model Number	836[1]
Revisions	None
Production Began	June 1937*
First Price List	January 1, 1938
Last Price List	August 22, 1946
Discontinued	Late 1946*
Length of Production	9.3 Years*
Colors: Red[†], Cobalt, Green, Yellow, Ivory, Turquoise	
*Estimate	
[†]Red discontinued in early 1944	
[1]Originally part of the Kitchen Kraft line	

Nested Mixing Bowls and Mixing Bowl Covers

Mixing bowls have been a standard item of household pottery for hundreds of years. In the first half of the twentieth century, before fast food restaurants or home delivery, a residential kitchen was not complete without a set of mixing bowls in several sizes. In order for Fiesta to be competitive with other lines of ware, Frederick Rhead had to include a mixing bowl set. Because the Fiesta mixing bowls could be purchased individually and were offered in a wide variety of sizes, the housewife could buy only the bowls she really needed.

The bowls Rhead designed had another attractive feature: the whole set was made to "nest" and would take no more shelf space than the largest bowl. The sizes produced ranged from a 5" diameter bowl for frostings and sauces to an 11" giant for meat loaf or turkey stuffing for the largest of families. The bowls were numbered one to seven, smallest to largest.

It isn't well known, but there was a bowl modeled for this set even smaller than a number one. The 4" mini bowl was not produced. And here's another bit of Fiesta trivia: at six and one half pounds the #7 mixing bowl is the heaviest item in the line.

Produced for less than nine years, the mixing bowls are somewhat difficult to find, especially in excellent condition. Most were well used and show it with rim chips and scratches inside the bowl. They were made in all colors until the Fall of 1942 when each size was offered in only one color: #7 cobalt, #6 turquoise, #5 yellow, #4 ivory, #3 green, #2 yellow, and #1 red. By the Spring of 1944 they were no longer being sold.

Mixing bowls were produced by jiggering. The #7 bowl was the largest jiggered piece in the Fiesta line. There are two major varieties of mixing bowl, one has a band of rings in the inside bottom of the bowl, and the other does not. There are also two marks, the "HLC USA" and "MADE IN USA". The earlier bowls have the inside bottom rings and almost all of them will have the "HLC USA" mark. Bowls made after the early months of 1938 have no inside rings and are usually marked "Fiesta/MADE IN USA". Both types are known to have both marks, but this is generally how they are found.

The most convenient sizes for the housewife to use, numbers two through five, are the easiest for collectors to find. The smallest one and the two largest are in the very hard to find category. For most collectors color plays less of a roll in determining value when the purchase of a number one or seven is being considered.

Lids for the mixing bowls were a nice afterthought—they were not modeled until June 1936—but apparently they just didn't sell. The lids were on only one Fiesta price list which made its appearance around August 1936 (it is not dated). It is assumed that the lids were made for less than half a year and thus had one the shortest production runs of any item in the line.

A lid for each size bowl was modeled, but only the four smallest were produced. However, a trial run of all seven sizes was made and a few collectors have been able to find a number five or six to put in their collection. So far the survival of an example of the largest lid is only a rumor.

Designed with the knob sunk in a depression, each lid permitted the next smaller size bowl to be stacked on top of it, which would save space in the refrigerator. Yet the bowls themselves were not shaped in a way that would save much space. Competition from other potteries, such as Hall China with it's multiple lines of refrigerator ware, could have been part of the reason the Fiesta mixing bowl lids did not sell. Another reason was the fact that they cost nearly as much as the bowl they were intended to cover.

While not in the same league as turquoise onion soups or medium green cream soups, these lids are definitely in the "rare" category. Even with chips, they still are highly valued.

Opposite page:
The complete set of vintage Fiesta nested mixing bowls. See appendix E for pricing information on these 42 bowls.

The seven sizes of vintage Fiesta nested mixing bowls in assorted colors. Number 1 in Red, $215-235; Number 2 in Green, $125-135; Number 3 in Ivory, $150-160; Number 4 in Yellow, $120-130; Number 5 in Turquoise, $170-180; Number 6 in Cobalt, $295-320; Number 7 in Red, $410-455

Cobalt and yellow mixing bowls.

Stacking mixing bowls.

A complete set of vintage Fiesta mixing bowl covers with their corresponding bowl. See Appendix E for pricing information on these 20 lids.

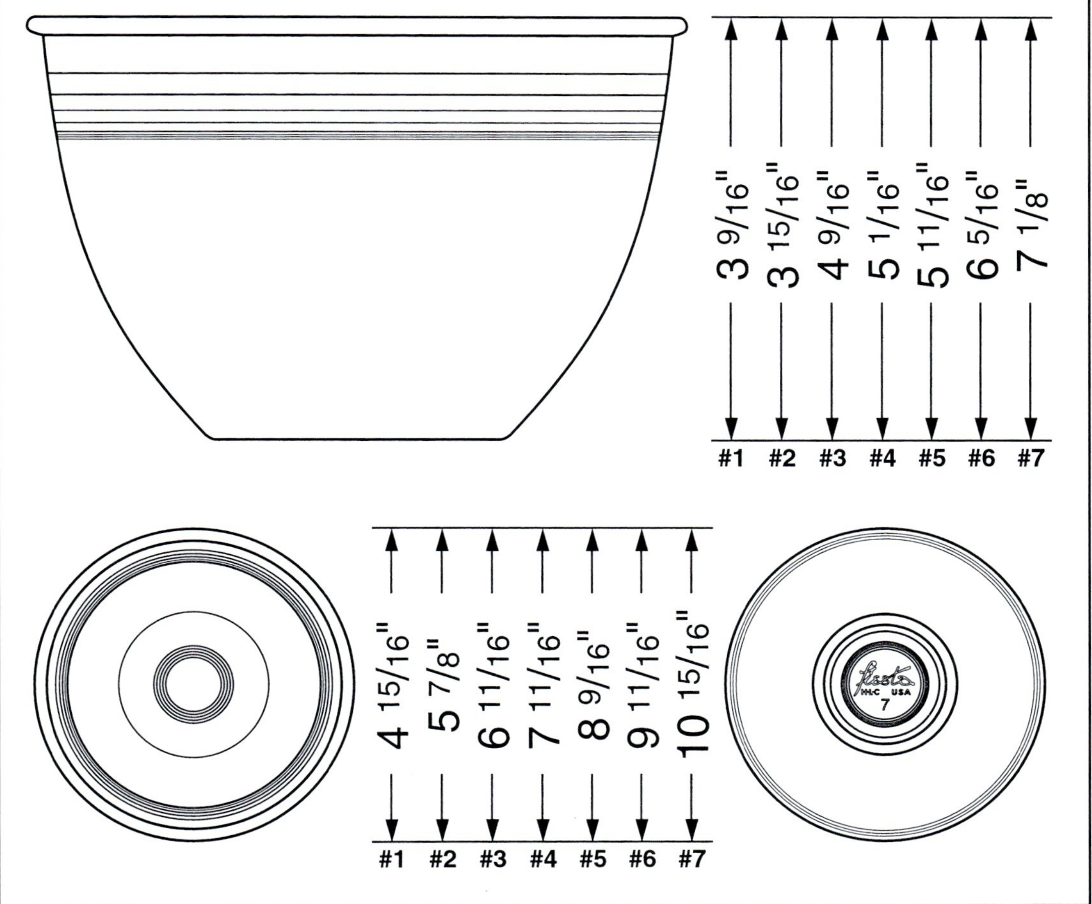

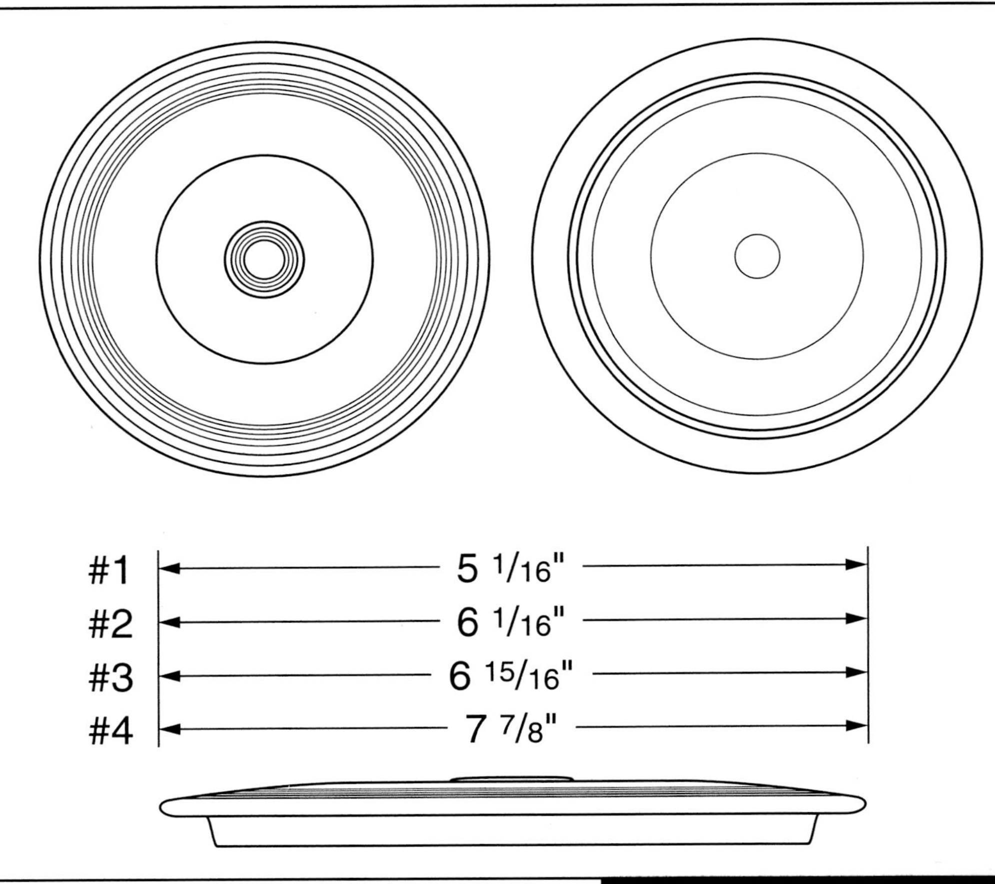

Fiesta Nested Mixing Bowls

Modeling Dates .... June-July 1935
Model Numbers .... #6 385, #5 387, #4 396,
.... #3 403, #7 406, #2 407,
.... #1 410, 414[1]
Revisions .... None
Production Began .... November 1935*
First Price List .... Early 1936 (undated)
Last Price List .... October 1, 1942
Discontinued .... Early 1944*
Length of Production .... 8.7 Years*
Colors: Red, Cobalt, Green, Yellow, Ivory, Turquoise
*Estimate
[1]Smallest bowl, 4" diameter, not produced

Fiesta Mixing Bowl Covers

Modeling Date .... June 1936
Model Numbers .... 629-635[1]
Revisions .... None
Production Began .... August 1936*
First Price List .... Late 1936 (undated)
Last Price List .... Late 1936 (undated)
Discontinued .... Early 1937*
Length of Production .... 0.5 Year*
Colors: Red, Cobalt, Green, Yellow, Ivory
*Estimate
[1]Only sizes 1-4 produced for sale, 5 & 6 known to exist

Fiesta 8 1/2″ Nappie

Nappie (or nappy) is an old English term for an open, earthenware serving bowl and seems to have been in common use by American potters during the 1930s. The serving bowl was a much-needed piece in the days of large, rural families and the Fiesta line had two. This one was in production for more than 33 years and is one of 14 items (out of 75) made for the entire time Fiesta was in production.

The mold for the 8 1/2″ nappie seems to have been made in two versions and each had a slightly different jiggering tool to go with it. Thus, collectors will note different impressed marks and accompanying internal ring patterns. The "Fiesta/HLC USA" mark is the earlier one and appears on nappies in the original five colors. The mark was changed to "Fiesta/MADE IN USA" sometime in 1937 or early 1938 and will be the mark most often seen. Like the small fruit bowls, this one features a flange or lip on the rim.

Until the 1950s most bowls of this type were placed in saggers for their trip through the kiln after being glazed. Three indentations in the glaze, under the rim of the bowl, will be noted on pieces processed in this manner. With the introduction of the Fifties color glazes, nappies had the glaze wiped from the foot of the bowl and were sent through the kiln on shelves. They will have a white ring of clay showing on the bottom.

Except for those in medium green, 8 1/2" Fiesta nappies are not difficult to find. Those in the elusive green glaze of the Sixties are valued at three or four times those in other colors.

Fiesta 8 1/2″ nappy in colors available at shape introduction. Yellow, $43-44; Cobalt, $56-59; Green, $42-43; Red, $54-56; Ivory, $53-56.

Fiesta 8 1/2″ nappy in colors added after introduction. Turquoise, $42-43; Forest, $57-61; Gray, $56-60; Chartreuse, $60-62; Rose, $57-60.

Fiesta 8 1/2″ nappy in medium green. Medium Green, $155-165.

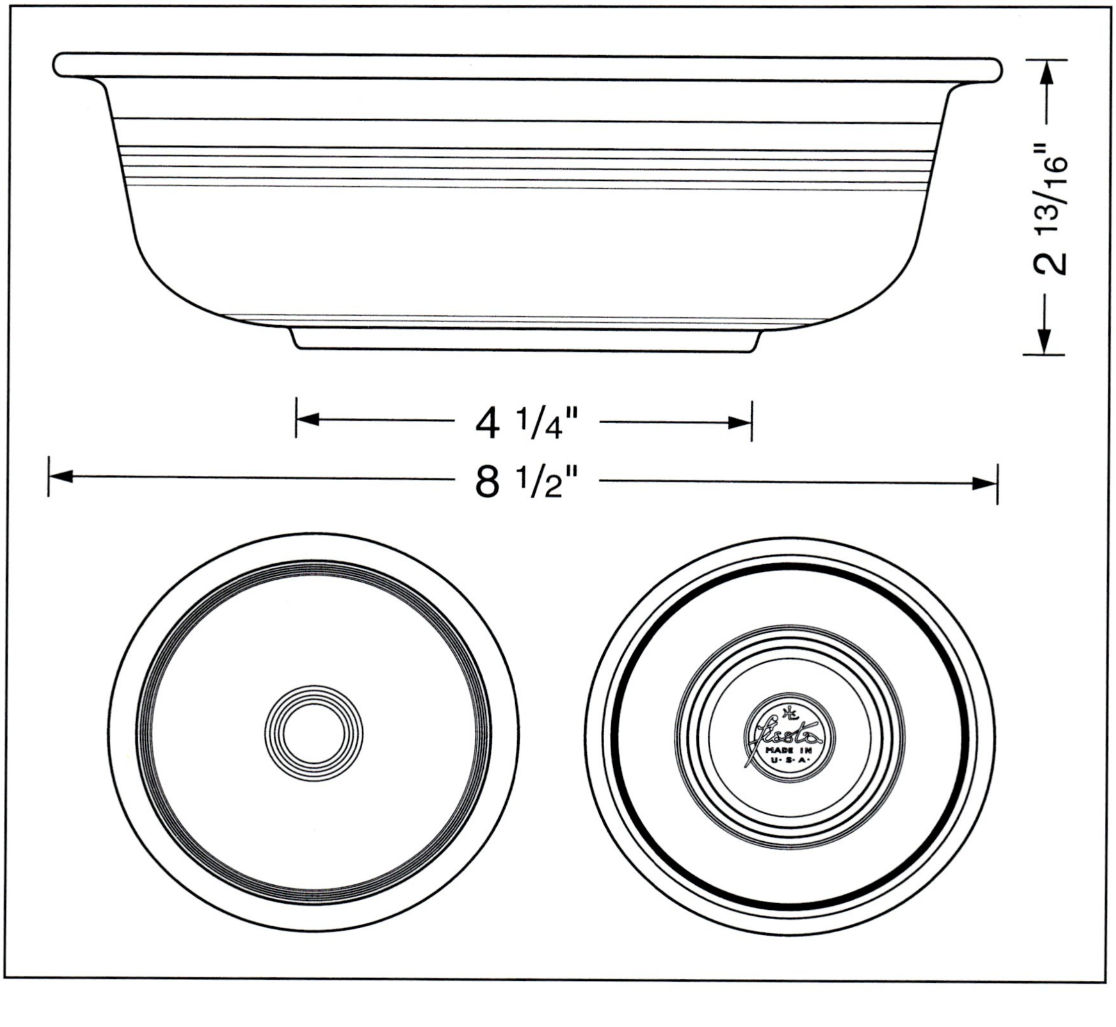

2 13/16"

4 1/4"

8 1/2"

Fiesta 8 1/2" Nappie

Modeling Date	March 1935
Model Number	356
Revisions	None
Production Began	November 1935*
First Price List	Early 1936 (undated)
Last Price List	January 1, 1968
Discontinued	Early 1969*
Length of Production	33.2 Years*

Colors: Red[†], Cobalt, Green, Yellow, Ivory, Turquoise, Rose, Gray, Chartreuse, Forest, Medium Green

*Estimate

[†]Red discontinued in early 1944, reintroduced mid-1959

Fiesta 9 1/2" Nappie

While the 8 1/2" nappie holds 32 ounces, this larger one will bring 48 ounces of food to the table. Modeled within a week or so of the smaller one, this bowl was produced for approximately eleven years. It was discontinued in late 1946, along with 14 other pieces, in the largest reduction of available items in the line's history.

This bowl has the same variations found on the other nappie. Two types of "HLC USA" marks exist, one larger than the other, while the "MADE IN USA" mark is also found. There are slight differences of the inside ring patterns, which is expected with jiggered bowls made over a period of time. All large nappies have a wet foot and sagger pin marks under the rim.

The 9 1/2" nappie is not as common as the 8 1/2" one, but still available. Red ones were made for only eight years and usually bring a higher price than the others.

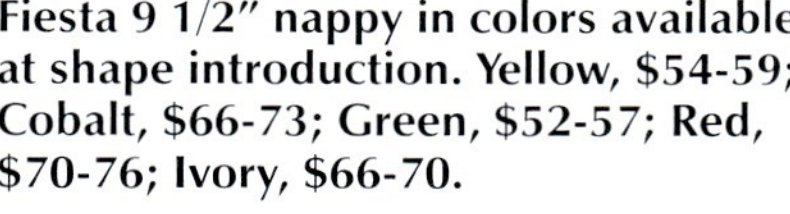

Fiesta 9 1/2" nappy in colors available at shape introduction. Yellow, $54-59; Cobalt, $66-73; Green, $52-57; Red, $70-76; Ivory, $66-70.

Fiesta 9 1/2" nappy in turquoise, added after introduction. Turquoise, $50-55

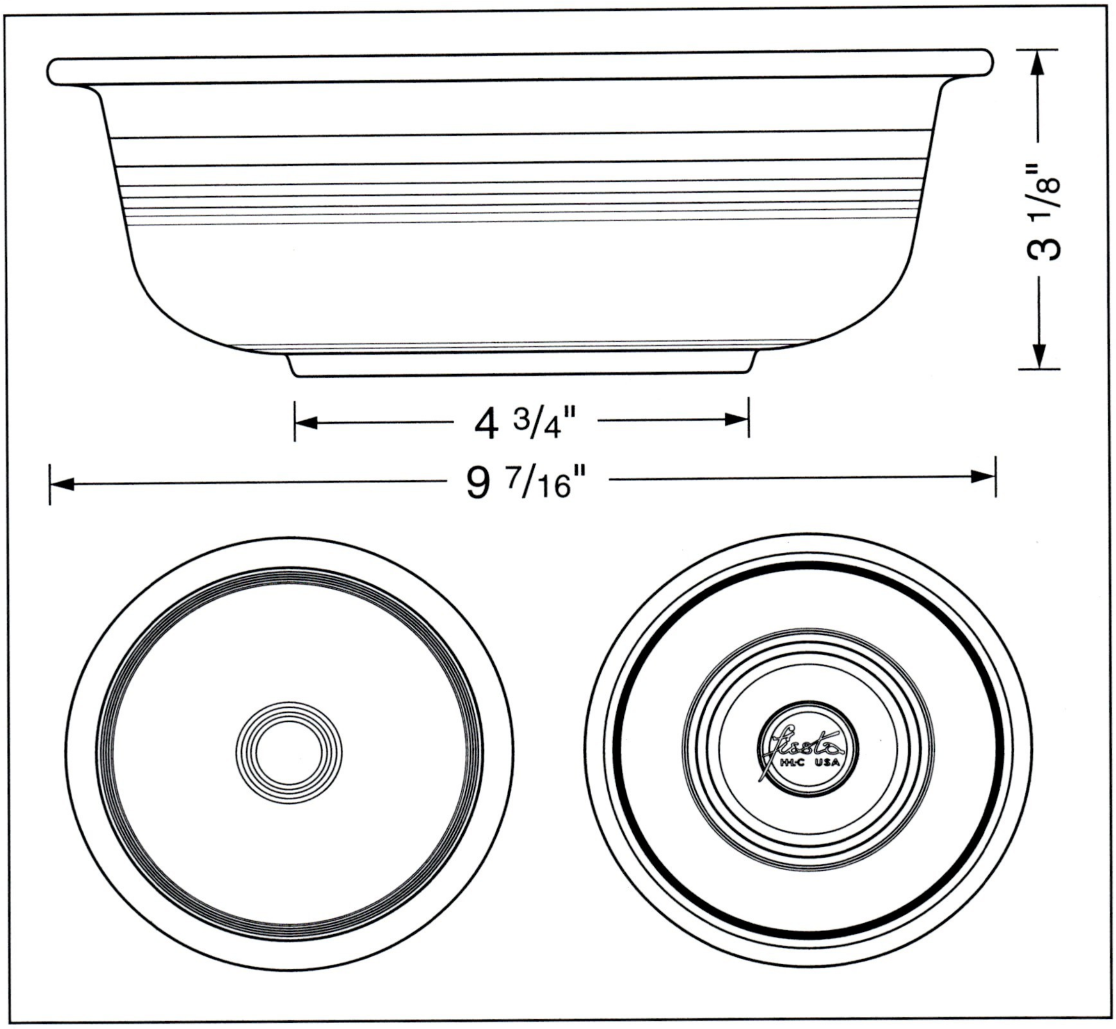

3 1/8"

4 3/4"

9 7/16"

fiesta HLC USA

Fiesta 9 1/2" Nappie

Modeling Date .... April 1935
Model Number 361
Revisions .... None
Production Began .... November 1935*
First Price List .... Early 1936 (undated)
Last Price List .... August 22, 1946
Discontinued .... Late 1946*
Length of Production .... 11 Years*
Colors: Colors: Red†, Cobalt, Green, Yellow, Ivory, Turquoise
*Estimate
†Red discontinued in early 1944

Footed Salad Bowl

It's not the tallest Fiesta piece, or the heaviest or widest, but it is a very large bowl and one of the most sought after items in the line. Priced at $2.25 in 1936 it was big piece for the money. This bowl was introduced and discontinued along with the 9 1/2" nappie, but they are much harder to find than that bowl. No doubt this is due to the relative few sold when they were in production. Yellow ones are reportedly the most elusive. This bowl was also used in the Fiesta Tom and Jerry set and can be found with hand-applied gold band decorations on the rim and foot, and "Tom & Jerry" stamped in gold on the side.

Another jiggered piece, this one has two known variations. It seems early bowls had a foot that was cast separately and hand applied, like the 12" comport. These apparently proved unstable and the design was changed. Indications are that the problem was related to the foot coming off the bowl in the bisque stage. At least one of these, minus its foot, was glazed in cobalt and made it into a collector's hands. There is a narrow band of rings on the inside edge of the bowl, which stop about 1.5" from the rim. This type has an in-mold "Fiesta/HLC USA" mark.

The second variety has a much thicker foot, which appears to be hand turned. That is, it was made as part of the bowl and was shaped by hand after the bowl was removed from the mold. The inner ring pattern descends 2" into the bowl from the rim and the rings are more widely spaced compared to the other type. These bowls are usually marked with the "Genuine Fiesta" backstamp.

Both types will have three imperfections in the center of the completely glazed foot. This is due to the tripod stilt used in the glazing kiln.

Fiesta Footed Salad Bowl

Modeling Date	April 1935
Model Number	366
Revisions	None
Production Began	November 1935*
First Price List	Early 1936 (undated)
Last Price List	August 22, 1946
Discontinued	Late 1946*
Length of Production	11 Years*

Colors: Red†, Cobalt, Green, Yellow, Ivory, Turquoise

*Estimate

†Red discontinued in early 1944

Fiesta footed salad bowls in colors available at shape introduction. Green, $335-370; Ivory, $360-385; Cobalt, $375-405; Red, $350-375; Yellow, $350-385.

Fiesta footed salad bowl in turquoise, added after introduction. Turquoise, $335-380.

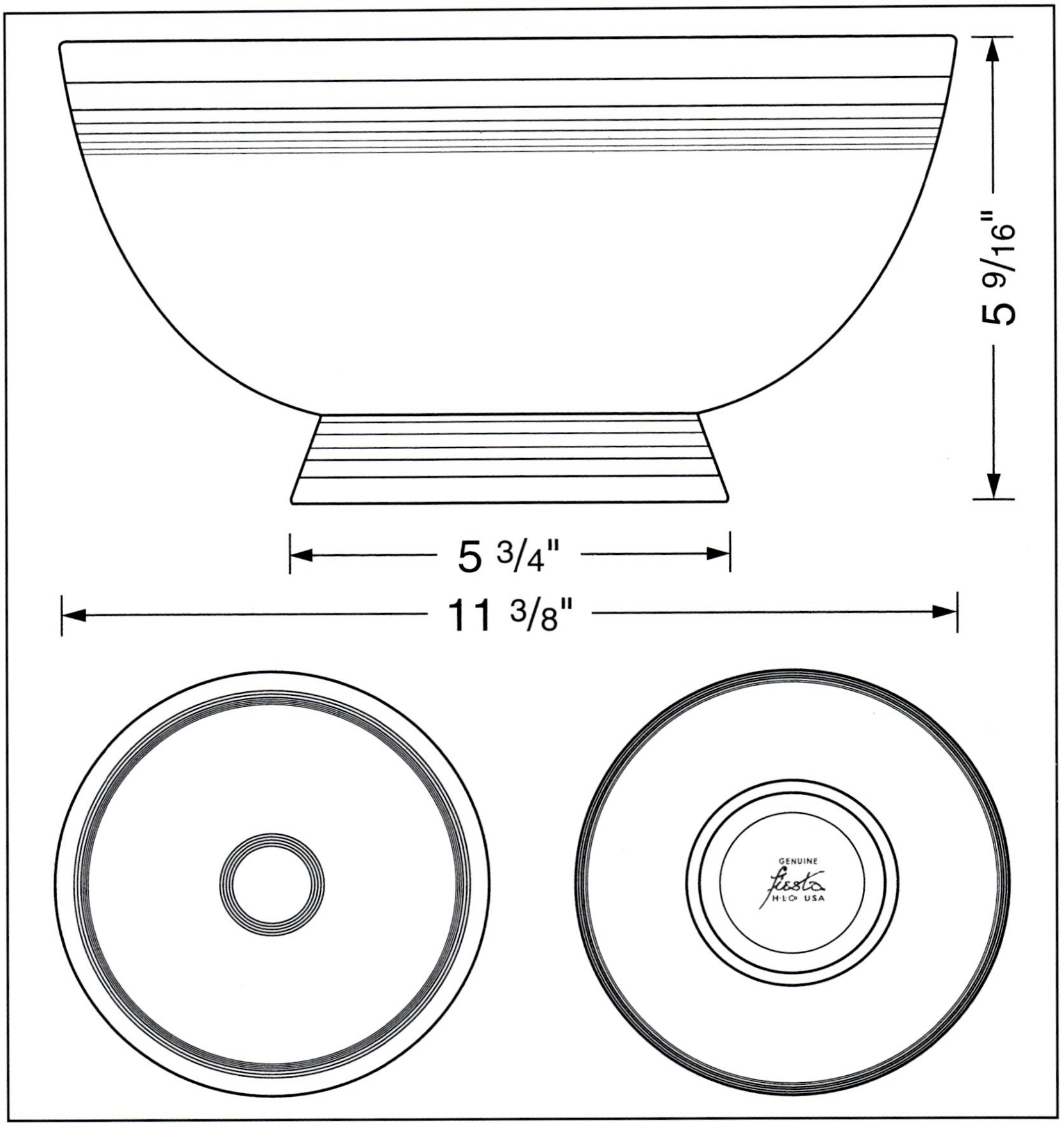

5 9/16"

5 3/4"

11 3/8"

GENUINE
Fiesta
HLC USA

Individual Salad Bowl

In September 1939 a salad bowl was modeled for Fiesta. It measured approximately 7-1/2 inches wide by 2 inches tall and had rings inside and out. It was not produced. Instead the inside rings were removed, the outside rings modified, and the shape used for Harlequin. It can be found today in all twelve Harlequin colors.

The Fiesta individual salad bowl modeled in 1959 was the first new item added to the line since the sugar, creamer, and tray set in January 1940. Although not a revision of the original Fiesta salad, or the Harlequin bowl, it is approximately the same size. It was made only in the colors of the Sixties. This bowl has two major types. One features the familiar inside and outside rings; the other has outside rings only with a completely smooth interior. Both types have an unglazed foot

The HLC modeling log lists this bowl as, *"Harlequin, Fiesta bowl, released July 8, [plant] #4"*. It is believed that the salad bowl was made for both Fiesta and Harlequin. The bowls without inside rings being the Harlequin version.

This bowl was made on the automatic jiggering machine. A spinning metal blade or tool formed the inside. The outside was shaped by a plaster mold. Initially, two molds were used. One created the impressed "Fiesta/MADE IN USA" mark, the other left a plain, unmarked bottom. The Fiesta marked bowls were made with inside rings, the unmarked Harlequin bowls had no inside rings.

Later it was decided to use only the plain bottom mold while continuing to use the two different tools, one that formed inside rings and one that did not. The bowls with inside rings then received the "Genuine Fiesta" backstamp. This was a cost saving measure because the same mold could be used for both dinnerware lines and the jiggering tools already in use did not have to be changed.

There are several variations to note. The Fiesta bowls have thicker sides to accommodate the inside rings and they weigh more than the Harlequin version. The bowls with inside rings may have the impressed mark or the hand applied backstamp. These bowls were made in Fiesta yellow as well as the other Sixties glazes. The bowls without inside rings are not marked and have been found in Harlequin yellow, red, turquoise and medium green.

The amount of Fiesta sold during the Sixties was less than it had been during previous decades. Even though this bowl was made for nearly ten years, they are somewhat difficult to find these days and values for all colors are perhaps higher than might be expected for a bowl of this size.

Fiesta Individual Salad Bowl

Modeling Date	June 1959
Model Number	2552
Revisions	None
Production Began	July 1959
First Price List	June 1, 1959
Last Price List	January 1, 1968
Discontinued	Early 1969*
Length of Production	9.6 Years*

Colors: Red, Yellow, Turquoise, Medium Green

*Estimate

Fiesta individual salad bowl in all available colors. Yellow, $78-85; Medium Green, $120-125; Red, $97-100; Turquoise, $82-88.

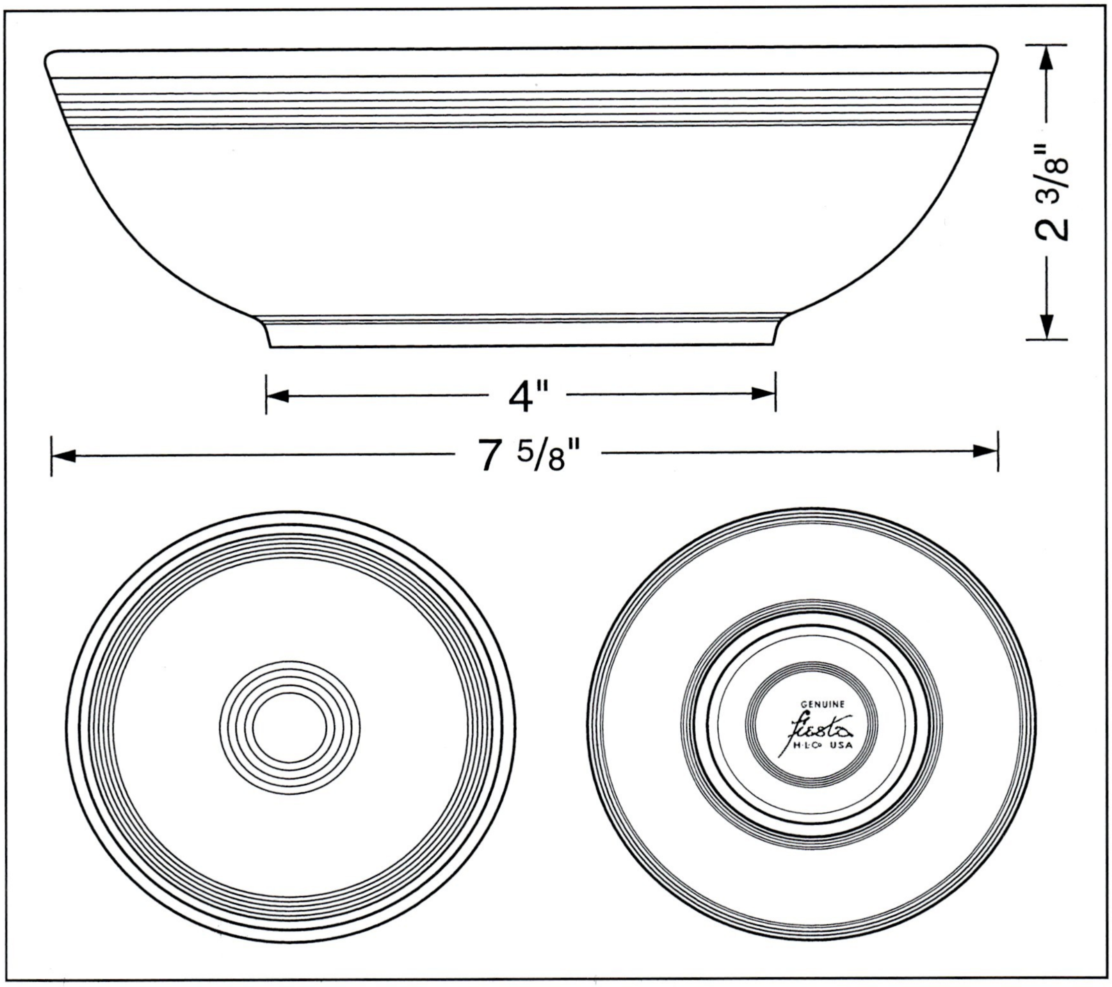

Bulb Candle Holder

During 1935, Frederick Rhead showed his designs for Fiesta to many long-time clients. As suggestions came in from the retail buyers, Rhead discussed them with HLC management, created drawings, had models made, and added new items to the growing Fiesta line. Late in the year, he added a second candle holder. The HLC modeling log gives a brief glimpse of three alternatives in tiny marginal drawings, but the final design is one of the few pieces that clearly shows an Art Deco influence. It resembles candle holders by other manufacturers already on the market and was itself an inspiration for more than one American pottery.

Bulb candle holders were made by the slip casting method. The design did not change during the eleven years they were made. An in-mold mark is present on two adjacent sides on the underside of the square bottom. Frequently, mold seams can be seen on the globe.

This style of candle holder seems to have been more popular than the tripod as they are not that difficult for the collector to find today. Values tend to be slightly higher for those in the popular red and cobalt glazes.

Fiesta Bulb Candle Holder	
Modeling Date	September 1935
Model Number	435[1]
First Revision	September 1935, 443
Production Began	November 1935*
First Price List	Early 1936 (undated)
Last Price List	August 22, 1946
Discontinued	Late 1946*
Length of Production	11 Years*

Colors: Red[†], Cobalt, Green, Yellow, Ivory, Turquoise

*Estimate

[†]Red discontinued in early 1944

[1]First model not produced

Fiesta bulb candle holders in turquoise, added after introduction. Turquoise, $115-120 pair.

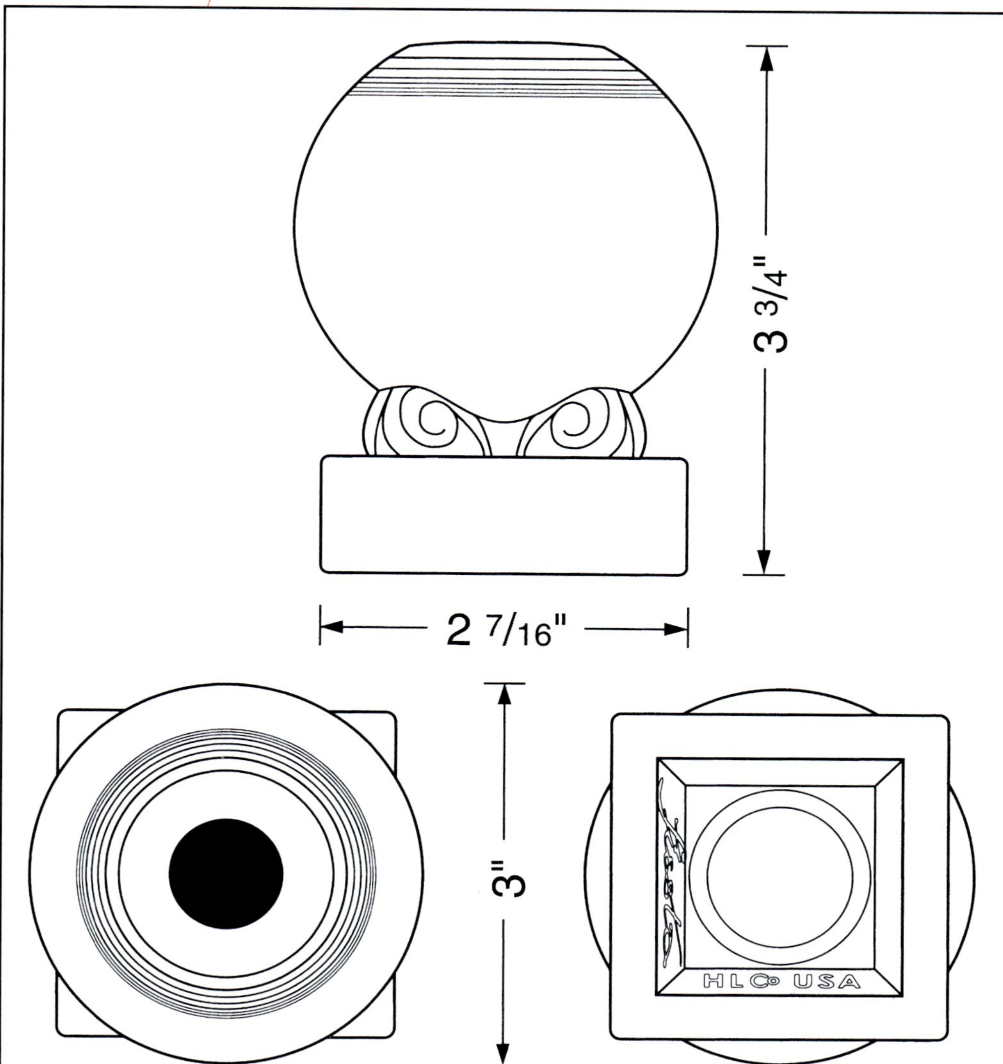

Fiesta bulb candle holders in colors available at shape introduction. Yellow, $100-105 pair; Red, $115-120 pair; Cobalt, $120-125 pair; Green, $99-105 pair; Ivory, $115-120 pair.

Tripod Candle Holder

The name for this interesting piece comes from vintage Fiesta price lists. In Rhead's *Record of Sketches and Drawings* he refers to the design as "candlestick, three supports." Two models were made and the final selection is one of the most sought after items for current collectors. They were produced for approximately seven years and discontinued for apparent lack of sales.

Like any complicated shape, this one was slip cast. It took an intricate four-part mold to shape the item from the liquid clay. An impressed "Fiesta/HLC USA" mark can be found on the bottom. Two varieties of the tripod candle holder are known. Almost all of them have a completely glazed foot with the three pinpoint marks left by the kiln stilt. In fact, the "wet foot" is a feature that distinguishes the vintage item from those produced today. However, a few of the earlier candle holders have been found with a wiped foot. These are very rare, but they are known to exist in more than one color.

Fiesta candle holders of both types are usually sold in pairs. With the tripods being highly valued even individually, adding a set to a collection is an expensive proposition. Again, the popular red glaze tends to be more desirable and thus commands a higher price. Due to their relatively short production time, tripods are in the "hard to find" category.

Fiesta Tripod Candle Holder

Modeling Date	May 1935
Model Number	379[1]
Revision	July 1935, 399
Production Began	November 1935*
First Price List	Early 1936 (undated)
Last Price List	August 1, 1941
Discontinued	Late 1942*
Length of Production	7 Years*

Colors: Red, Cobalt, Green, Yellow, Ivory, Turquoise

*Estimate

[1]First model not produced

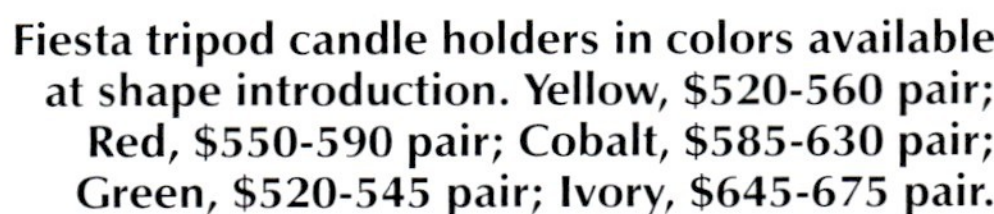

Fiesta tripod candle holders in colors available at shape introduction. Yellow, $520-560 pair; Red, $550-590 pair; Cobalt, $585-630 pair; Green, $520-545 pair; Ivory, $645-675 pair.

Fiesta tripod candle holders in turquoise, added after introduction. Turquoise, $620-670 pair.

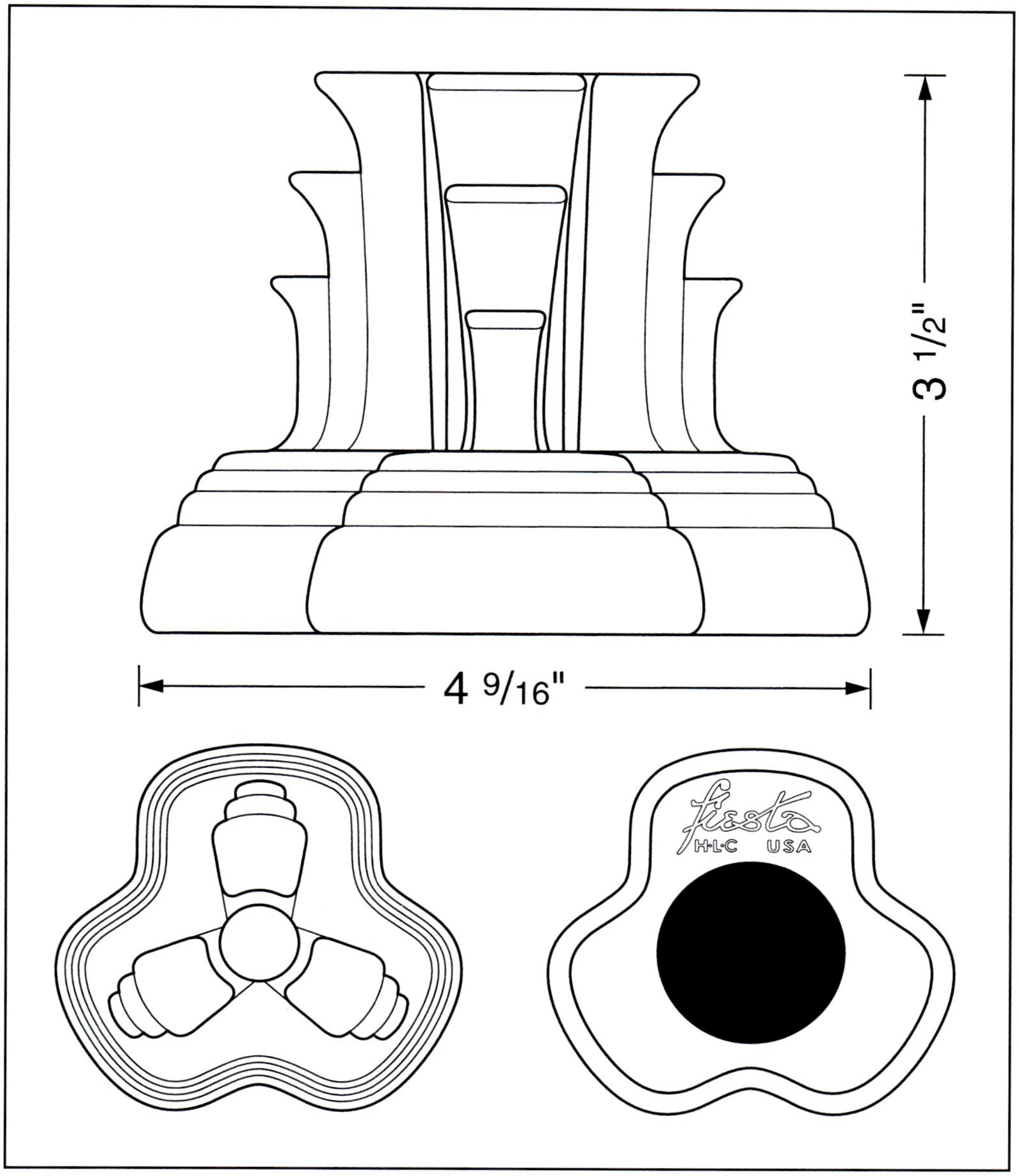

3 1/2"

4 9/16"

fiesta
H·L·C USA

Carafe

The Fiesta carafe is one item that is usually on the list as a "must have" for collectors. The shape is distinct among 1930s ware and is often used in drawings or photographs to represent the essence of Fiesta. Occasionally a debate develops over the purpose of the carafe. Rhead's own notes, the record of drawings, and the HLC modeling log all refer to this item as a water bottle. The stated capacity of the carafe is three pints.

As with almost all hollowware, this piece was slip cast. There are two varieties of impressed marks, both the "Fiesta/HLC USA" type. One is slightly larger and is surrounded by three rings, while the other consists of the logo and text only. Carafes with the latter mark weigh about two pounds. For some reason the other variety can be considerably heavier. This is probably the result of a slight change in the way they were made. By allowing the liquid slip to stay in the mold longer, a thicker and heavier side wall would develop. The lid has an attached cork stopper for the 1 1/2" diameter opening and sports a hand-applied finial.

Fiesta carafes are somewhat difficult to locate. Red ones more so than the other colors, since HLC stopped making them approximately three years earlier than those in other colors. The lid is frequently missing or damaged and chips on the foot of the vessel are not uncommon. Carafes in excellent shape, in any color, are a prize and can be an expensive acquisition.

Fiesta Carafe

Modeling Date	July 1935
Model Number	398
Revisions	None
Production Began	November 1935*
First Price List	Early 1936 (undated)
Last Price List	August 22, 1946
Discontinued	Late 1946*
Length of Production	11 Years*

Colors: Red†, Cobalt, Green, Yellow, Ivory, Turquoise

*Estimate

†Red discontinued in early 1944

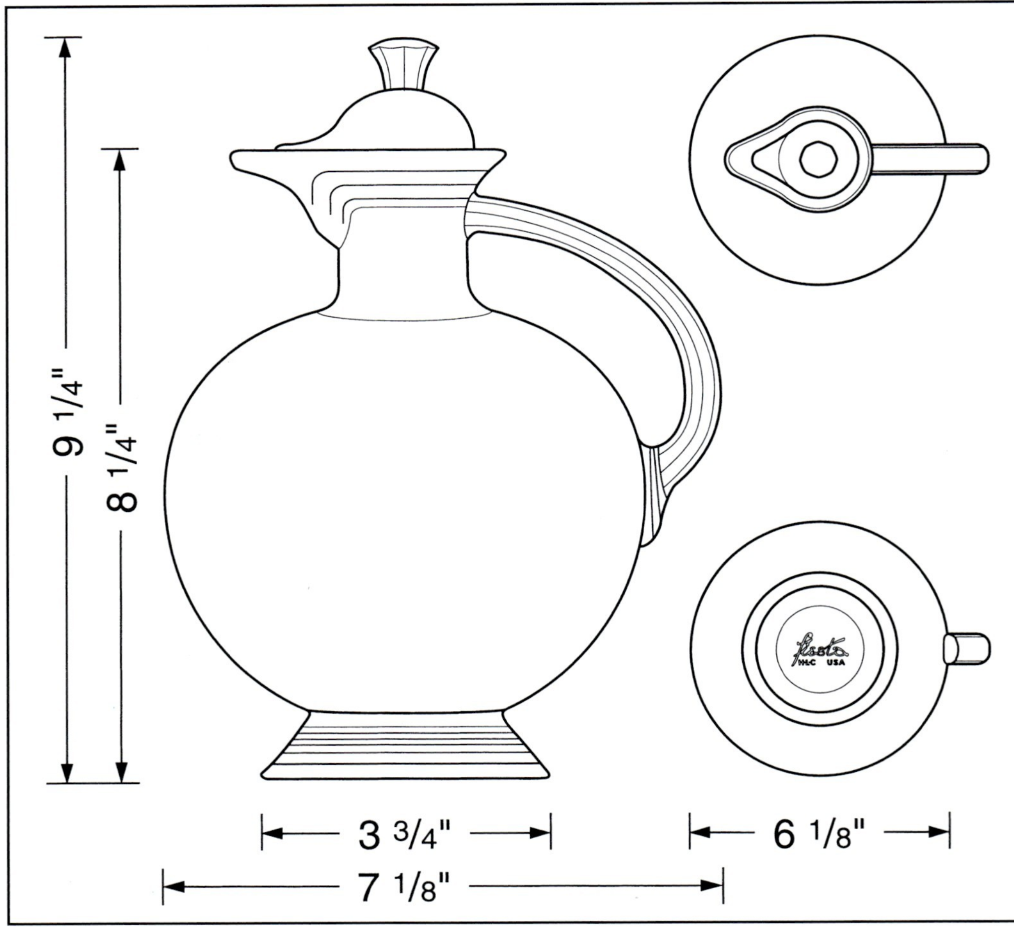

Fiesta carafe in turquoise, added afte introduction. Turquoise, $280-295.

Covered Casserole

Frederick Rhead's first casserole idea for Fiesta was a single-handled French casserole. This was modeled in April 1935 and may have been the one revived for the promotional campaign of the early 1940s, but it was not produced for the main dinnerware line. In August of 1935 the casserole that collectors are familiar with was modeled. In spite of a couple early attempts at changing the lid, this design was made for the entire time the vintage line of Fiesta was in production.

Rhead was likely inspired to reshape the onion soup bowl after he made the casserole. Both share the same shape and have a family resemblance to the Fiesta sugar bowl. The revised onion soup was created only a few days after the final casserole shape was determined.

While the basic shape of the casserole and lid did not change during the more than 30 years it was made, there are a few variations to note. The bowls themselves were jiggered and can be found with three different impressed marks. As with the large nappy, two "Fiesta/HLC USA" marks were used, one smaller than the other. The third type is the "Fiesta/MADE IN USA" mark, which is generally found on pieces after 1938. The ring pattern inside the rim of the casserole is also known in three varieties, which correspond to the three types of marks. These changes were due to slight alterations in the jigger tools used and do not affect the value.

The earliest casseroles had a separately cast foot ring which was applied by hand like the early footed salad bowls and 12" comports. In November 1936 the mold was changed to include the foot, which was then hand turned to its final shape. Throughout it's production run the casserole had hand applied handles.

An interesting feature of the casserole lid is a group of four rings in the center of the underside; a side usually not seen. The lids were jiggered and have the flared, eight-sided finial that was attached by hand.

In spite of the fact that they were produced for a long time, the Fiesta casserole is not easy to find. This is especially true for casseroles in the medium green glaze, which can have three to four times the value of those in the Fifties colors.

An even more difficult to find variation of this bowl was made for Tricolator Products in early 1938. It wasn't simply a casserole without the foot, but a separately modeled shape that has the Tricolator name impressed in the base. They have been found in all six early Fiesta colors and are not known to have a lid.

Fiesta Covered Casserole

Modeling Date	April 1935
Model Number	369[1]
First Revision	August 1935, 419[2]
Second Revision	September 1935, 427[3]
Third Revision	September 1935, 429[4]
Fourth Revision	January 1938, 1028[5]
Production Began	November 1935*
First Price List	Early 1936 (undated)
Last Price List	January 1, 1968
Discontinued	Early 1969
Length of Production	33.2 Years*

Colors: Red[†], Cobalt, Green, Yellow, Ivory, Turquoise, Rose, Gray, Chartreuse, Forest, Medium Green

*Estimate

[†]Red discontinued in early 1944, reintroduced mid-1959

[1]French style casserole, not produced

[2]Two handled casserole with cover

[3]Cover with turned knob, not produced

[4]Inside cover, not produced

[5]Tricolator bowl (see text)

Fiesta carafes in colors available at shape introduction. Yellow, $270-280; Red, $295-310; Cobalt, $325-340; Green, $300-310; Ivory, $300-330.

Fiesta covered casserole in medium green. Medium Green, $1305-1405.

Fiesta covered casseroles in colors available at shape introduction. Yellow, $155-160; Red, $195-205; Cobalt, $200-210; Ivory, $195-205; Green, $135-150.

Fiesta covered casseroles in colors added after introduction. Turquoise, $130-140; Gray, $255-275; Rose, $285-300; Forest, $285-305; Chartreuse, $250-260.

Fiesta covered casserole in red, covered onion soup in cobalt, and covered sugar in yellow. ; Covered Casserole in Red, $195-205; Covered Onion Soup in Cobalt, $710-755; Covered Sugar in Yellow, $41-43.

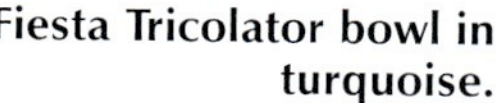

Fiesta Tricolator bowl in turquoise.

The marking from the Tricolator bowl.

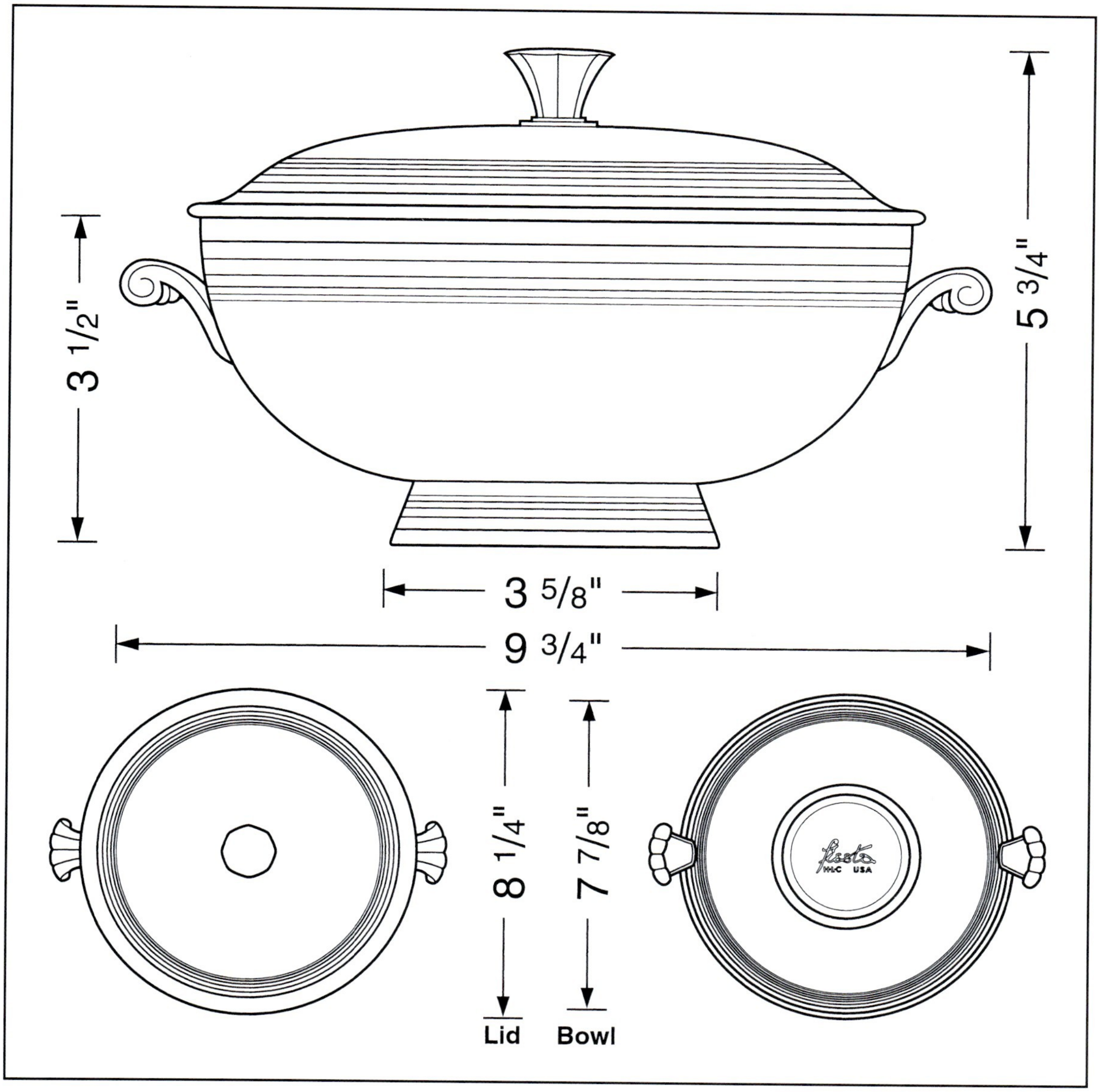

3 1/2"

5 3/4"

3 5/8"

9 3/4"

8 1/4"

7 7/8"

Lid

Bowl

After Dinner Coffeepot

In French, *demi tasse* means "small cup." In English it can also mean the type of strong, black coffee drunk from these small cups, usually after the evening meal. Instead of demitasse, Homer Laughlin used the term "After Dinner," or A.D., when referring to the small cups and to the elegant coffeepot made for use with them. This piece is another on the list of all-time favorite shapes for many collectors. The stick handle and shapely profile seem to give it an air of sophistication that other items in the line do not have.

Originally called a chocolate pot by Rhead, the after dinner coffeepot holds eight demitasse cups. It was made by the slip casting method from four parts—the body, handle, lid, and finial—that were assembled by hand. The size of the opening for the spout can vary somewhat because they were created manually. Some lids have been found with steam vent holes. There are two varieties of marks; both the "HLC USA" type. One is plain and the other has three rings around it. This piece was made in the first six colors for a period of approximately seven years.

For some reason, the turquoise "demi pots" are harder to find than the other colors and may command a higher price. None of them are easy to find and are therefore another highly valued item.

Fiesta after dinner coffee pots in colors available at shape introduction. Yellow, $425-465; Red, $530-560; Ivory, $505-535; Cobalt, $475-505; Green, 465-505.

Fiesta After Dinner Coffeepot

Modeling Date	May 1935
Model Number	370
Revisions	None
Production Began	November 1935*
First Price List	Early 1936 (undated)
Last Price List	August 1, 1941
Discontinued	Late 1942*
Length of Production	7 Years*

Colors: Red, Cobalt, Green, Yellow, Ivory, Turquoise

*Estimate

Fiesta after dinner coffee pot in turquoise, added after introduction. Turquoise, $620-665.

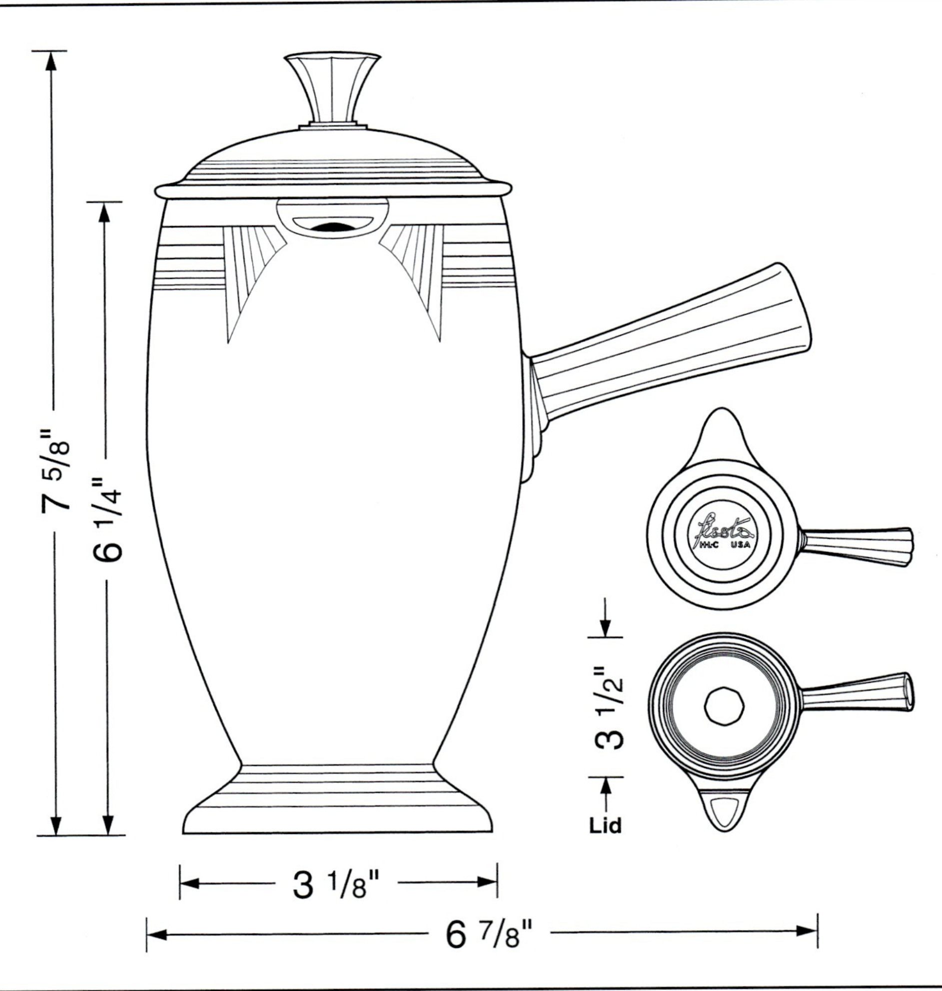

Fiesta regular coffee pot in colors available at shape introduction. Yellow, $175-185; Red, $235-240; Cobalt, $235-245; Ivory, $230-240; Green, $175-185.

Regular Coffeepot

At a little over ten inches, the Fiesta coffeepot is the second tallest piece in the line. It was part of the original offering in 1936 and was made for more than twenty years. Although it was called an "eight cup" pot in HLC records, it really holds only seven.

The coffeepot was slip cast as a single piece, including the handle. The lid and finial were cast separately and put together by hand. This item can be found with three different impressed marks—the plain "Fiesta/HLC USA", the same mark with three rings around it, and the "MADE IN USA" mark.

With declining sales probably because more people were using electric coffee makers instead of preparing coffee on the stove, HLC decided to stop making Fiesta regular coffee pots in the late 1950s. They last appear on the October 1, 1957 price list, but must have been made well into the next year. By 1959 they were gone and not officially produced in the medium green glaze.

Gray coffeepots seem to be in very short supply and a gray one will cost the collector more than those in the other Fifties colors. The others are also scarce and can be added to the "hard to find" list. Original color coffeepots are not common, but can be found without too much trouble.

Fiesta Regular Coffeepot

Modeling Date	July 1935
Model Number	400
Revisions	None
Production Began	November 1935*
First Price List	Early 1936 (undated)
Last Price List	October 1, 1957
Discontinued	Early 1959*
Length of Production	23.2 Years*

Colors: Red†, Cobalt, Green, Yellow, Ivory, Turquoise, Rose, Gray, Chartreuse, Forest

*Estimate

†Red discontinued in early 1944

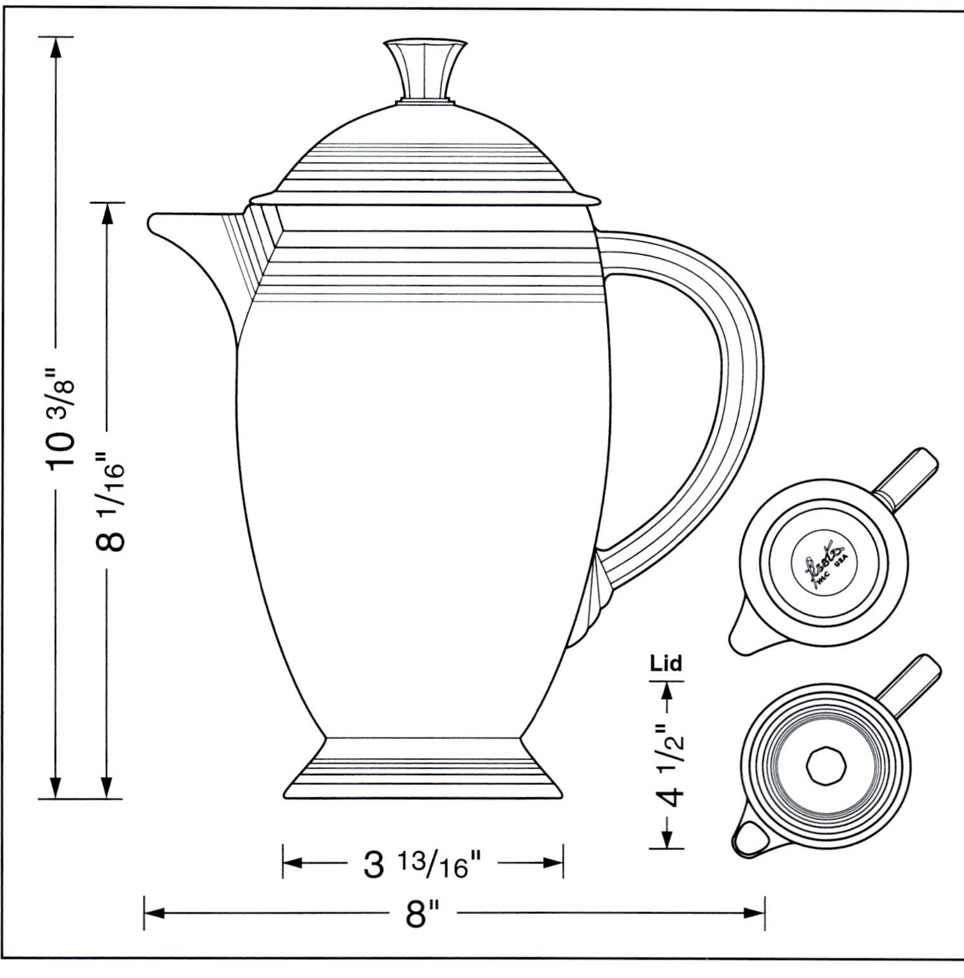

Fiesta regular coffeepot in colors added after introduction. Turquoise, $200-205; Gray, $600-645; Forest, $450-515; Rose, $490-550; Chartreuse, $435-485.

Sweets Comport

New collectors of Fiesta usually have a problem with the name of this dish. They are used to *comport* being a verb. "To comport oneself with dignity." But the word is a noun, too. Since the late Eighteenth Century it's been used as an alternate form of *compote*. Especially, it seems, by potters. A compote is "a dessert of fruit cooked in syrup." It is also the dish in which that sweet dessert is served. Since Homer Laughlin used "comport" on its price lists for Fiesta, that's what we're using here.

This shallow bowl on a pedestal was made between 1936 and 1946, so it can be found only in the original colors. It is one of nine vintage Fiesta items that are usually not marked. It also has the distinction of being an unmarked piece that is found marked about 25% of the time. When it is marked, a rubber stamp that says "HLCo USA" was used inside the bottom of the pedestal.

Other than the presence or absence of a mark, there really are no variations of this piece. Both parts, the bowl and the pedestal, were created on a jigger machine then put together by hand. Collectors may occasionally find a bowl that is not quite level, but in general they are all pretty much the same.

They're surprisingly available, as well. There isn't too much difference in the value among colors. Red ones were discontinued nearly three years before the others, so they may be a bit harder to find.

Fiesta sweets comport in turquoise, added after introduction. Turquoise, $74-78.

Fiesta Sweets Comport

Modeling Date	May 1935
Model Number	380
Revisions	None
Production Began	November 1935*
First Price List	Early 1936 (undated)
Last Price List	August 22, 1946
Discontinued	Late 1946*
Length of Production	11 Years*

Colors: Red†, Cobalt, Green, Yellow, Ivory, Turquoise

*Estimate

†Red discontinued in early 1944

Fiesta sweets comport in colors available at shape introduction. Yellow, $77-81; Red, $98-105; Cobalt, $93-97; Ivory, $83-88; Green, $76-80.

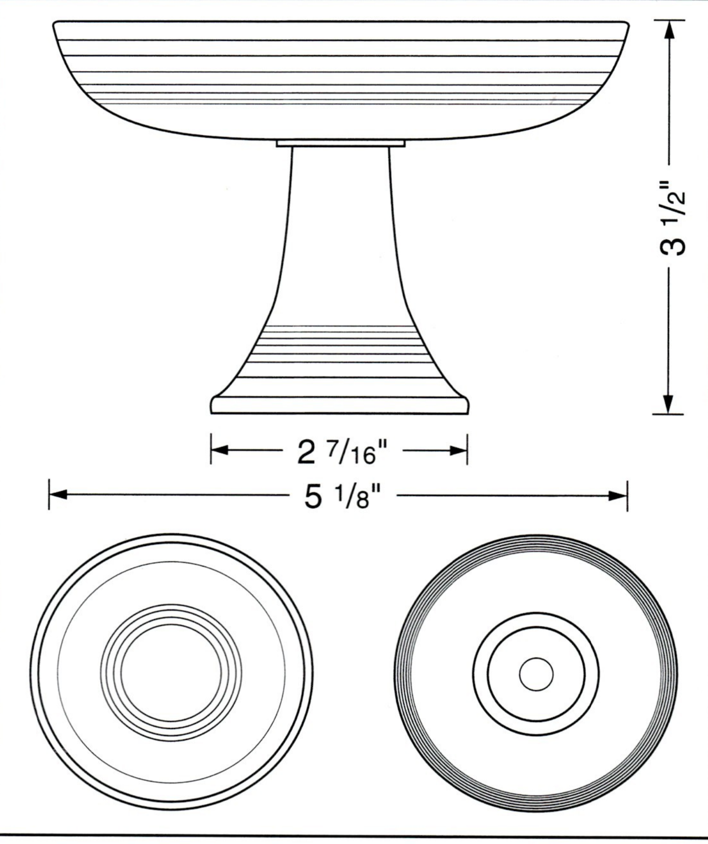

Fiesta 12" Comport

This great looking bowl on a pedestal foot could really dress up a Depression Era table for about $2.00 ($24 in today's dollars). It could be used to serve a dessert or even a salad, or for displaying fruit or perhaps a flower arrangement. Rhead's earliest version was ten inches in diameter, but it was soon changed to a more generous 12 inches and was then produced for about eleven years.

The bowl was made on a jigger machine and the foot was slip cast. The two pieces were joined by hand using slip as glue. When fired in the bisque kiln, the two became one. Glazed comports were sent through the glost kiln in saggers, so these bowls will have three points of disturbed glaze under the rim from the tips of the sagger pins. If they are marked, it will be with the "Genuine Fiesta" backstamp.

The large comport disappeared from the price lists with 14 other items in late 1946. Red ones were gone three years before. They are not particularly easy to find in any color and values reflect their scarcity.

Fiesta 12" Comport	
Modeling Date	April 1935
Model Number	363[1]
Revision	May 1935, 377
Production Began	November 1935*
First Price List	Early 1936 (undated)
Last Price List	August 22, 1946
Discontinued	Late 1946*
Length of Production	11 Years*
Colors: Red†, Cobalt, Green, Yellow, Ivory, Turquoise	

*Estimate

†Red discontinued in early 1944

[1]First model, 10" diameter, not produced

Fiesta 12" comports in colors available at shape introduction. Yellow, $155-160; Cobalt, $170-180; Green, $135-140; Red, $180-190; Ivory, $165-170.

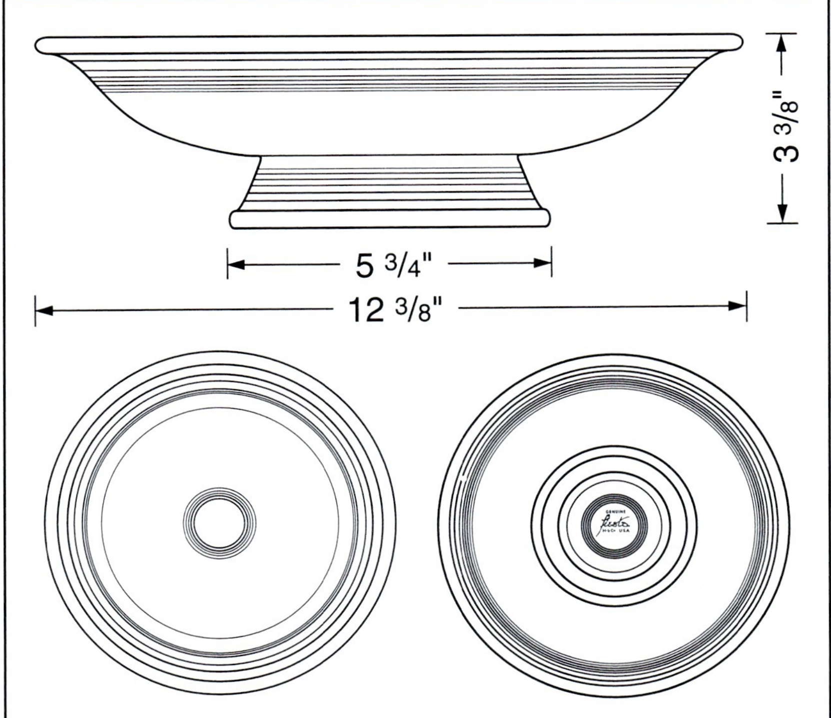

Fiesta 12" comport in turquoise, added after introduction. Turquoise, $150-160.

Cream (Stick Handle)

The cream and sugar set is a standard item in almost every dinnerware line. For Fiesta, Frederick Rhead's first design in March 1935 was quite different from the one that was eventually produced. Both pieces had a resemblance to the final shape of the covered onion soup and had reing handles. The cream featured a large raised spout similar to the high-lip creamers of the Harlequin line. His redesign in June was labeled "small cream" in the HLC modeling log. The volume of the original is not given, but photographs of the trial pieces indicate the capacity was several ounces more than the final design.

The A.D. coffeepot had already been modeled and Rhead's use of a stick handle on the new cream allowed it to complement the coffeepot on the table. Another cream was modeled in November 1935, which sported a ring handle like the teacup, but it was not produced. Perhaps Rhead had a premonition about the acceptance of the stick-handled cream. If he did, it was proved right less than three years later.

Creams with the stick handle were produced for only 30 months. Clearly easier to use by right-handed individuals, this may have contributed to it's redesign. On July 2, 1938 Rhead sent a memo to Guy Pittenger, supervisor of plant #4: *"J.M.W. has ordered the regular Fiesta cream with side stick handle (model No. 389) discontinued. The Fiesta cream for future production will consist of the same body, but with round handle, model No. 1104."*

It is assumed, because of this memo, that production of the stick handle cream ceased during the month of July 1938. The ring-handled model that replaced it is discussed below since most collectors consider it a separate item in their collections.

The body of the cream and its stick handle were both slip cast items joined by hand. All stick-handled creamers have the "HLC USA" type impressed mark. This early piece of Fiesta is not common, but can be found with a bit of effort. Those in the turquoise glaze were produced for a period of less than a year and are therefore the most difficult to find.

Fiesta Cream (Stick Handle)

Modeling Date	March 1935
Model Number	354[1]
First Revision	June 1935, 389[2]
Second Revision	November 1935, 469[3]
Third Revision	July 1938, 1104[4]
Production Began	November 1935*
First Price List	Early 1936 (undated)
Last Price List	July 1, 1938
Discontinued	Mid 1938*
Length of Production	2.8 Years*

Colors: Red[†], Cobalt, Green, Yellow, Ivory, Turquoise

*Estimate

[1]First model not produced

[2]Stick-handled model

[3]Early ring-handled model, not produced

[4]Ring handle for cream, see next entry

Fiesta cream (stick handled) in turquoise, added after introduction. Turquoise, $70-79.

Fiesta creams (stick handled) in colors available at shape introduction. Yellow, $43-46; Cobalt, $62-65; Green, $45-47; Red, $62-65; Ivory, $62-65.

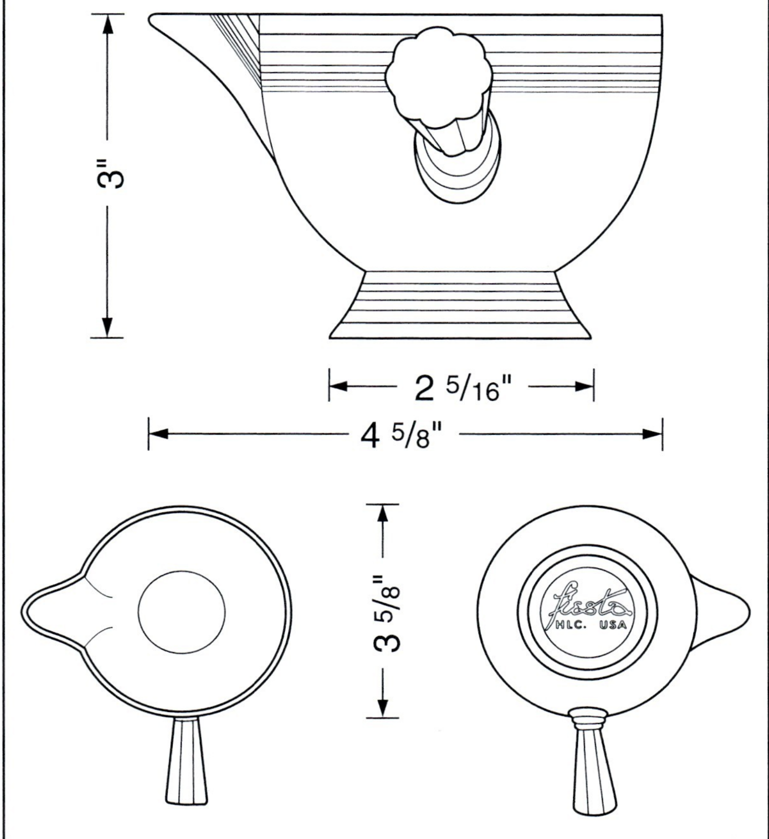

Cream (Ring Handle)

As noted in the previous section, the standard ring-handled creamer was a replacement for the original model that had a stick handle. Production began in July 1938 and continued until the line was restyled in 1969. The black and white image on the back of Fiesta price lists continued to show the stick-handled cream until late in 1940. No doubt this has contributed to collector confusion regarding the date the shape was changed.

It can be found in all eleven vintage colors and has no variations. All ring-handled creams have the "MADE IN USA" impressed mark and they were made the same way as the original creams—slip casting. The cream is the most often seen serving piece after nappies and is not at all hard to find. Creamers in the red glaze had a combined production time (pre-1944 and post-1959) that is less than half as long as the other colors, so they may be a bit more difficult to locate.

Fiesta cream (ring handled) in colors available at shape introduction. Cobalt, $34-36; Green, $25-27; Red, $33-35; Ivory, $30-31; Turquoise, $23-25; Yellow, $24-26.

Fiesta Cream (Ring Handle)

Modeling Date .... July 1938
Model Number .... 1104[1]
Revisions .... None
Production Began .... Mid 1938*
First Price List .... January 1, 1939[2]
Last Price List .... January 1, 1968
Discontinued .... Early 1969*
Length of Production .... 30.5 Years*
Colors: Red†, Cobalt, Green, Yellow, Ivory, Turquoise, Rose, Gray, Chartreuse, Forest, Medium Green

*Estimate
†Red discontinued in early 1944, reintroduced mid-1959
[1]Ring handle only, used on original body
[2]Stick-handle image used on price lists until October 1940

Fiesta cream (ring handled) in colors added after introduction. Forest, $39-41; Gray, $40-42; Chartreuse, $40-43; Rose, $38-40.

Fiesta cream (ring handled) in medium green. Medium Green, $110-115.

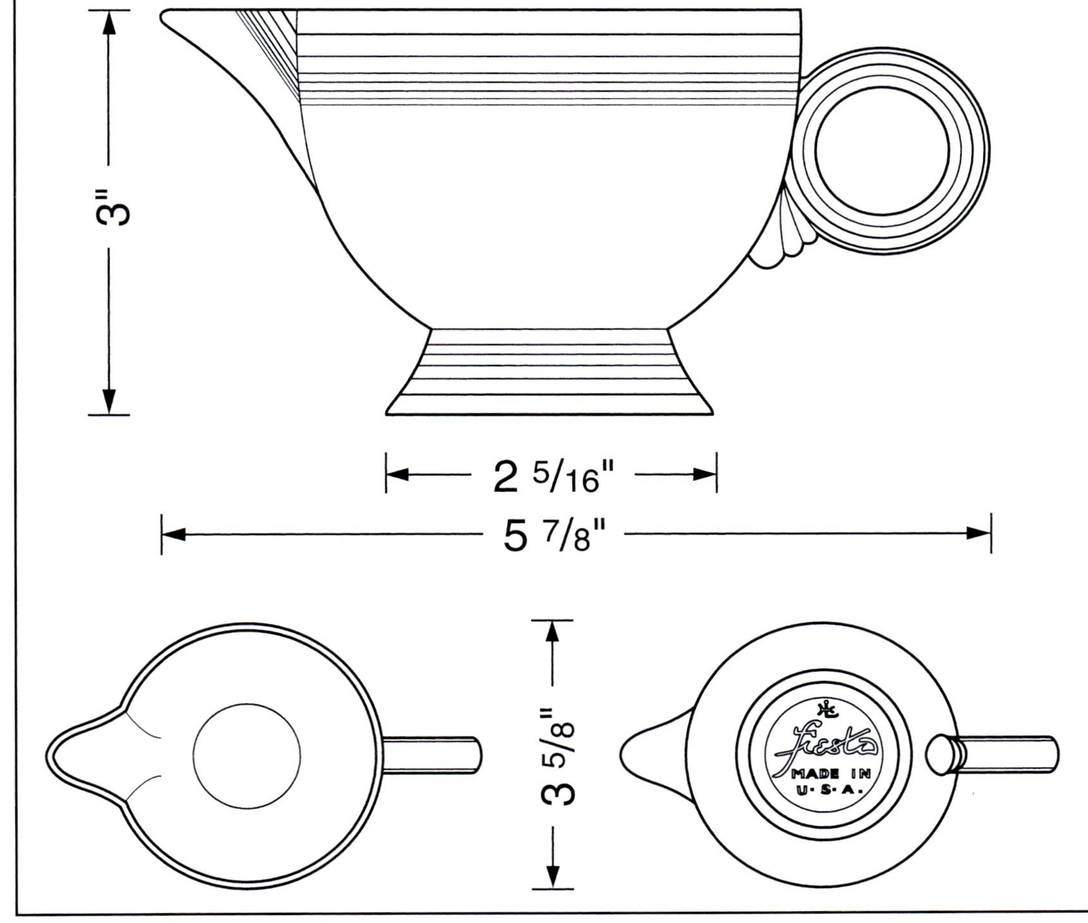

After Dinner Coffee Cup and Saucer

If a piece of pottery could be called "cute," this is it—little stick-handled cups for drinking espresso after dinner. In the Thirties it wasn't espresso, but demitasse or Turkish coffee. These cups hold approximately 2 1/2 ounces, about half the volume of a Fiesta teacup. The A.D. coffee cup was one of the first items modeled for the new line in early 1935.

Like most cups, this piece was jiggered. The stick handle was a slip cast piece and the two were joined by hand. After the cup was formed, but before the handle was attached, the foot was hand turned to give it a flared shape. The A.D. saucer was made on the jigger machine, too, like all Fiesta flatware.

The cup is one of the nine rarely marked pieces in the line. If they are marked, it is with a rubber stamp that says "HLCo USA". It has been explained that the marking was required for export, more than likely to Canada where a lot of normally unmarked Fiesta has been found with the HLCo stamp.

There are two variations to note. Early A.D. cups have a flat bottom inside the cup. A change in September 1937 resulted in cups with a round bottom. This is due to the use of a different jiggering tool, which also created one of three variations in the rings inside the rim. The saucers come in two varieties as well. Early ones are not marked and have two rings around the foot. The later ones have a single ring around the foot and almost always carry the "Genuine Fiesta" backstamp.

Even though the A.D. coffeepot was discontinued in 1942, the cups and saucers were made until 1958 or 1959. Those in the glazes of the 1950s can be quite difficult to locate and are valued at approximately five times those in the original six glazes.

Fiesta After Dinner Coffee Cup & Saucer

Modeling Date	March 1935
Model Numbers	341[1], 342[2], 344[2]
Revision	September 1937, 943[3]
Production Began	November 1935
First Price List	Early 1936 (undated)
Last Price List	October 1, 1957
Discontinued	Early 1959*
Length of Production	23.2 Years*

Colors: Red†, Cobalt, Green, Yellow, Ivory, Turquoise, Rose, Gray, Chartreuse, Forest

*Estimate

†Red discontinued in early 1944

[1]Cup body

[2]Saucer

[3]Stick handle

[3]A.D. cup "lines deepened"

Fiesta A.D. coffee cups and saucers in colors available at shape introduction. Cup, Saucer; Yellow, $57-60, $17-19; Cobalt, $74-76, $19-21; Red, $78-80, $24-25; Green, $69-71, $20-22; Ivory, $74-79, $23-25.

Fiesta A.D. coffee cups and Saucers in colors added after introduction. Cup, Saucer; Turquoise, $71-75, $20-21; Forest, $380-400, $110-120; Chartreuse, $385-400, $110-115; Gray, $395-430, $112-120; Rose, $385-420, $110-120.

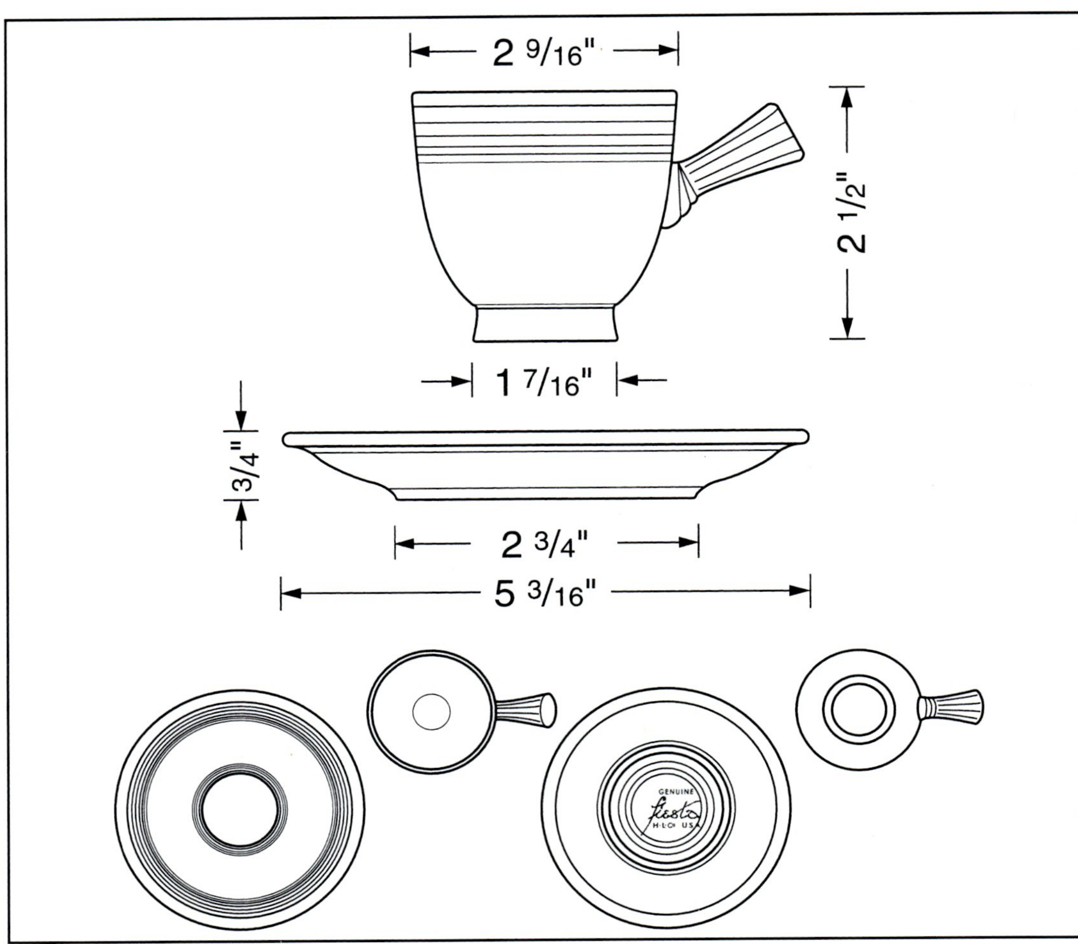

Teacup and Saucer

It seems Frederick Rhead's usual practice when starting a new line was to first model a small plate as well as a cup and saucer. That's exactly what he did with Fiesta. Originally called the "colored glaze" line, he later referred to it as "ringed." The final name was not decided upon until May 1935, even though work on the line began in February. The Fiesta teacup was first modeled in that month with a choice of four handles, none of which were approved. A saucer for the cup was modeled next.

Later that same month the familiar ring shaped handle was created and selected for use on the new ware. It would remain on the teacup for more than thirty years. The saucer was revised as well and was approved and produced for the better part of the next two years.

Teacups, like all cup shaped objects, are made on a jigger. The outside of the cup body is formed by a plaster mold, the inside by metal blade or tool. Saucers are also jiggered, the top formed by a mold, the bottom by the jigger tool. Cup handles are slip cast and hand applied before glazing.

Most Fiesta teacups and quite a few other items in the line have a hand turned foot. Because the cup is formed in a mold, it must be shaped for easy removal. There cannot be any part of the cup narrower than the part below it. To obtain the flared shape of the foot, it was formed by hand after the cup was removed from the mold. The cup could have been placed on a potter's wheel for this operation, but more than likely a cup lathe was used. (See explanation under Tom & Jerry mug.) When the clay had dried to a workable stage, a metal tool in a precise shape was pressed into the cup foot as it spun on the wheel or lathe. The tool removed clay and formed the flared foot.

Vintage Fiesta teacups and saucers can be found in three varieties. If one counts the changes made for Fiesta Ironstone, there are actually four types, but in this context only items in the original line will be discussed.

Two features can distinguish the first production cups and saucers from later ones. The cups have a flat inside bottom and the saucers have five closely spaced rings around the foot. Like all teacups made until 1960, these have a band of rings inside the cup and a hand turned foot. Neither the cup nor the saucer was marked. This pair was made until late 1937 and might be called "Type I".

The most common style of Fiesta cups and saucers were modeled in August 1937 and produced until the Sixties. The teacups have a round inside bottom with inside rings and a hand

turned foot. The saucers are identified by a single thick ring just under the rim and were usually marked with the "Genuine Fiesta" backstamp. The teacups were not marked except for export (see previous entry). These can be called "Type II".

The molds were changed again sometime in the early 1960s although modeling log entries to verify it eluded our researchers. The hand turned foot was eliminated and that is the key point of identification for the cups. The inside rings were also removed and the entire cup was made slightly larger. The new saucers were remodeled with a more concave shape and thus have taller rims than previous types. Their major identifying feature is two thick rings just under the rim. The new saucers continued to receive the usual backstamp. "Type III" cups and saucers will be found only in the four glazes of the 1960s.

Type I cups and saucers were made for less than two years and are not easy to find yet they do not command a premium over other types in the same colors. They were made in the first six colors, but very few have been found in the turquoise glaze. Type II cups and saucers are the most common type and are easy to find in the first ten colors. Medium green pairs are more difficult to locate and tend to command a higher price than Type III cups and saucers in that color. The final type of vintage cups and saucers are Type III. They have not been found in the colors of the Fifties. Those in medium green are valued higher than the other 1960s colors.

Fiesta Teacup & Saucer

Modeling Date	February 1935
Model Number	326[1], 330[2]
First Revision	February 1935, 336[3], 337[4]
Second Revision	August 1937, 902[5], 904[6]
Third Revision	Early 1960s[7]
Production Began	November 1935*
First Price List	Early 1936 (undated)
Last Price List	January 1, 1968
Discontinued	Early 1969*
Length of Production	33.2 Years*

Colors: Red[†], Cobalt, Green, Yellow, Ivory, Turquoise, Rose, Gray, Chartreuse, Forest, Medium Green

*Estimate

[†]Red discontinued in early 1944, reintroduced mid-1959

[1]Teacup and four handles

[2]First saucer, not produced

[3]New ring handle

[4]Saucer with five rings around foot (see text)

[5]Handle "lines sharpened"

[6]Cup "lines sharpened"

[7]Modeling log confirmation not found for straight foot cup (see text)

Fiesta teacup and saucer in colors available at introduction. Cup, Saucer; Yellow, $22-23, $6-7; Cobalt, $26-28, $7-9; Red, $28-30, $8-10; Green, $22-24, $6-7; Ivory, $28-30, $5-7.

Fiesta teacup and saucer in colors added after introduction. Cup, Saucer; Turquoise, $23-24, $7-8; Forest, $31-33, $11-14; Chartreuse, $31-33, $7-8; Gray, $27-30, $7-8; Rose, $30-32, $6-7.

The inside rings of a Fiesta teacup.

This teacup's foot was glazed without being turned to shape it.

Fiesta teacup and saucer in medium green. Cup, Saucer; Medium Green, $43-45, $14-16.

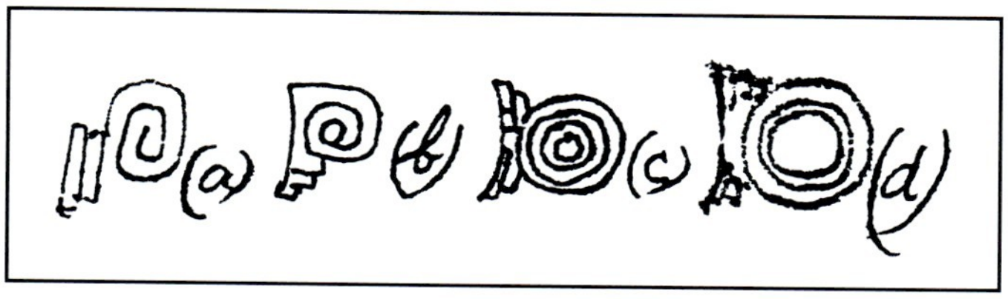

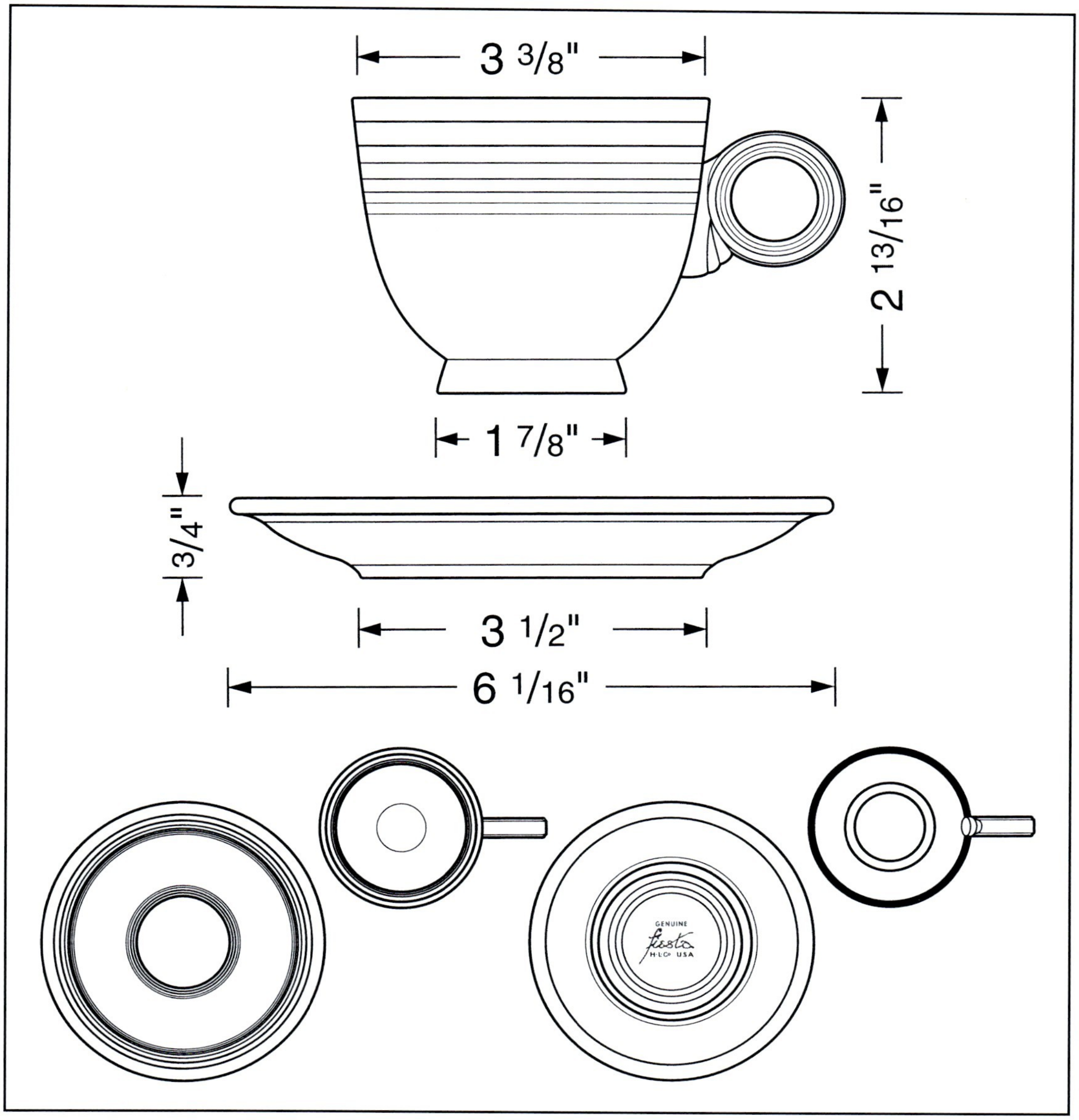

(a) (b) (c) (d)

3 3/8"
2 13/16"
1 7/8"
3/4"
3 1/2"
6 1/16"
GENUINE
fiesta
HLC USA

Egg Cup

After Fiesta was on the market for a few months, Frederick Rhead began to work on adding pieces to the line. Before the end of the first year, fourteen new items were added. The egg cup was one of them.

Unlike most HLC egg cups, this one was not designed to serve an egg in the shell. It seems to have been made large enough to serve poached eggs.

Another jiggered piece, the egg cup also has a hand turned foot. Some variation of the shape and ring pattern on the foot will be noted as several tools were used. Egg cups can have the impressed "MADE IN USA" mark, or they can be unmarked.

Egg cups were not made past 1959 and are not known in the medium green glaze. Those in the Fifties colors are valued at two to three times those in the original colors.

Fiesta Egg Cup

Modeling Date	May 1936
Model Number	606
Revisions	None
Production Began	June 1936*
First Price List	Late 1936 (undated)
Last Price List	October 1, 1957
Discontinued	Early 1959*
Length of Production	22.7 Years*

Colors: Red†, Cobalt, Green, Yellow, Ivory, Turquoise, Rose, Gray, Chartreuse, Forest

*Estimate

†Red discontinued in early 1944

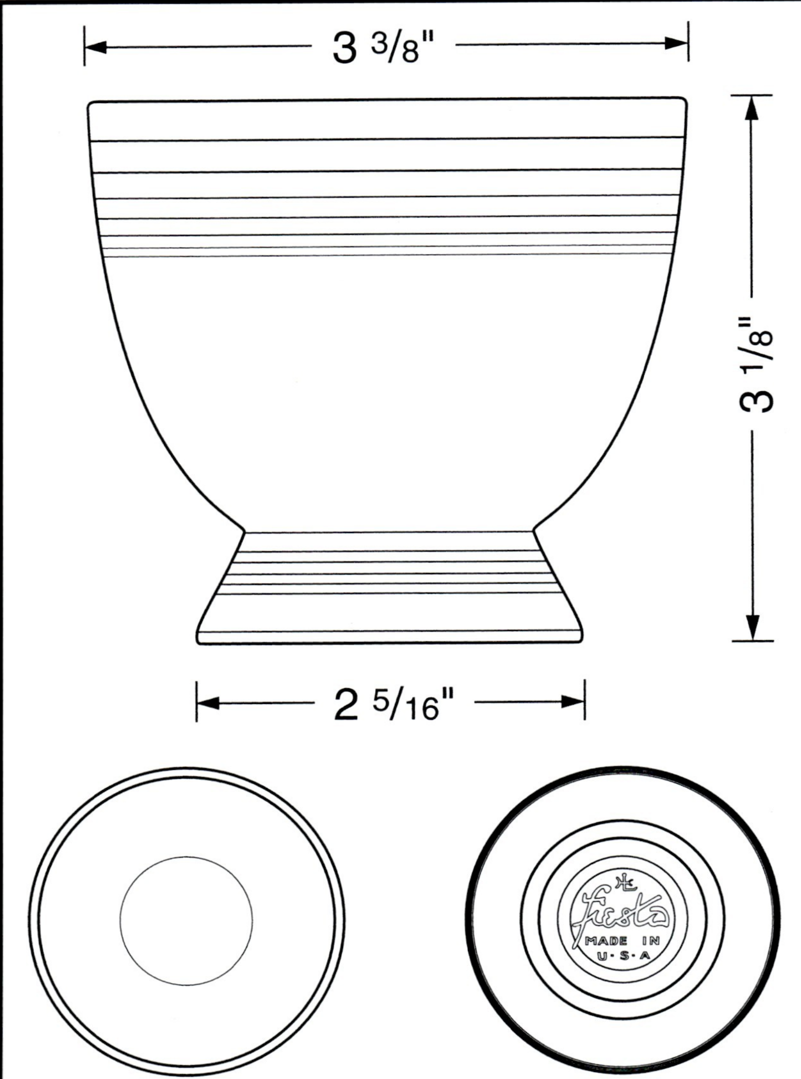

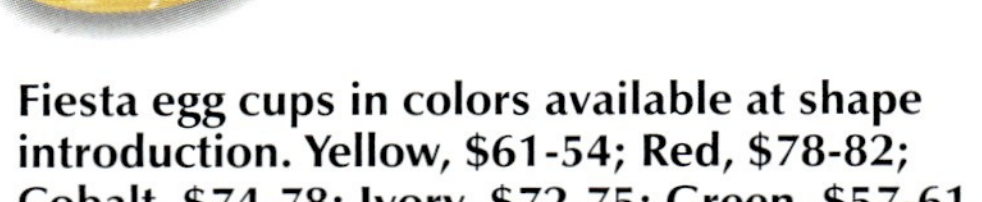

Fiesta egg cups in colors available at shape introduction. Yellow, $61-54; Red, $78-82; Cobalt, $74-78; Ivory, $72-75; Green, $57-61.

Fiesta egg cups in colors added after introduction. Turquoise, $57-60; Chartreuse, $150-155; Forest, $145-155; Rose, $155-160; Gray, $155-165.

Fiesta covered marmalade jar in turquoise, added after introduction. Turquoise, $310-340.

Covered Marmalade Jar

Another of the mid-1936 additions, the marmalade was originally designed as the Fiesta mustard. Apparently Rhead decided it was too large for that purpose and remodeled it to a smaller size. After the mustard was finished he went back to his larger design and renamed it. First it was called a "honey jar," then "marmalade."

It was made from three pieces—a slip cast body and finial, and a jiggered lid. The spoon slot was hand punched from the lid before the clay dried, so the shape and depth will vary a bit. The finial was hand applied to the lid. All marmalades are marked with the "HLC USA" in-mold mark.

Although the marmalade was made for more than ten years their scarcity is apparently due to the number sold. Red ones are slightly more difficult to find because that color was discontinued approximately three years before the others. No matter what the color, a Fiesta marmalade in excellent condition is a highly valued item.

Fiesta Covered Marmalade Jar

Modeling Date	February 1936
Model Number	550[1]
Revisions	None
Production Began	June 1936*
First Price List	Late 1936 (undated)
Last Price List	August 22, 1946
Discontinued	Late 1946*
Length of Production	10.3 Years*

Colors: Red†, Cobalt, Green, Yellow, Ivory, Turquoise

*Estimate

†Red discontinued in early 1944

[1]This was the original mustard later renamed

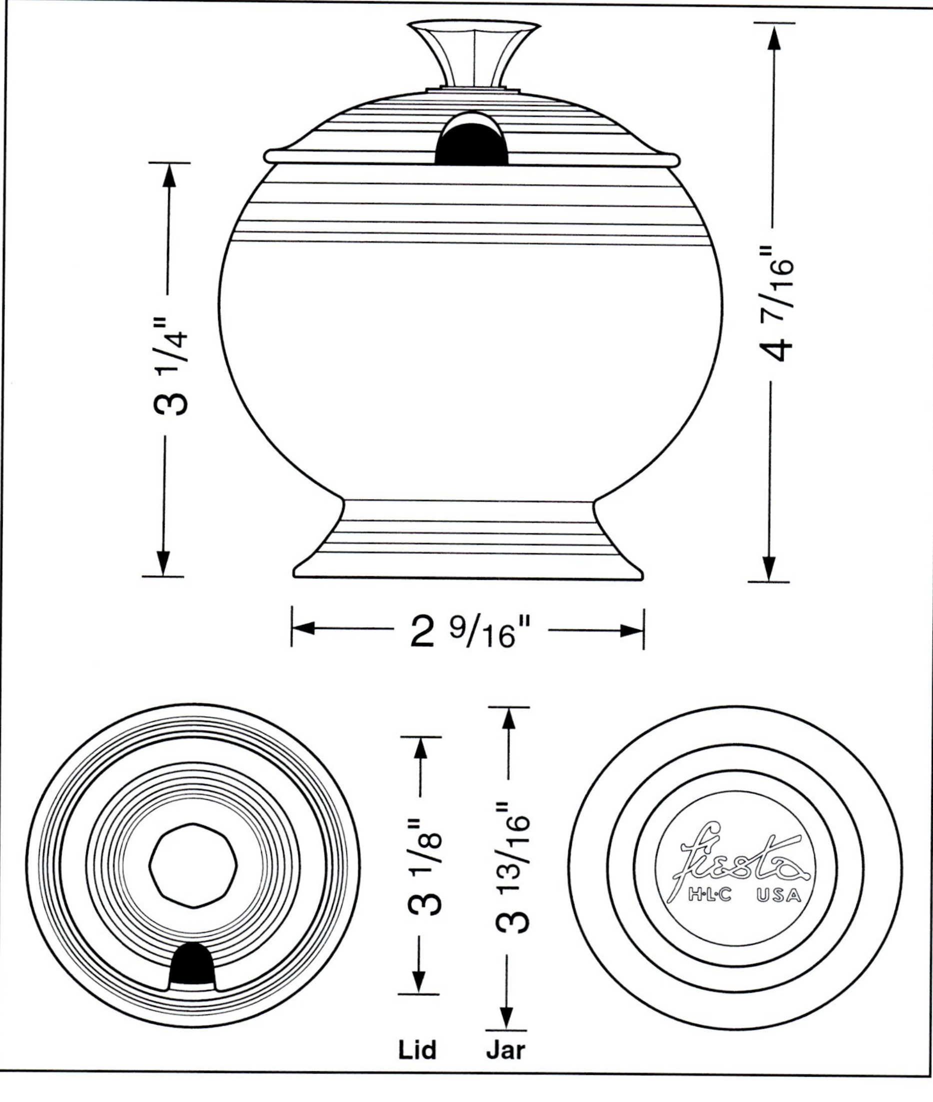

Fiesta covered marmalade jars in colors available at shape introduction. Yellow, $245-265; Red, $325-345; Cobalt, $320-345; Ivory, $315-345; Green, $280-300.

Tom & Jerry Mug

This is another item with a name that new collectors sometimes have trouble with. The "Tom and Jerry" is an alcoholic drink based on an egg and milk mixture. It was popular during the winter months in the 1930s to the 1950s and was served warm from a large bowl into handled mugs. Homer Laughlin had been making this mug for several years with a different handle when Rhead decided to add it to the Fiesta line in mid-1936.

In the HLC modeling log, Rhead wrote, "Fiesta mug. Tom & Jerry with round handle." The Fiesta mugs were to be the same shape as the mug already being made, but in the Fiesta clay body (a different formula than the one used for other items made by HLC) and it was to have the distinctive round handle. This is one of two items in the Fiesta line that has no ring pattern, the other being the Dripcut® syrup that was also brought into the line from somewhere else. The T&J mug is sometimes called a coffee mug. More Fiesta trivia: the Tom and Jerry mug holds the same amount of liquid as the regular Fiesta teacup.

In addition to glazing it in the Fiesta colors, HLC also used the new mug in a true Tom and Jerry set with the Fiesta footed salad bowl. Both items were glazed in ivory and received the gold stamped "Tom and Jerry" name as well as hand applied gold band decorations.

The unusual concave shape of this mug cannot be achieved by jiggering alone, yet the mugs are jiggered. Hand processing on a cup lathe is what gave this mug its unique shape as well as its variations. When the jiggered cylinder of clay had dried to a workable stage it was turned in a horizontal lathe much like a woodworker might use. The sides and foot were shaped with metal tools.

Because of this hand work, there are several variations seen in the Fiesta mug. These include different thickness of the sides, a slight hump or rim at the foot, and mugs may be the correct hourglass shape or only curve in from the rim with straight sides below. Sometimes "chatter" is seen. Chatter is a potter's term for corrugations or ripples in the sides of the cup caused by vibrations in the turning tool. This usually occurs when the clay is too dry. In the finished mug, chatter appears as faint horizontal rings under the glaze.

Since the foot was shaped by hand, the mug could not have an in-mold mark and the "Genuine Fiesta" handstamp was used instead. As with other backstamped items, some mugs may not be marked.

The Fiesta T&J mug was in production from mid-1936 until the line was restyled in 1969. They are readily available in all colors. As expected, those in the glazes of the 1950s and medium green are a bit more difficult to find and carry the higher price tags.

Fiesta Tom & Jerry Mug

Modeling Date	May 1936
Model Number	612
Revisions	None
Production Began	June 1936*
First Price List	Late 1936 (undated)
Last Price List	January 1, 1968
Discontinued	Early 1969*
Length of Production	32.7 Years*

Colors: Red†, Cobalt, Green, Yellow, Ivory, Turquoise, Rose, Gray, Chartreuse, Forest, Medium Green

*Estimate

†Red discontinued in early 1944, reintroduced mid-1959

Fiesta Tom and Jerry mug in medium green. Medium Green, $105-110.

Fiesta Tom and Jerry mugs in colors available at shape introduction. Red, $78-80; Cobalt, $72-75; Ivory, $75-79; Yellow, $56-57; Green, $57-59.

Fiesta Tom and Jerry mugs in colors added after shape introduction. Turquoise, $51-53; Forest, $79-82; Chartreuse, $83-85; Rose, $79-82; Gray, $80-84.

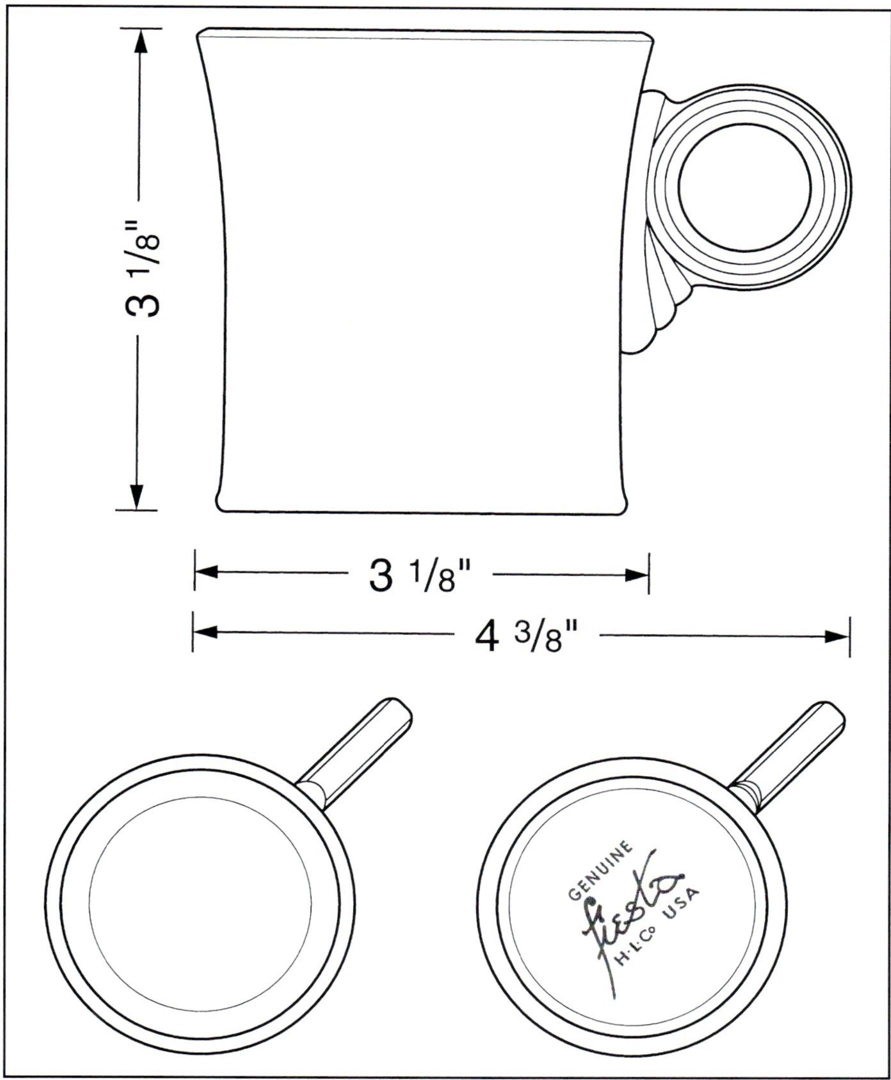

Covered Mustard

When it was decided that the original mustard was too large (see *Covered Marmalade* above) Rhead set about making it smaller. Over several months three additional models were made and finally one that had dimensions similar to the salt and pepper shakers was deemed to be the right size. Released to production in June 1936, this item joined several other new pieces added to the line at that time. The mustard is another of the nine vintage items that did not routinely receive a mark. Marked mustards were probably for export and have the "HLCo USA" rubber stamp.

The mustard and its lid were slip cast. The mustard lid has the distinction of being one of only two one-piece lids in the line. Most others had a hand applied finial. This lid, and that of the medium teapot, was cast as a single piece.

The mustard was produced for about ten years (red ones for seven) and is not easy to find. Like the marmalade, it will cost the collector a fair amount of their collecting budget to add a mustard in excellent shape to their collection.

Fiesta Covered Mustard

Modeling Date	February 1936
Model Number	550[1]
First Revision	April 1936, 582[2]
Second Revision	May 1936, 605[3]
Third Revision	May 1936, 610
Production Began	June 1936*
First Price List	Late 1936 (undated)
Last Price List	August 22, 1946
Discontinued	Late 1946*
Length of Production	10.3 Years*

Colors: Red[†], Cobalt, Green, Yellow, Ivory, Turquoise

*Estimate

[†]Red discontinued in early 1944

[1]First model renamed "covered marmalade"

[2]Second model not produced, "smaller than 550"

[3]Third model not produced, "too small"

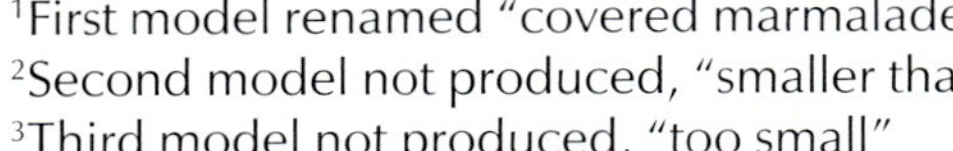

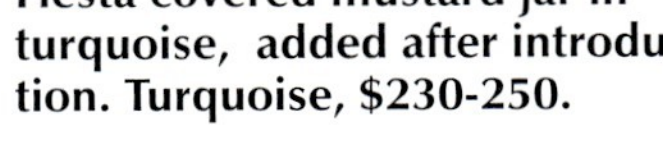

Fiesta covered mustard jar in turquoise, added after introduction. Turquoise, $230-250.

Fiesta covered mustard jars colors available at shape introduction. Yellow, $260-275; Red, $300-310; Cobalt, $290-305; Ivory, $270-285; Green, $240-260.

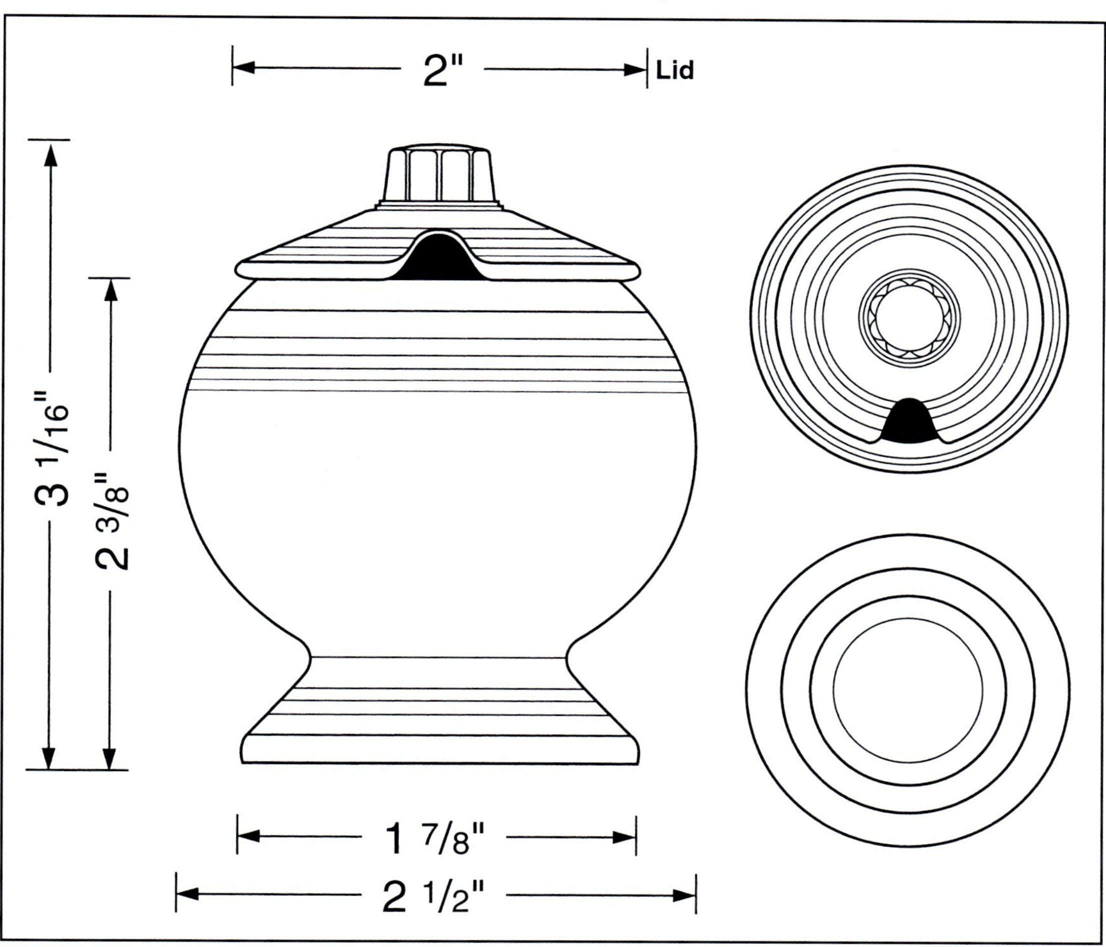

Disc Water Jug

This endearing symbol of the line was not originally a part of it. Fiesta had been in production for more than two years when Frederick Rhead began work on the new water jug. A year earlier he had proposed a water jug for Fiesta in the shape of a ball jug. That design was modified and used instead for Harlequin. See Fiesta Developmental Pieces for a photo of this early design.

In March 1938 there were several types of jugs being worked on at HLC. The modeling log is not clear if the others were being considered for Fiesta, but the disc shaped one was chosen and several sizes were created. The largest was 90 ounces, nearly three quarts, which would have made it very heavy to lift when full. Three other sizes were made: 71 ounces, 53 ounces, and 30 ounces. The 71 ounce jug was selected as the most appropriate size.

Disc shaped jugs were not unique to Homer Laughlin. Over the years several would be made by a number of different potteries. Unknowing dealers will sometimes label these other jugs as Fiesta, but the genuine article is always marked with the "Fiesta/MADE IN USA" variety of in-mold mark. This shape, and several others, is still being produced by HLC and the mark is exactly the same. It cannot be used to tell the difference between vintage and contemporary Fiesta items. Color is the best way to do that.

This piece was in production for nearly the entire time that Fiesta was made and is fairly easy to find. Jugs in the Fifties colors are valued at approximately double that of the original colors. Those in medium green are much less available than the other colors and frequently sell for considerably more.

Fiesta Disc Water Jug

Modeling Date .... March 1938
Model Number .... 1057[1]
First Revision .... April 1938, 1075[2]
Second Revision .... April 1938, 1088[3]
Third Revision .... June 1938, 1095[4]
Production Began .... June 1938*
First Price List .... July 1, 1938
Last Price List .... January 1, 1968
Discontinued .... Early 1969*
Length of Production .... 30.6 Years*
Colors: Red[†], Cobalt, Green, Yellow, Ivory, Turquoise, Rose, Gray, Chartreuse, Forest, Medium Green

*Estimate
[†]Red discontinued in early 1944, reintroduced mid-1959
[1]First model, 90 oz. capacity, not produced
[2]Spout changed on 1057, not produced
[3]Size reduced to 71 oz.
[4]Size reduced to 53 oz., not produced

Fiesta disc water jugs in colors available at shape introduction. Green, $110-115; Cobalt, $155-160; Red, $150-160; Turquoise, $115-120; Yellow, $115-120; Ivory, $155-165.

Fiesta disc water jugs in colors added after introduction. Gray, $230-240; Forest, $240-250; Rose, $230-240; Chartreuse, $245-255.

Fiesta disc water jug in medium green. Medium Green, $1515-1585.

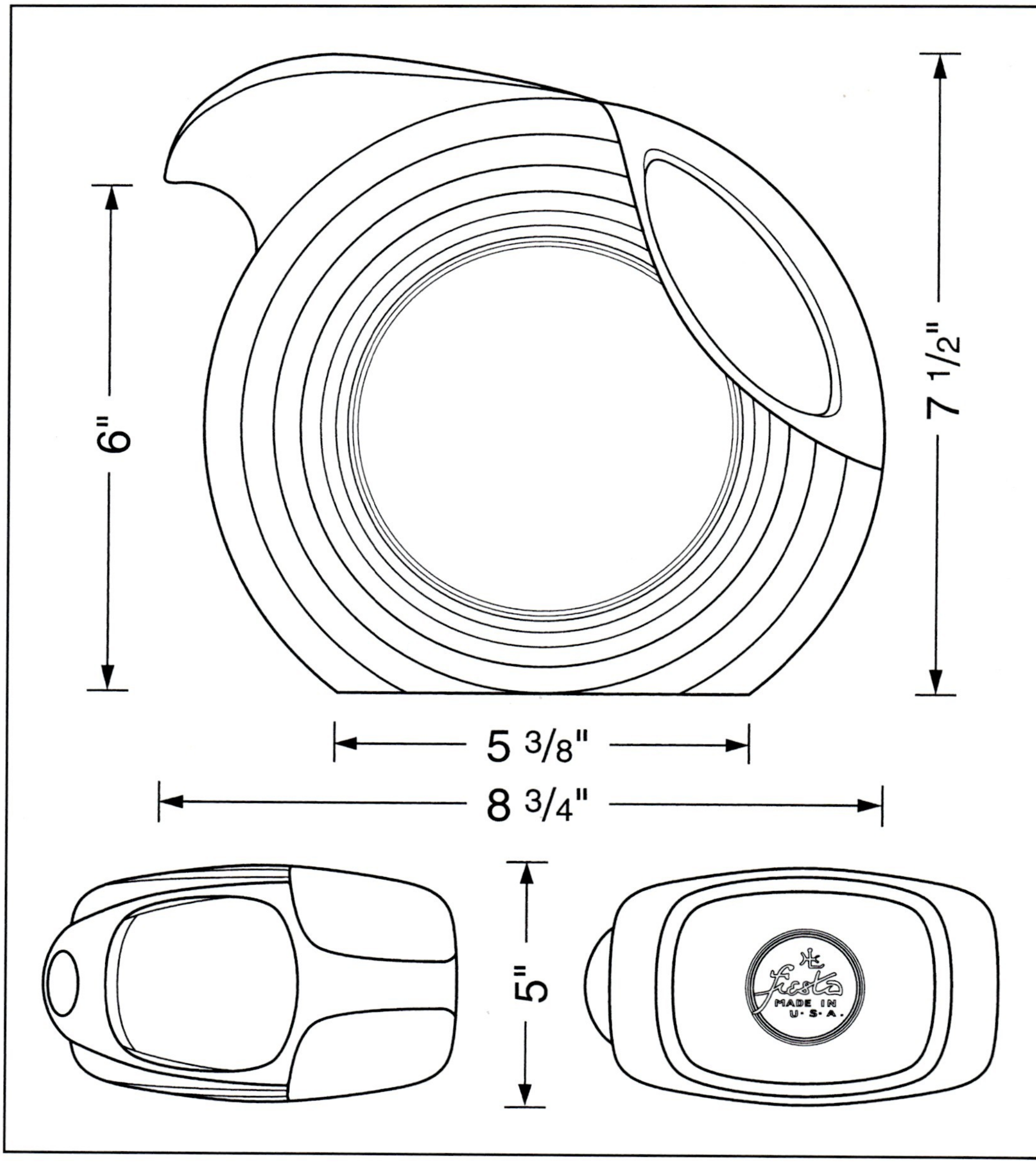

6"

7 1/2"

5 3/8"

8 3/4"

5"

Fiesta MADE IN U.S.A.

Fiesta ice pitchers in colors available at shape introduction. Green, $145-150; Yellow, $130-135; Cobalt, $150-160; Ivory, $155-165; Red, $150-160.

Ice Pitcher

This pitcher looks like a giant, open mustard with a handle. The resemblance was intentional and showed Rhead's attempt to create a coherent style for the line. The name comes from the "ice lip" that covers the spout and prevents pieces of ice from flowing from the pitcher when ice water is poured into a glass or tumbler. It was a part of the original offering and was in production until late 1946 when it and fourteen other items were removed from the line at one time.

The pitcher was slip cast and had a hand applied separately cast handle. It can be found with the two versions of the "HLC USA" mark, one small and plain, the other larger and surrounded by three rings. The pitcher holds nearly two quarts (64 ounces). It does not have a lid.

This is another item that is not all that easy to find. It was made in only the first six colors, but red ones were made for a shorter period of time and are even more difficult to locate.

Fiesta Ice Pitcher	
Modeling Date	June 1935
Model Number	394
Revisions	None
Production Began	November 1935*
First Price List	Early 1936 (undated)
Last Price List	August 22, 1946
Discontinued	Late 1946*
Length of Production	11 Years*

Colors: Red†, Cobalt, Green, Yellow, Ivory, Turquoise

*Estimates

†Red discontinued in early 1944

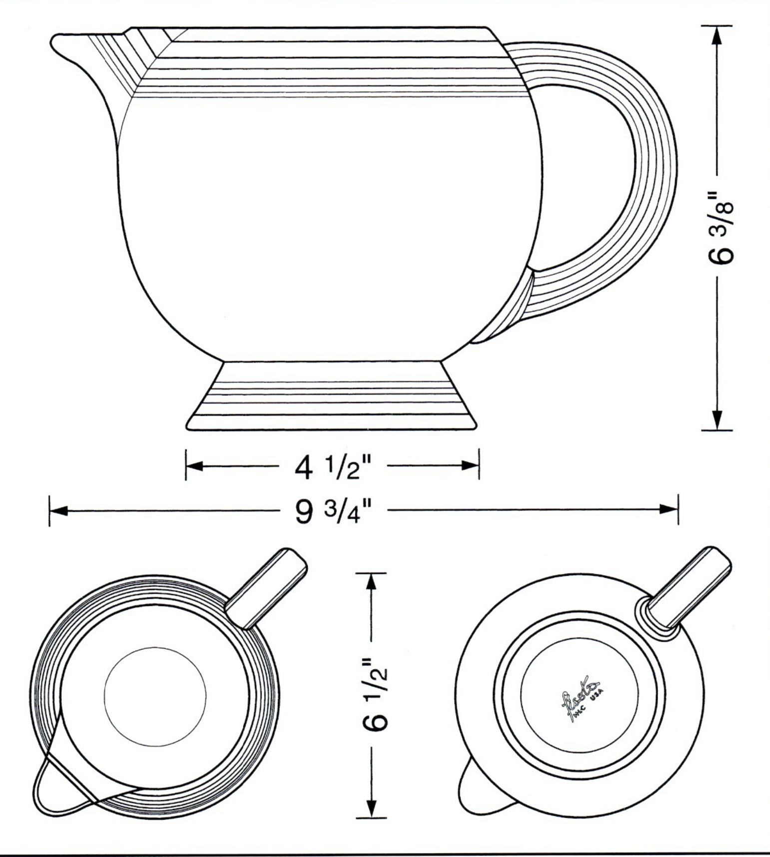

Fiesta ice pitcher in turquoise, added after introduction. Turquoise, $145-150.

Two Pint Jug

Rhead developed a very interesting series of open jugs for Fiesta in May 1936. There were five sizes, all in the same shape, but the largest was the only one produced. The range of sizes was 4 ounces (half cup), 8 ounces (one cup or half pint), 16 ounces (one pint), 24 ounces (1-1/2 pint or 3 cups), and 32 ounces (two pints). In HLC's modeling log, they were numbered 1 to 5. A few of the trial pieces for the other sizes have made it into collector hands—a number four in red and a number two in cobalt are known.

The jug that was produced was made by the slip casting method with the large ring handle as part of the mold. These jugs have a wiped foot and will show a ring of white clay on the bottom. Two variations exist, both involving the in-mold mark. One is the familiar "HLC USA," the other is the "MADE IN USA" type. The first mark is usually accompanied by a hand inscribed "5" above the script Fiesta logo and is the earlier version. The number is not present on the second type.

Even though they were probably produced in smaller quantities, there is only a slight increase in the value of jugs in the 1950s colors compared with those in the original six. The jug was not made in medium green since production of it stopped just before that color was introduced.

Fiesta two pint jugs in colors added after introduction. Turquoise, $81-84; Chartreuse, $120-130; Forest, $130-135; Rose, $140-145; Gray, $150-155.

Fiesta 2 Pint Jug

Modeling Date	May 1936
Model Number	590[1]
Revisions	None
Production Began	May 1936*
First Price List	Late 1936 (undated)
Last Price List	October 1, 1957
Discontinued	Early 1959*
Length of Production	22.7 Years*

Colors: Red[†], Cobalt, Green, Yellow, Ivory, Turquoise, Rose, Gray, Chartreuse, Forest

*Estimate

[†]Red discontinued in early 1944

[1]Largest in a series of jug models (see text)

Fiesta two pint jugs in colors available at shape introduction. Yellow, $80-85; Red, $110-115; Cobalt, $115-120; Ivory, $105-110; Green, $86-87.

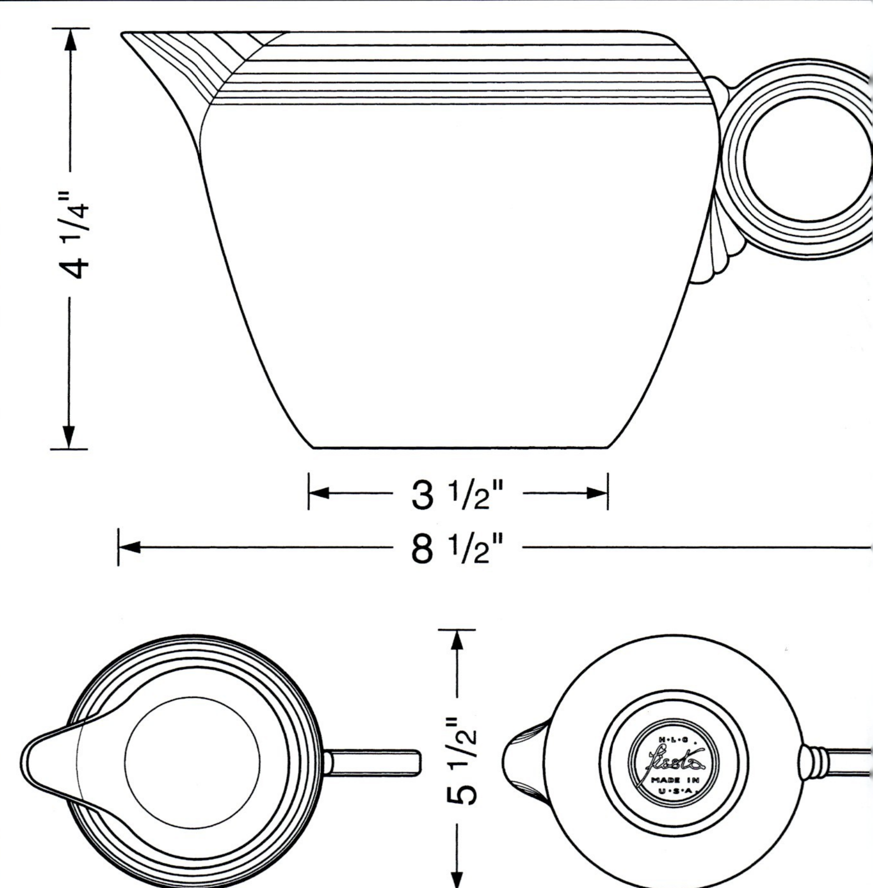

Cake Plate

Our researchers could find only two references to a Fiesta cake plate in Rhead's journal or the HLC modeling log. Model 771, created in February 1937, was for a "Plate 8 [inch] flat cake, Fiesta." Remembering that Rhead used the "English measurements", this eight inch plate was approximately ten inches in diameter when it came out of the kiln. That is the size of the flat Fiesta cake plate known to collectors.

The other reference is from Rhead's journal for February 10, 1937. He wrote, "Royal Metal returned drawing of flat cake plate for Fiesta line. To be 10-1/2 inches in diameter, we will make the surface slightly concave to avoid edge drop and practical difficulties." HLC had made several items for Royal Metal Manufacturing throughout the late 1930s. Some were done in the Fiesta glazes, but none had the familiar pattern of rings. Even if they were done in Fiesta colors, they were distinguished from that line by their different form of decoration or by the absence of it.

Was the Fiesta cake plate made for Royal Metal? Should they all have a metal frame? For how long were they made? In what colors? Only the last two questions can be answered, and not without some uncertainty. So far, this very hard to find plate has been confirmed in Fiesta's five original glazes. That means it was probably not made past July or August 1937. Turquoise cake plates, in our opinion, have not been proved to exist.

Like all Fiesta plates, this one was jiggered. It has a unique pattern of rings on the bottom, they are thick and there are a lot of them; no other Fiesta item has so many rings. The top surface is indeed absolutely flat and unmistakable should one be found in a stack of other ten inch plates (which as been done as recently as last year).

As stated, these are a true rarity in the Fiesta line. In excellent condition they are very highly valued and near the top of collector's "most sought after" list.

Fiesta Cake Plate

Modeling Date	February 1937
Model Number	771
Revisions	None
Production Began	March 1937*
First Price List	None[1]
Last Price List	None[1]
Discontinued	Late 1937*
Length of Production	0.5 Year*

Colors: Red, Cobalt, Green, Yellow, Ivory

*Estimate

[1]Not found on any price list

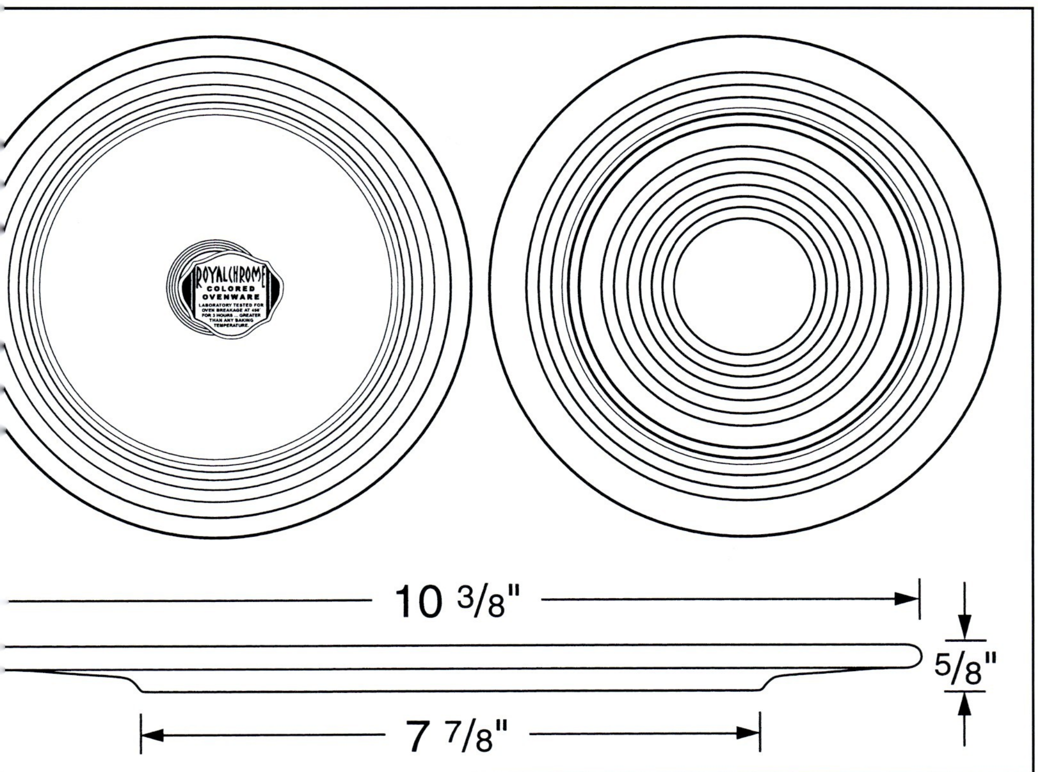

Fiesta cake plates. ; Red, $1415-1475; Cobalt, $1360-1485; Green, $1080-1190; Yellow, $1195-1330.

13" Chop Plate

Once the design of the Fiesta plate was finished, it was fairly easy for the modeling shop to create variations in different sizes. Round serving platters were used for serving "steaks and chops", thus the name for this one. The 13" plate was original to the line and was made until 1969.

Made by jiggering, the plates changed very little over the years. There are slight variations in the pattern or number of rings in the center of the foot, which may identify the individual jigger machines. Like all plates, this one was marked with the "Genuine Fiesta" backstamp, but some occasionally missed being marked. Missing backstamps should have no effect on a plate's appeal to collectors. All vintage Fiesta plates have a glazed foot and three sagger pin marks in the glaze on the bottom.

There is one notable variation that is the cause of a frequently asked question by new collectors: the double foot ring. Various explanations are given, but two are prominent. The one given by Homer Laughlin is that the smaller ring was to support the center of the plate. There is a precedent for that in the 12" compartment plate, which had such a support ring. Why only some 13" chops have this ring, and why the others don't need it, has never been fully explained by the company.

The alternate explanation, generated by collectors, is that these plates were specially made to go with a "lazy Susan" revolving stand. Two types have been found, and both fit in the space between the foot rings of the chop plate. Almost all of the double foot plates have been found in the original six colors, but some collectors claim to have seen them in Fiesta's 1950s colors as well.

Except for those in the elusive medium green glaze, Fiesta 13" chop plates are not difficult to find.

Fiesta 13" Chop Plate

Modeling Date	May 1935
Model Number	378
Revisions	None
Production Began	November 1935*
First Price List	Early 1936 (undated)
Last Price List	January 1, 1968
Discontinued	Early 1969*
Length of Production	33.2 Years*

Colors: Red†, Cobalt, Green, Yellow, Ivory, Turquoise, Rose, Gray, Chartreuse, Forest, Medium Green

*Estimate

†Red discontinued in early 1944, reintroduced mid-1959

Fiesta 13" chop plate in colors added after introduction. Forest, $89-92; Gray, $91-95; Chartreuse, $83-87; Rose, $93-100; Turquoise, $42-45.

Fiesta 13" chop plate in colors available at shape introduction. Cobalt, $48-51; Green, $39-42; Red, $48-51; Ivory, $43-47; Yellow, $37-39.

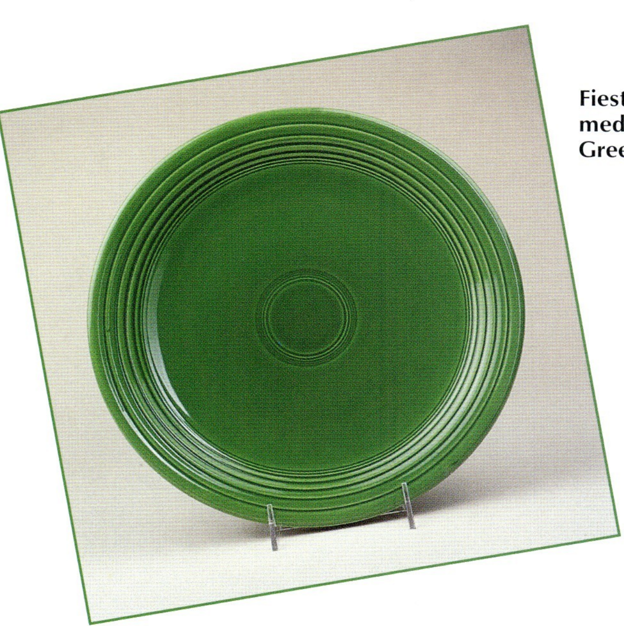

Fiesta 13" chop plate in medium green. Medium Green, $390-420.

Lazy susans for the Fiesta chop plate.

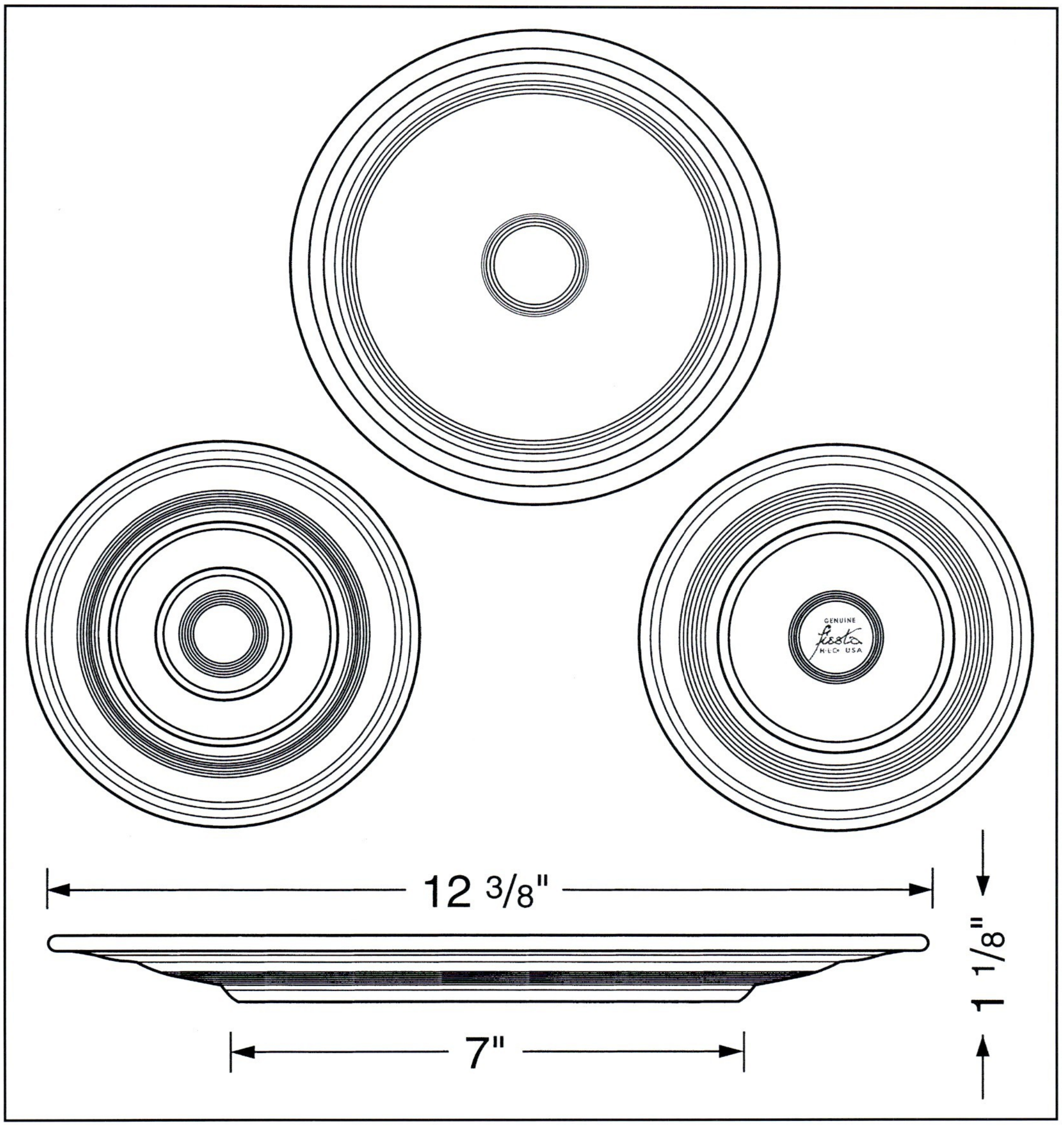

GENUINE fiesta HLC USA

12 3/8"

7"

1 1/8"

15" Chop Plate

Large enough for a good size turkey, this plate has the distinction of being the widest piece in the line. Like the 13" variety, the name comes from Fiesta price lists. It actually is slightly over 14 inches in diameter. Made for serving a lot of food to a large family, these plates were part of the original line, but were made only until the late 1950s. None have been found in medium green.

Because they are so large and heavy they probably could not be made on the automatic jigger installed in 1940 and were no doubt made by hand until the end. The jigger machine mold and tool didn't change much and collectors will find the same two types as are found on the smaller chop plate. The double foot ring on this plate is slightly larger and takes a different lazy Susan mechanism (if that is the purpose of the two rings). They were marked in the same manner as the 13" chop.

Finding a plate in the Fifties colors may be more difficult than one in the original colors. Because of the way they were used, chop plates often have surface scratches, which will effect the value.

Fiesta 15" Chop Plate

Modeling Date	March 1935
Model Number	352
Revisions	None
Production Began	November 1935*
First Price List	Early 1936 (undated)
Last Price List	October 1, 1957
Discontinued	Early 1959*
Length of Production	23.2 Years*

Colors: Red†, Cobalt, Green, Yellow, Ivory, Turquoise, Rose, Gray, Chartreuse, Forest

*Estimate

†Red discontinued in early 1944

Fiesta 15″ chop plates in colors added after introduction. Forest, $105-110; Gray, $105-110; Chartreuse, $100-110; Rose, $95-100; Turquoise, $53-56.

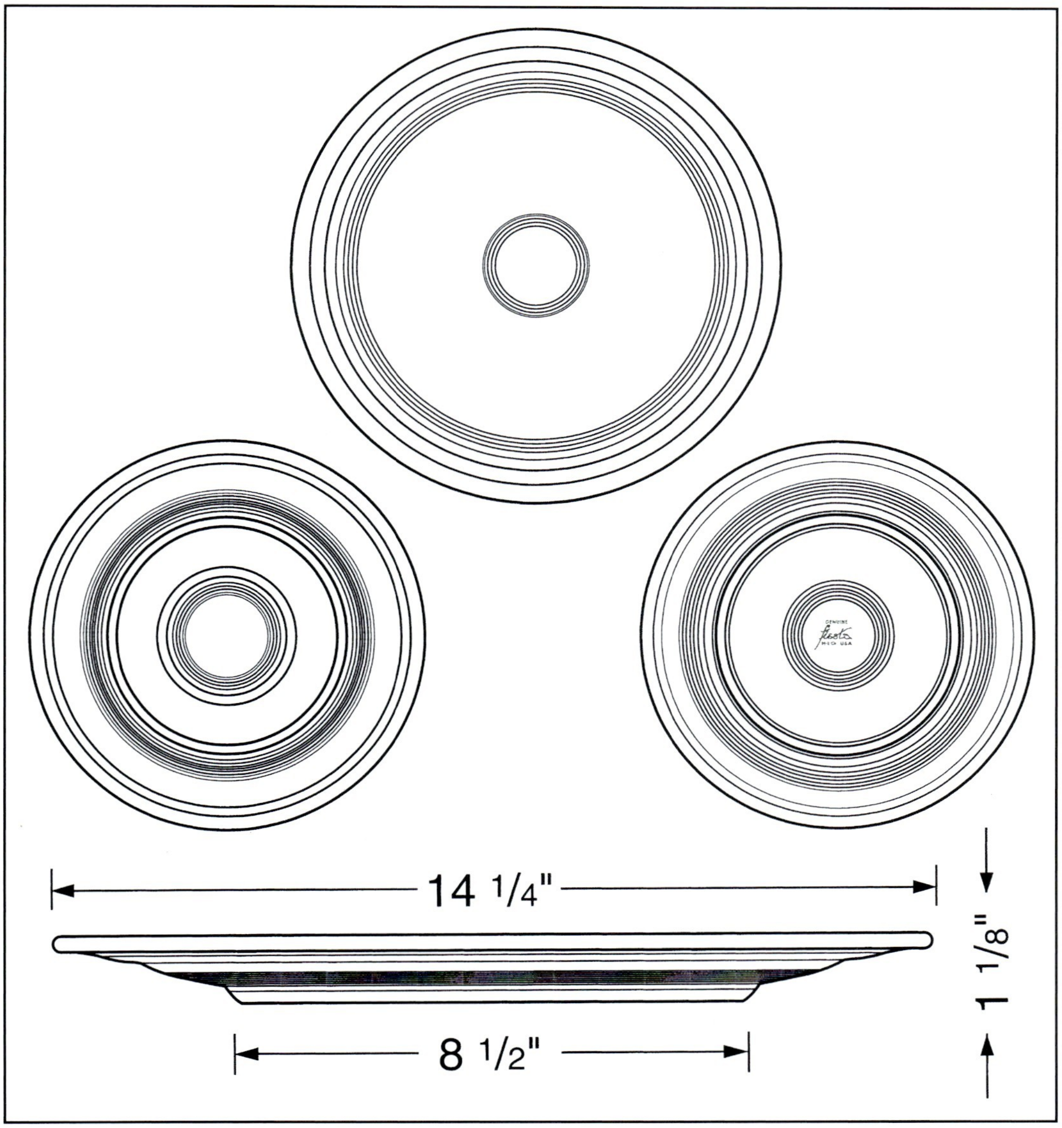

14 1/4"

8 1/2"

1 1/8"

Opposite page:
Fiesta 15″ chop plates in colors available at shape introduction. Cobalt, $75-79; Green, $46-48; Red, $72-78; Ivory, $64-67; Yellow, $46-48.

12" Compartment Plate

Sometimes called a "grill plate" or "divided plate", this large, heavy item didn't last long as a member of the Fiesta family. Production stopped in early March 1937, making it among the first pieces in the line to be discontinued. Grill plates were a popular item in dinnerware sets of the time and Rhead made sure Fiesta had one. Unfortunately, his first design proved to be too large. Its weight made it especially unwieldy when full of food.

The dividers on the plate added enough weight that a support ring had to be included on the bottom to prevent the center from slumping in the kiln. This distinctive feature and the fact that these plates were not marked are aids in identifying it when a ruler is not handy. Like all plates, this one was jiggered. They were glaze fired in a sagger and will have three sagger pin marks on the back.

These plates were made before Fiesta had a turquoise glaze, so they are found only in the first five colors. They are surprisingly affordable considering their short production lifetime.

Fiesta 12" Compartment Plate	
Modeling Date	March 1935
Model Number	395
Revisions	None
Production Began	November 1935*
First Price List	Early 1936 (undated)
Last Price List	Late 1936 (undated)
Discontinued	Early 1937*
Length of Production	1.2 Years*
Colors: Red, Cobalt, Green, Yellow, Ivory	
*Estimate	

Top: **Fiesta 12" compartment plate in all available colors. Cobalt, $68-73; Green, $54-57; Red, $69-78; Ivory, $63-67; Yellow, $52-55.**

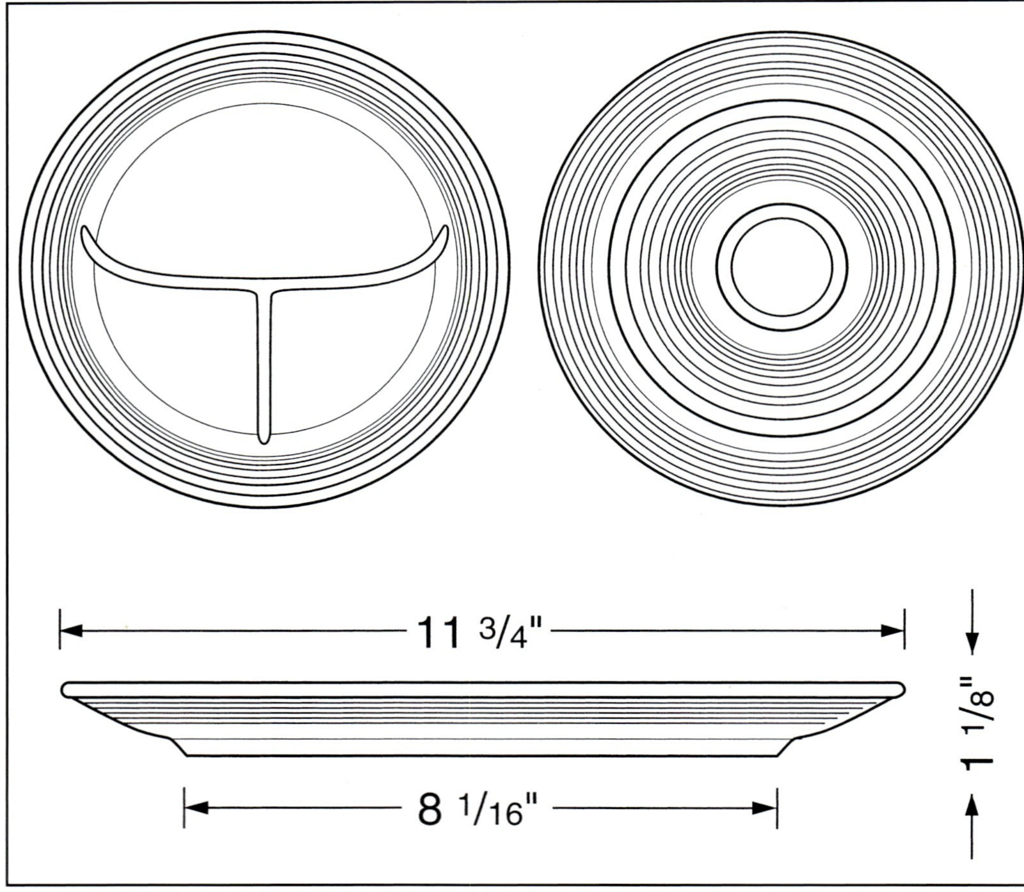

Fiesta 10 1/2" Compartment Plate

A note in Frederick Rhead's journal for February 1, 1937 says, "Returned from Columbus yesterday... Lazarus [department store] suggests compartment plate same size as 10" plate and deeper compartment wells." And that's exactly what he did. This is another example of the commitment Rhead and HLC had to the retailers. It also shows how suggestions were often turned into items in the line. The new plate was well received and stayed in the line until the late 1950s.

Made the same way as all Fiesta plates, and displaying the same sagger pin points, the smaller compartment plate was usually marked with the "Genuine Fiesta" backstamp. Red plates and those made after 1951 are more difficult to find and have a correspondingly higher value. They were not made in medium green.

Fiesta 10 1/2" Compartment Plate

Modeling Date	February 1937
Model Number	775
Revisions	None
Production Began	March 1937*
First Price List	March 15, 1937
Last Price List	October 1, 1957
Discontinued	Early 1959*
Length of Production	22 Years*

Colors: Red†, Cobalt, Green, Yellow, Ivory, Turquoise, Rose, Gray, Chartreuse, Forest

*Estimate

†Red discontinued in early 1944

Center: **Fiesta 10 1/2" compartment plates in colors available at shape introduction. Cobalt, $44-45; Green, $40-44; Ivory, $46-50; Red, $61-70; Yellow, $40-43.**

Bottom: **Fiesta 10 1/2" compartment plates in colors added after introduction. Forest, $86-95; Gray, $79-84; Chartreuse, $77-79; Rose, $78-81; Turquoise, $40-43.**

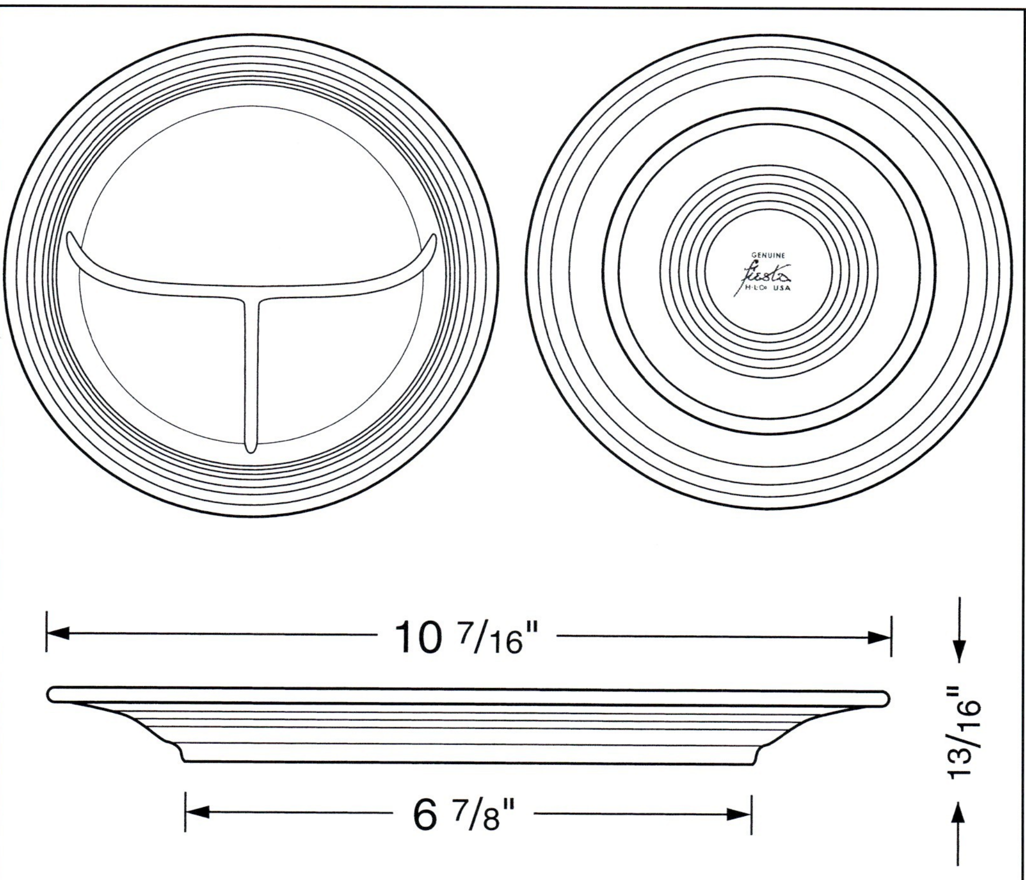

Fiesta Deep Plate

Often called a "soup plate" or "rimmed soup" this bowl was a needed addition to the line when it was modeled in May 1936. Part of a list of fourteen new items, it appeared for the first time on an undated price list sometime around August 1936. As the name implies, it is an 8" diameter plate with a deep well and was used for serving soup. Other bowls in the line at that time could not provide the volume needed for serving soup in an appropriate shape for the table.

Another jiggered piece, this one shows the same subtle variations in the ring pattern of the foot. It is fully glazed and has three sagger pin marks just under the rim. Made in all eleven vintage colors, it is relatively easy to find, even in medium green.

Fiesta Deep Plate	
Modeling Date	May 1936
Model Number	598
Revisions	None
Production Began	June 1936*
First Price List	Late 1936 (undated)
Last Price List	January 1, 1968
Discontinued	Early 1969*
Length of Production	32.7 Years*

Colors: Red†, Cobalt, Green, Yellow, Ivory, Turquoise, Rose, Gray, Chartreuse, Forest, Medium Green

*Estimate

†Red discontinued in early 1944, reintroduced mid-1959

Fiesta deep plates in colors available at shape introduction. Cobalt, $56-57; Green, $37-38; Red, $56-58; Ivory, $54-54; Yellow, $35-37.

Fiesta deep plates in colors added after introduction. Forest, $53-55; Gray, $54-56; Rose, $55-57; Chartreuse, $49-52; Turquoise, $38-39.

Fiesta deep plate in medium green. Medium Green, $130-135.

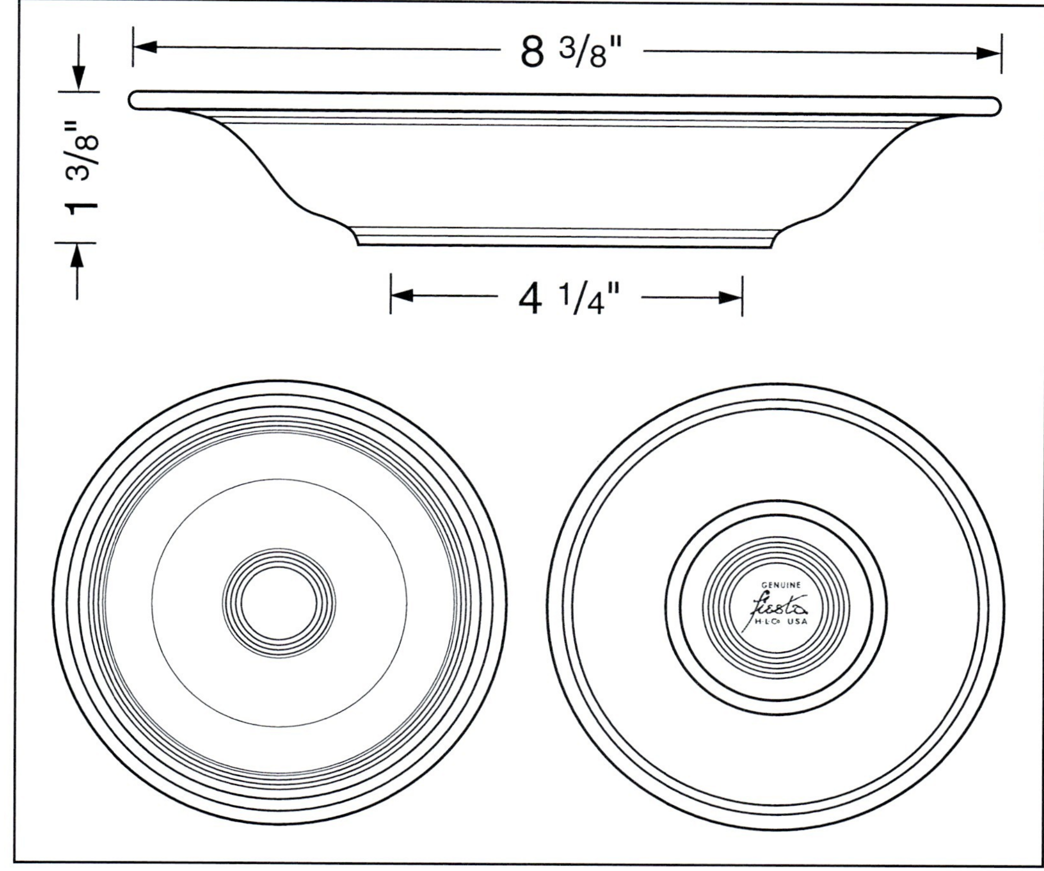

Fiesta 6" Plate

Just before production of Fiesta began, Frederick Rhead added the bread and butter plate to the line. His original design was not altered during the next 33 years and, except for color, these little plates are pretty much all the same. It is one of the 14 longest running items in the line.

Made on a jigger machine and completely glazed, they have three sagger pin marks under the rim. Most of them have the "Genuine Fiesta" backstamp. They are easily found in all colors with the Fifties glazes and medium green costing a little more.

Fiesta 6" Plate

Modeling Date .... November 1935
Model Number 468
Revisions .... None
Production Began .... November 1935*
First Price List .... Early 1936 (undated)
Last Price List .... January 1, 1968
Discontinued .... Early 1969*
Length of Production .... 33.2 Years*
Colors: Red†, Cobalt, Green, Yellow, Ivory, Turquoise, Rose, Gray, Chartreuse, Forest, Medium Green

*Estimate
†Red discontinued in early 1944, reintroduced mid-1959

Fiesta 6" plate in colors available at shape introduction. Cobalt, $7; Green, $6; Red, $6-7; Ivory, $7; Yellow, $6.

Fiesta 6" plate in medium green. Medium Green, $22-23.

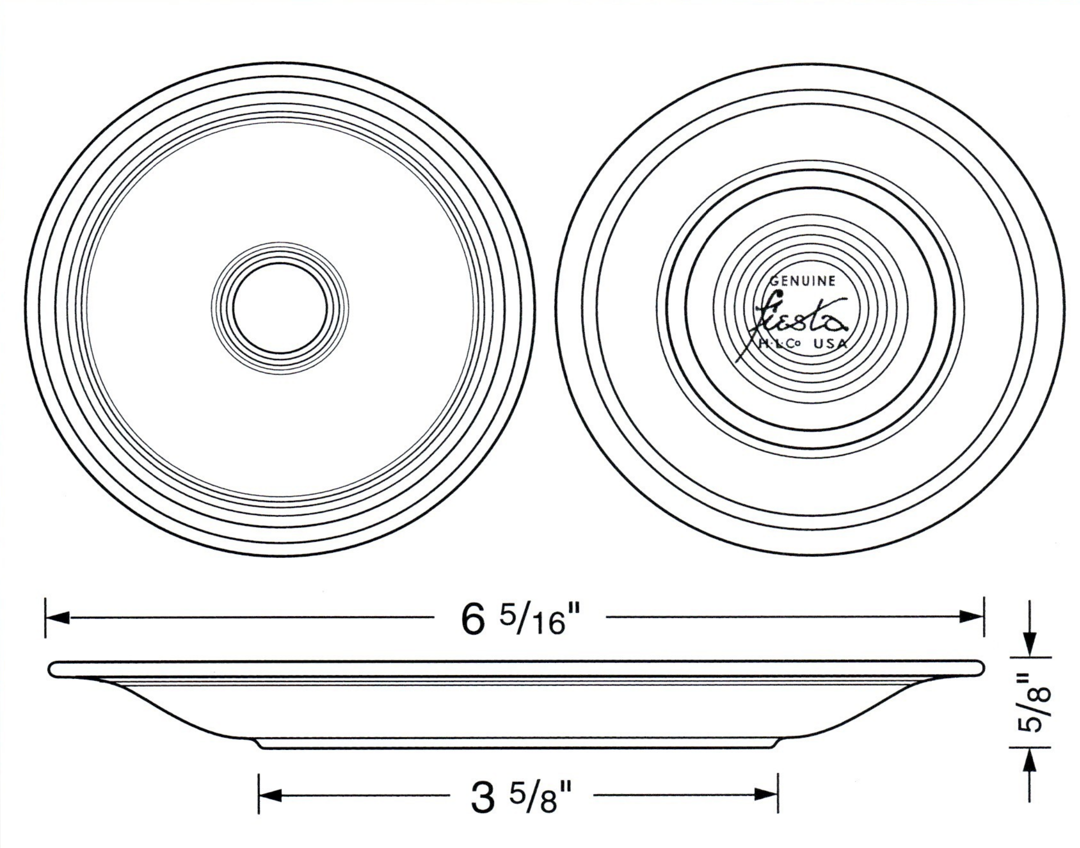

Fiesta 6" plate in colors added after introduction. Forest, $8-9; Gray, $10; Rose, $9; Chartreuse, $9-10; Turquoise, $6.

Fiesta 7" Plate

Here is another of the 14 items made for the entire time Fiesta was in production and it never really changed. Made like all the other plates and having the same sagger pin scars and backstamp, this one is sometimes called (confusingly) a "cake plate" or often a "salad plate."

They are readily available, with the expected difference in value for those from the 1950s and in the medium green glaze.

Fiesta 7" Plate

Modeling Date	March 1935
Model Number	350
Revisions	None
Production Began	November 1935*
First Price List	Early 1936 (undated)
Last Price List	January 1, 1968
Discontinued	Early 1969*
Length of Production	33.2 Years*

Colors: Red†, Cobalt, Green, Yellow, Ivory, Turquoise, Rose, Gray, Chartreuse, Forest, Medium Green

*Estimate

†Red discontinued in early 1944, reintroduced mid-1959

Fiesta 7" plates in colors available at shape introduction. Cobalt, $10-11; Green, $9-10; Red, $11-12; Ivory, $10-11; Yellow, $8-9.

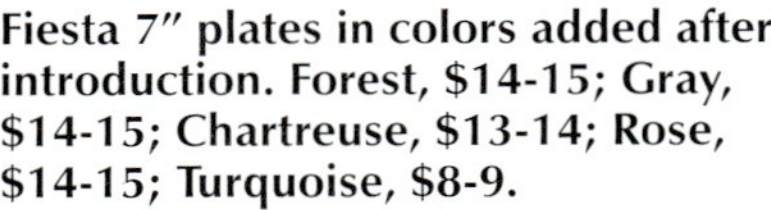

Fiesta 7" plates in colors added after introduction. Forest, $14-15; Gray, $14-15; Chartreuse, $13-14; Rose, $14-15; Turquoise, $8-9.

Fiesta 7" plate in medium green. Medium Green, $38-39.

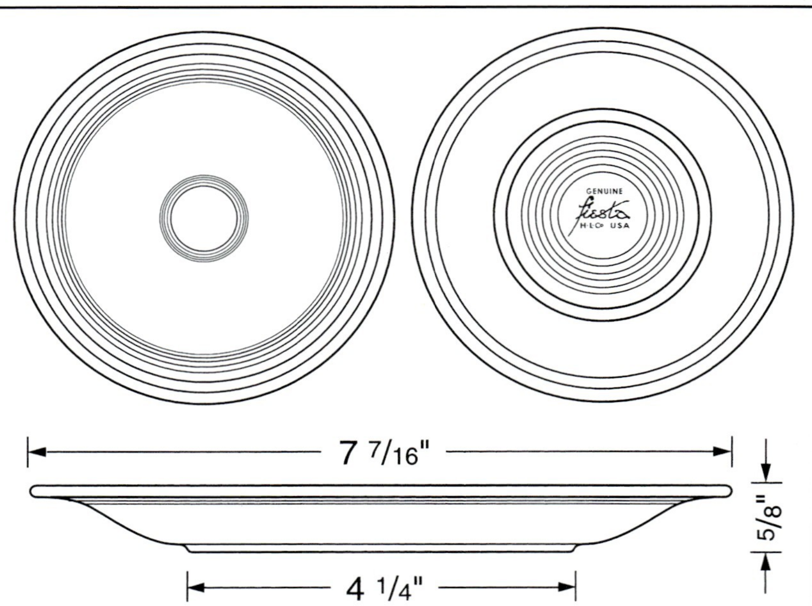

Fiesta 9" plates in colors available at shape introduction. Cobalt, $17-18; Green, $12-13; Red, $17-18; Ivory, $15-16; Yellow, $12-13.

Fiesta 9" Plate

This plate was the first item modeled for Fiesta. Like all the other plates, it has no real variations to speak of, was jiggered, has sagger pin marks, and the "Genuine Fiesta" backstamp. These are often called "luncheon plates".

Reports indicate that many prepackaged sets of Fiesta included the 9" plate, not the ten inch as one might expect. Perhaps this is the reason the smaller plate is still relatively easy to find and at reasonable prices.

Fiesta 9" Plate	
Modeling Date	February 1935
Model Number	324[1]
Revisions	None
Production Began	November 1935*
First Price List	Early 1936 (undated)
Last Price List	January 1, 1968
Discontinued	Early 1969*
Length of Production	33.2 Years*

Colors: Red†, Cobalt, Green, Yellow, Ivory, Turquoise, Rose, Gray, Chartreuse, Forest, Medium Green

*Estimate

†Red discontinued in early 1944, reintroduced mid-1959

[1]First item modeled for Fiesta

Fiesta 9" plates in colors added after introduction. Forest, $20-21; Gray, $20-21; Chartreuse, $20-21; Rose, $20-21; Turquoise, $12-13.

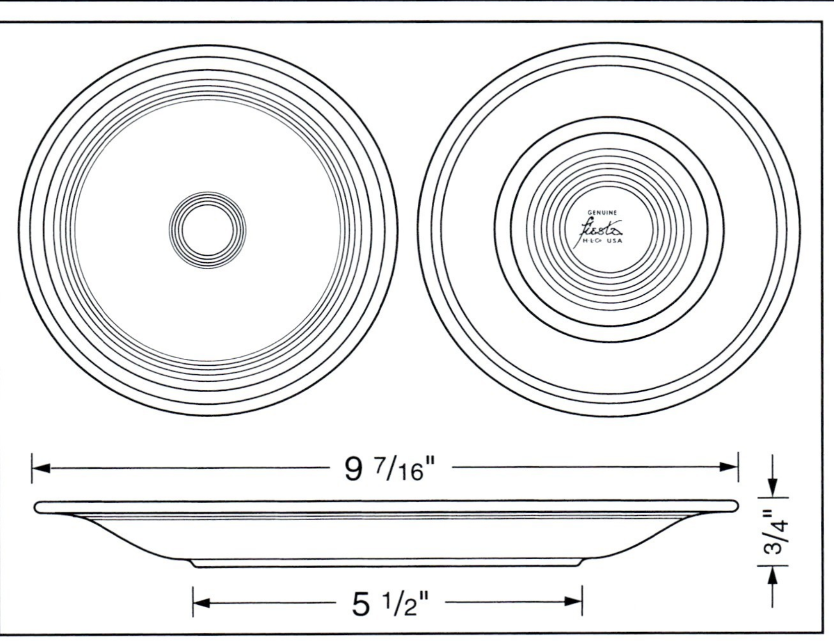

Fiesta 9" plate in medium green. Medium Green, $51-54.

Fiesta 10" Plate

The dinner plate is the one that is a bit more difficult to find. Like the others, there is some variation in the ring patterns within the foot due to the different jigger tools used. This plate also has the sagger pin marks and most of them are marked with the usual Fiesta backstamp.

Medium green plates in this size generally are the most highly valued, while those in the Fifties colors are also desirable collection pieces. All colors can be found with a little searching.

Fiesta 10" Plate

Modeling Date	February 1935
Model Number	338
Revisions	None
Production Began	November 1935*
First Price List	Early 1936 (undated)
Last Price List	January 1, 1968
Discontinued	Early 1969*
Length of Production	33.2 Years*

Colors: Red†, Cobalt, Green, Yellow, Ivory, Turquoise, Rose, Gray, Chartreuse, Forest, Medium Green

*Estimate

†Red discontinued in early 1944, reintroduced mid-1959

Fiesta 10" plate in medium green. Medium Green, $130-135.

Fiesta 10" plates in colors available at shape introduction. Cobalt, $41-42; Green, $29-31; Red, $39-41; Ivory, $40-41; Yellow, $28-30.

Fiesta 10" plates in colors added after introduction. Forest, $51-53; Gray, $45-47; Chartreuse, $49-52; Rose, $49-51; Turquoise, $28-29.

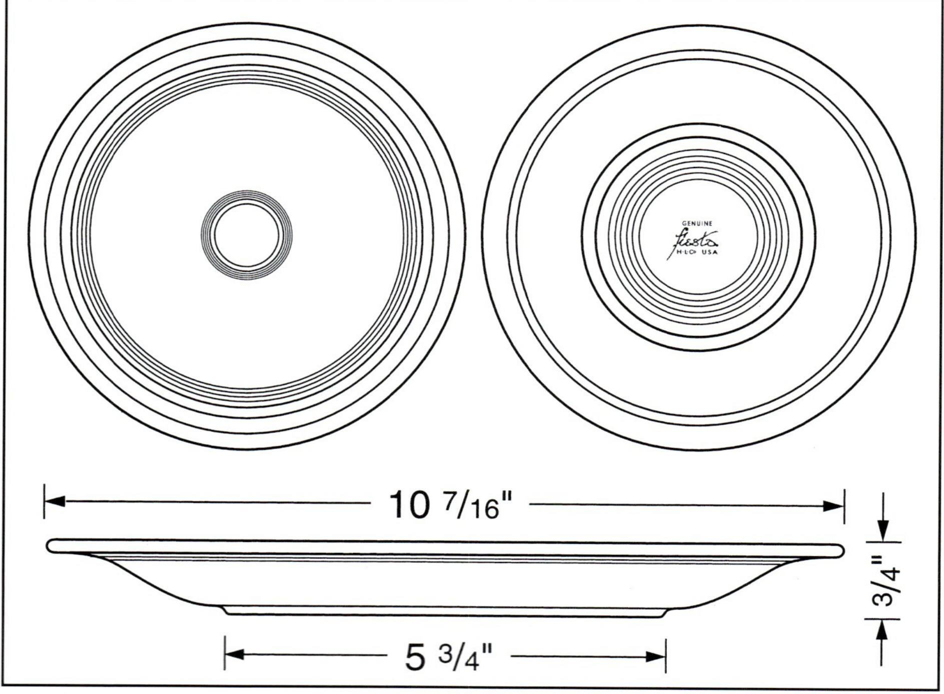

Oval Platter

Another of the mid-1936 additions, the oval platter was made using the ram press method. Items that are not round cannot be jiggered. Sometimes pieces like this are slip cast, but often they are made in a ram press. Semi-moist clay is put between two plaster molds, or "dies", which are then pressed together hydraulically.

The Fiesta platter was revised in 1947. The original model was 12 3/4" in length; the newer one was 12 1/2". The reason for the revision is not known, but may have been due to an attempt to correct problems with warping. Items made in the ram press can twist when being removed from the dies and, if allowed to dry in that manner, will result in a warped piece of pottery.

Most oval platters have the "Genuine Fiesta" backstamp. They are fairly easy to find in all colors.

Fiesta oval platter in medium green; Medium Green, $160-165.

Fiesta Oval Platter	
Modeling Date	February 1938
Model Number	1046
First Revision	January 1947, 2043[1]
Production Began	March 1938*
First Price List	July 1, 1938
Last Price List	January 1, 1968
Discontinued	Early 1969*
Length of Production	31 Years*

Colors: Red[†], Cobalt, Green, Yellow, Ivory, Turquoise, Rose, Gray, Chartreuse, Forest, Medium Green

*Estimate

[†]Red discontinued in early 1944, reintroduced mid-1959

[1]Reason for revision not known

Fiesta oval platter in colors added after introduction. Forest, $61-63; Gray, $58-60; Chartreuse, $56-58; Rose, $56-57.

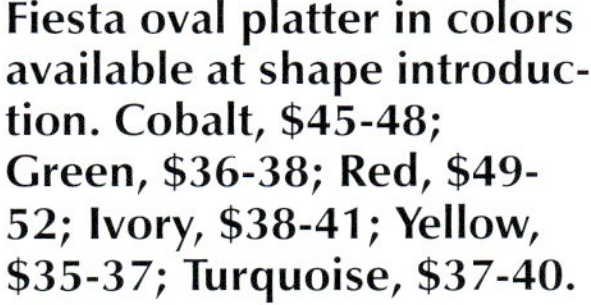

Fiesta oval platter in colors available at shape introduction. Cobalt, $45-48; Green, $36-38; Red, $49-52; Ivory, $38-41; Yellow, $35-37; Turquoise, $37-40.

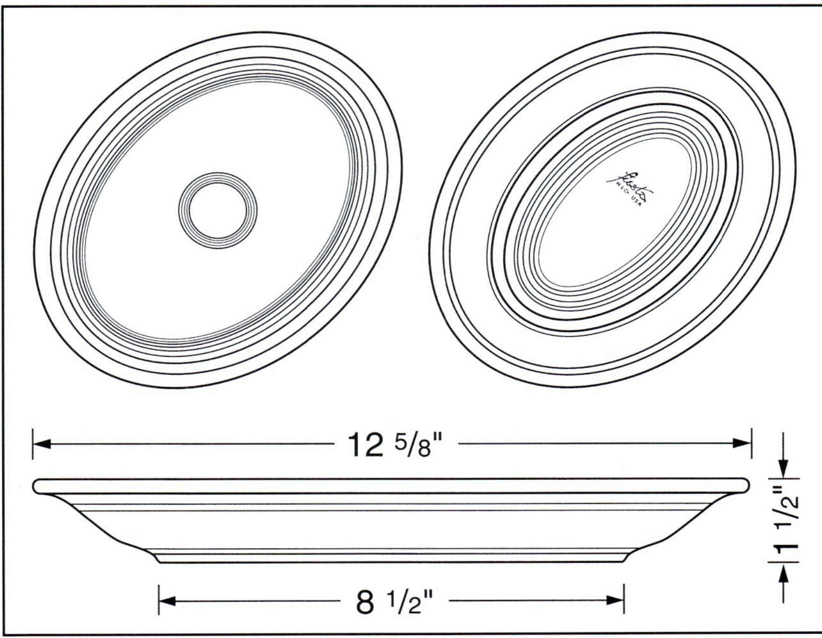

Relish Tray

Part of the fun of collecting the Fiesta relish tray involves finding all the pieces. Originally sold by HLC to wholesalers in one color, the parts were often mixed by retailers to provide a variety of color schemes from which their customers could choose. Today some collectors want a relish tray as it came "from the factory." But many others find the mixed color relish more appealing. Because of this, values for the individual pieces will vary by color.

Frederick Rhead was known for copying a design when it suited his purpose. In her excellent catalog, "Frederick Hurten Rhead: An English Potter In America," for the Erie Art Museum in 1986 Sharon Dale said, "...Rhead was not an especially original designer. Despite his oft-voiced contempt for lack of originality in art, Rhead's best designs are usually brilliant adaptations from other sources. Historical ceramics such as Chinese and Persian wares often served as prototypes, but most designs were based upon more recent models." Such could be the case with the Fiesta relish tray.

Attempts to verify the date of a relish tray marked "Maple Ware, Made in Japan" have not been successful. Shown in an accompanying photo, it very much resembles the Fiesta piece. Slight differences indicate it was not copied from the Fiesta item; more than likely the Fiesta relish was a copy of the Japanese.

First of all, the Japanese tray is larger. It has a diameter of 11 3/8" compared to 10 7/8" for the Fiesta relish. The Japanese tray has four rings on the rim of the base; the Fiesta tray has three or five. The inserts of the Japanese relish have a lip, or inner rim, while the Fiesta inserts do not.

Because the Japanese relish is marked "Made in Japan", it was clearly for export. Why would a foreign company copy a well-known and popular ware like Fiesta, then try to sell the copy in the same country as the original? That would not make economic sense, especially since Fiesta was relatively inexpensive. The more likely scenario is that the Japanese piece was already being sold in the United States when Rhead was designing the shapes for Fiesta.

Knowing that some pieces in the Fiesta line were copied from existing items does not lessen the importance of Rhead's contribution to American mass-produced dinnerware. He utilized existing designs or concepts to their fullest advantage in rounding out the line with pieces needed by the retail customer of the time.

There are several variations of the Fiesta relish tray that need to be addressed, starting with the base. When sold by itself this part is often called a "pie plate." All are marked with the "HLC USA" mark and most have five equally spaced rings on the rim. Occasionally a marked Fiesta base will have three rings. Unmarked relish tray bases in turquoise, with three rings on the rim, were made for the Harlequin line. The relish tray base was jiggered and glaze fired in saggers, so they will have three glaze disturbances from sagger pins under the rim.

The center inserts are also marked with the "HLC USA" mark, which may be plain or enclosed in a band of rings. They were also jiggered. This piece will have a triangular pattern of glaze scars on the bottom from the tripod stilts used in the glost kiln. When sold by itself, a center insert may be called a coaster.

There are several types of the side inserts. Made by two different processes, they may not fit together well if mixed. The oldest were made by slip casting and come in three versions, two marked and one unmarked. The two marked ones are the same size and will have the familiar "HLC USA" or "MADE IN USA" impressions. The unmarked sides are slightly smaller, not in

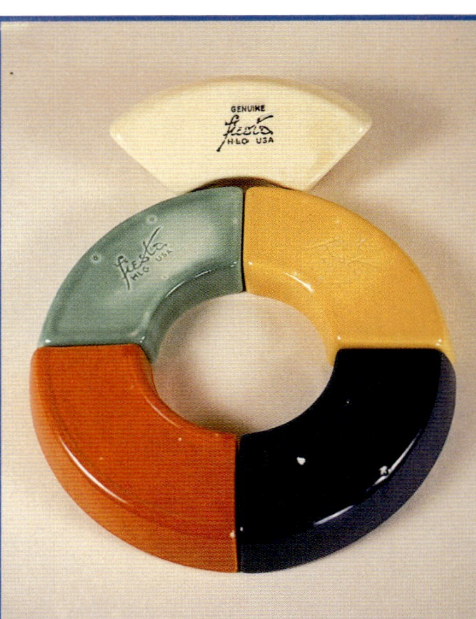

Various types of relish tray side inserts (see text).

The Maple Ware relish tray.

Fiesta relish tray in turquoise, added after introduction. Turquoise, $305-315.

height, but in width. The short, straight sides are approximately 1/8" shorter than on marked pieces. When four unmarked, slip cast sides are in a tray, the center insert will have a large gap all around it. All of the slip cast pieces have smooth rounded edges and the faintest impression of a rim all around the bottom. All will display three glaze dimples on the bottom from the glaze kiln stilt. Side inserts, in-mold marked or not, will sometimes feature the "Genuine Fiesta" backstamp.

The other type of side insert was made on a ram press. They are usually not marked and have distinct edges on the bottom of the curved sides only. This type is also taller than the slip cast inserts by at least 1/16". That may not seem like much, but when the ram pressed and slip cast types are mixed, the height difference is very noticeable.

The relish tray is often the centerpiece of a collection because of its multiple part design and the collector's ability to put together several combinations of colors. This item can also be found decorated with decals, usually over the ivory or yellow glaze. The relish tray was made by HLC for approximately eleven years (red ones for about seven). They are somewhat hard to find intact as solid colors and most often will be put together piece by piece. Color seems to matter in the value, with red ones topping the list.

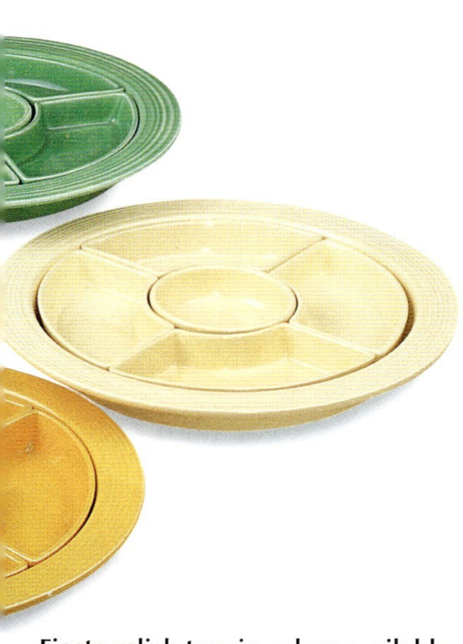

Fiesta relish tray in colors available at shape introduction. Cobalt, $310-325; Red, $295-310; Yellow, $285-300; Green, $290-300; Ivory, $310-325.

Fiesta Relish Tray

Modeling Date	June 1935
Model Number	383
Revisions	None
Production Began	November 1935*
First Price List	Early 1936 (undated)
Last Price List	August 22, 1946
Discontinued	Late 1946*
Length of Production	11 Years*

Colors: Red†, Cobalt, Green, Yellow, Ivory, Turquoise

*Estimate

†Red discontinued in early 1944

The backstamp for the Maple Ware relish tray.

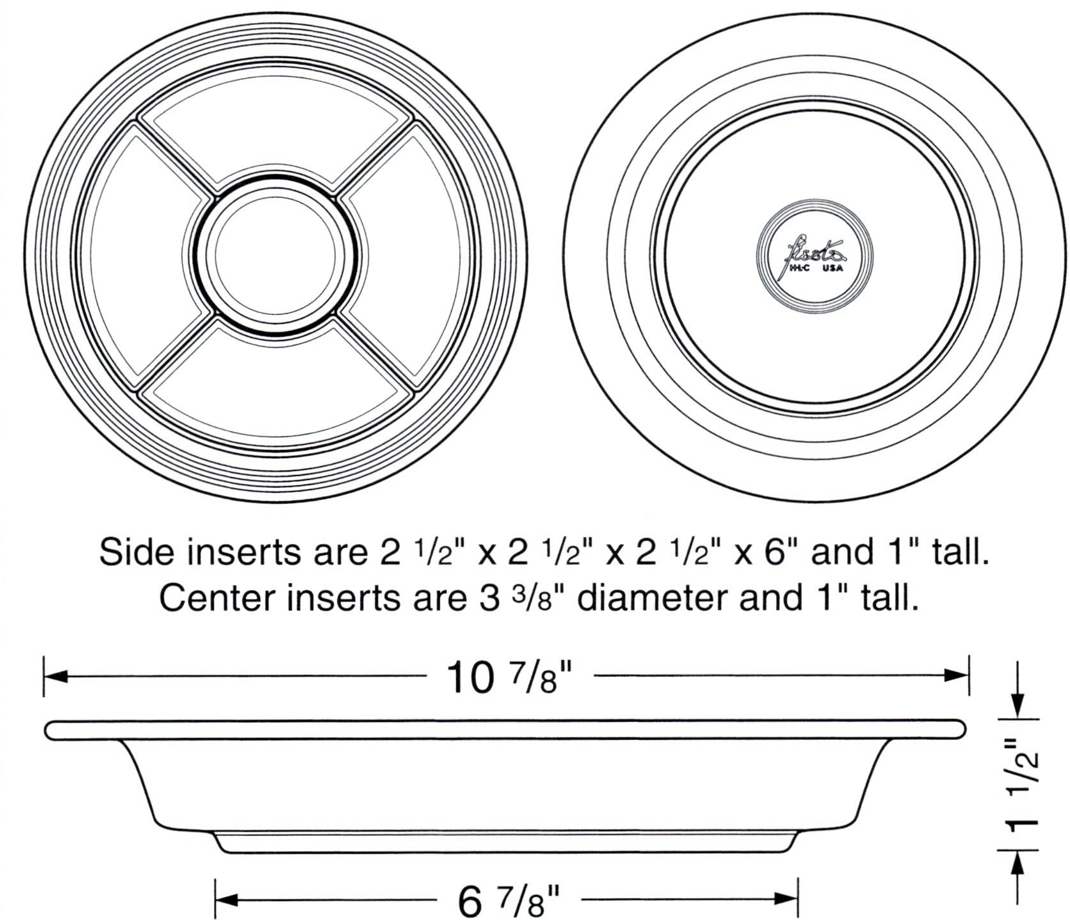

Sauce Boat

Slightly fat when viewed from the top, but curvaceously streamlined from the side; the Fiesta sauce boat was part of the line for more than 30 years. It was one of the few items that made the transition to Fiesta Ironstone without much change (only the loss of its impressed mark) and is once again part of the Fiesta lineup today.

Like most hollowware it was slip cast and had one of two in-mold marks, the "HLC USA" or "MADE IN USA". The former is the older mark and was changed in late 1937 or early 1938.

Sauce boats in most colors are relatively easy to add to a collection. Those in medium green, of course, command a much higher price and present more of a challenge to the collector seeking one.

Fiesta Sauce Boat

Modeling Date	April 1937
Model Number	801
Revisions	None
Production Began	June 1937*
First Price List	January 1, 1938
Last Price List	January 1, 1968
Discontinued	Early 1969*
Length of Production	31.7 Years*

Colors: Red†, Cobalt, Green, Yellow, Ivory, Turquoise, Rose, Gray, Chartreuse, Forest, Medium Green

*Estimate

†Red discontinued in early 1944, reintroduced mid-1959

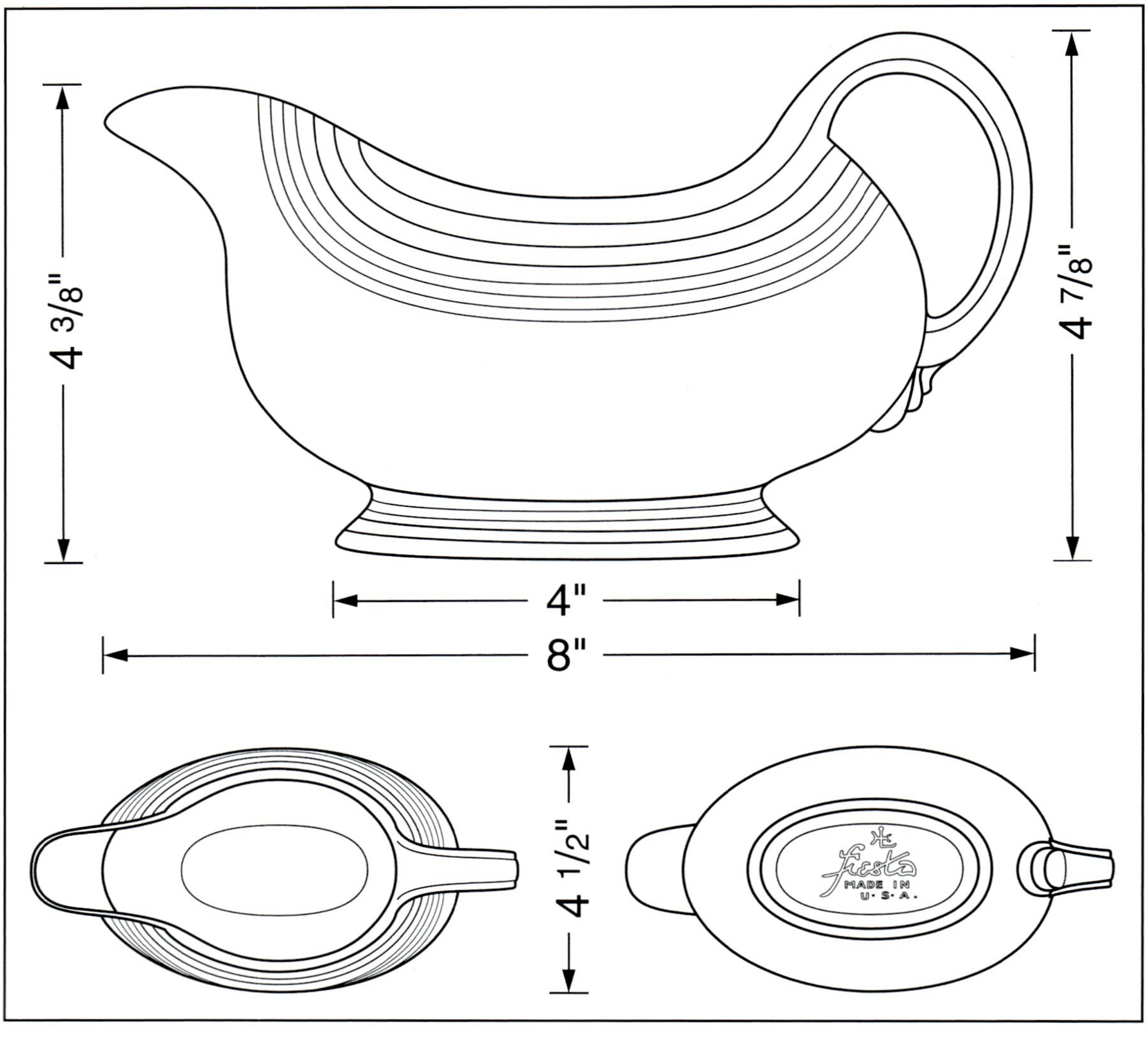

4 3/8"

4 7/8"

4"

8"

4 1/2"

HLC fiesta MADE IN U.S.A.

Fiesta sauce boats in colors available at shape introduction. Yellow, $43-45; Red, $76-84; Cobalt, $70-73; Ivory, $69-71; Green, $47-50.

Fiesta sauce boats in colors added after introduction. Turquoise, $41-44; Chartreuse, $69-72; Forest, $77-80; Rose, $78-81; Gray, $70-74.

Fiesta sauce boat in medium green. Medium Green, $185-195.

Salt and Pepper Shakers

These little ball-shaped shakers are members of several elite groups. First, they are two of the 14 items made for the whole time Fiesta was in production (HLC usually sold them separately). Second, they are two of the nine items that were rarely marked. Three, they were among the few items moved to the Fiesta Ironstone line with only minor changes (the number of holes in the pepper). Finally, they were the first salt and pepper shakers in any line of ware produced at Homer Laughlin up to the time of their introduction. Today collectors find them fun and easy to collect while readily available and (generally) inexpensive.

HLC's modeling log says the shakers had their "lines sharpened" in August 1937, but there does not seem to be a detectable difference to let collectors know the revised shakers from the original. Both shakers have seven holes in a hexagonal pattern. The pepper shaker has smaller holes and the pattern of holes is smaller as well. After Amberstone was put into production in 1967, the pepper shaker lost its center hole. Collectors may find shakers in the colors of the Sixties with this type of pepper.

The shakers were slip cast and will often show the mold seam on the globe part. They originally came with cork stoppers and many still have them. They have an unglazed foot.

Usually sold in pairs, Fiesta salt and pepper shakers are easily found and not all that expensive. Those in medium green are the exception to that rule and can be rather hard to find.

Fiesta Salt & Pepper Shakers

Modeling Date .... July 1935
Model Number 397
Revision .... August 1937, 903[1]
Production Began .... November 1935*
First Price List .... Early 1936 (undated)
Last Price List .... January 1, 1968
Discontinued .... Early 1969*
Length of Production .... 33.2 Years*
Colors: Red†, Cobalt, Green, Yellow, Ivory, Turquoise, Rose, Gray, Chartreuse, Forest, Medium Green
*Estimate
†Red discontinued in early 1944, reintroduced mid-1959

Fiesta salt and pepper shakers in colors added after introduction. Turquoise, $12-13 each; Forest, $24-25 each; Chartreuse, $24-25 each; Gray, $23-24 each; Rose, $23-24 each.

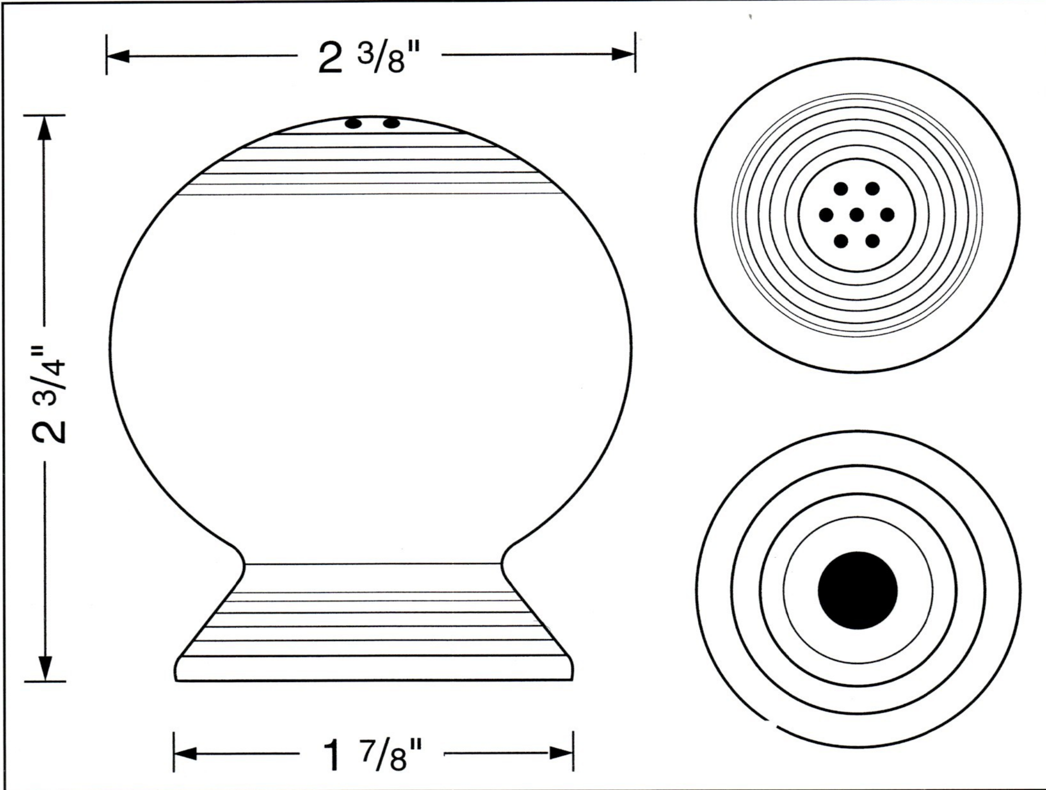

Fiesta shaker in medium green. Medium Green, $79-83 each.

Fiesta salt and pepper shakers in colors available at shape introduction. Yellow, $12-13 each; Cobalt, $15-16 each; Red, $16-17 each; Green, $12-13 each; Ivory, $16-17 each.

Covered Sugar

The first model creamer (see *Cream* above) had a companion sugar which looked very much like a ring handled version of the later-designed onion soup bowl. Shown nearby is that early model in what looks like a chocolate brown glaze. It actually was glazed in Fiesta red, which burned off in a kiln with the temperature set too high. This sugar has remnants of red glaze in the deep crevices. Whatever his reasons, Frederick Rhead decided the first model sugar was too large. His revision a few months later was labeled "small sugar."

The new model was put into production and is the shape with which collectors are familiar. This early production sugar had four key differences from those made later - (1) It was slip cast; (2) it had a flat inside bottom; (3) it had a deeper foot, like a Fiesta creamer; and (4) the lid was also slip cast and had a flange that was 3/8" deep. The separately slip-cast finial was hand applied. This model featured the "HLC USA" in-mold mark and was made only in the first five colors. They are very rare today because the next revision occurred only three months after Fiesta's introduction.

In March 1936 major modifications were made. The new sugar was made by jiggering and had a hand turned foot. Some unusual foot variations can be found due to the hand work involved. The new model had a round inside bottom and the foot was shallow. The lid flange was only 1/8" deep; this lid was also jiggered and had a hand applied, slip-cast finial. These sugars can be found with no mark at all or the "HLC USA" mark surrounded by three rings.

The model that began production around October 1937 is the one most often seen today. The HLC modeling log states the sugar and its cover had the lines "deepened" and made "heavier". It is believed that the slogan on the foot was changed to "MADE IN USA" at this time. The turning tool used to shape the foot was modified in the 1950s and sugars in the Fifties glazes may appear to have a foot that is less flared than those made previously.

The sugar bowl was a standard tableware item and anyone who bought the dishes usually purchased a sugar and cream as well. Fiesta sugar bowls are fairly easy to find in most colors. As expected, those in medium green are the most elusive.

Fiesta Covered Sugar

Modeling Date .... March 1935
Model Number .... 349[1]
First Revision .... June 1935, 388[2]
Second Revision .... February 1936, 538[3]
Third Revision .... September 1937, 942[4], 962[5]
Production Began .... November 1935
First Price List .... Early 1936 (undated)
Last Price List .... January 1, 1968
Discontinued .... Early 1969*
Length of Production .... 33.2 Years*
Colors: Red†, Cobalt, Green, Yellow, Ivory, Turquoise, Rose, Gray, Chartreuse, Forest, Medium Green

*Estimate
†Red discontinued in early 1944, reintroduced mid-1959
[1]First model not produced
[2]Slip cast (flat bottom) produced until March 1936
[3]Jiggered (round bottom)
[4]Sugar "lines deepened" (see text)
[5]Lid "lines heavier" (see text)

Fiesta covered sugars in colors available at shape introduction. Yellow, $41-43; Red, $54-57; Cobalt, $56-60; Green, $46-49; Ivory, $56-58.

Fiesta covered sugar in medium green. Medium Green, $155-165.

Fiesta covered sugars in colors added after introduction. Turquoise, $44-46; Chartreuse, $73-74; Forest, $67-70; Rose, $73-74; Gray, $66-69.

The original production model of the covered sugar featured a flat bottom inside the bowl.

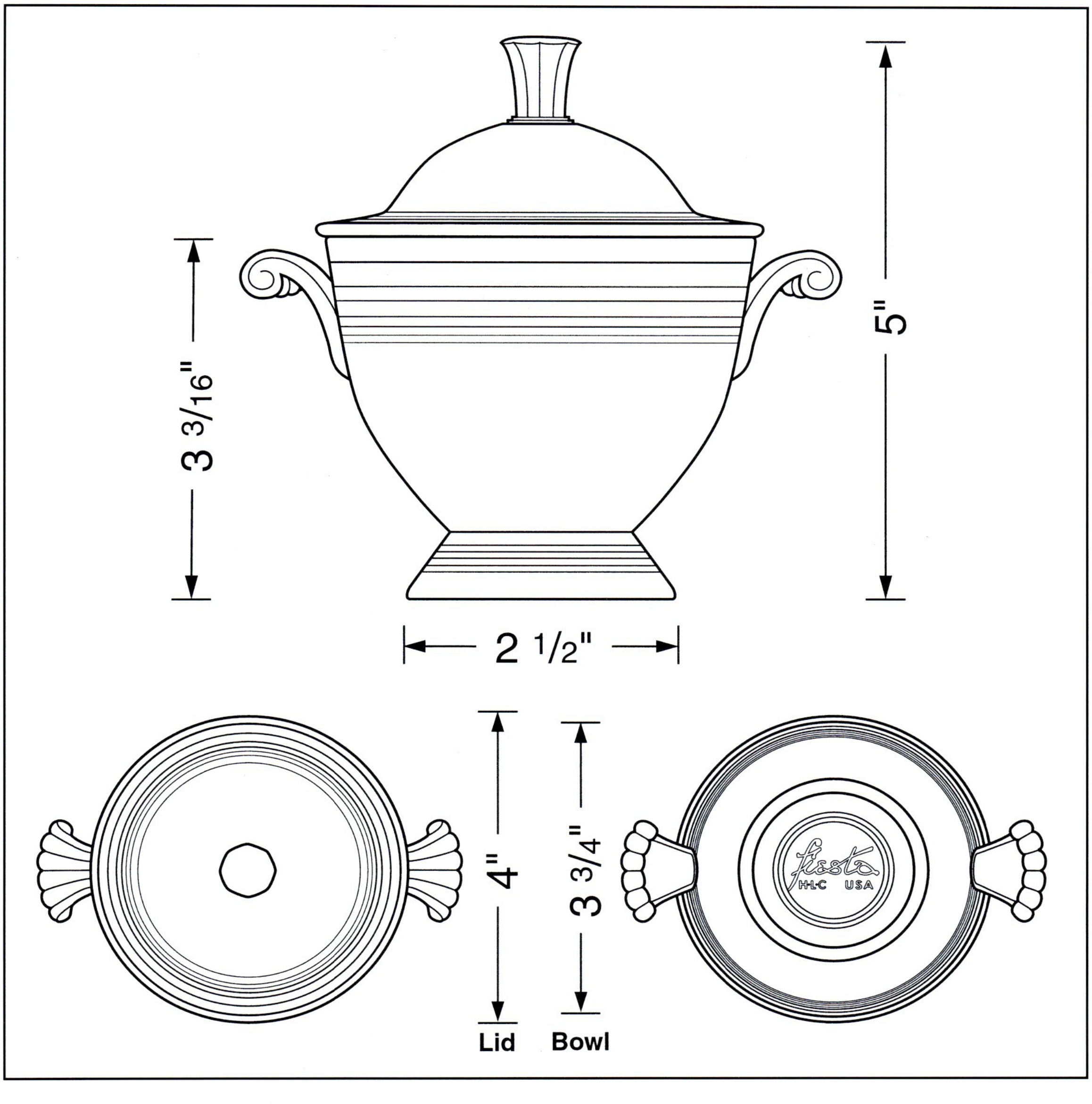

3 3/16"
5"
2 1/2"
4"
3 3/4"
fiesta HLC USA
Lid
Bowl

Dripcut® Syrup

The Dripcut Corporation was a southern California company founded in the 1930s. According to company literature, the patent on their spring loaded, metal slide syrup dispenser was applied for in 1935. The company made that product for more than 50 years in glass, plastic, and ceramic versions. Traex®, a division of the Menasha Corporation, acquired Dripcut Corporation in the mid-1980s. Traex® still makes items with the Dripcut® name, including several styles of syrup dispensers, some of which resemble the vintage models.

In July 1938 a model for the Fiesta version was created. Contrary to popular belief, HLC did not purchase molds from the Dripcut Corporation. They did purchase the rights to create an item shaped like the Dripcut® container and which used the same metal slide lid. The lids did come from the Dripcut Corporation in colors to match the Fiesta and Harlequin syrups.

In Frederick Rhead's journal, on August 12, 1938 he wrote, "J.M.W. brought in syrup jug with spring top. This is to be modeled to the metal cap." (J.M.W. was Joseph M. Wells, Sr., HLC's general manager and the executive who approved everything that went into production.)

There had been a previous model created in the same shape, albeit larger, in June 1937. It was made for L. Friedlman, an HLC executive mentioned frequently in Rhead's journal. The earlier model apparently was not produced and its relationship with the one finally made is not known.

The only known appearance of the Fiesta Dripcut® syrup in a retail publication was in the Larkin Company's catalog #124 of 1940. It was offered in only one color, however, so there must have been other retailers who sold this item. No other information from HLC was available to our researchers.

The syrups were slip cast and have the "MADE IN USA" impressed mark. The lids tend to fade when exposed to light and may be a slightly different color than the base when found today. The cobalt lids are especially prone to discoloration and are often dark purple instead of blue. Collectors who find syrup bases without a lid may have a difficult time trying to find the correct top. The Dripcut Corporation made several sizes of syrups, mostly of glass, with lids that resemble those used on the Fiesta syrups. Some of these lids may fit, but the color will probably not match.

There are some distinctive features to watch for when looking for an original Fiesta syrup lid. The color, obviously, should be the first consideration. Original lids may be marked "Dripcut" on the metal slide, but most were not. The thumb piece is cast metal, without decoration, and says "Made in U.S.A." on the underside of the rounded end. It also has a spur, hidden under the slide, that engages a hole in the plastic top. The hinge pin, which is surrounded by the spring, has usually darkened with age and the exposed head is less than 1/8" in diameter. The plastic bracket that holds the hinge pin is curved and extends below the handle.

The plastic part of genuine Fiesta lids was made in two styles. The one presumed to be older has a handle that curves tightly and nearly touches the side of the base when the lid is on. The later model has a handle that rests approximately 5/8" away from the body when in place. Both fit on a syrup jar that measures exactly two inches at the rim (outside diameter). If the syrup jug from which a substitute lid is removed measures more than 2" at the rim, the lid will not fit on a Fiesta syrup base.

The syrup shape was used for two other Fiesta/HLC collectibles: the "boudoir" lamps and Dutchess Tea jars. The source of the syrups for these items was more than likely overruns, seconds, or leftover stock that was sold by the pound to outside companies. The lamps have a brass filigree base and ivory colored shades with golden fringe trim. They are approximately 10" tall without the shade. The tea jars were packed by Dutchess Food Specialties, a company known to use unusual ceramic containers for cheese and tea. The syrups used this way had a cork seal, paper label, and a card attached by a yellow cord with tassel.

Fiesta syrups are on the "all time favorite" list of many collectors and are very desirable additions to a collection. They were probably produced for a little more than two years, perhaps ending when production of the Harlequin syrup began. No matter what the color, Fiesta syrups with the proper lid are difficult to find and are usually highly valued when purchased in excellent condition.

Fiesta Dripcut® Syrup

Modeling Date	August 1938
Model Number	1119
Revisions	None
Production Began	September 1938*
First Price List	None[1]
Last Price List	None[1]
Discontinued	Late 1940*
Length of Production	2.2 Years*

Colors: Red, Cobalt, Green, Yellow, Ivory, Turquoise

*Estimate

[1]Not found on any price list

Dutchess brand tea container, still filled with tea leaves, is the Fiesta syrup in turquoise with intact cork, label, and tag, . No established value.

Fiesta Dripcut® syrup in all available colors. Red, $445-470; Cobalt, $445-465; Yellow, $350-375; Ivory, $410-440; Turquoise, $380-425; Green, $350-375.

Boudoir lamps were made using Fiesta syrup bases. No Established value.

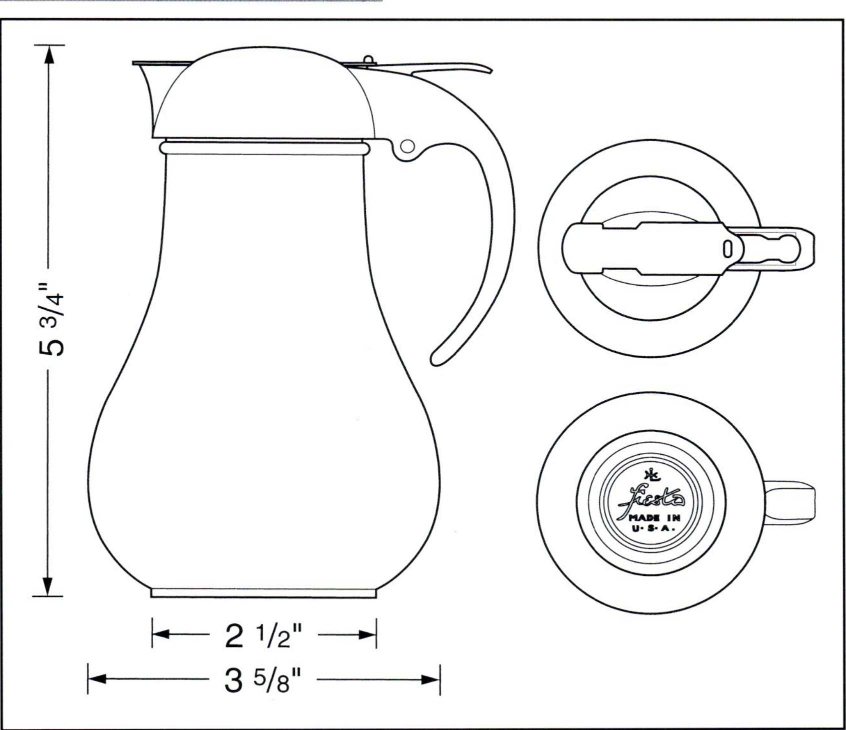

Fiesta WARE

Drip-Cut Server

Now you can get the famous Drip-Cut Server in Fiesta Ware! The patented drip-cut top cuts the flow and contents positively cannot drip when closed and are kept sanitary. Perfect for serving syrup, honey, cream, salad dressing, etc.

Base of this gracefully-shaped, new pitcher is of genuine Fiesta pottery in soft-green color. Capacity, 13 oz. Height, 5¾ in. Mailing weight 1 lb.

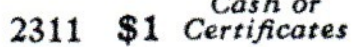

2311 **$1** *Cash or Certificates*

Fiesta Juice Set

Imagine getting this smart, new 7-piece set of genuine Fiesta pottery with all its color, charm and usefulness—for so little! Either to supplement your other Fiesta Ware, or as a charming set to use alone, adding a bright touch, it is thoroughly delightful.

Consists of one-quart pitcher of distinctive style and six tumblers in green, blue, yellow and red—all in assorted colors. All pieces have the quality, grace, smartness of line, and characteristic texture for which Fiesta pottery is famous.

Height of pitcher, 5¾ in.; tumblers, 3½ in. Ideal for serving fruit juices and beverages. Mailing weight 4 lbs.

2514 **$1** *Cash or Certificates*

Large Teapot

The stated capacity of this piece is eight cups and when it is full of boiling water, it can be heavy and difficult to hold by the ring handle alone. This may be one of the reasons it was discontinued, along with 14 other items, in November 1946.

The large tea pot, like all vessels, was slip cast in a plaster mold. The ring handle was part of the casting and was not separately applied. The lid was also cast and has a hand placed finial. Hand-made steam vent holes may vary in their location on the lid, but almost all lids will have one. There were three in-mold marks used: the plain "HLC USA", the same slogan surrounded by three rings, and the "MADE IN USA" mark. It is difficult to date when the marks changed, but it is believed the "MADE IN USA" mark was applied to most slip-cast items in the line by mid-1938. Other than the different marks, there are no major variations of this teapot.

As time passes, early items like this become harder to find. The red large teapots were discontinued before the others, but the ivory ones appear to be the most difficult to locate. In excellent condition this piece is another highly valued item.

Fiesta large tea pot in turquoise, added after introduction. Turquoise, $185-195.

Fiesta Large Teapot

Modeling Date	November 1935
Model Number	470
Revisions	None
Production Began	November 1935*
First Price List	Early 1936 (undated)
Last Price List	August 22, 1946
Discontinued	Late 1946*
Length of Production	11 Years*

Colors: Red†, Cobalt, Green, Yellow, Ivory, Turquoise

*Estimate

†Red discontinued in early 1944

Fiesta large tea pot in colors avaialable at shape introduction. Red, $215-230; Cobalt, $220-230; Ivory, $210-220; Yellow, $195-200; Green, $180-190.

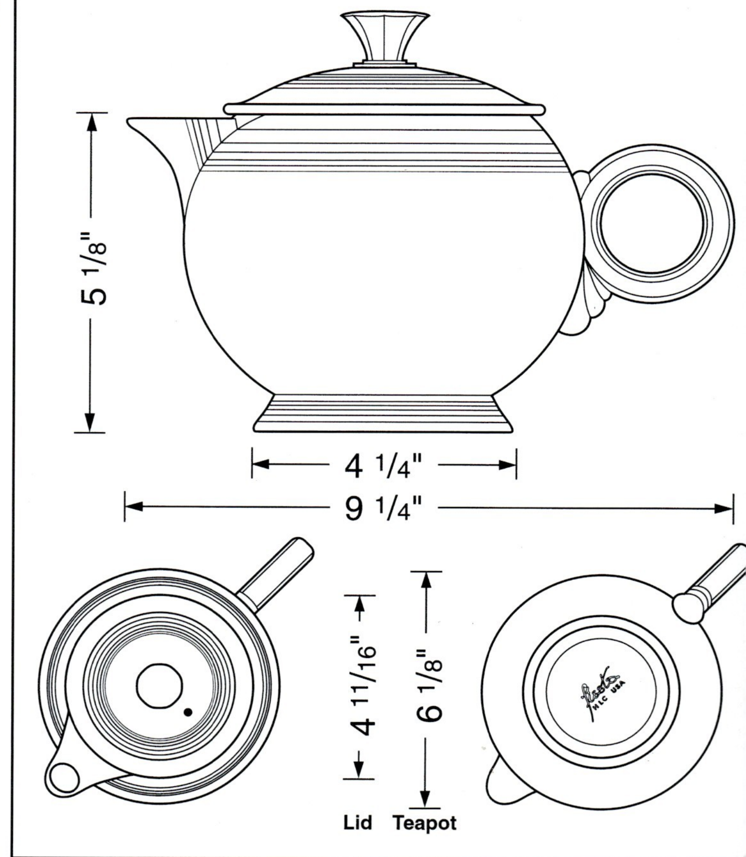

Medium Teapot

Fiesta's medium tea is named that way because a smaller one was modeled, but never produced (see the trial items section). This one was added after about a year of production, coming into the line in early 1937, and was likely the result of a suggestion by the retailers. Rhead sketched two lid designs, one was like the lid of the large teapot and the other resembled the lid of the mustard jar. The one-piece lid was produced.

This piece and its lid were slip cast and the tea pot features the same three marking variations as the larger one. Some medium tea pots have been found in the Sixties colors without any marking at all, but those are considered errors created when an Amberstone tea pot received the wrong color glaze. The lids have manually created vent holes, which may not always be in the same place or may be missing entirely.

The medium teapot was made in all eleven vintage colors and is only somewhat difficult to find. Not unexpectedly, those in the glazes of the 1950s and medium green will be more of a challenge. After the cream soup cup and disc water pitcher, a medium green tea pot is the most expensive item in that color to add to a collection (with the covered casserole not far behind).

Fiesta medium teapot in medium green. Medium Green, $1480-1645.

Fiesta Medium Teapot

Modeling Date	January 1937
Model Number	741
Revisions	None
Production Began	January 1937*
First Price List	March 15, 1937
Last Price List	January 1, 1968
Discontinued	Early 1969*
Length of Production	32.1 Years*

Colors: Red†, Cobalt, Green, Yellow, Ivory, Turquoise, Rose, Gray, Chartreuse, Forest, Medium Green

*Estimate

†Red discontinued in early 1944, reintroduced mid-1959

Fiesta medium tea pots in colors available at shape introduction. Yellow, $155-160; Red, $195-200; Cobalt, $215-225; Ivory, $200-205; Green, $160-165.

Fiesta medium tea pots in colors added after introduction. Turquoise, $160-165; Gray, $340-360; Forest, $330-350; Rose, $310-330; Chartreuse, $315-325.

Utility Tray

This serving piece was named "utility" because it could perform a variety of functions—as a base for the sugar and cream, for serving celery or carrot sticks, or a handy place for relishes or condiments. It was among the first additions to the line in mid-1936 and was produced for about ten years. There are two major varieties.

This piece was originally produced on the ram press. Two plaster dies were pressed together after a mass of clay had been put between them. The nature of the clay used for this process, which could be quite stiff, resulted in the retention of deformities due to uneven release from the dies. This problem often presented itself as bowing or warping of the finished tray. After nearly two years of production, the utility tray was redesigned for slip casting.

The earlier utility trays have a narrow, unglazed foot (although a few have been found fully glazed) and are not marked. They also feature straight sides and resemble the profile of the small fruit bowls when viewed from the short end. The slip cast model has a wider, glazed foot and is usually marked with the familiar "Genuine Fiesta" backstamp. The newer tray has slanted sides and features sagger pin marks under the rim. In spite of the change in production method, the later trays also had problems with deformities. This is most often seen as twisting on the long axis.

Both types of utility tray were made in the first six colors, although the ram press variety in the turquoise glaze will be more difficult to find. All colors are fairly easy to find in the later model, with red being a bit more difficult since it was discontinued before the others.

Fiesta Utility Tray	
Modeling Date	May 1936
Model Number	591[1]
First Revision	April 1938, 1071[2]
Second Revision	April 1938, 1077[3]
Production Began	June 1936*
First Price List	Late 1936 (undated)
Last Price List	August 22, 1946
Discontinued	Late 1946*
Length of Production	10.3 Years*

Colors: Red†, Cobalt, Green, Yellow, Ivory, Turquoise

*Estimate

†Red discontinued in early 1944

1Ram press, dry foot, produced until mid-1938

2Revised for slip casting, not produced

3Length increased, slip cast, wet foot

Fiesta utility trays in colors available at shape introduction. Cobalt, $45-48; Green, $38-40; Yellow, $40-42; Red, $43-47; Ivory, $39-43.

Fiesta utility tray in turquoise, added after introduction. Turquoise, $39-41.

Comparison of the two types of Fiesta utility tray.

Comparison of end shapes of the two varieties of utility tray.

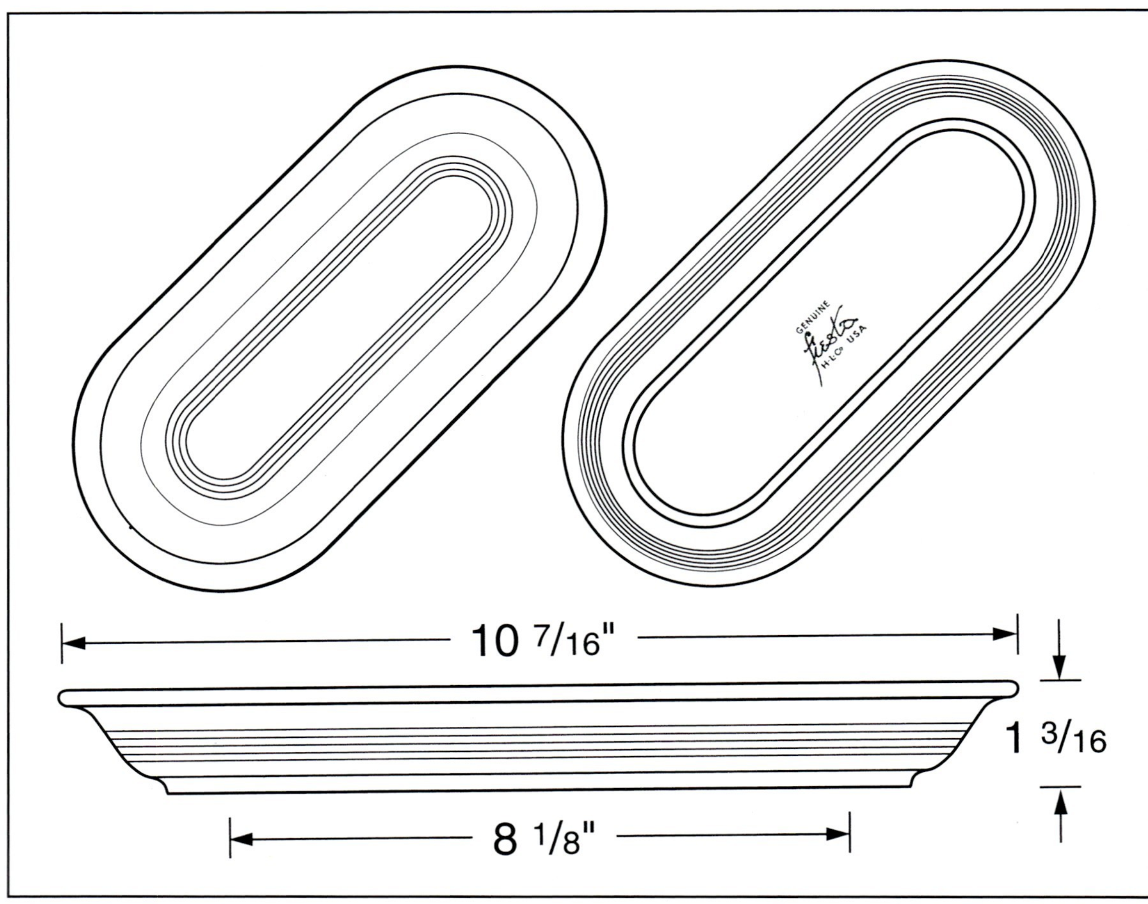

Fiesta water tumbler in turquoise, added after introduction. Turquoise, $60-62.

Water Tumbler

Introduced in March 1937, the tumbler reached retail shelves just in time for lemonade or iced tea with a summer meal. No doubt a welcome addition to the line and one probably suggested by the department stores where Fiesta was sold. In HLC's modeling log, items with this shape were called mugs. Frederick Rhead designed two "mugs" for Fiesta, one with convex sides and one concave. The mug with inner curving sides proved easier to produce and is the item found today. (See the sample modeling log page in the Appendix for a look at Rhead's original sketches.)

This tumbler was jiggered, like all cup shaped objects. It was made with two impressed marks during its nearly ten years in production—the now familiar "HLC USA" and "MADE IN USA". Some collectors have questioned whether the occasional difference in height is important. It may be due to the production method, or a slight change in the jiggering tool, and should not effect the value or collectability.

For its size, the water tumbler can seem expensive. Red ones were made for a shorter period of time and may command a higher price.

Fiesta Water Tumbler	
Modeling Date	December 1936
Model Number	735[1]
Revision	736[2]
Production Began	January 1937*
First Price List	March 15, 1937
Last Price List	August 22, 1946
Discontinued	Late 1946*
Length of Production	9.7 Years*

Colors: Red[†], Cobalt, Green, Yellow, Ivory, Turquoise

*Estimate

[†]Red discontinued in early 1944

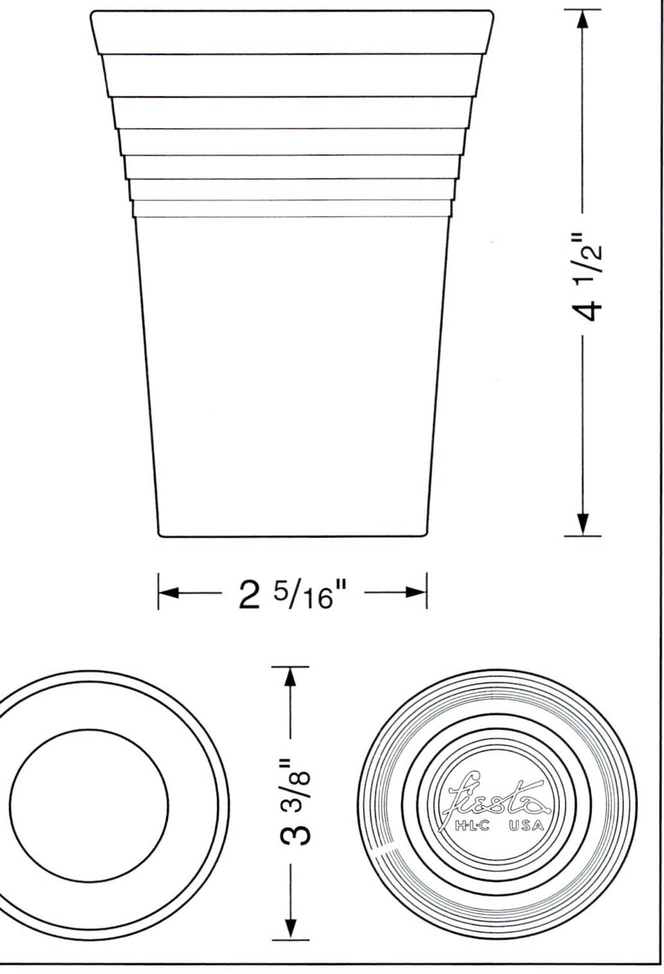

Fiesta water tumbler in colors available at shape introduction.. Red , $71-74; Cobalt, $73-75; Ivory, $69-72; Yellow, $62-63; Green, $60-62.

Bud Vase

The shape of the Fiesta bud vase is not exactly the same as one made by the Van Briggle Art Pottery Company, but it's very, very close. One must wonder which came first. The answer is the Van Briggle vase which was made in the early 1930s - certainly before 1935 when Frederick Rhead had his version modeled for Fiesta. As previous stated, Rhead had no trouble borrowing designs, or at least ideas for designs, from others. The bud vase appears to be another case of his use of this method for creating new shapes for Fiesta.

Of course, both Rhead and the art director at the Colorado pottery could have been influenced by, or directly copied the shape from, another source. It certainly shows a heavy Art Deco influence, much more so than most pieces in the Fiesta line. Whatever the origin, the bud vase fits nicely with Fiesta's other items and is a piece found in many collections today.

This vase, like other hollowware, was slip cast. Sometimes mold seams can be seen on the gently curved sides. It was made for more than ten years and was an original item in the line. There are two slight varieties, with only the impressed mark making the difference. One has the "HLC USA" and the other reads "MADE IN USA."

Although the value is pushing steadily upward, these little vases are still readily available in all of the first six colors. Red ones were made for a shorter period of time and are therefore a bit more difficult to find.

This shape is also part of the currently produced line of Fiesta and is almost the same size as the vintage vases. Knowing the original colors well will prevent collectors from paying a vintage price for a contemporary product.

Fiesta Bud Vase

Modeling Date	May 1935
Model Number	374
Revisions	None
Production Began	November 1935*
First Price List	Early 1936 (undated)
Last Price List	August 22, 1946
Discontinued	Late 1946*
Length of Production	11 Years*

Colors: Red†, Cobalt, Green, Yellow, Ivory, Turquoise
*Estimate
†Red discontinued in early 1944

Fiesta bud vase in turquoise, added after introduction. Turquoise, $93-97.

Fiesta bud vases in colors available at shape introduction. Yellow, $85-88; Red, $91-98; Cobalt, $100-105; Ivory, $105-110; Green, $84-89.

The Van Briggle bud vase.

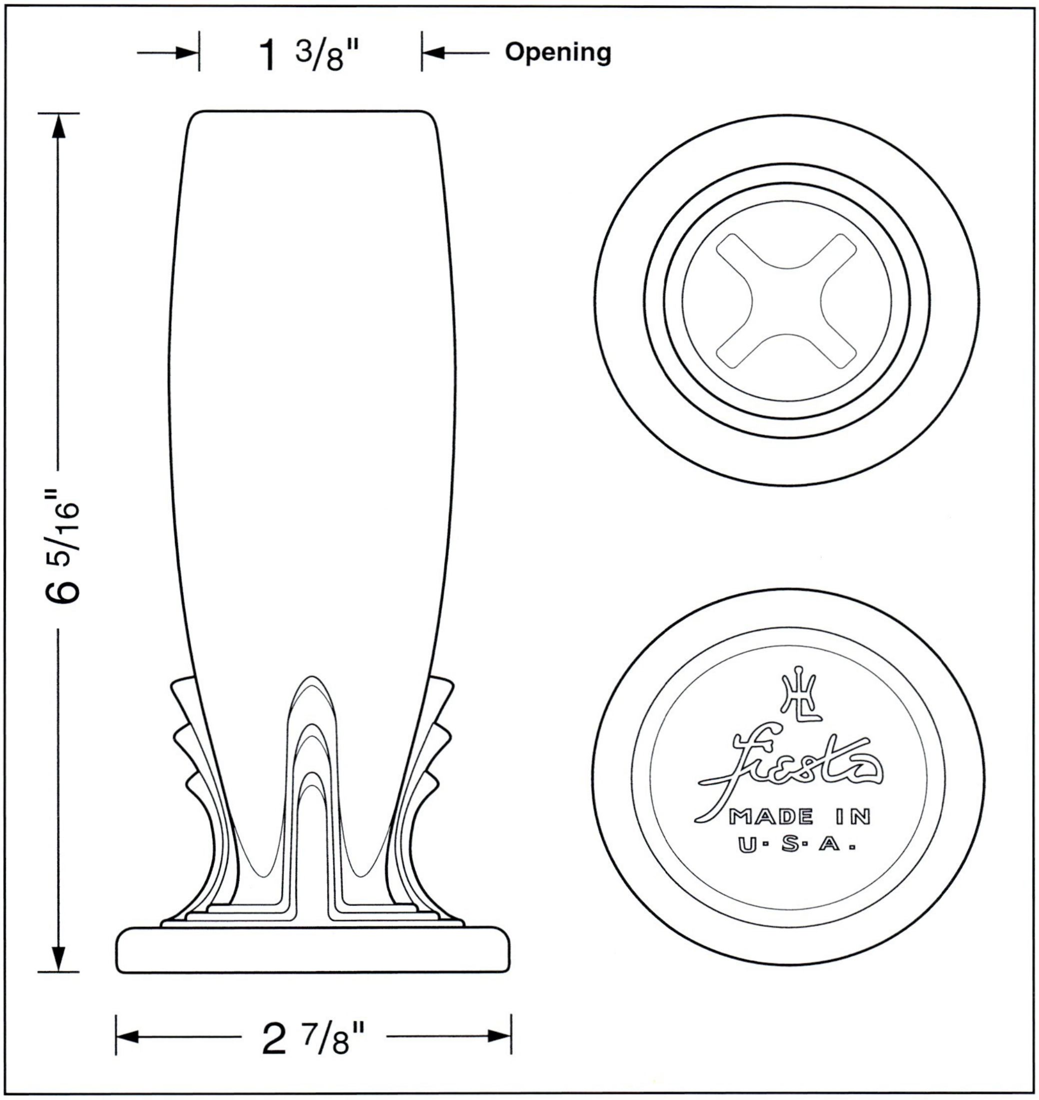

1 3/8" Opening

6 5/16"

2 7/8"

HL Fiesta MADE IN U·S·A.

Fiesta 8", 10", and 12" flower vases in turquoise, added after introduction. 8", $550-600; 10", $855-905; 12", $1285-1365.

Flower Vases

As mentioned before, Frederick Rhead was not averse to copying a design. And more than one collector has noticed that the fluted shape of the Fiesta flower vases has little in common with the rest of the line. Now comes a white clay vase, with a clear, age-crackled glaze, that very much resembles the Fiesta vase, but is not one of them. Found by a Colorado collector, this vase is one of three currently known. Some believe it is the original that Rhead used as a model for the Fiesta flower vases.

A story has been told about a bride in 1934 who had such a vase at her wedding. It was seen many years later by an experienced collector who noted it was marked "Japan" in red. None of the three known vases are marked, but could well be the same item.

This vase was not made from a cast of a Fiesta 10" vase. There are subtle differences: (1) It is 1/8" taller, (2) the foot is not as wide, (3) it is also narrower at the top of the band of rings on the base, and (4) it was not marked in the mold. The vase has a clear glaze that has crazed and it weighs less than the Fiesta vase.

One might wonder how such an exact copy (by Rhead) could be made. The answer is another question: How could the 12" vase be an exact, although larger, copy of the 10" model? Skilled craftsmen provide the answer to both questions. The modelers, Kraft, Watkin, and Berrisford, were wonderful technicians with an immense talent. Their skill at duplicating shapes was truly amazing. More importantly, they could take the sketches done by Rhead and turn them into physical reality. Items rarely had to be revised. The modelers were the final step between an idea and a piece of ware on the production line and the ones working at HLC during the 1930s and 1940s were among the best in the business.

Like the relish tray, it does not matter from where Rhead drew his inspiration. The flower vase in three sizes became part of the line and is now one of the most sought after additions to a modern collection. The 10" size was modeled first, just after production of Fiesta began in late 1935, with the other two arriving about a month later. The models were held for approximately six months before they were released to production in the Summer of 1936. The 10" and 12" vases were discontinued in mid-1942 giving them one of the shortest production runs of any Fiesta piece, just six years. The 8" vase was continued for four years more (except red ones) with production stopping in mid-1946.

These vases were slip cast in complicated four part molds. The two larger sizes will have the "HLC USA" in-mold mark, the 8" vase can be found with that mark and the "MADE IN USA" impression as well. No vase actually measures its stated size, but they all are within a fraction of an inch of their named height.

Judging from recent Internet auctions, vases are much easier to find these days than in the past. Still, they are some of the most expensive additions one can make to a collection. The larger sizes, and those in the popular red glaze, will be in the highest price range.

A comparison of the Japanese vase (right) with a Fiesta one (left).

Fiesta 8" Flower Vase

Modeling Date	January 1936
Model Number	528
Revisions	None
Production Began	July 1936*
First Price List	Late 1936 (undated)
Last Price List	May 1, 1944
Discontinued	Mid 1946*
Length of Production	10 Years*

Colors: Red†, Cobalt, Green, Yellow, Ivory, Turquoise
*Estimate
†Red discontinued in early 1944

Fiesta 10" Flower Vase

Modeling Date	December 1935
Model Number	510
Revisions	None
Production Began	July 1936
First Price List	Late 1936 (undated)
Last Price List	August 1, 1941
Discontinued	Mid 1942*
Length of Production	6 Years*

Colors: Red, Cobalt, Green, Yellow, Ivory, Turquoise
*Estimate

Fiesta 12" Flower Vase

Modeling Date	January 1936
Model Number	527
Revisions	None
Production Began	July 1936
First Price List	Late 1936 (undated)
Last Price List	August 1, 1941
Discontinued	Mid 1942*
Length of Production	6 Years*

Colors: Red, Cobalt, Green, Yellow, Ivory, Turquoise
*Estimate

Discarded four-piece medium vase molds used in current production.

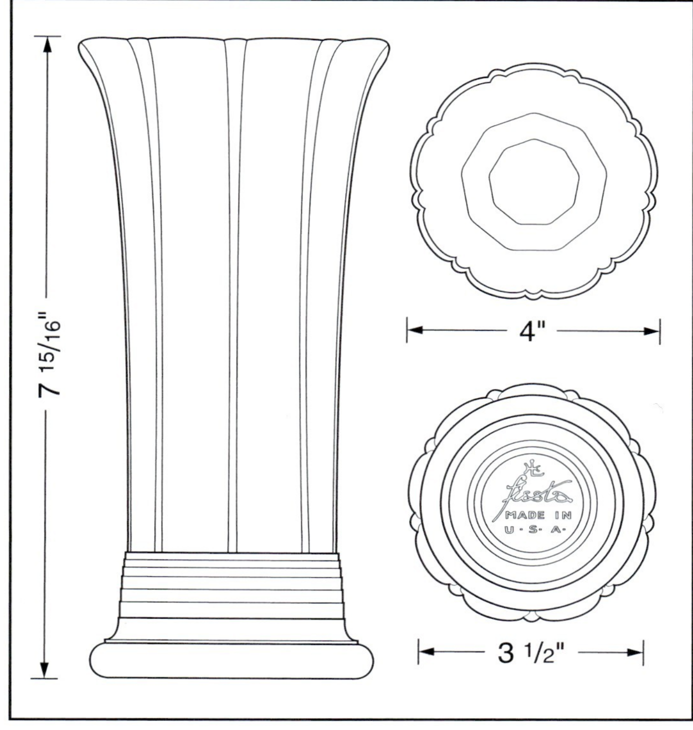
7 15/16"
4"
fiesta
MADE IN
U.S.A.
3 1/2"

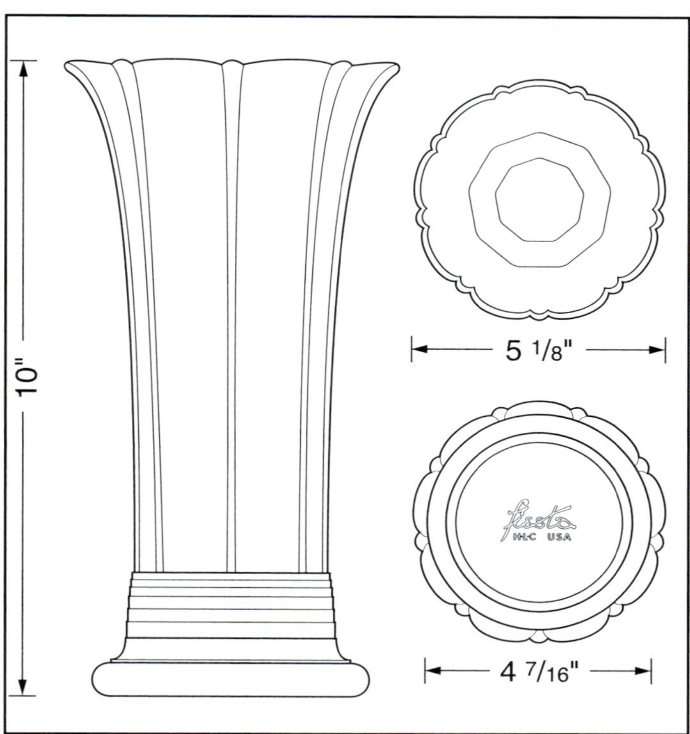
10"
5 1/8"
fiesta
HLC USA
4 7/16"

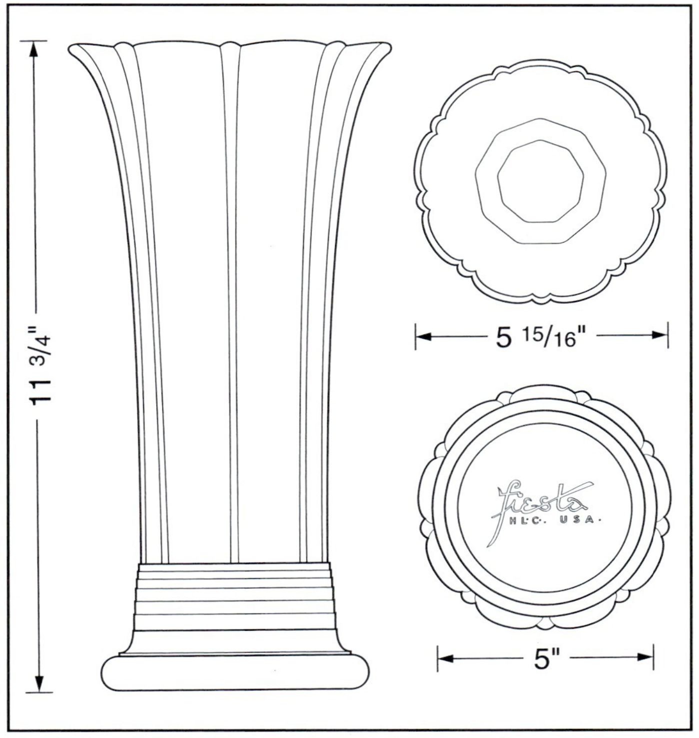
11 3/4"
5 15/16"
fiesta
HLC. USA.
5"

Fiesta 8", 10", and 12" flower vases in colors available at shape introduction. See appendix E for pricing for these 15 vases.

Marketing

HOMER LAUGHLIN
THE WORLD'S LARGEST POTTERIES
THE HOMER LAUGHLIN CHINA CO.
NEWELL, W. VA.
1938

The Paper Side

For more than 60 years, people have loved Fiesta ware, Fiesta Kitchen Kraft, and their cheerful companion Harlequin. That deep devotion to dishes has centered largely on the pottery itself for obvious reasons. But in recent years a lesser known and under appreciated side of dish collecting has blossomed. Once the niche effort of a small band of Fiesta veterans and dish-advertising buffs, paper and ephemera has now emerged as a major realm of pottery collecting on all levels. Items of interest in this category would include original price lists, advertising, promotional campaigns, news articles, packaging, store displays, and even the price guides that have been written over the years by various authors.

While the "paper side of Fiesta" has always warranted some attention by the Huxford's and other authors, it has not captured wide and deep attention. Collectors want the pottery first. Just as one might start with dinner plates and nappies, then move to demitasse pots and marmalades so have many Fiesta collectors moved from the ware to the paper. Not only does ephemera provide interesting history on the beloved dinnerware line (and its various HLC cousins), but many items make great display items, whether in the scrapbook or on the kitchen wall.

In this section, we present just a few of the major areas related to Fiesta/HLC paper and ephemera. Unlike the pottery side of Fiesta and Harlequin where most of the pieces are now known (although each day brings hope of a new glaze or shape or pattern discovery), the paper and emphera arena still holds many treasures yet uncovered. Whether a new date for a factory price list, a page from a department-store catalog, or a one-time-only newspaper ad, there are many bits of Homer Laughlin history still awaiting the patient sleuth's eye.

Front of HLC 1938 pocket calendar featuring Fiesta.

Fiesta shelf paper.

Opposite page, bottom:
Back of HLC 1938 pocket calendar featuring Fiesta.

Factory Price Lists

For a collector wanting to add a bit of accent as well as historical reference to their pottery, vintage factory price lists are an excellent place to start. Price lists are the most prevalent Fiesta paper and representative dates can be found spanning four decades from the 30s into the 60s. These small, envelope-sized folded brochures were distributed by the factory via retail stores, mail requests, and field sales representatives. They are frequently found ink stamped by individual merchants of the day lending an additional bit of nostalgia to the vintage story line. Many different dates and versions can be located with careful sleuthing. Not too surprisingly, Fiesta price lists are more frequently found than Fiesta Kitchen Kraft versions due to the larger selection and greater demand of the day. Vintage Harlequin lists are virtually nonexistent and our researchers were unable to verify even one, although there are known examples of functional Harlequin "sales flyers" (sans prices) from the Re-issue series of the late 70s and early 80s.

Price lists give us our best record of piece and color introductions, retirements, and original price points and are therefore invaluable research aids. Whether one is interested in finding every piece in every color of the original 1936 selection or perhaps the line of the 1950s, price lists offer a relatively affordable way to have an exact look at just what comprises that selection.

The Fiesta price lists can usually be located in two versions of each date – both east-of-the Mississippi (not labeled) and west-of-the Mississippi (marked WOM). Likely due to added transportation costs associated with moving the pottery to the west, the prices found on the WOM lists are higher across the entire line. The dates known range from ones in 1937 and extend into 1968 with usually a new date presented every 2-3 years on average. New lists were printed when colors were dropped, selection changes occurred, or price changes were needed. There is also a very scarce and undated Fiesta price list that appears to be the original list available as the line debuted in 1936. A highly valued item for anyone interested in HLC paper for sure!

Newpaper Advertising

Strangely, when it comes to the familiar advertising medium of newspapers, Fiesta is rather under-advertised. There are two primary challenges for the person interested in locating dishes in print – identifying the actual location and/or dates where it's found and finding of these materials intact after more than a half century. Newspapers, and to some degree magazines, were never designed to last more than the day, week, or month following their publication. An unread daily from 1939 is uncommon in any form let alone one featuring our favorite dishes.

In 1939, HLC offered a Fiesta Ensemble set that featured a compete service for eight inclusive of go-along glassware, flatware, and serving pieces. This type of marketing appears to have been limited to a short period from early 1939 into mid-1941 based on the dates found to this point. These colorful ads were designed to promote the relatively new Fiesta dinnerware line and bring the opportunity of purchase into homes in all the major markets across the country without the need to have stock on hand in retail stores. There was even the lure of a "payment plan" and the ads offer the buyer to pay with "50¢ down, 50¢ a week." Shown nearby are a couple examples of the very scarce, full-page advertisements that arrived in homes via the Sunday newspaper. These highly valued items are extremely desirable and make a wonderful display addition to the dish collection.

Other forms of vintage advertising that can be found include store catalogs such as Sears and Wards annuals, wholesaler catalogs such as those from Omaha Crockery or Sommers, and numerous small references within home-related magazines of the 40s and 50s. Whether big or small, color or black-and-white, or simply showing HLC dishes in an ad these paper items are all gaining acceptance amongst collectors at all levels.

One of the elusive Fiesta ensemble advertisements. This example is on display at the HLC outlet store.

An easier-to-find ensemble advertisement.

Original Packaging

Shown nearby are a couple examples of vintage Fiesta in original packages. For the die-hard collector, items like these represent the best examples of "mint" ware that can be found. If it was never opened or never used, a piece of dinnerware is essentially the same as it left the factory. A fun and challenging area of collecting to compliment the "unpackaged" ware we're all familiar with, original boxes, wrappers, and master packs are scarce and coincidentally highly valued.

Turquoise saucers in their orginal packaging.

Collector Price Guides

Like this publication, collector's guides are always desired by the buyer, seller, or dealer for current pricing and identification purposes. Once that edition is updated or outdated and the need arises to purchase a new one, the book itself often becomes just as collectable as the pottery presented within. Known authors of guides in this category include the Huxford's, Nancy Berkow, the Fiesta Finders series, and the Fiesta Club of America's Guide. Newsletters such as the "Dish" and early editions of the Fiesta Collector's Quarterly are also very collectable. Many of the complete titles and dates for these publications can be found in our bibliography.

Special Promotional Campaign

To stimulate sales of Fiesta, Homer Laughlin began a sales campaign in early 1940 that offered special items not normally found in the Fiesta line. There was a mixture of new pieces created for the promotion as well as existing items at special prices, in special combinations, or with a special enhancement. Announcements were sent to the trade press, which appeared in the February 1940 journal issues: *"...dollar retailers in Fiesta ware—covered French casserole, 4-piece refrigerator sets; sugar, cream and tray set; salad bowl with fork and spoon, casserole with pie plate; chop plate with detachable metal holder; jumbo coffee cups and saucers in blue, pink, and yellow."*

The announcement was part of a much larger press release that covered everything from the newest shape, "Piccadilly," to retail groupings such as the "All Fiesta" ensemble. It also discussed new decal treatments on several shapes, new underglaze prints, and new merchandising programs. In the context of all the other information, it can be said that the inclusion of the blue, pink, and yellow jumbo coffee cups and saucers in the Fiesta portion of the statement was probably a mistake. Although a coffee cup was modeled for Fiesta in mid-1935, it was never produced.

The other six items can be considered part of the line, but it must be recognized that they were made for a specific reason and a specific period of time. The history of the items, for the most part, is not well documented. What is presented here is an interpretation of the information about the promotional items gathered from Frederick Rhead's journal, the HLC modeling log, and reports from other authors, collectors, and dealers.

Juice Set

The Fiesta juice set was an early promotional item not initially related to the campaign, but it may have been the inspiration for the series of pieces that came later. The small jug and tumblers were not originally designed as a set, but came together seemingly by accident. The two parts have separate and interesting histories.

In March 1938 Frederick Rhead had models made of a variety of different water jugs. One of them was the disc shaped pitcher for Fiesta. During the course of its development over the next few months the disc jug was modeled in several sizes. The smallest design had a capacity of just 30 ounces. Eventually the final size of the disc water jug was selected and the other, rejected models were put away in a storeroom like so many others before them. It would be nearly a year before the smallest jug model was taken out of storage and put into production as the Fiesta juice pitcher.

Fiesta juice set in standard colors. See appendix E for pricing information on the items in this set.

The story behind the juice tumbler is one of the best documented of any item in the line. It tells of Frederick Rhead's determination to make the client happy and his personal frustration when he was unable to do so.

Rhead's personal journal for June-July 1935 recalls his struggles with the Kraft-Phenix Cheese Corporation over the size, shape, color, and capacity of ceramic crocks to hold their processed cheese spreads. Multiple samples in various clay and glaze formulations were made and sent to Kraft over the two-month period. Several attempts were made to fine-tune the capacity that the cheese maker needed the jars to have for consistency in filling them with their product. In the end, Homer Laughlin's plan to produce 200,000 crocks in two sizes was successful, but not without a lot of effort on the part of Rhead, the modelers, and the production staff at HLC.

Therefore, Rhead understood very well what he was getting into two years later, in 1937, when Kraft asked for another ceramic jar for processed cheese. It is unfortunate that Rhead's journals from 1937 and the first half of 1938 are missing. We were not able to determine the particulars of the new project, but did note the first model was created in May of that year.

Over the next fourteen months more than twenty models were created for the new cheese jar. Each was dutifully made into a dozen samples and sent for evaluation to Kraft, only to be rejected as insufficient. Rhead tried several variations on the band of rings theme. He also tried changing the height, the width, the amount of flare at the rim, and several other parameters. After this extraordinary amount of work Rhead sent a July 6, 1938 memo to Plant #4 supervisor Guy Pittenger: "Final model number of Kraft Cheese jar will be 1107... Diameter to be 62 mm at the top, and capacity to have minimum of 162 cc. Mr. Wells instructs this to be released when ready..."

A comparison between a water tumbler (top) and juice tumber (bottom).

Rhythm juice set on Fiesta shape. Gray pitcher, $2550-2800; Chartreuse tumbler, $865-970; Forest tumbler, $825-980, Harlequin yellow, $755-895.

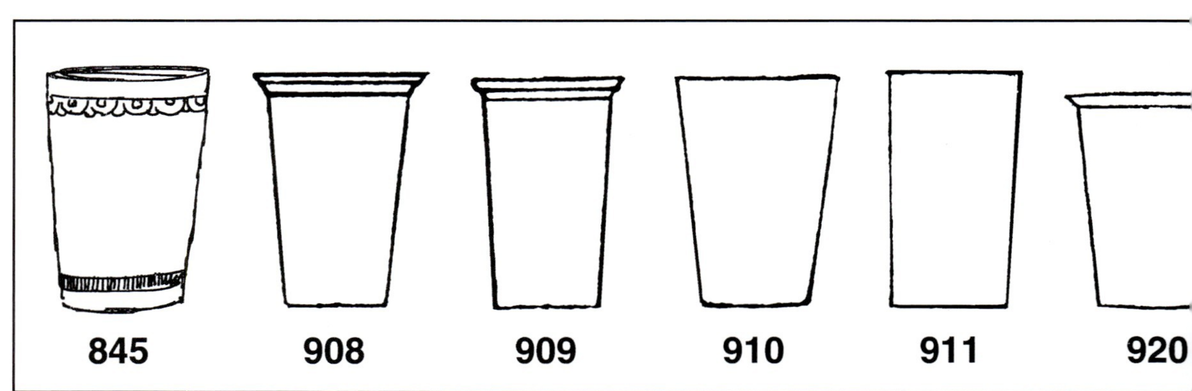

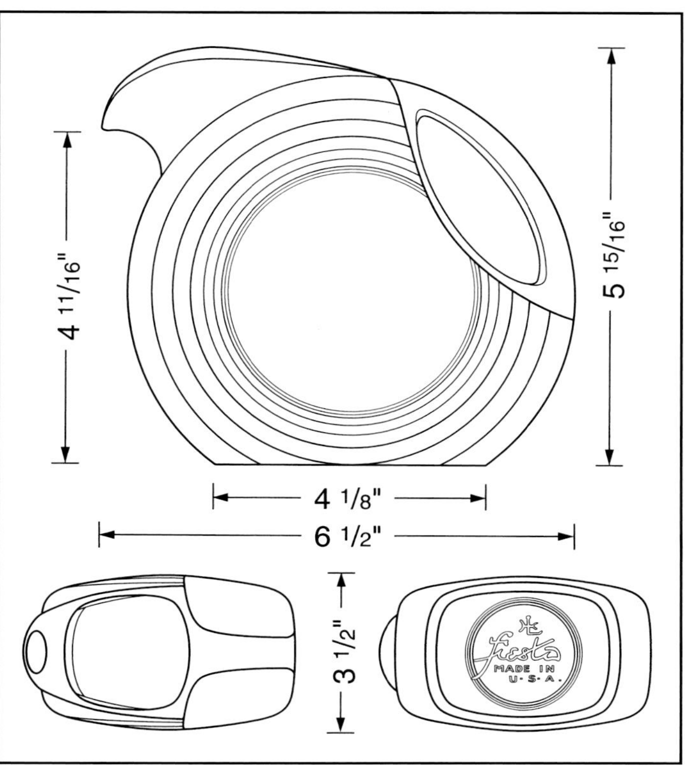

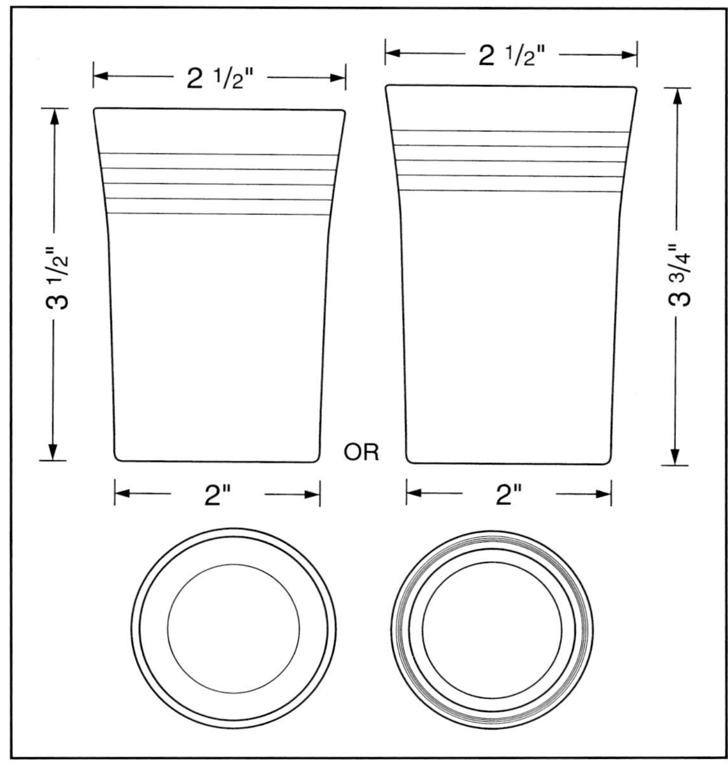

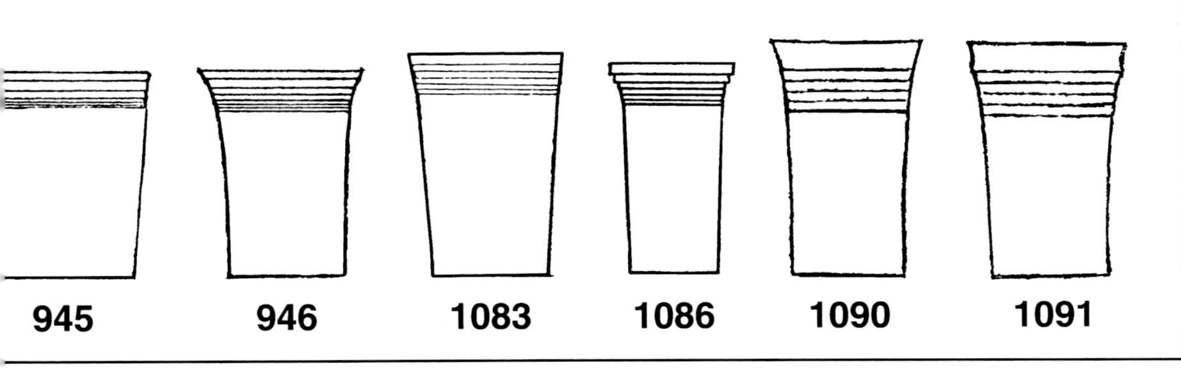

Drawings from the HLC modeling log for the juice tumbler.

The tumbler was released to production and molds were made, but it was apparently not produced at that time. There is nothing more about the cheese jar in Rhead's journal until eight months later. On March 24, 1939 he wrote, "Saw Hazel Atlas glass copies of Kraft Cheese jars. Copy of our Fiesta jar. Ours was to sell for 35¢ each (with cheese). Glass jars, Fiesta colors and shape, sell for two for 35¢. Last of Kraft Cheese, after months of development and over two dozen models."

Throughout the time Frederick Rhead was in charge of the art department at HLC many projects failed to produce a product, but this was one of the few about which he expressed his feelings in writing. Happily, in the end, all of the work done on the cheese jar design would be put to good use.

Someone got the idea to use the existing cheese jar molds to make small tumblers for Fiesta and pair them with the little jug left from the development of the disc water pitcher. The cheese jar was remodeled one more time, its height lowered by 1/4 inch, and it was finally put into production as the Fiesta juice tumbler in March 1939.

Ads in the trade journals began in May 1939 and offered "a colorful, 7-piece Juice Set, calculated to fill a real need in the summer refreshment field." The sets consisted of the "30-oz. disc jug in Fiesta yellow, and six 5-oz. tumblers, one each in the Fiesta blue, turquoise, red, green, yellow and ivory." They were to be sold for minimum retail price of one dollar and came packed one set to a carton. With that, the successful series of promotional products began.

Determining when the juice set promotion was over has proved difficult. Others have referred to it as a 1939-1943 campaign, but at least one wholesale catalog shows the set for sale as late as 1944. The one offered there includes the red tumbler, so it's likely that the wholesaler was selling from old stock and not something in production at the time. The juice set seems to have been a promotion separate from the campaign that began the next year, although the set was also part of it.

In addition to the "standard" juice set mentioned above, there were three other sets produced. A set with the same tumblers, but with a red disc pitcher was made for Old Reliable Coffee. A product of the Dayton Mills Spice Company, Old Reliable Coffee had a long history of offering premiums to its customers over the years. The Fiesta juice set was only one of them. This set was more than likely produced at the same time as the standard one.

In 1948, with the release of "Jubilee" for it's seventy-fifth anniversary, Homer Laughlin again used the small jug and tumblers to augment a new line. This set consist of a celadon green pitcher and two each tumblers in shell pink, mist gray, and cream beige.

Again, in 1951 or 1952, the little juice pitcher and tumblers were used for a promotion. This time it was for Woolworth's "Rhythm" and it was made in the colors used for that line: a gray pitcher and six tumblers, two each in forest green, chartreuse, and Harlequin's yellow.

There are only a few variations to report. The disc jugs do not vary except for color. In addition to Fiesta yellow, they are easy to find in Harlequin yellow as well. The tumblers can be of two sizes, 3 1/2" tall or 3 3/4" tall. This is probably the result of both the 1938 Kraft cheese mold and the 1939 Fiesta tumbler mold being used at the same time. Rose colored tumblers exist in sufficient quantity to suspect they were made for a specific purpose. Either to substitute for a color in the sets or as a result of a special order. The reason has not been determined.

Fiesta gray and Harlequin maroon tumblers have been reported. The gray ones are probably only a heavy application of Jubilee's mist gray, but the possibility of a true Fiesta gray tumbler cannot be dismissed. This confusion has caused the gray tumblers to be valued higher than others in the Jubilee set. Maroon tumblers have not bee proved to be Fiesta and were more than likely made by another company. Cameron Clay Products, of Cameron, West Virginia is the most likely place of origin.

Like all cup-shaped objects, the tumblers were made on a jigger machine. They were not marked, except for export. If marked they will have the "HLCo USA" rubber stamp. The disc pitchers were slip cast and all carry the impressed "Fiesta/HLC USA" mark.

Fiesta and Harlequin yellow juice pitchers are easily found as are the tumblers in the first six Fiesta colors. Rose tumblers may be a bit more difficult. Red juice pitchers are on the hard to find list and can cost eight times the amount a collector would pay for a yellow one. The Jubilee sets are in the "extremely hard to find" category and items in the Rhythm sets are all considered rare.

Old reliable coupon.

Fiesta 30 Ounce Disc Jug

Modeling Date .... April 1938
Model Number .... 1084[1]
Revision .... May 1938, 1093[2]
Production Began .... April 1939*
Discontinued .... Mid 1952*
Length of Production[3] .... 4.2 Years*
Colors: Red, Yellow, Harlequin Yellow, Celedon Green, Gray
*Estimate
[1]First model not produced
[2]Same as first model with "changed snip"
[3]Continuous production until mid-1943, two special production runs in 1948 and 1951

Fiesta Juice Tumbler

Modeling Dates .... May 1937-March 1939
Model Numbers .... 839, 840, 841, 845, 908, 909, 910, 911, 920, 932, 945, 946, 952, 953, 955, 993, 1083, 1086, 1090, 1091, 1107[1], 1210[2]
Revisions .... 22 models (see text)
Production Began .... March 1939*
Discontinued .... Mid 1943*
Length of Production[3] .... 4.2 Years*
Colors: Red, Cobalt, Green, Yellow, Ivory, Turquoise, Rose, Chartreuse, Forest, Harlequin Yellow, Shell Pink, Mist Gray, Cream Beige
*Estimate
[1]Released to production July 1938, apparently not used until March 1939
[2]Released to production March 1939
[3]Continuous production until mid-1943, two special production runs in 1948 and 1951

Fiesta juice pitchers. Red: $520-560; Yellow, $45-46; Harlequin Yellow, $56-62.

Salad Set

The first item specifically created for the promotion was a new salad bowl. The footed salad already in the line was too large and heavy to be sold as one of the dollar specials. The 11 3/4" bowl, which had been modeled as a salad bowl for Kitchen Kraft, was called a "fruit bowl" when it was added to the Fiesta line and couldn't be used either. The new bowl, a generous 9 1/2" in diameter, was modeled in November 1939. It was revised a month later by adding a half inch to its depth and was released to production just before the end of December 1939.

While this bowl would best be called the Fiesta "promotional salad" collectors have adopted another name for it. There were three competing collector books for Fiesta in the 1970s. Two of them essentially ignored this bowl and the authors of the other could not locate it in any HLC documents, so it was said to be "unlisted." That name stuck and today collectors refer to it as the "unlisted salad bowl."

For the promotion, the new salad was glazed in Fiesta yellow and offered with the Kitchen Kraft fork in green and spoon in red. Some of these bowls have been discovered in cobalt blue and are said to exist in ivory and red, but we have not been able to confirm that.

Like most bowls and cup-shaped items, this one was made on a jigger machine. It is different from most other Fiesta bowls in that is has no rings on the inside. The ring motif is prominently featured on the outside as well as on the bottom, where a unique impressed Fiesta mark is present. These bowls have three sagger pin scars under the rim.

Because it was produced for less than three years the promotional salad bowl is somewhat hard to find. They are rarely found with the fork and spoon that came with them. Almost all will be in yellow with the rare cobalt one commanding a value four to five times that of the standard color. See the Kitchen Kraft section for details and values of the fork and spoon.

Fiesta Promotional Salad Bowl

Modeling Date	November 1939
Model Number	1341[1]
Revision	December 1939, 1345[2]
Production Began	January 1940
Discontinued	Mid 1943*
Length of Production	2.5 Years*

Color: Yellow, Cobalt[3]

*Estimate

[1]First model not produced

[2]Revised 0.5" deeper

[3]Other colors reported (see text)

***Above:* Promotional salad bowl in yellow. $99-105.**
***Below:* Promotional salad bowl in cobalt. $2620-3380.**

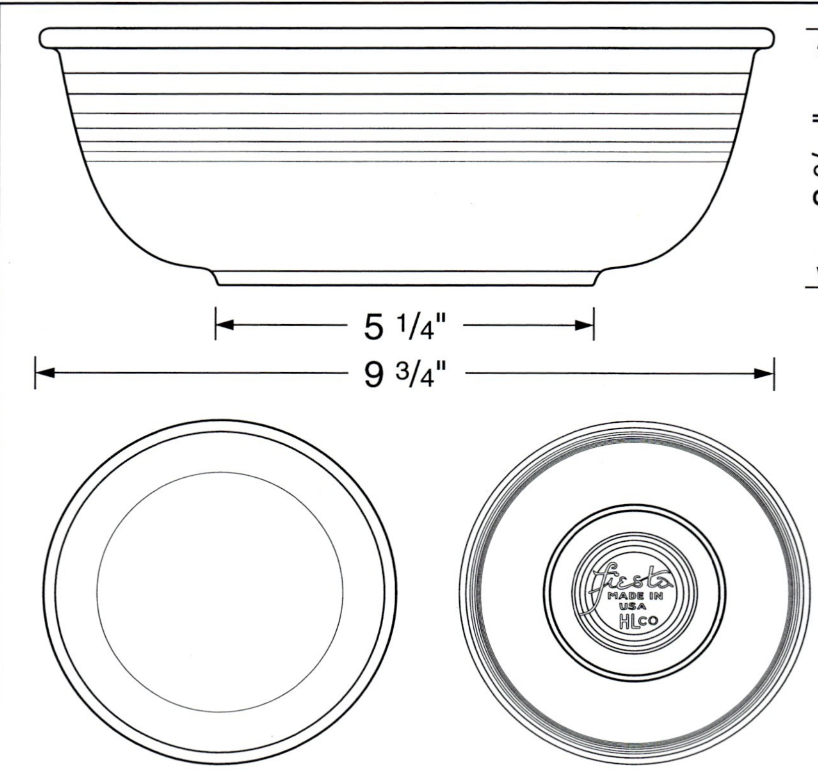

French Casserole

One of the earliest items modeled for Fiesta, in April 1935, was labeled "ringed shape casserole (one handle)". Although not produced at the time, it was probably the design Frederick Rhead used in 1939 for another new item for the sales promotion—the French casserole. His original design had a hand-applied foot and a few of the trial run pieces of the footed casserole have been located by collectors in the area around the HLC plant in Newell, West Virginia. The design used for the promotional campaign was essentially unchanged except for the removal of the foot.

The French casserole has a hand-applied stick handle similar to the one on the Fiesta After Dinner coffeepot. The finial on the cover resembles one on the earliest Fiesta sugar (shown in the *Fiesta* section), which is straight sided and not flared like most of the lid handles in the line. Like the promotional salad, the French casserole has no inside rings. This item was sent through the glazing kiln on a tripod stilt, so it has three glaze disturbances in a triangular pattern on the bottom. The casserole has a "MADE IN USA" type in-mold mark.

Yellow was the common theme of the promotional pieces and almost all French casseroles were glazed in the familiar Fiesta hue. Some, which were probably trial run pieces, have been found in cobalt, ivory, and light green. A rare few of these are said to have a lid.

Yellow French casseroles, in excellent condition with the lid, are hard to find and are valued in excess of two hundred dollars.

Fiesta yellow covered French casserole. $295-310.

Fiesta cobalt french casserole bottom. $4295-4705.

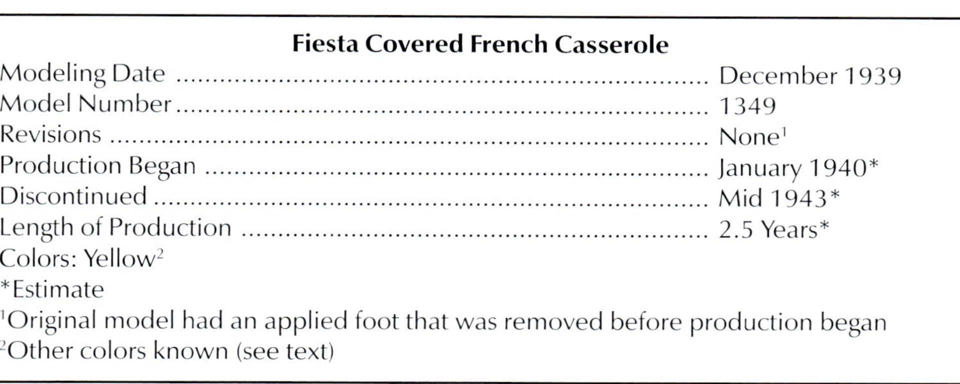

Fiesta Covered French Casserole

Modeling Date	December 1939
Model Number	1349
Revisions	None[1]
Production Began	January 1940*
Discontinued	Mid 1943*
Length of Production	2.5 Years*

Colors: Yellow[2]

*Estimate

[1]Original model had an applied foot that was removed before production began

[2]Other colors known (see text)

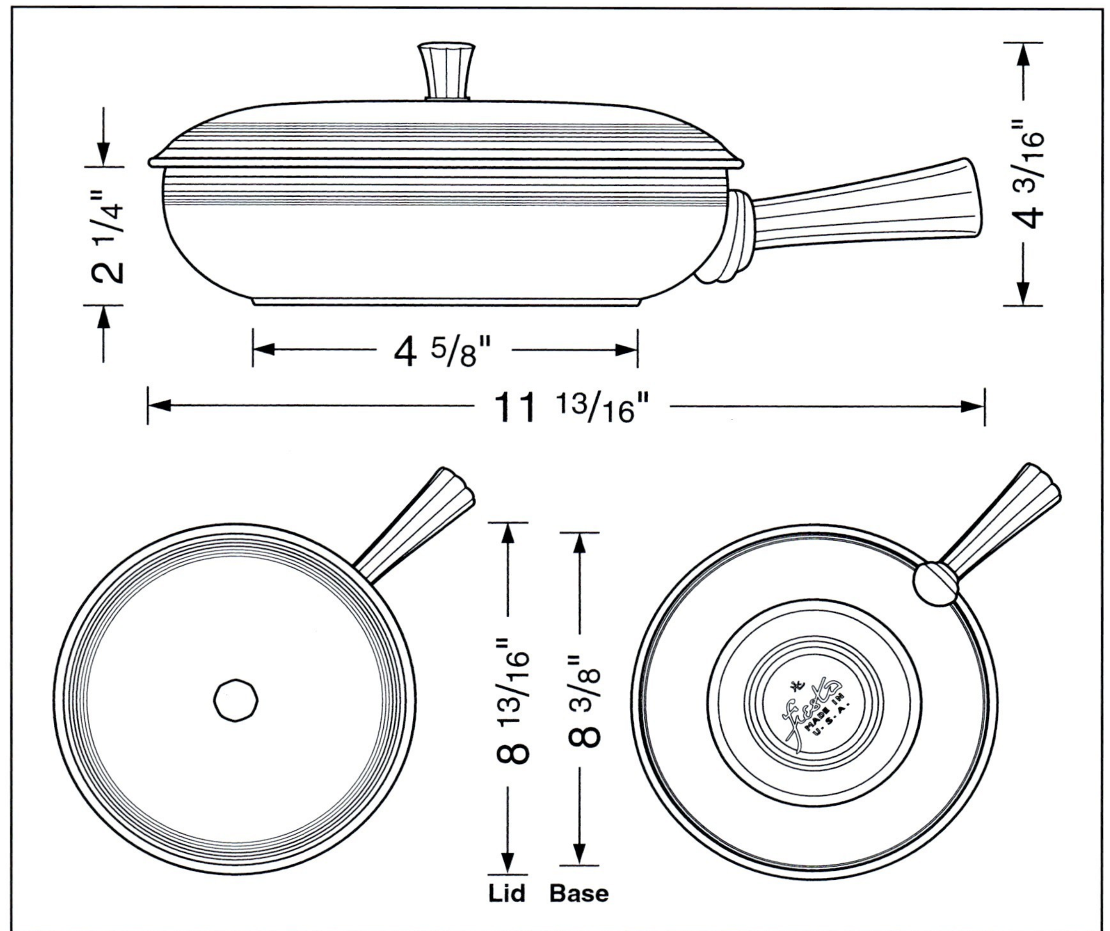

Sugar, Cream, Tray Set

Another item created just for the promotional campaign, and something high on the "must have" list of many collectors, is the sugar, cream, and tray set. The pieces in the set were the last designed by Frederick Rhead for Fiesta, and they were the last items added to the line until the individual salad bowl of 1959.

Modeled in January 1940, the cream and sugar were produced in the prominent color of the promotion, Fiesta yellow. The figure-eight shaped tray was made in cobalt blue. That was the standard configuration, but other colors exist. Trays in turquoise turn up from time to time and yellow ones have been reported, but at present are unverified. In addition to yellow, the creams were made in the Fiesta red glaze, although not in a large quantity. Both the cream and (lidless) sugars exist in vintage turquoise, but these were no doubt trial pieces as only a couple have been found. A few sugars glazed in Harlequin yellow also exist.

It is believed the turquoise trays and red creamers were made to fulfil special orders. The two pieces are often photographed together (even for this book), but more than likely were not sold that way. The turquoise trays have been found in original sets with the yellow cream and sugar. The red creams may have been sold with a "normal" sugar and tray in a red, yellow, and blue set. That color combination is particularly striking.

All pieces of the set were slip cast in plaster molds. The sugar and cream have impressed "MADE IN USA" type marks. The handles on these two items were a part of the mold. The finial on the sugar lid was separately cast and hand applied. The trays can have slight variations in weight and thickness, especially of the foot, depending on how long the slip was left in the mold. A longer time allowed more water to be absorbed and the thickness of the clay therefore increased. When they were marked, the trays received the "Genuine Fiesta" backstamp.

Condition, as with any piece of Fiesta, has a bearing on value. The trays are rarely found in "mint" condition. They almost always have surface scratches from the unglazed feet of the sugar and cream. The sugar lid is often missing or will have small chips or missing flakes of glaze. Collectors often put a set together from the individual pieces.

Fiesta yellow individual sugar and individual creamer with cobalt figure-8 tray. Sugar, $125-130; Creamer, 73-76; Tray, $94-100.

Fiesta Sugar, Cream, and Tray Set

Modeling Date, Number	December 1939, 1350[1]
	January 1940, 1351[2]
	January 1940, 1352[3]
Revisions	None
Production Began	January 1940*
Discontinued	Mid 1943*
Length of Production	2.5 Years*

Colors: Sugar in Yellow[4]; cream in Yellow, Red[4]; Tray in Cobalt, Turquoise[4]

*Estimate

[1]Tray

[2]Sugar

[3]Cream

[4]Other colors known (see text)

Fiesta yellow individual sugar and red individual creamer with turquoise figure-8 tray. Sugar, $125-130; Creamer, $305-325; Tray, $365-395.

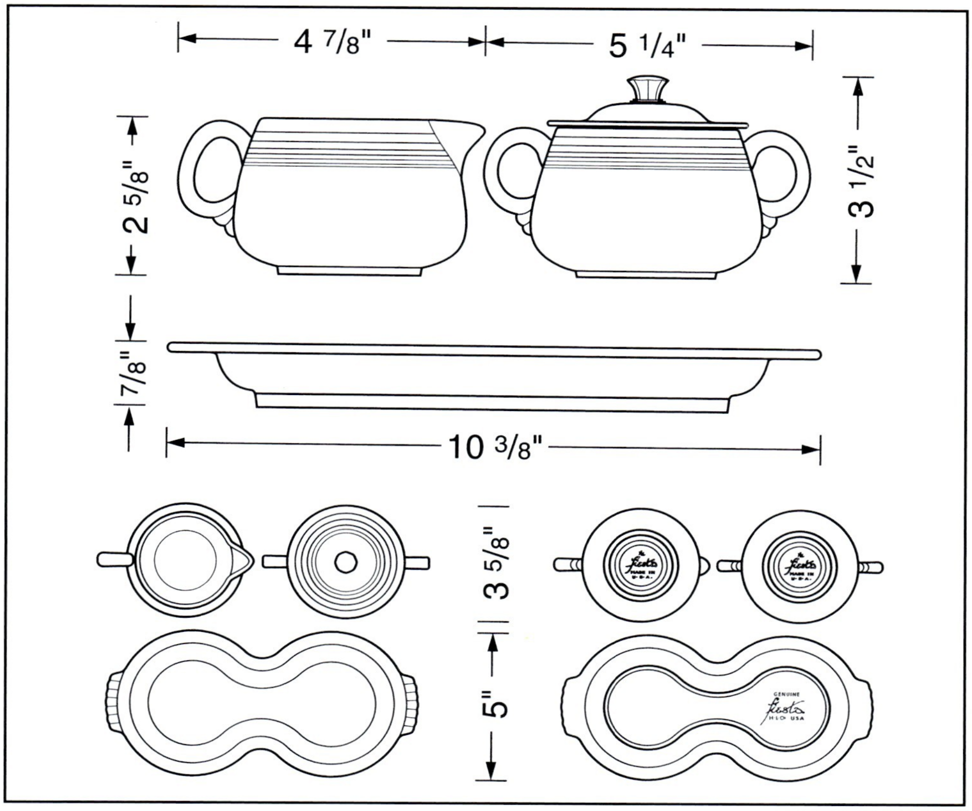

Kitchen Set

One of the combinations of existing items offered during the promotion was a "Kitchen Set" which consisted of a covered casserole and a pie plate. There may have been two different casseroles used for the set depending on which retailer was selling it. A 1942 wholesale catalog shows this set made up of a Kitchen Kraft 8 1/2" casserole in green with a red cover and yellow 9" Kitchen Kraft pie plate. Another set, first shown in the seventh edition of *The Collector's Encyclopedia of Fiesta*, includes the yellow 9" pie plate with a covered casserole made for Royal Metal Manufacturing in the same green/red color scheme (see below for information on the Royal Metal casserole).

The casserole's color combination of a green bowl with a red lid may seem odd, but it is in keeping with the colors used for other promotional sets such as the salad bowl with fork and spoon. The wholesale catalog referenced above included this statement: "Colors of these special items are standard with the manufacturers and cannot be substituted." However, any retailer with open stock Kitchen Kraft items could switch the red/green casserole for one in a single color and the set may have been offered to the public in other color combinations at the promotional price.

However they were sold, the Kitchen Set is rarely found intact today. The Kitchen Kraft components are not too difficult to find and can be combined to create the original promotional offering. Values would be the same as they are for the individual items (see the *Kitchen Kraft* section of the book).

The Fiesta "Kitchen Set."

Chop Plate with Metal Handle

An unusual item that was part of the promotion was a regular Fiesta 13" chop plate accompanied by a raffia-wrapped metal handle. The strap-like handle clipped onto the edges of the plate, allowing a fully loaded one to be easily carried to the table or buffet. This handle was an item used by several dinnerware manufacturers in the 1940s and was made in copper and steel. Available in five or six sizes, only the one that fit a 13" chop plate was offered during the promotion.

The handles are not easy to find and may show up in some unusual places, such as thrift shops or garage sales. Should one come with a Fiesta chop plate, expect to pay almost as much for the handle as for the plate itself.

Five sizes of raffia wrapped metal handles.

Refrigerator Set

The final item offered in the campaign was the standard Kitchen Kraft stacking refrigerator set in mixed colors. It consisted of three bowls or "units", one each in green, yellow, and cobalt, and a lid in Fiesta red.

The components of the set are somewhat hard to find today. Values for the individual pieces can be found in the Kitchen Kraft section.

Kitchen Kraft units with red lid.

Royal Metal Manufacturing Covered Casserole

Although it is considered by some to be part of the early 1940s promotions, this casserole, as well as the 10" pie plate and plain 13" oval platter often associated with Kitchen Kraft, were all designed several years earlier for the Royal Metal Manufacturing Company of Chicago. During the late 1930s HLC created several items for this client. Many were produced in the solid-color glazes used for Fiesta and Harlequin. Therefore, it's easy to understand how collectors would want to include some of these pieces in their collections.

The casserole was first modeled in May 1936. There is a note added to the modeling log entry for the casserole that references Rhead's Record of Sketches and Drawings. In that notebook an entry for the piece says, "Casserole, Fiesta, Royal Metal." The "Fiesta" in the note could refer to the glaze colors, the clay body used for Fiesta, or to the line itself. Since the casserole does not feature the standard Fiesta decorative motif of a band of graduated rings, it is believed the reference is to the glaze colors. The modeling log itself includes the note "talc body" next to the casserole listing.

Over the next few weeks two revisions were made to the casserole design before it was accepted by Royal Metal. In Rhead's journal for July 2, 1936 he wrote, "Telegram from Royal Metal Co. approving bisque new model casserole. Released to [plant #4 supervisor Guy] Pittenger model No. 628." The 10-inch pie plate and oval platter had been approved a few days earlier.

Once production began, serious flaws in the molds were discovered. A little over two weeks later Rhead wrote, "Trouble with Royal casserole. Verge tears off and inside is too deep... the body hangs in the mold and must be taken out in the plastic state... Am having [modeler Al] Kraft change both top and base and will try these before changing present molds. Something must be done because the situation is bad. Saw the jiggerman working and most of the work was spoilt in the molds."

The problems were evidently worked out because the casserole is not mentioned again in Rhead's journal. Collectors have found this casserole in Fiesta's red, blue, yellow, and green glazes. At the time it was in production, the final decision was being made on the glaze colors for Harlequin and Tango. Eventually, this casserole was also produced in the four colors of those other two lines: Harlequin yellow, blue, spruce, and maroon.

The length of time this casserole was made has been difficult to determine. The first full year of production occurred before there was a turquoise glaze for Fiesta, yet a statement in the seventh edition of *The Collector's Encyclopedia of Fiesta* implies turquoise is a frequently found color. This would extend production into 1938. In the same edition, the authors report the discovery of a casserole and pie plate set in the colors used for the 1940s promotions. Perhaps the "Kitchen Set" (above) was made with two different casseroles. Based on this information the shape was probably made from 1936 to 1943, although production may not have been continuous.

It should be noted that the report of the casserole's possible connection to the promotional campaign has caused some to refer to it as the "promotional casserole."

Both the bowl and lid were jiggered, with the lid knob being finished by hand. The unmarked bowls have three sagger pin scars under the rim. Because the casserole was made for Royal Metal Manufacturing, they will sometimes be found in a metal frame. In such cases, the frame should probably be considered original.

For some reason there is an abundance of red lids for this casserole. They are frequently found by themselves and range in price from $20 to $80. It cannot be explained why so many in a single color exist. Perhaps they were produced for the promotional campaign and not used, being sold as seconds or overstock to outside companies.

A casserole and cover in excellent condition and glazed in the Fiesta colors is valued in excess of a hundred dollars. In Harlequin/Tango colors it can command two to four times that amount.

Royal Metal Mfg. Covered Casserole

Modeling Date .... May 1936
Model Number .... 604[1]
First Revision .... June 1936, 620[2]
Second Revision .... June 1936, 628
Production Began .... July 1936
Discontinued .... Mid 1943*
Length of Production .... 7 Years*
Colors: Fiesta Red, Cobalt, Green, Yellow, Turquoise[3]; Harlequin Yellow, Blue, Maroon, Spruce

*Estimate
[1]First model not produced
[2]Second model not produced
[3]Turquoise not verified

Fiesta Royal Metal Manufacturing covered casserole in Harlequin blue.

Fiesta Royal Metal Manufacturing covered casseroles.

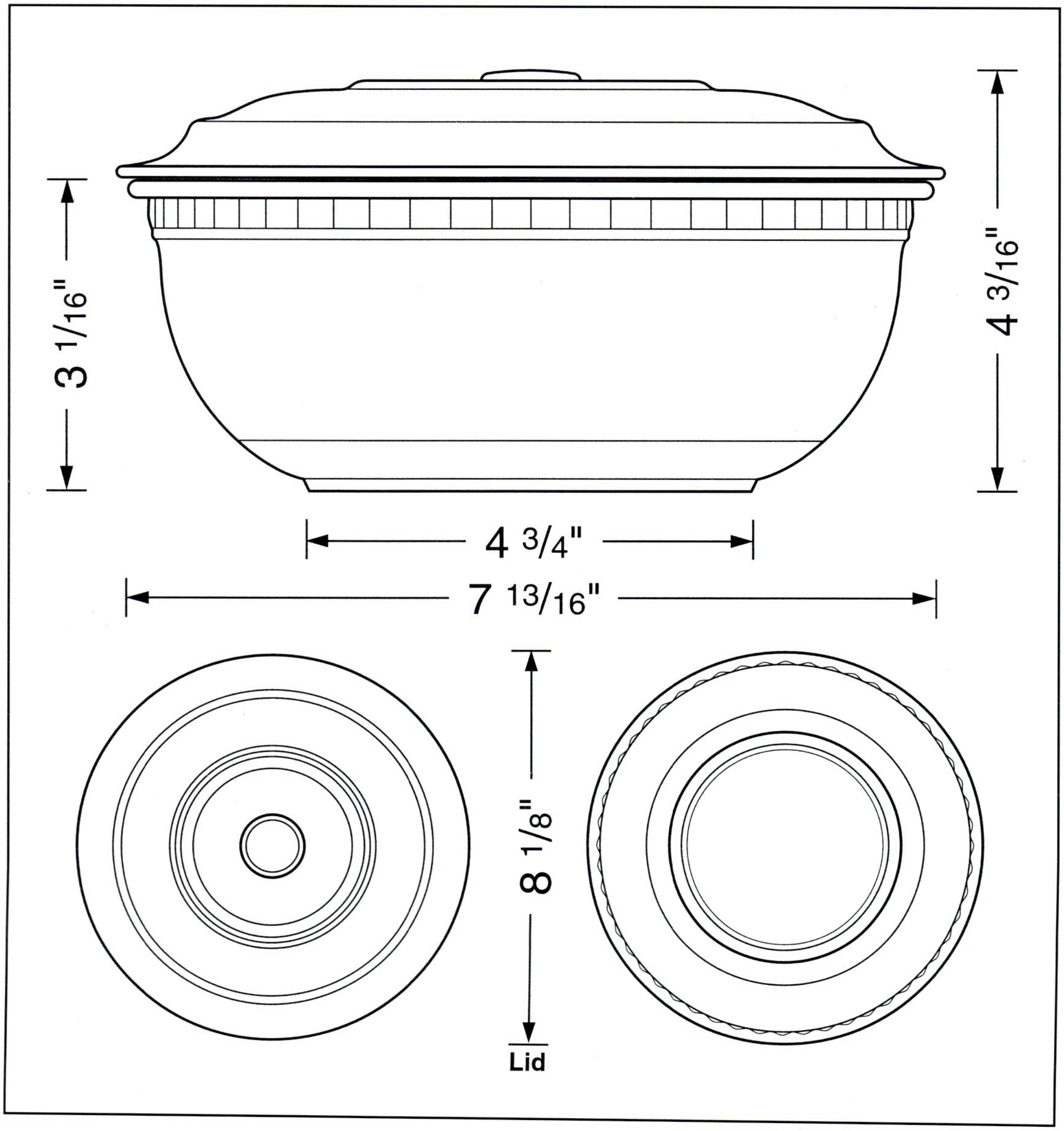

4 3/16"
3 1/16"
4 3/4"
7 13/16"
8 1/8"
Lid

Chapter 3

Fiesta Evolves

Decals and Decoration on Fiesta

Fiesta Casuals

Perhaps the reasoning behind the Fiesta Casuals was that the Fiesta line, having been in production for nearly 30 years, needed something new to renew buyers' interest. Or, maybe the underglaze decorations were done at the request of a specific retailer. Whatever the reason, this interesting stepchild of the vintage line was produced for a relatively short time and can make a fun addition to a collection.

No existing company records could be located that would verify the dates of production for the Fiesta Casuals. One author of an early Fiesta collector book reported a range of 1962 to 1965, with others extending the end of production to 1968. Most agree that the line was sold primarily by the E. F. MacDonald Company through their Plaid Stamp premium program. However, a 1965 wholesale catalog from A. C. McClurg & Co. of Chicago offered the Casuals in service sets for four or eight to any retailer.

There were two patterns. One featured a ring of turquoise flowers with brown centers, the other a chain of yellow flowers with brown stems and accents. The designs appear to be spayed onto the plates through a stencil. For place settings, the colored flowers were applied to white glazed Fiesta 10-inch plates, 7-inch plates, and tea saucers.

The yellow flowers are carnations and the name for that pattern is, appropriately, "Yellow Carnation." The turquoise flowers have been called daisies or cornflowers. The name used by collectors for this pattern is "Hawaiian 12-Point Daisy", although it doesn't seem to correspond to anything in nature with that name. Both patterns first became to the attention of collectors in the second edition (1976) of *The Collectors Encyclopedia of Fiesta.* HLC pattern numbers were also provided in the book, which lends support to the probability that those names were official.

Opposite page:
Fiesta Casuals "Yellow Carnation."

Accompanying the decorated Fiesta flatware were teacups and 5 1/2" fruit bowls in standard Fiesta colors that matched the underglaze decoration—yellow for Carnation and turquoise for Daisy. Serving pieces in the same colors were also available and included the 8 1/2" nappie, covered sugar, and cream. The oval platter made for the Fiesta Casuals sported the same flower decoration as the plates.

These dishes are not all that common. However, when found they are usually reasonably priced. The solid color pieces, of course, are valued the same as their normal vintage counterparts.

Fiesta Casuals "Hawaiian 12-Point Daisy."

Amberstone

J & H International of Wilmette, Illinois, was a dinnerware distribution company that promoted both domestic and foreign ware. During the 1960s and 1970s they offered several patterns made by Homer Laughlin, a few of which were sold under the brand name "Sheffield." Among HLC collectors, the best known of the Sheffield lines is Amberstone. Beginning in mid-1967 J & H International distributed Amberstone to major grocery store chains for use in promotions to attract customers.

A deep, coffee-brown glaze was used on modified Fiesta shapes for Amberstone. The final color was selected from among several trial glazes. A few pieces of one of them were recently found in eastern Ohio. The brown is flat and resembles milk chocolate. A 9" plate and two shakers in the trial color were glazed. The shakers have nine individually created holes. The extra holes perhaps added by a playful employee who knew they were a test piece and not for production.

In addition to the brown glaze, plates and other flatware had a mechanically applied decoration in black. No doubt HLC's positive experience with the decorated Fiesta Casuals was partly responsible for the use of an underglaze design on Amberstone. The addition of it helped make the 30-year-old shape more attractive to new buyers. Normal Fiesta markings were removed from the hollowware.

The redesigned shapes would also be used for Fiesta Ironstone two years later. A complete description of the changes made to the vintage Fiesta line can be found in the Ironstone section of this book.

In addition to the redesigned items, several existing or new pieces were also used only for Amberstone and Casualstone (see *Casualstone* below). The Fiesta deep plate and ashtray were not changed and received the brown glaze for the Sheffield line. The Fiesta marmalade had the impressed mark removed and the lid was given the new knob designed for the Amberstone sugar. The covered butter dish was an HLC design used for several dinnerware patterns. The base stayed the same and slight modifications were made to the lid for each line. Likewise, the pie plate offered with Amberstone was not specifically made for it, but was shared with other lines.

There was a form available at the store display that customers could use to order Amberstone serving pieces and additional place settings. On one side is a drawing of the items available. Obviously done before the shapes were actually modeled, a few pieces are not accurately depicted. The sauceboat stand is not shown although a covered mustard is.

One Fiesta mustard is known to exist in the brown Amberstone glaze. However, based on the order form, the mustard was not offered as part of the line. The one that exists is believed to be unique and more than likely was part of a display set up at HLC for the representative from J & H International when the final selection of items was made. Collectors should not expect to find an Amberstone mustard to add to their collection.

During the time that Amberstone was in production, the regular Fiesta line was still being made in the colors of the Sixties: red, yellow, turquoise, and medium green. Collectors may occasionally find items from one line glazed in the color(s) of the other. Amberstone sauceboats, disc water pitchers, and teapots have been found with the impressed Fiesta mark, even though all marks were removed from the molds intended for use with that line. A few Amberstone plates are known to have a backstamp that says "Fiesta" instead of the expected "Sheffield."

Sometimes the errors appear on the Fiesta side. A few Fiesta medium teapots in the medium green glaze have been found missing the impressed Fiesta mark, indicating that an Amberstone mold was used. Collectors should be on the lookout for other unmarked teapots in yellow, red, and turquoise. Some Fiesta pepper shakers in the Sixties colors will be missing the center hole. This was the pattern used for Amberstone.

Teacups with Amberstone style "C-shaped" handles are known in the 1960s colors as well. The red ones, of course, are indistinguishable from Fiesta Ironstone red teacups. The yellow, turquoise, and medium green cups with this handle can make an interesting addition to a collection of Amberstone. In the accompanying photos we show a variety of Amberstone/Casualstone oddities including an Eggshell Nautilus teacup in the Amberstone glaze, one of a set of eight recently found.

It is a major undertaking when the shapes and glaze colors of a dinnerware line change. Much more so than when a minor line, like Amberstone, is run at the same time as the main one. At the time Fiesta Ironstone was put into production in 1969, the old glazes were taken off the production line and the possibility of such errors was eliminated. Not so during the time Amberstone was being made. The logical explanation is that these mistakes were made during Amberstone's production period, which probably lasted for about two years, instead of during a so-called "transitional" period at the end of regular Fiesta production.

Amberstone plates, cups, and small bowls are very easy to find. Serving pieces, especially casseroles, teapots, and coffee servers, will prove to be more difficult. Nothing in the line is considered rare, but the large salad bowl, coffee mug and ashtray are the most difficult pieces to add to a collection.

***Top, Center & Right:* Fiesta Amberstone.**

"C-handled" teacups in Fiesta medium green, turquoise, and yellow.

Items Available in Amberstone/Casualstone

Dinner Plate
Salad Plate
Bread & Butter Plate
Large Soup Plate
Soup/Cereal Bowl
Dessert Dish
Coffee Cup
Saucer
Jumbo Mug
Covered Sugar Bowl
Creamer
Covered Jam Jar
Covered Butter Dish
Salt & Pepper Shakers
Vegetable Bowl
Jumbo Salad Bowl
Oval Platter 13"
Round Serving Platter
Handled Relish Tray
Covered Casserole
Sauceboat
Sauceboat Stand*
Disc Serving Pitcher
Coffee Server
Tea Server
Ash Tray
Pie Plate

*The sauceboat stand is not on the Amberstone order blank although they are known to exist in some quantity. It is not on the Casualstone order form either and may not have been part of that line.

Some Fiesta Amberstone oddities.

Coupon for an Amberstone relish tray.

Casualstone

The name "Casualstone" was originally intended for a different line of dinnerware. More than a dozen new shapes, including cups, plates, bowls, and serving pieces were prepared in 1968 for the dinnerware distributor Cunningham & Pickett, a long-time HLC customer. The new line was to be called Casualstone, but it was never produced.

In 1970 Coventry Ware, Inc., of Barberton, Ohio, picked up the name and applied it to the modified Fiesta shapes that were being used for Fiesta Ironstone. Clearly a cost saving measure for HLC, Ironstone's antique gold glaze was also used for Casualstone production. Like J & H International before them, Coventry Ware offered the new design to grocery store chains for use in promotions.

There are many similarities between Casualstone and Amberstone. The same items were offered in both lines, both had an underglaze design on the flat pieces, and both had an identical printed form for ordering additional items direct from the factory. Interestingly, the sauceboat stand is not on either order form and may have been used only as a special incentive item. While they certainly exist in the Amberstone glaze, those in Casualstone's antique gold may simply be Fiesta Ironstone pieces and not part of the promotional line. No documentation was located to verify the history of these lines except the order forms and HLC's modeling log.

Although it was in production at the same time as Fiesta Ironstone, and shared the antique gold glaze, the two lines did not have identical items. Like Amberstone, the Fiesta deep plate, marmalade (with new lid), and ashtray were used for Casualstone. These three items were not part of the Fiesta Ironstone line and will be found only in Casualstone's gold glaze. The butter dish and pie plate that were shared with several HLC lines also received the golden underglaze stamped design and antique gold glaze for Casualstone.

Coventry Ware, Inc. went out of business shortly after Casualstone production began, so the length of time the line was in production was not very long. The actual date it was discontinued is unknown.

As easy to find as Amberstone, if not more so, Casualstone place setting pieces are inexpensive. The five major serving pieces, salad bowl, coffee server, teapot, casserole, and disc pitcher, were shared with Fiesta Ironstone (all made only in the antique gold glaze) and may prove harder to find. The coffee mugs and ashtrays, again, are among the more difficult items to locate.

Fiesta Casualstone.

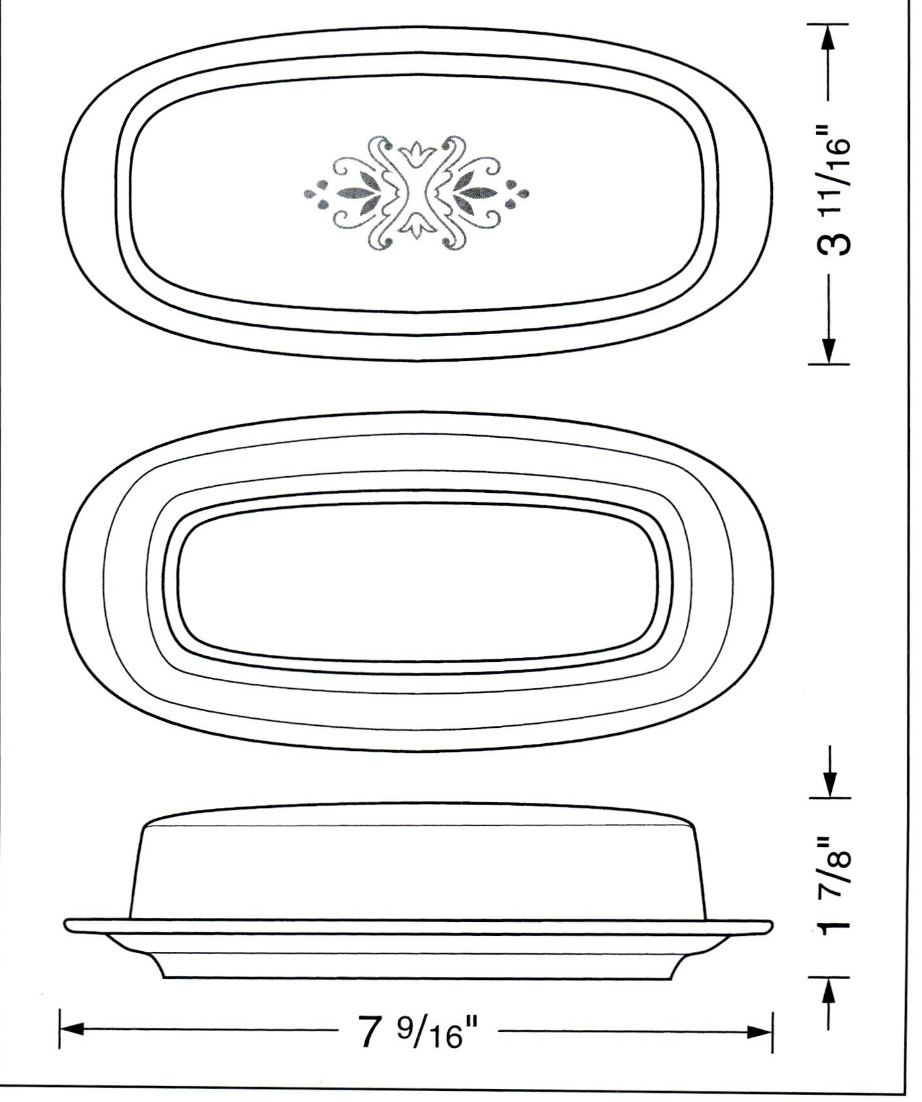
3 11/16"
1 7/8"
7 9/16"

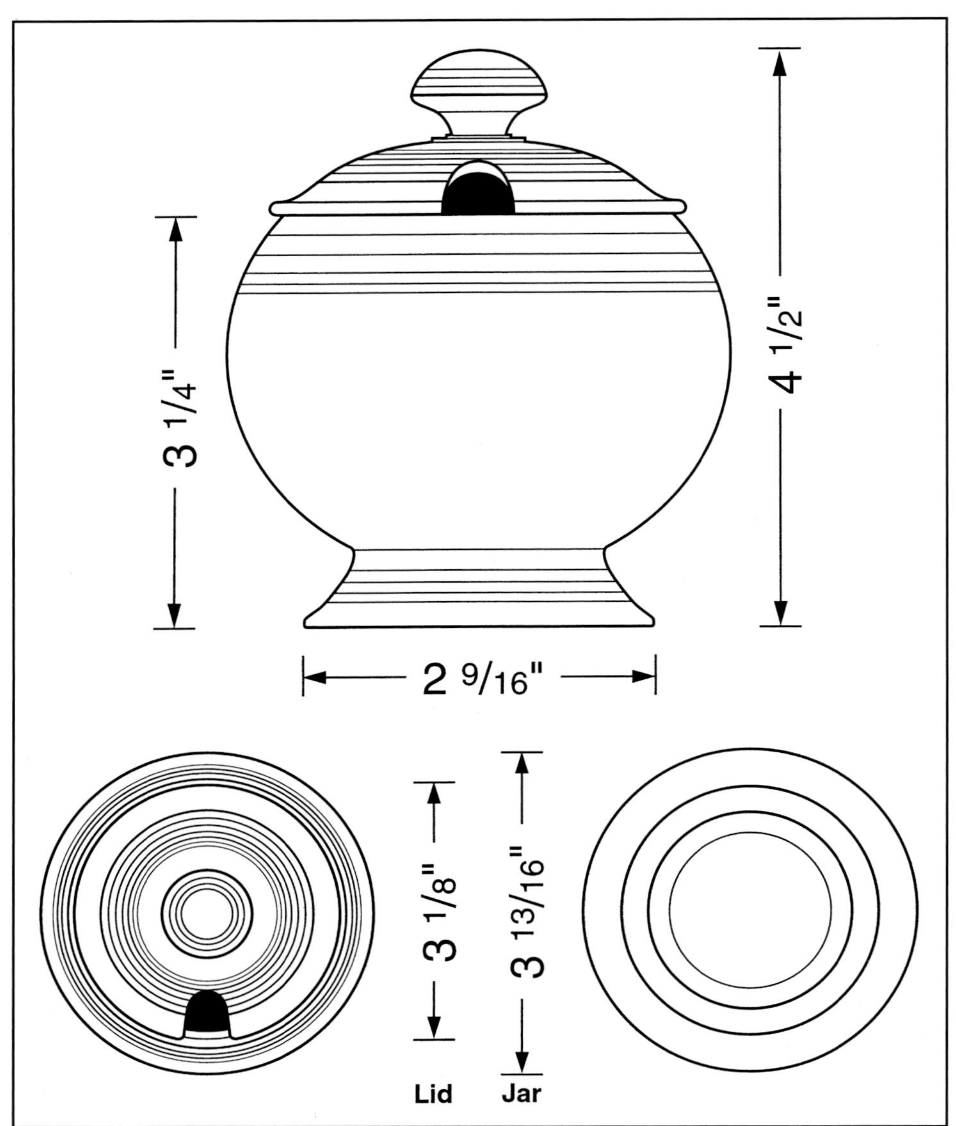
3 1/4"
4 1/2"
2 9/16"
3 1/8"
3 13/16"
Lid
Jar

OVEN-PROOF ★ DETERGENT-PROOF ★ DISHWASHER-SAFE ★
★ ★ ★
CASUALSTONE
by
CUNNINGHAM
INDUSTRIES
ALLIANCE, OHIO
44601
AVOCADO GREEN

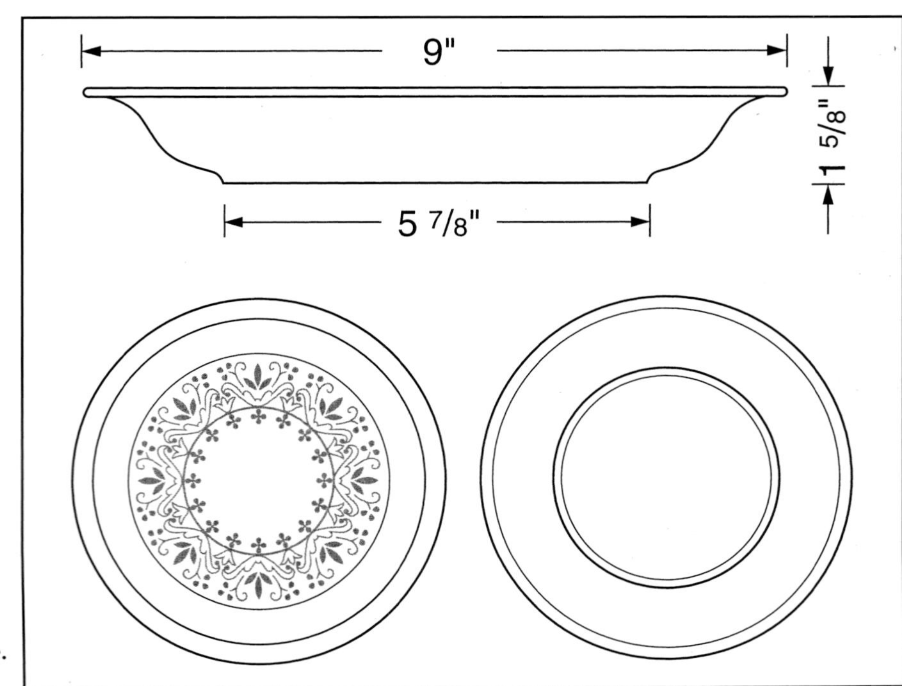
9"
1 5/8"
5 7/8"

Pie plate.

Fiesta Tom and Jerry Set

The Tom and Jerry is a cold weather drink similar to eggnog made from hot milk, eggs, sugar, and two types of liquor, usually brandy and rum. It is served warm in mugs from a large serving bowl. The drink was invented in the 1860s and the name is either a tribute to the alleged inventor, a New Yorker named Jerry Thomas, or recalls two characters from the English work of fiction, "Life in London."

If the Fiesta set was produced for the entire time the footed salad bowl was made, then it would have been available from mid-1936 to late 1946. The gold stamped mugs are the same as the ivory Tom and Jerry mugs produced for the regular Fiesta line. There are two varieties of the gold stamped design on the bowl. The older one has open "Old English" style lettering and the later, more common one has solid lettering. The characters stamped on the mugs always seem to have been done with solid lettering. As with many pieces of Fiesta, the bowl and mugs may or may not have the "Genuine Fiesta" backstamp. Some of the older bowls may have an impressed "HLC USA" mark.

Homer Laughlin already had a Tom and Jerry set in production when Fiesta was introduced, and the mugs from it were adapted to the new line. It is sometimes called a Fiesta set by retailers who don't know the difference, so it is being included here to avoid such confusion. The bowl is 9.5" wide and 4.5" tall. It can be found with the same two styles of gold lettering as the Fiesta set. These bowls are usually marked with the Homer Laughlin date code backstamp.

There are two types of mugs found with these bowls as shown in the accompanying photo. The mugs are usually unmarked, but may have the same stamp as the bowl. These HLC sets were sold for about 25 years beginning in the early 1930s. The mug with the flared rim replaced the original in 1951.

The Fiesta Tom & Jerry set.

Another HLC Tom & Jerry set.

Fiesta Calendar Plates

Homer Laughlin was making calendar plates as far back as the early 1900s and they seem to have been a regular item by the 1950s and 1960s. They were made on a variety of HLC shapes.

Fiesta calendar plates were made for 1954 and 1955. Those for 1954 appear only on ivory 10 inch plates and have the year prominently shown in the center of the decal. The 1955 plates were made in two sizes and three colors. Ten inch 1955 plates can be found in ivory, light green, and Fiesta yellow. The 1955 decal was also applied to ivory glazed nine-inch plates. Only a few 9" examples have been reported in the green and yellow glazes and we were unable to verify if they really exist.

The Fiesta calendar plates.

It is sometimes asked why ivory and green plates were used when those glazes were not Fiesta colors by 1954-55. There are several possible explanations.

Anyone who has visited the Homer Laughlin factory in Newell, West Virginia knows how huge the buildings are. Built between 1905 and 1928, the five buildings cover acres of space. It is very easy for a pallet or two of glazed ware to disappear for a few years. Some feel that this could be the source for the ivory and green plates. Found a few years later, the colors were right for displaying a gold decal so the leftover plates were put to good use. This sounds like the most reasonable explanation.

Others think the colors used were specifically applied to show off the calendars. Ivory was still used on other lines in the early 1950s and it would have been easy for HLC to glaze a bunch of Fiesta plates just for these decals. However, that does not explain the green plates. This explanation is not as likely as the first, but still possible.

Finally, there are those who believe the calendar plates were made several years in advance. The decals for future years could have been put on plates in the late 1940s or early 1950s when Fiesta was being made in these colors. HLC did not usually produce items without having a buyer waiting, so this last explanation is not likely to be the correct one.

These fun additions to a collection are not seen everyday, but can be located with a little effort. No matter what year, size, or color, the Fiesta calendar plates all seem to be share a reasonable range of values.

Fiesta With Decals

Before Fiesta production began, buyers from all the major department stores and wholesale firms were invited to the Homer Laughlin plant to see the new line. Many made suggestions or had special requests. One was Macy's of New York. In Rhead's personal journal he notes, on November 12, 1935, "Series of samples of Vellum [ivory] Fiesta with bands and decal decorations for [Gerald] Stone of Macy's... Likes contemporary patterns on yellow Fiesta."

Without actual production records we have no way of knowing if Macy's eventually sold Fiesta with decals, but we do know they were interested in doing so. There have been quite a variety of decals found on vintage Fiesta, although they are not easy for most collectors to locate. Most often seen on ivory, but occasionally on yellow or other colors, the decorations tend to be floral patterns. Turkeys, butterflies, and intricate designs that include people or pastoral scenes are also known.

No doubt HLC's decorating department applied some of the decals, but outside firms, such as Royal China and Vogue, are also known to have purchased the ware and resold it after applying decals or gold bands and accents.

It would be logical to assume that plates and bowls received the majority of these decorations, but many serving pieces have also been found including relish trays, footed salad bowls, nappies, etc. Values for Fiesta with decals tend to be higher than for the same item with out them.

Some interesting decorated Fiesta.

Fiesta With Stripes

The concentric ring pattern that is present on Fiesta was sometimes enhanced by the application of overglaze stripes. Two styles seem to have been used. One was very early, within the first two years of production, and involved a band of three stripes of varying widths. The stripes were placed on the outer edges of plates, saucers, and lids, and under the rims of bowls, cups, and casseroles. Two colors are known, blue and red, both applied to ivory glazed Fiesta ware.

The other known pattern of stripes was used on a "cake set" sold by Sears in the mid-1940s. An ivory or yellow ten-inch plate was accompanied by four or sometimes six 7" plates in the same color. Two stripes were used to decorate both sizes, one at the rim and one at the verge. Stripes in green or dark red (maroon) were applied to either color plates. The seven plates were sold as a set for less than three dollars, and the 5-piece for even less.

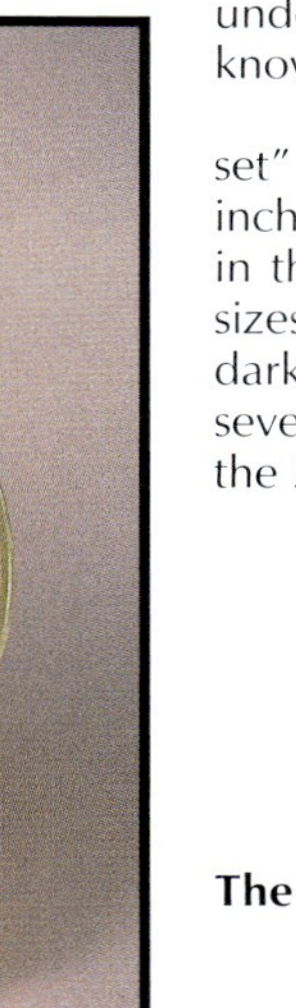

The Sears striped cake set.

Fiesta Developmental Pieces

Of the 157 models created for the Fiesta line between February 1935 and January 1969, 138 were made under the direction of Frederick Hurten Rhead during the first five years. He had ideas and designs for several items that were never produced. Many of the original models have long since disappeared and none of Rhead's original drawings have been found, according to officials at Homer Laughlin. The modeling log does contain a few sketches of items that were not added to the line, but these drawings frequently cannot give a sense of the size or details of the piece.

Luckily most models had trial runs, usually producing a dozen pieces. Some of those samples have survived and found their way into collector hands. The reason for the trials was to see how difficult it was for the plant worker to make the item, how the shape would tolerate the bisque firing, and how it looked when glazed. The samples were often glazed in the color being used on that day, which may not have been a Fiesta color. These so-called "experimental" pieces have become some of the most unusual and highly collectible examples of early Fiesta design.

This section will list a few of those never produced items and, if possible, show an image of the piece being discussed. We are indebted to the advanced collectors and dealers who graciously allowed us to examine and photograph their treasures.

The original sugar bowl. No established value.

Models 349 & 354, Original Cream and Sugar

Only half a dozen items had been modeled for Fiesta when the first sugar was designed. Rhead's sketch of March 14, 1935 came to life in plaster before the end of the month. Both pieces featured the new ring handle he had created for the line a few weeks before. It's apparent that Rhead was beginning to work out the general look that would be used for other serving pieces, but he had not yet widened the top of the finial.

The example of the sugar shown nearby suffered from being exposed to an overheated kiln, which burned off most of the red glaze. That color is still present in the deep crevices, but has turned a root beer brown over most of the surface of the piece. Other examples of this sugar, and the cream, have been found in an ivory glaze.

The lid for this sugar, which looks very much like the lid on the later designed covered onion soup, has turned up on an onion soup bowl. This has led some to believe that the Fiesta onion soup had an earlier, different lid. That is not documented in the log and the lid shown is more than likely from an early sugar.

The lid for this onion soup appears to be for an early sugar model.

Model 363, 10" Comport

The compote, or comport, is a "wide, low bowl usually on a pedestal." Rhead recognized the need for one in the new line, but his first design proved to be too small. His April 1935 model was ten inches in diameter and had a look that fit the description of a compote exactly. The design was faithfully reproduced a month later when the 12" version was created.

Like many of the early pieces, the example shown here is glazed in ivory. Fiesta's colored glazes had not yet been formulated at the time most of the early pieces were designed, so the available ivory glaze used on OvenServe and the Century shape was applied instead.

The early 10" comport atop the production 12" variety.

Model 369, First Fiesta Casserole

Rhead's first idea for a Fiesta casserole, in April 1935, had a single handle and a pedestal foot. The design was later used, without the foot, for the promotional campaign of the early Forties. All of the trial pieces of this early casserole that have surfaced are in the ivory glaze.

An early model for a Fiesta casserole. No established value.

An ivory two-cup teapot. No established value.

Model 386, "Two-cup" Teapot

This piece is listed in the HLC modeling log as "Ringed teapot, sketch No. 381." Sketch 381, in Rhead's "Record of Sketches and Drawings", is an early design for a 6-cup After Dinner coffeepot. So although many collectors refer to the ball shaped server with a stick handle as a two-cup or "individual" teapot, it was originally intended for A.D. coffee service. The shape of the lid and spout, as well as the stick handle, are shared with the demitasse coffeepot that was later produced for this purpose within the line.

Model 423, Cracked Ice Bowl

This bowl was designed after the mixing bowls and bears a resemblance to them, except this piece has an attached pedestal foot. According to Homer Laughlin documents, the bowl is 9-3/4" wide and 6-3/4" tall. Few, if any, are in private collections. One is known to have been in storage at HLC and it featured the ivory glaze.

Models 433 & 437, Pie Plates

Two pie plates were modeled for Fiesta, but neither was produced. The initial one measured 9" x 1-1/2" and the second was 10-1/2" x 2". No design features are known, but they likely had the familiar Fiesta's rings somewhere on them. There is some speculation that a piece some call a "spaghetti bowl" may be one of the pie plate trials. We were unable to examine a copy of that bowl to obtain accurate measurements, so a connection to the Fiesta pie plates cannot be made. It is said to have a band of rings under the rim.

Model 519 & 520, Beaker and Coaster/Saucer

Just after production began on Fiesta, in January 1936, Frederick Rhead had a "beaker" and "coaster" modeled for the new line. In HLC's modeling log, the word "mug" was written next to the beaker entry, then crossed out. Throughout the log, Rhead uses the term "mug" the way collectors today use the term "tumbler", to designate a tall, rimless cup without a handle used for drinking cold liquids. Perhaps a beaker was a large mug. Whatever the case, no examples are known and the log contains no drawings of it.

At least one example of the coaster or saucer made to go with the beaker is known to exist. It was glazed in Fiesta red and resembles a flattened fruit bowl. There is a fairly wide, thick rim and it has short, straight sides.

Model 549, Teapot Stand

A teapot stand was like a small trivet that protected the table and linens from the hot pot and caught drips like a coaster. Many potteries made them during the Thirties and Forties. Frederick Rhead designed one for Fiesta in February 1936. It was essentially a flat disk with a small lip or rim and resembled the lid to the Kitchen Kraft stacking refrigerator bowls that were made more than a year later. The familiar concentric ring pattern decorated the top.

Models 586/587/588/589, Small Jugs

The two-pint jug is a familiar piece to collectors of vintage Fiesta since it was made for more than 20 years in ten colors. However, not many realize that there were four smaller jugs in the original series. The jugs were made in one-cup increments from four cups (2 pints) down to one-half cup. They were numbered 5 for the largest to 1 for the smallest.

Known to exist are at least two examples of the trial run pieces in collections, a number 4 and a number 2. The jugs all have the same shape no matter the size and are marked with the "size" number, which is impressed in to the clay on the bottom.

Models 633/634/635, Mixing Bowl Covers 5/6/7

Covers, or lids, for Fiesta's mixing bowls were made for a very short period of time in 1936. They were produced in four sizes to fit the four smallest bowls. Trial run examples of the three larger bowls were made and some of them have survived to this day. There are rumors of at least two number seven lids, but so far no one has proved that they exist. Fives and sixes are extremely rare and command prices above $10,000 each. A few examples are shown nearby.

Fiesta mixing bowl covers in green - size 5 and 6. No established value.

Models 791 & 804, Water Jug

Collectors of HLC's Harlequin will recognize the ball-shaped jug as belonging to that line, but it was originally to be used for Fiesta. The modeling log includes drawings and written entries that identify this shape as a "Fiesta water jug." It was modeled in March 1937, a full year before the familiar disc pitcher. The first attempt had a long, sweeping handle and a high-necked spout. The revision, done four months later, was inspired by a similar product made by Hall China and features a shorter handle and a redesigned spout. Both jugs have Fiesta's band of graduated rings at the bottom.

We're aware of only one example of the early jug and are pleased to be able to display a photograph of it in this book. The revised jug of July 1937 was used for Woolworth's line and was eventually produced in all twelve Harlequin colors.

A Harlequin service water pitcher on the left, and the early prototype for the Fiesta water jug on the right. No established value.

Models 897/899/907/918, Divided Plate

Quite a bit of work was done on this piece. Four different models were made during August 1937, yet it never was integrated into the Fiesta line. Apparently a one-piece replacement for the relish tray, this item measured 10 1/2 inches in diameter and had five deep compartments. The modeling log indicates this plate was attempted both by slip casting and jiggering, but it likely proved too difficult to make in full production.

One of these plates, in the cobalt glaze, was in storage at Homer Laughlin. A red glazed example also recently surfaced and was featured on an Internet auction site. It is not known how many more may be out there in collector hands.

The prototype divided plate. No established value.

Swirl Sherbet

Even with diligent searching by several researchers we could not locate this item in the HLC modeling log. It is clearly marked "Fiesta", but is a most unusual piece. Made up of three colored clays with a clear glaze, it may have been made in the early 1950s when HLC was producing Skytone and Suntone. Those two lines were made with clays of similar hues.

The presence of the impressed "Fiesta" mark tends to make it difficult to classify this as an employee invention. Why the unusual clays were used is unknown. Without modeling log verification, it cannot be considered a legitimate item made for the Fiesta line, but should probably be viewed as someone's lunchtime fantasy made real.

The Fiesta sherbet dish.

Another view of this unusual Fiesta piece.

Chapter 4

Fiesta Ironstone

By the late 1960s sales of Fiesta were in decline. The bright colors were no longer in fashion and some of the shapes were looking very dated. In 1967 an attempt to continue the production of the famous line was made by reshaping some items and using a different method of decoration as well as a new distribution method. The new incarnation was called Amberstone. Using their Sheffield brand name, J & H International distributed the new line to supermarkets for use in promotions to attract new customers.

The changes made to the shapes were mainly confined to bowls, handles, and knobs. The coffeepot and marmalade were returned to the line and a few newly designed items were added. Because it was to be sold under a different name, the Fiesta marks were removed from existing pieces. Bowls were changed from straight sided to a more modern shape with slanted or sloped sides. Smooth, rounded knobs were created for the sugar, teapot, and coffee server. The sugar's side handles were removed and the ring handles on the teacup and creamer were changed to a more traditional shape.

Amberstone was in production until at least 1970 and its success may have served to stimulate Homer Laughlin to use the restyled shapes in Fiesta's main line. By July 1969 production of Fiesta in red, yellow, turquoise, and medium green had ended. Many items that had been standard in the line for more than 30 years were discontinued. Most of the revised shapes created for Sheffield Amberstone were substituted and the line was glazed in colors popular at the time: harvest gold, avocado green, and burnt orange. The new line was called Fiesta Ironstone. There was no change in the clay formula or production methods used. Ironstone was a name already attached to other HLC lines and using it with Fiesta was probably a marketing strategy.

A few shapes that had been used for Amberstone were not made when Fiesta Ironstone started production. The ashtray, deep plate, and marmalade were not part of the revised line, although all three items were made for Casualstone and can be found in the gold glaze used on that promotional line. For more information about Amberstone and Casualstone, see the section of the book that covers Fiesta with *Decals and Decoration*.

Fiesta Ironstone was made for about three and a half years. In her book on United States pottery marks, Lois Lehner quoted material sent to her by Homer Laughlin concerning Fiesta. It said, "...Fiesta Ironstone dinnerware was discontinued January 1, 1973 and there will be no further production." In spite of the strong statement, many of the Fiesta Ironstone shapes were revived in 1986 with the reintroduction of Fiesta. They are still in use today.

Colors

HLC's names for the new colors in 1969 were antique gold, turf green, and mango red. The gold and green were already in use on other HLC shapes and the red was the standard Fiesta red renamed. It had always required its own kiln, so the continued use of it was justified for the restyled line.

Several shades of a light caramel-colored glazed were in use at HLC on the Granada and Hearthside shapes during the Sixties. It was logical to extend this color to Fiesta Ironstone where the golden glaze was called "antique gold." It was also used for Coventry Casualstone in grocery store promotions and is the most common Fiesta Ironstone color found today.

This color can at times have a greenish cast to it and can be confused by nascent collectors with turf green. When this occurs on items made only in the gold glaze it can cause quite a stir. The large serving pieces of Fiesta Ironstone were only produced in antique gold. Disc water pitchers, coffee servers, teapots, 10" salad bowls, and covered casseroles were not officially made in turf green or mango red. Now and then a "turf green" disc pitcher is discovered. So far they have all proved to be only a greenish variety of antique gold.

Green was another popular glaze already in use on other shapes at HLC and the slight variant selected for Fiesta Ironstone was named "turf green." It actually has no resemblance to grass, unless it's a lawn in need of water. Light olive is probably the best description. Today this

color is not as easy to find as antique gold, but not as hard to find as mango red. Except for the five serving pieces mentioned above, turf green was used on all items in the Fiesta Ironstone line.

Mango red as a name may not make much sense to those outside of the Midwest. To many people a mango is a tropical fruit with a tangy-sweet flavor and a greenish-yellow skin with red highlights. In the Midwest, some old-timers refer to bell peppers as mangos. The peppers can turn various shades of orange-red when ripe and this is probably the source of the name for the Fiesta Ironstone glaze.

Items from the line in this glaze are not easily found these days. Some pieces are little changed from the original line and are sometimes unknowingly sold as the older red ware. Completing a collection of red Fiesta Ironstone will take quite a bit of time and effort to find all the pieces.

Items Available in Fiesta Ironstone

Fruit/Dessert Bowl

This bowl replaced the 5 1/2" fruit. It was the first item designed for Amberstone/Ironstone and featured the flared shape that was used on most bowls in the new line. It was made on a jigger machine, has no known variations, and was not marked. It is one of the more easily found Fiesta Ironstone pieces and is generally considered to be inexpensive.

Fiesta Ironstone Dessert Bowl	
Modeling Date	March 1967
Model Number	2929
Revisions	None
Production Began	May 1967*
Discontinued	December 1972*
Length of Production[1]	5.6 Years*
Colors: Amberstone Brown, Antique Gold, Mango Red, Turf Green	
*Estimate	
[1]Includes Amberstone production	

Fiesta Ironstone fruit/ dessert bowls. $6-7.

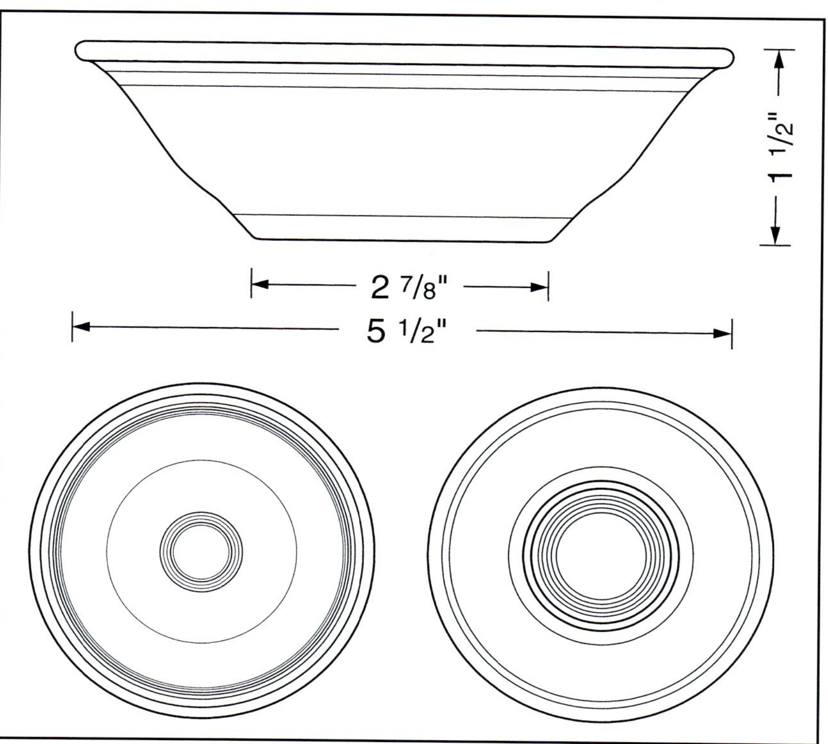

Soup/Cereal Bowl

This was an all-purpose, medium-sized bowl that took the place of the deep plate and the previously discontinued cream soup bowl. It has the same slope-sided shape as the new fruit bowl. Also made on a jigger and unmarked, these bowls have no variations. They're a bit harder to find than the smaller bowl, even more so in the mango red glaze.

Fiesta Ironstone Soup/Cereal Bowl	
Modeling Date	March 1967
Model Number	2931
Revisions	None
Production Began	May 1967*
Discontinued	December 1972*
Length of Production[1]	5.6 Years*

Colors: Amberstone Brown, Antique Gold, Mango Red, Turf Green

*Estimate

[1]Includes Amberstone production

Fiesta Ironstone soup/cereal bowls. $7-8.

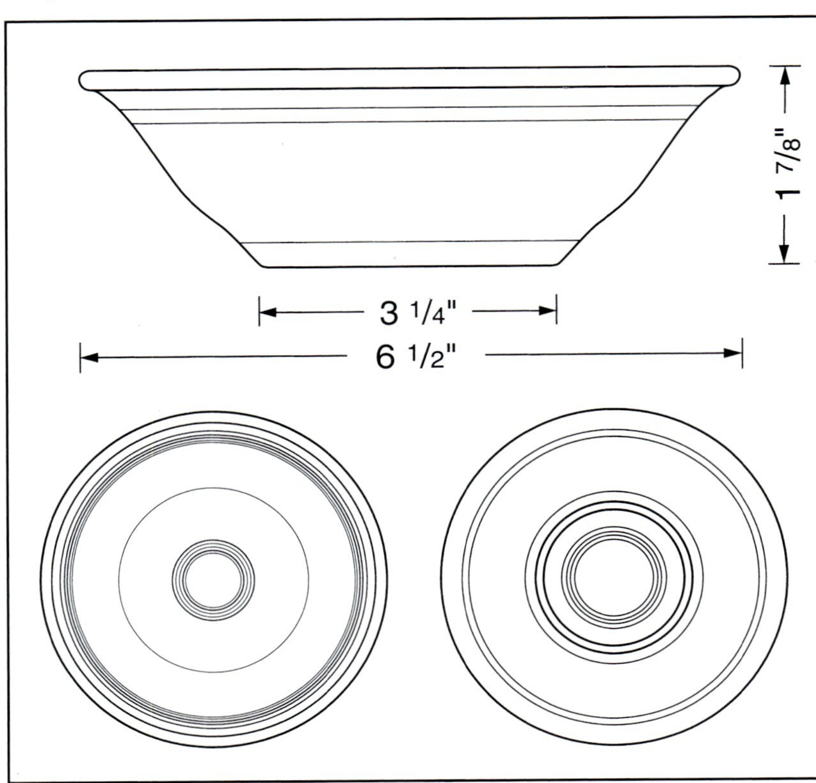

Salad Bowl

This hard to find bowl was one of the new additions for the restyled line. It features the familiar pattern of graduated rings just below the rim, but is completely smooth inside. Another jiggered piece, this bowl was made in only two glazes: Amberstone brown and antique gold. Like all Fiesta Ironstone items, the bowl was not marked.

Fiesta Ironstone Salad Bowl	
Modeling Date	April 1967
Model Number	2938
Revisions	None
Production Began	May 1967*
Discontinued	December 1972*
Length of Production[1]	5.6 Years*

Colors: Amberstone Brown, Antique Gold

*Estimate

[1]Includes Amberstone production

Fiesta Ironstone salad bowl. $27-35.

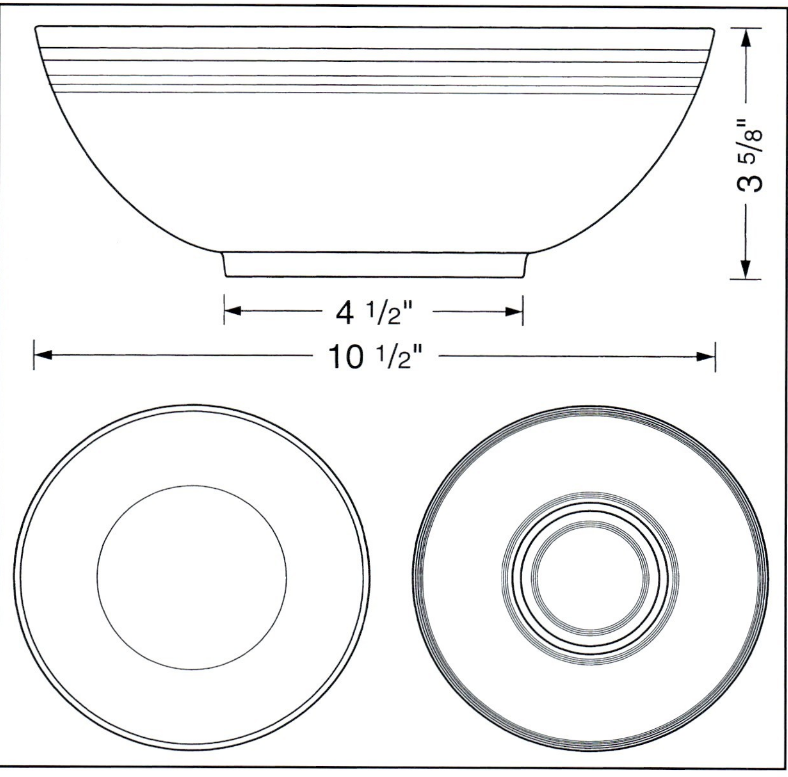

Vegetable Bowl

A larger version of the cereal and fruit bowls, the vegetable bowl was also made on a jigger machine. There are no variations, but some gold ones will be marked with the Coventry Casualstone backstamp. These bowls turn up now and again, but are not as easily found as their smaller counterparts.

Fiesta Ironstone Vegetable Bowl	
Modeling Date	March 1967
Model Number	2934
Revisions	None
Production Began	May 1967*
Discontinued	December 1972*
Length of Production[1]	5.6 Years*

Colors: Amberstone Brown, Antique Gold, Mango Red, Turf Green

*Estimate

[1]Includes Amberstone production

Fiesta Ironstone vegetable bowl. $21-23.

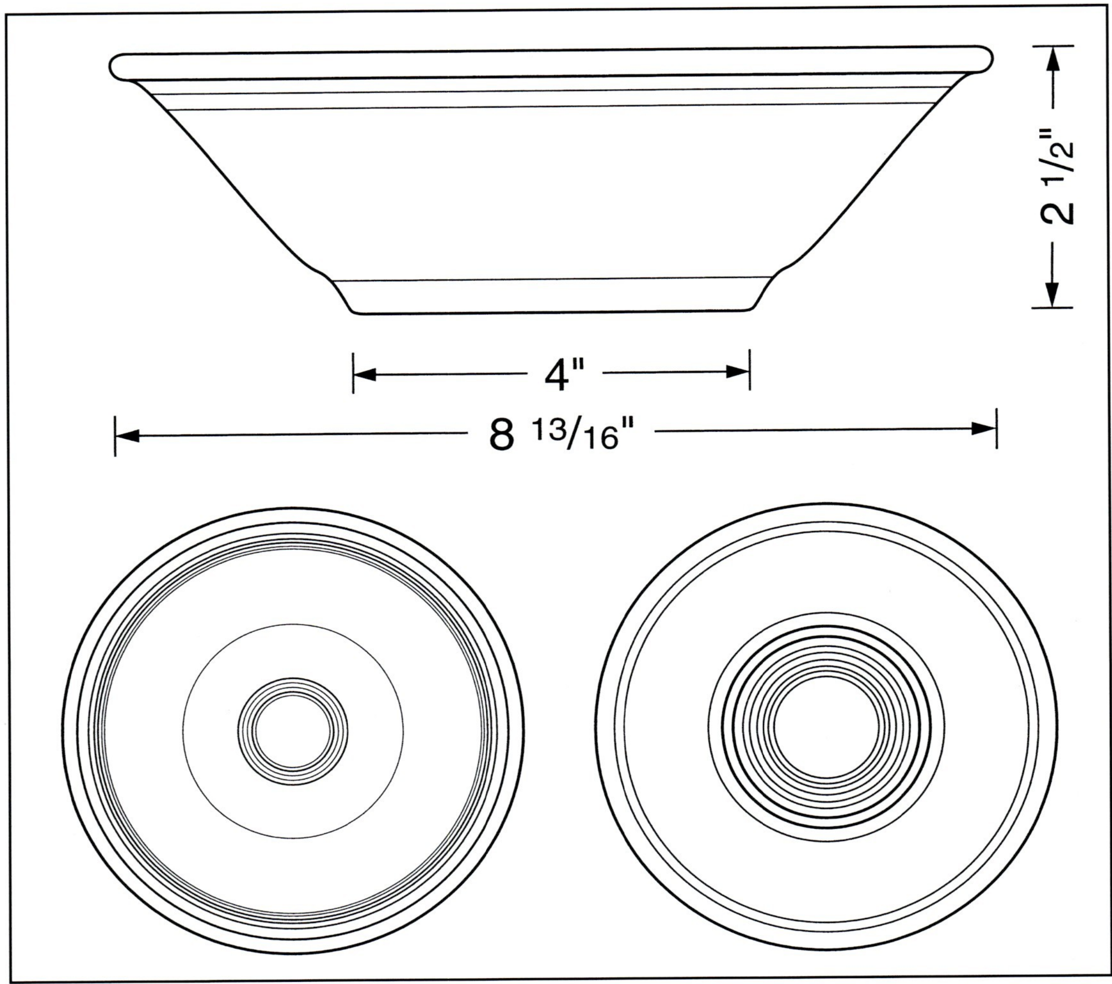

Covered Casserole

One of the most radical changes to the line was for the covered casserole. At first only the knob was restyled. Then it was decided to completely redesign the whole thing. The new casserole was made in one piece, including the handles. The cover and new bowl were slip cast items, as was the knob that was hand applied to the lid. This is another item made only in two colors, Amberstone brown and antique gold. The casserole was not marked.

Fiesta Ironstone Covered Casserole

Modeling Date	March, April 1967
Model Number	2935[1], 2939[2]
Revisions	None
Production Began	May 1967*
Discontinued	December 1972*
Length of Production[3]	5.6 Years*

Colors: Amberstone Brown, Antique Gold

*Estimate

[1]Casserole cover knob

[2]Casserole and cover

[3]Includes Amberstone production

Fiesta Ironstone covered casserole. $29-39.

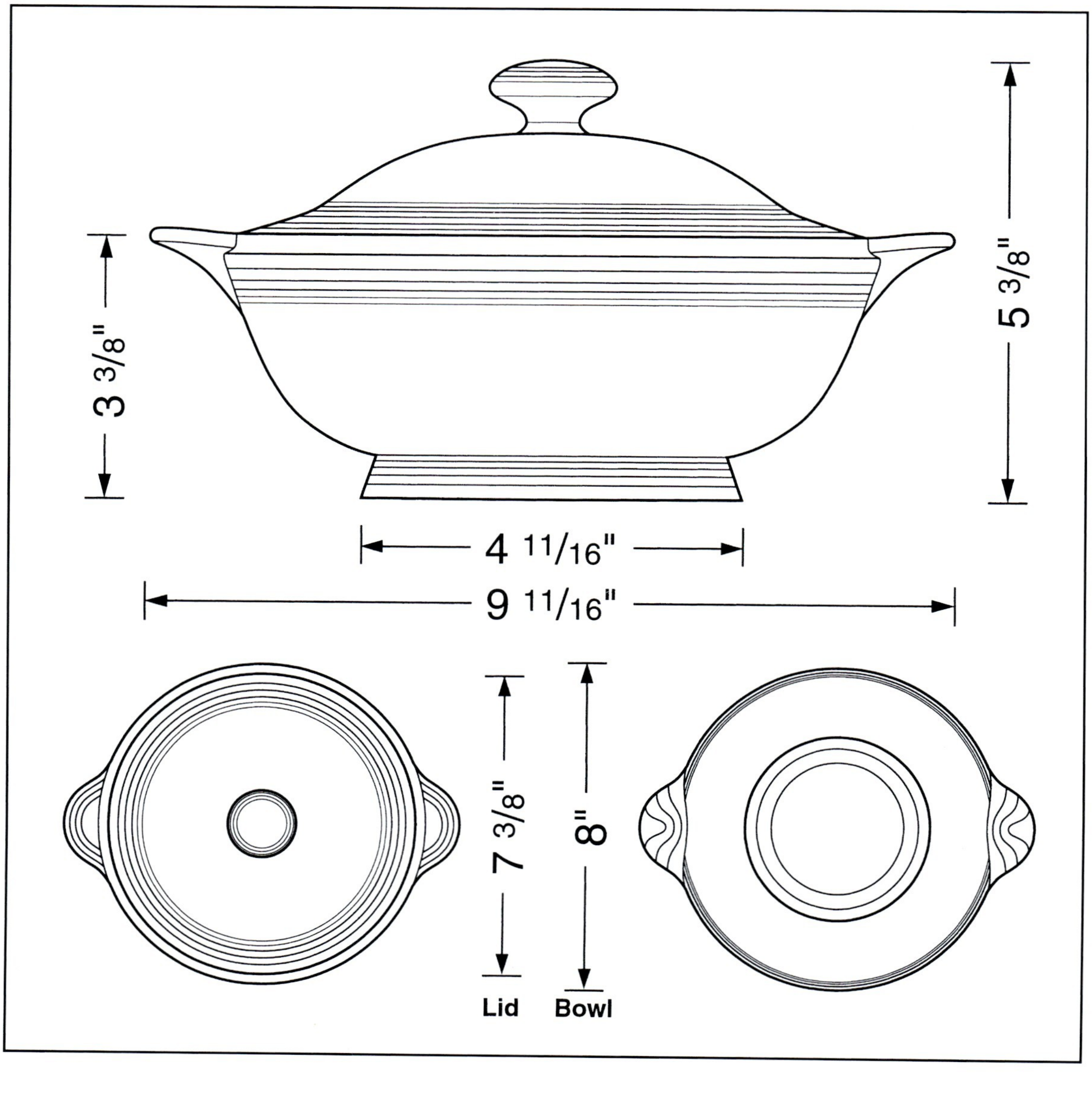

3 3/8"

5 3/8"

4 11/16"

9 11/16"

7 3/8"

8"

Lid

Bowl

Coffee Mug

This replacement for the Tom and Jerry mug was much easier to produce with its straight sides and simple ring handle. Made in the three Ironstone colors as well as Amberstone brown, this piece is so hard to find that some collectors don't believe they exist. Made like most cup-shaped objects, by jiggering, the mug was not marked.

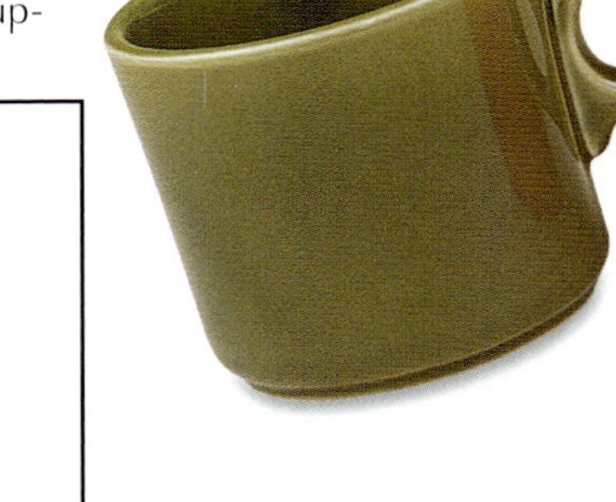

Fiesta Ironstone Coffee Mug	
Modeling Date	May 1967
Model Number	2948
Revisions	None
Production Began	May 1967*
Discontinued	December 1972*
Length of Production[1]	5.6 Years*
Colors: Amberstone Brown, Antique Gold, Mango Red, Turf Green	

*Estimate

[1]Includes Amberstone production

Fiesta Ironstone coffee mugs. $28-33.

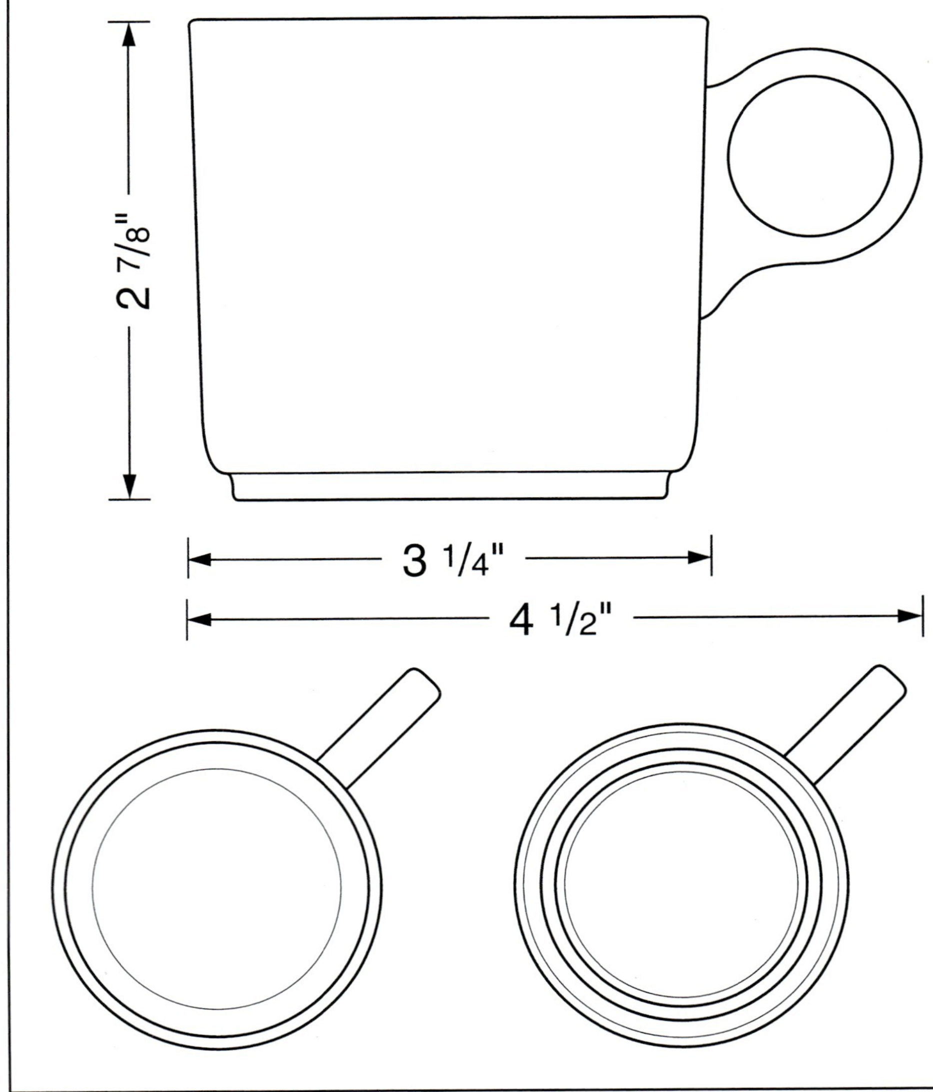

Fiesta Ironstone coffee server.
$79-89.

Coffee Server

The standard Fiesta coffeepot was returned to the line for Amberstone and it was also used for Fiesta Ironstone. A new knob for the lid was all that was needed to bring it into line with the other restyled pieces. The inscribed Fiesta logo was removed. This is another piece made only in brown and gold. Their scarcity is reflected in the relatively higher price compared to other Ironstone items.

Fiesta Ironstone Coffee Server

Modeling Date	April 1967
Model Number	2941[1]
Revisions	None
Production Began	May 1967*
Discontinued	December 1972*
Length of Production[2]	5.6 Years*

Colors: Amberstone Brown, Antique Gold

*Estimate

[1]Knob only, lid and coffee pot from original Fiesta line

[2]Includes Amberstone production

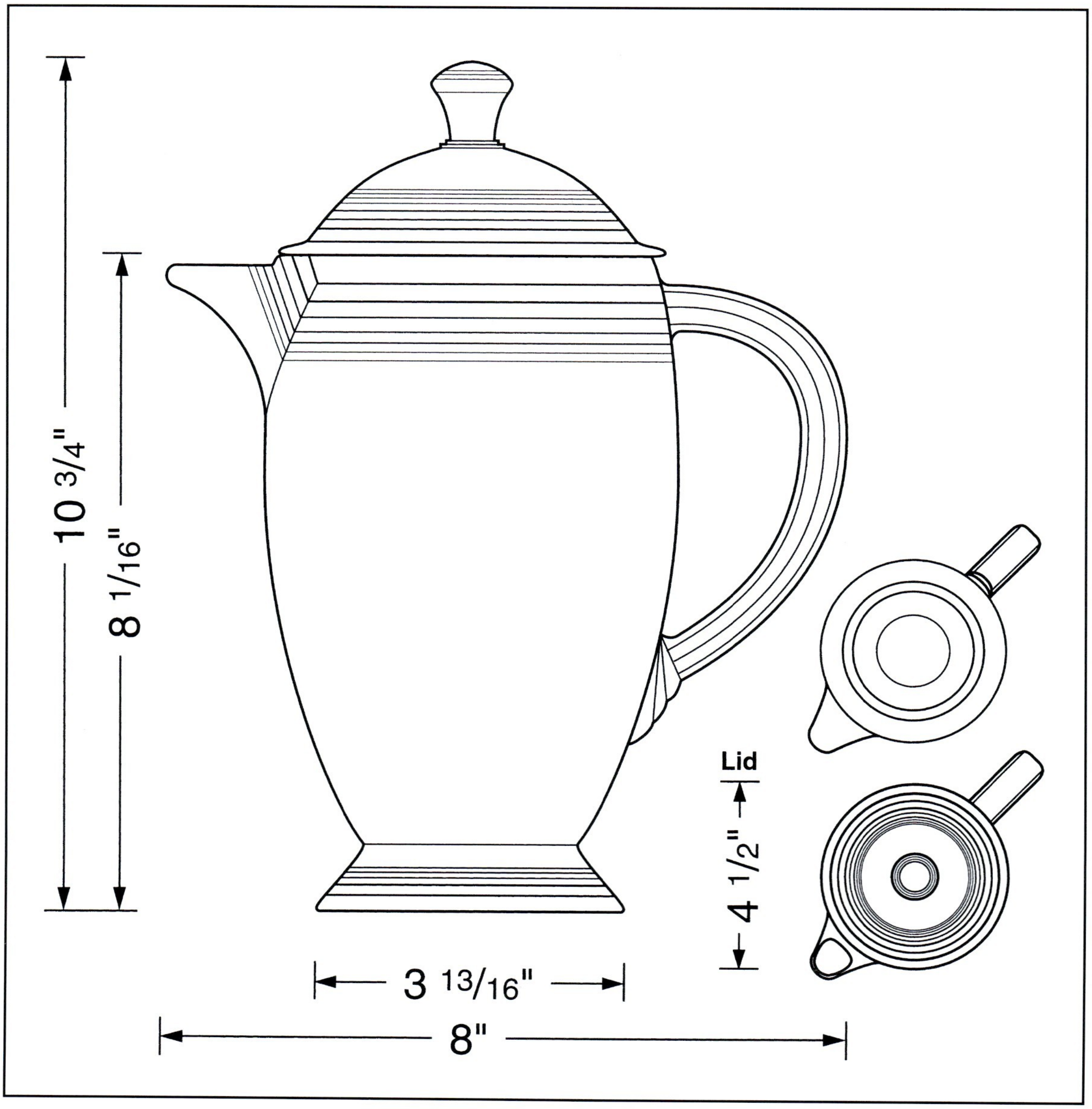

10 3/4"
8 1/16"
Lid
4 1/2"
3 13/16"
8"

Cream

A simple change of handles, from Fiesta's familiar ring to a "C-shaped" partial ring, completed the transformation to make the creamer part of the new line. The same body that had been used for Fiesta since 1936 was unchanged except for the removal of the impressed mark. The creamer was slip cast with a hand-applied handle. There are no variations of the Ironstone model.

Fiesta Ironstone Cream

Modeling Date	March 1967
Model Number	2933[1]
Revisions	None
Production Began	May 1967*
Discontinued	December 1972*
Length of Production[2]	5.6 Years*

Colors: Amberstone Brown, Antique Gold, Mango Red, Turf Green

*Estimate

[1]Handle only, used on cream body from original Fiesta line

[2]Includes Amberstone production

Fiesta Ironstone creams. $11-12.

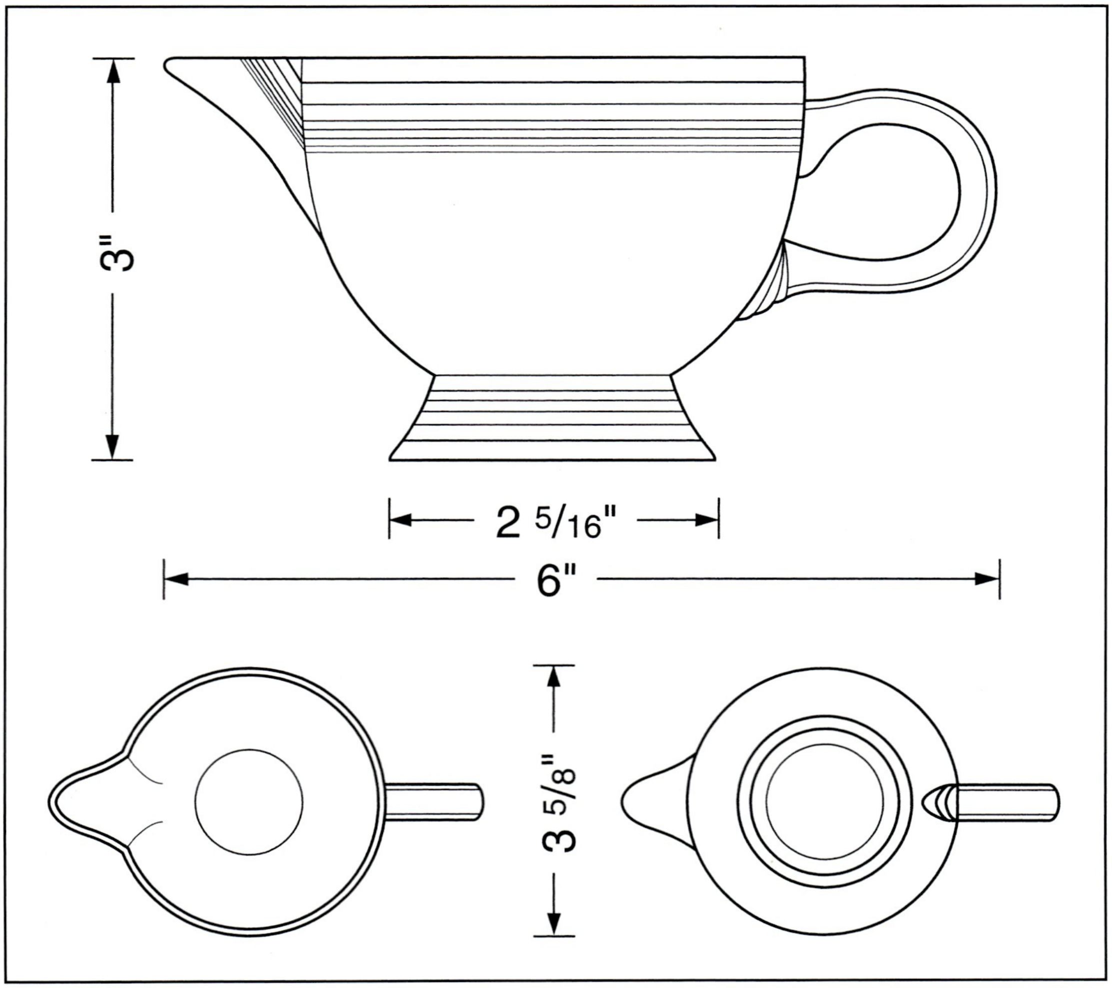

3"

2 5/16"

6"

3 5/8"

Cup and Saucer

Again, a handle change was the only difference between Fiesta Ironstone teacups and those used for the original line. There had been a shape change in the early 1960s. The inside rings were removed and the foot was shortened and no longer required hand turning to achieve its shape. This revised cup body was, of course, jiggered and was used until the end of Ironstone production in 1973.

The C-shaped handle was similar to the one on the new cream and can sometimes be found on cups in the colors of the 1960s. These were made during Amberstone production and should have received the brown glaze. See the Amberstone part of the *Decals and Decoration* section for more information on Amberstone oddities and errors.

The saucer was also revised in the early Sixties and was the same shape used for Fiesta Ironstone. There is a slight difference on the bottom that can be used to distinguish the two lines. Saucers from the original line, made after 1960, have two thick rings just under the rim. Fiesta Ironstone (and Amberstone) saucers have two thin rings in the same place.

Cups and saucers are the easiest items to find from the Ironstone line with red ones commanding a higher price. Red saucers from either the original line or Fiesta Ironstone may accompany red teacups and are usually valued the same. Not so for Ironstone saucers in green and gold, which are probably the most inexpensive items of vintage Fiesta available.

Fiesta Ironstone cups, saucers. $9-10, $3-4.

Fiesta Ironstone Cup and Saucer

Modeling Date	March 1967
Model Number	2932[1]
Revision	April 1967, 2940[2]
Production Began	May 1967*
Discontinued	December 1972*
Length of Production[3]	5.6 Years*

Colors: Amberstone Brown[4], Antique Gold[5], Mango Red, Turf Green

*Estimate

[1]Handle only, first model not produced

[2]Handle only, cup body and saucer from original Fiesta line

[3]Includes Amberstone production

[4]With stamped decoration in black

[5]Casualstone saucers have stamped decoration in brown

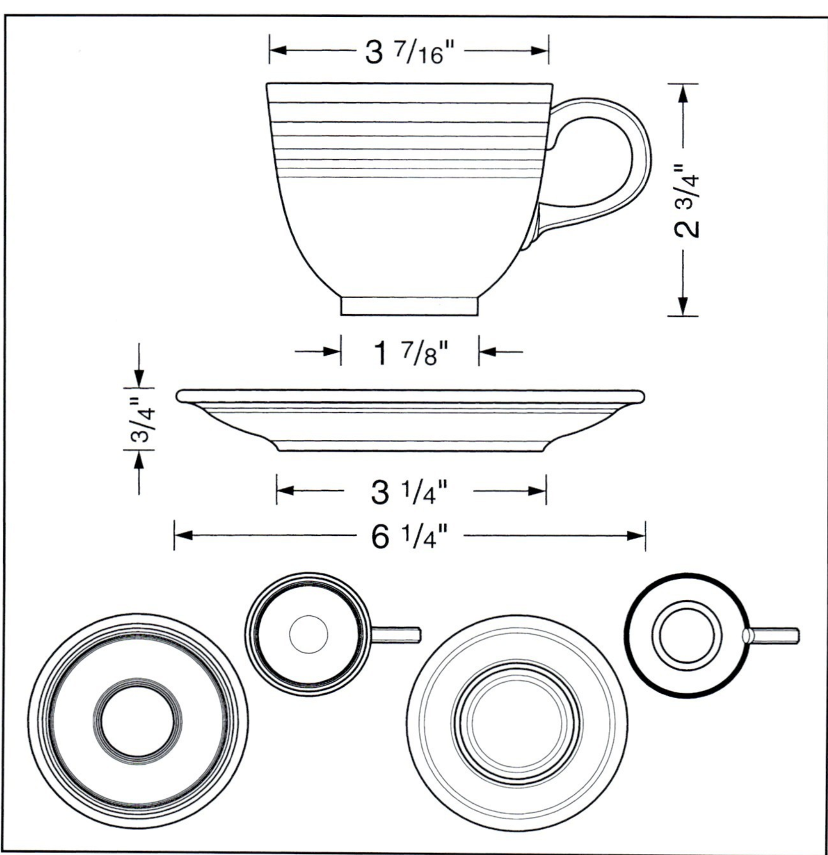

Disc Water Jug

The only change to the familiar disc water pitcher was the removal of the Fiesta logo. This is another item produced in only two colors, Amberstone brown and antique gold.

Fiesta Ironstone Water Jug

Modeling Date	April 1938
Model Number	1088[1]
Revisions	None
Production Began	May 1967*
Discontinued	December 1972*
Length of Production[2]	5.6 Years*

Colors: Amberstone Brown, Antique Gold

*Estimate

[1]Impressed mark removed from original design

[2]Includes Amberstone production

Fiesta Ironstone disc water jug. $62-67.

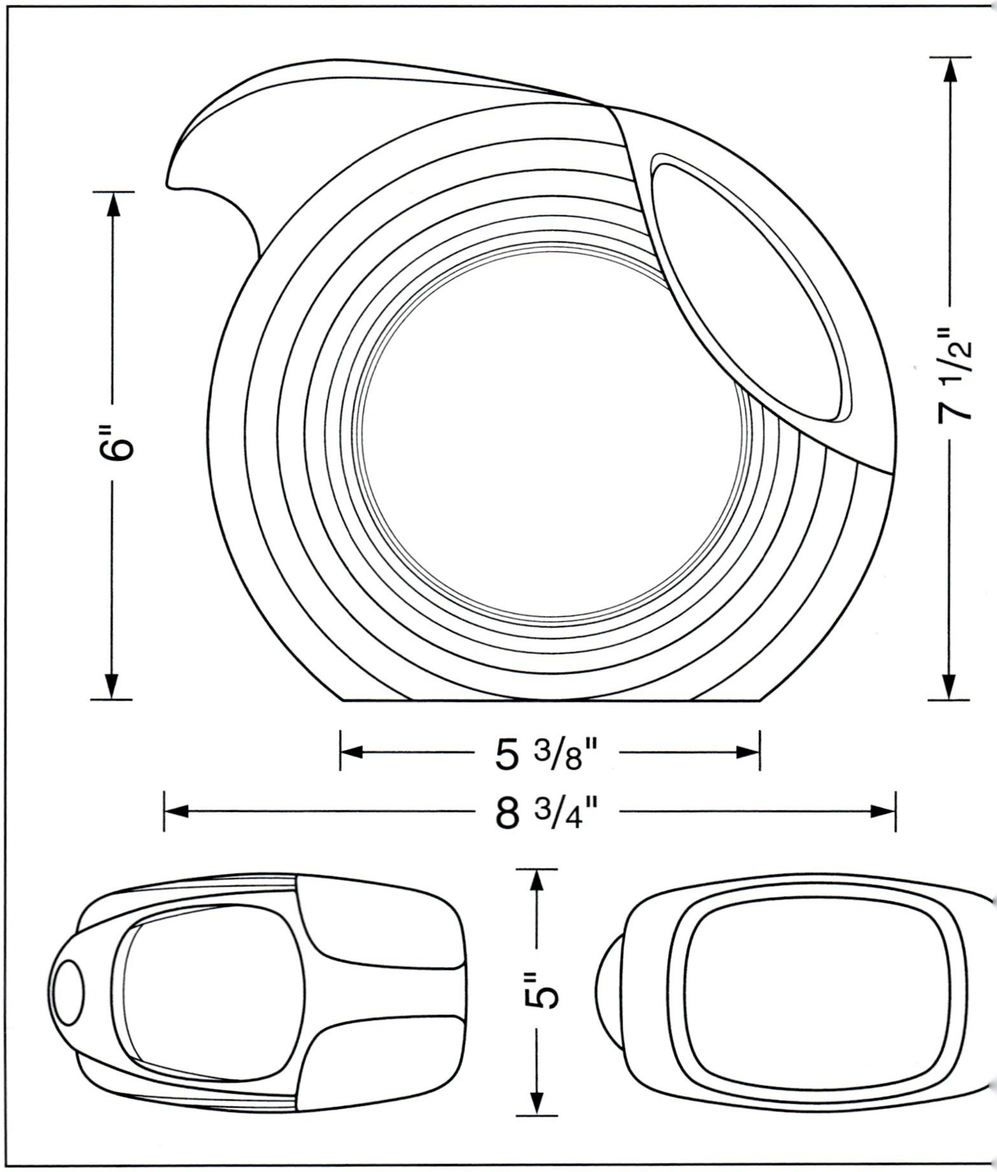

6"

7 1/2"

5 3/8"

8 3/4"

5"

Fiesta Ironstone 10" dinner plates. $12-13.

10" Dinner Plate

The standard Fiesta ten inch plate was revised for Amberstone. It was made slightly deeper by raising the rim one-eighth inch. The dinner plate was revised again for Fiesta Ironstone, but it was only a cosmetic change of the bottom. The two thin rings under the rim were removed. This created two inches of smooth surface that is the easiest way to tell red Ironstone plates from red plates of the original line.

Some 10" Ironstone plates received the "Genuine Fiesta" backstamp. They weren't supposed to, but human nature being what it is some workers may have continued in a "business as usual" mode in spite of the change in the marking policy. The marked plates while a curiosity are not valued any higher than unmarked ones.

As with most items in the Ironstone line, antique gold plates are the most available, with turf green ones not far behind. Red plates are more difficult to find, probably because those who don't know how to tell the difference often sell them as plates from the original line. Gold colored plates made for Casualstone will have the brown stamped design.

Fiesta Ironstone Dinner Plate

Modeling Date	June 1967
Model Number	3031
Revisions	None
Production Began	June 1967*
Discontinued	December 1972*
Length of Production[1]	5.5 Years*

Colors: Amberstone Brown[2], Antique Gold[3], Mango Red, Turf Green

*Estimate

[1]Includes Amberstone production

[2]With stamped decoration in black

[3]Casualstone plates have stamped decoration in brown

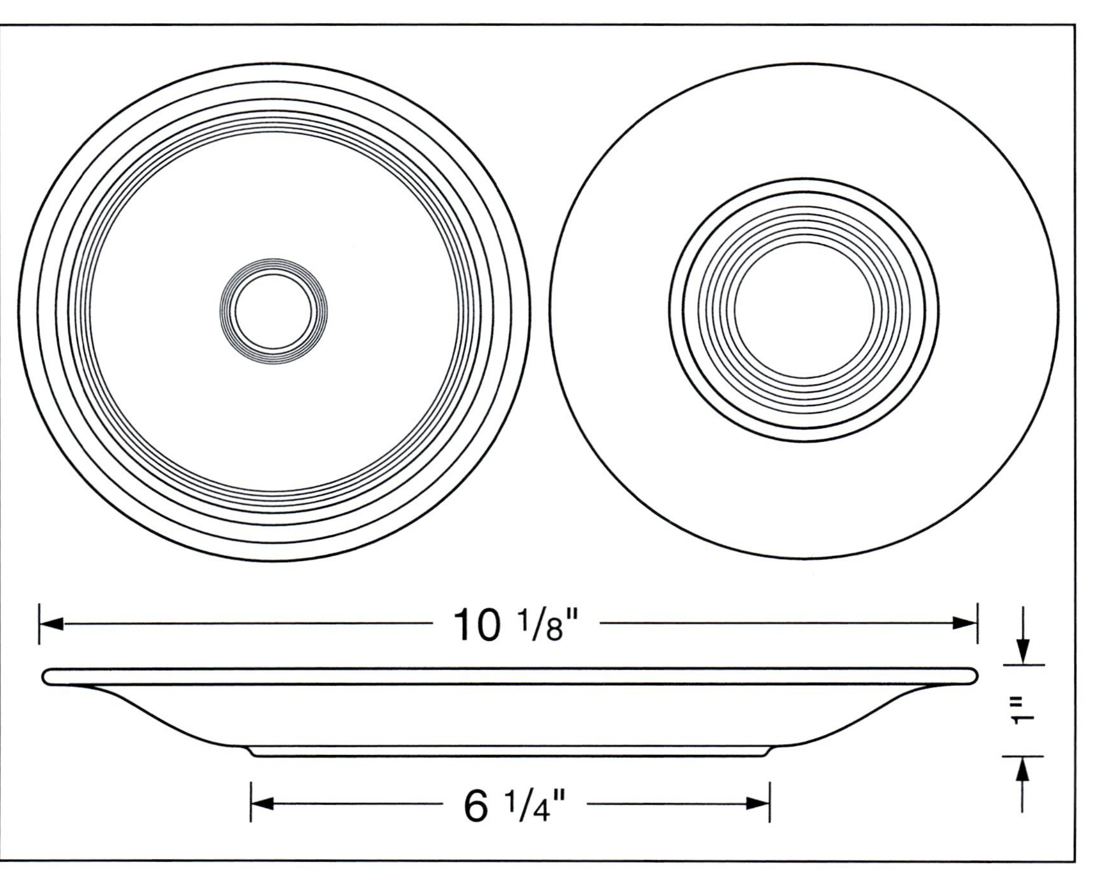

7" Salad Plate

The salad plate was carried over from the original line without much change. The two thick rings under the rim became two thin ones and that is the distinguishing sign of a Fiesta Ironstone plate. Of course that only matters when one is examining red plates, the gold and green ones are easy to recognize by the glaze color alone.

This plate was also used for Amberstone and Casualstone and is one of the harder items to find of those lines. It was not part of the "normal" place setting, but had to be purchased separately. Apparently not many were sold since they appear to be rather scarce with the decoration of the two promotional lines.

Fiesta Ironstone Salad Plate

Modeling Date	March 1935
Model Number	350[1]
Revisions	None
Production Began	June 1967*
Discontinued	December 1972*
Length of Production[2]	5.5 Years*

Colors: Amberstone Brown[3], Antique Gold[4], Mango Red, Turf Green

*Estimate

[1]Essentially unchanged from original line

[2]Includes Amberstone production

[3]With stamped decoration in black

[4]Casualstone plates have stamped decoration in brown

Top: **Fiesta Ironstone 7" salad plates. $5-6.**

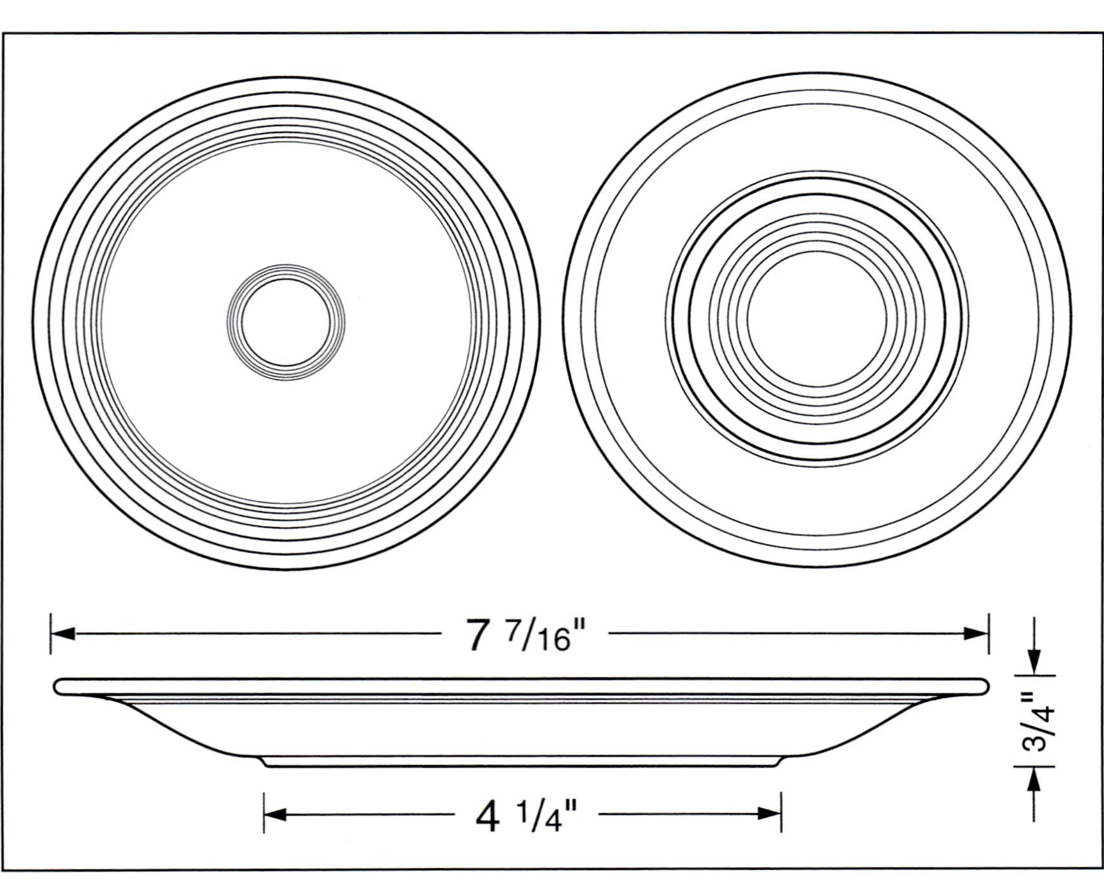

Oval Platter

On price lists for Fiesta Ironstone the oval platter is said to be 13 inches in length. On vintage Fiesta price pamphlets, it was listed as 12 inches. Some collectors believe that two sizes of platters were produced and that the piece was enlarged for the Ironstone line. This is not true. The platter was revised, but the change took place in 1947 when it was made slightly smaller. The only differences between Ironstone platters and those from the original line are the glaze colors and the fact that they do not have the Fiesta backstamp.

While the platter is fairly easy to find in Amberstone brown and in gold with the Casualstone stamped design, they are a bit harder to locate in the Ironstone colors. Red platters are especially difficult to add to a collection of Fiesta Ironstone. Once again this is most likely due to the difficulty distinguishing them from those of the vintage line.

Fiesta Ironstone Oval Platter	
Modeling Date	January 1947
Model Number	2043[1]
Revisions	None
Production Began	June 1967*
Discontinued	December 1972*
Length of Production[2]	5.5 Years*

Colors: Amberstone Brown[3], Antique Gold[4], Mango Red, Turf Green

*Estimate

[1]Essentially unchanged from 1947 revision

[2]Includes Amberstone production

[3]With stamped decoration in black

[4]Casualstone platters have stamped decoration in brown

Fiesta Ironstone oval platters. $25-28.

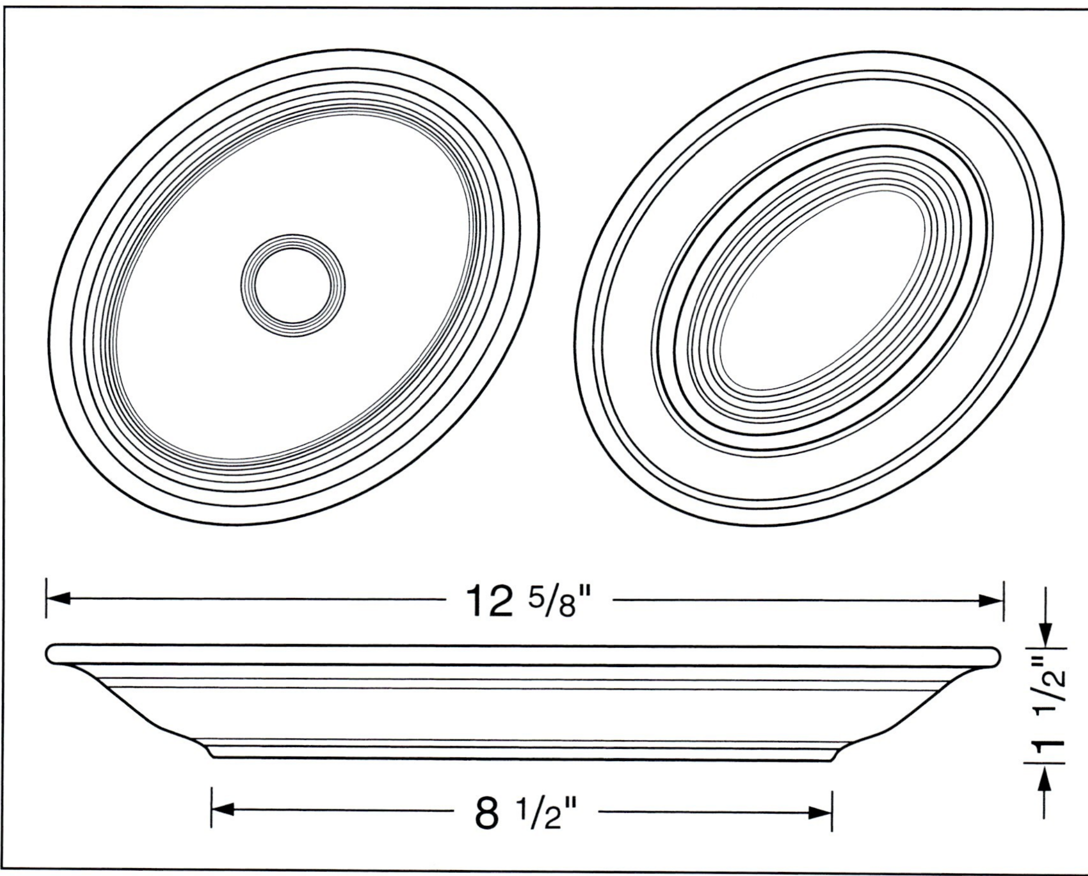

Sauce Boat

Here's another item that was carried over from the original line unchanged except for the removal of the inscribed mark. They were made in the three Ironstone colors and are not that easy to find.

Fiesta Ironstone Sauce Boat

Modeling Date	April 1937
Model Number	801[1]
Revisions	None
Production Began	June 1967*
Discontinued	December 1972*
Length of Production[1]	5.5 Years*

Colors: Amberstone Brown, Antique Gold, Mango Red, Turf Green

*Estimate

[1]Impressed mark removed

[2]Includes Amberstone production

Fiesta Ironstone sauce boats. $32-35.

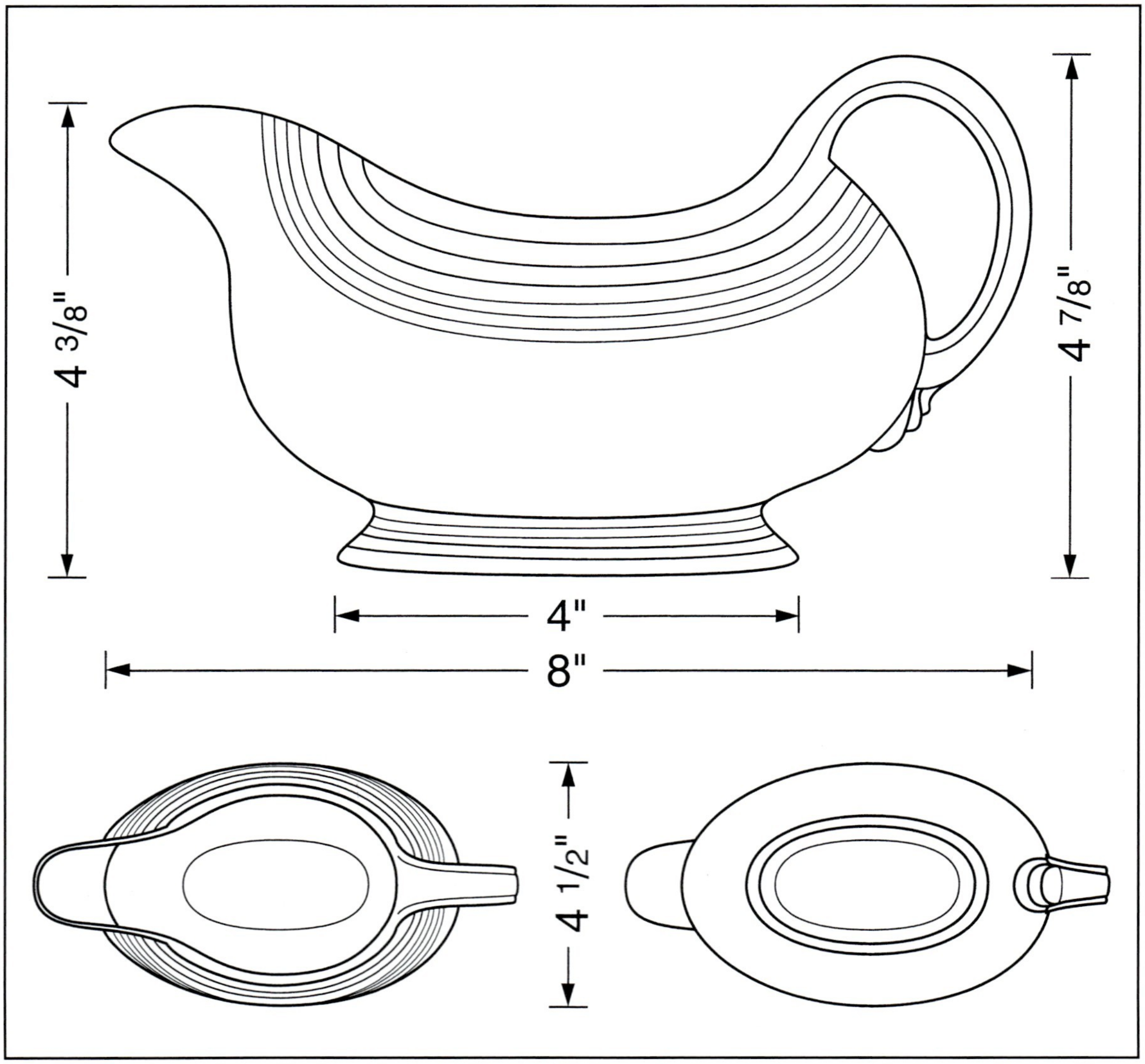

4 3/8"

4 7/8"

4"

8"

4 1/2"

Sauce Boat Stand

Many collectors wish this piece had been part of the original line. The demand for them in red has caused the sauce boat stand in that color to be valued at five times those found in green and gold. Made on the ram press like the larger platter, these mini versions are not that easy to find. The gold ones seem to turn up more often than the other two colors.

Fiesta Ironstone Sauce Boat Stand	
Modeling Date	March 1967
Model Number	2936
Revisions	None
Production Began	May 1967*
Discontinued	December 1972*
Length of Production[1]	5.6 Years*
Colors: Amberstone Brown, Antique Gold, Mango Red, Turf Green	
*Estimate	
[1]Includes Amberstone production	

Fiesta Ironstone sauce boat stands. Mango Red: $165-205. Other colors: $55-74.

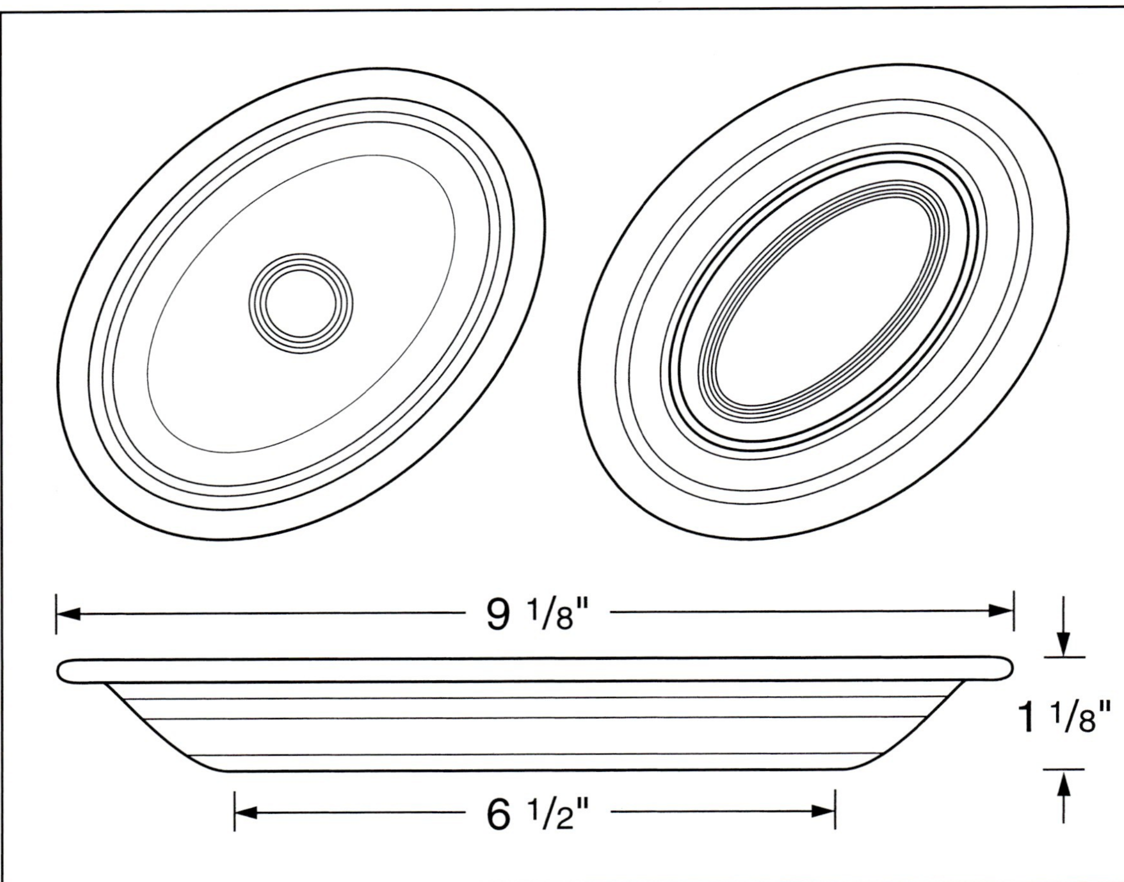

Salt & Pepper Shakers

Shakers in the original line had seven holes in a hexagonal pattern. Salt shakers had larger holes than pepper shakers and the pattern of holes was slightly larger, too. Starting with the shakers made for Amberstone, HLC changed the design so that both shakers had holes the same size, but pepper shakers lost their center hole. This design was continued with Fiesta Ironstone.

Shakers are reasonably easy to find, but like many Fiesta Ironstone items, the red ones are more difficult to locate than the other colors.

Fiesta Ironstone Salt & Pepper Shakers	
Modeling Date	August 1937
Model Number	903[1]
Revisions	None
Production Began	May 1967*
Discontinued	December 1972*
Length of Production[1]	5.6 Years*

Colors: Amberstone Brown, Antique Gold, Mango Red, Turf Green

*Estimate

[1]Essentially unchanged from 1937 revision

[2]Includes Amberstone production

Fiesta Ironstone salt and pepper shakers. $13-14 pair.

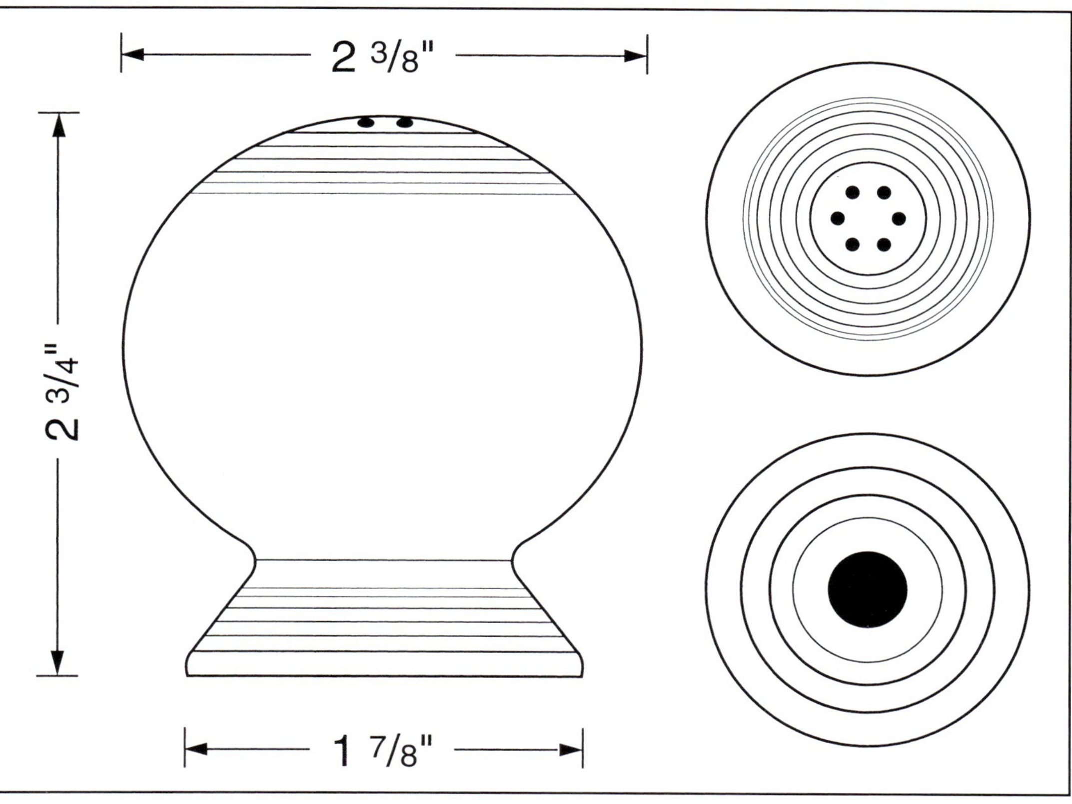

Covered Sugar

After a brief period during the first year of production when they were made by slip casting, Fiesta sugar bowls were made on a jigger machine for more than thirty years. They had a hand-turned foot and hand-applied handles. For Amberstone a new sugar was modeled that was similar to the older shape, but didn't require as much work to produce. A cover with a smooth, rounded knob was made for the new model. This jiggered sugar was in production for approximately two years and only in the Amberstone glaze. It had a rounded bottom inside the bowl like almost all vintage sugars in the original line.

In January 1969 a slip cast version that was apparently less labor intensive to make was designed. It was used throughout the years that Fiesta Ironstone was in production. The slip cast sugar featured a flat inside bottom and can also be found in Amberstone's brown glaze.

Sugar bowls and creamers are fairly easy to find in all three Ironstone colors. For years some collectors believed that there were egg cups in the Fiesta Ironstone glazes. Our research has not shown this to be true. More than likely the items sold as Fiesta Ironstone egg cups were sugar bowls missing their lids.

Fiesta Ironstone Covered Sugar

Modeling Date	March 1967
Model Number	2930[1]
Revisions	January 1969, 3047[2]
Production Began	May 1967*
Discontinued	December 1972*
Length of Production[3]	5.6 Years*

Colors: Amberstone Brown, Antique Gold, Mango Red, Turf Green

*Estimate

[1]Jiggered, produced in Amberstone glaze only

[2]Revised for slip casting

[3]Includes Amberstone production

Fiesta Ironstone covered sugars. $15-16.

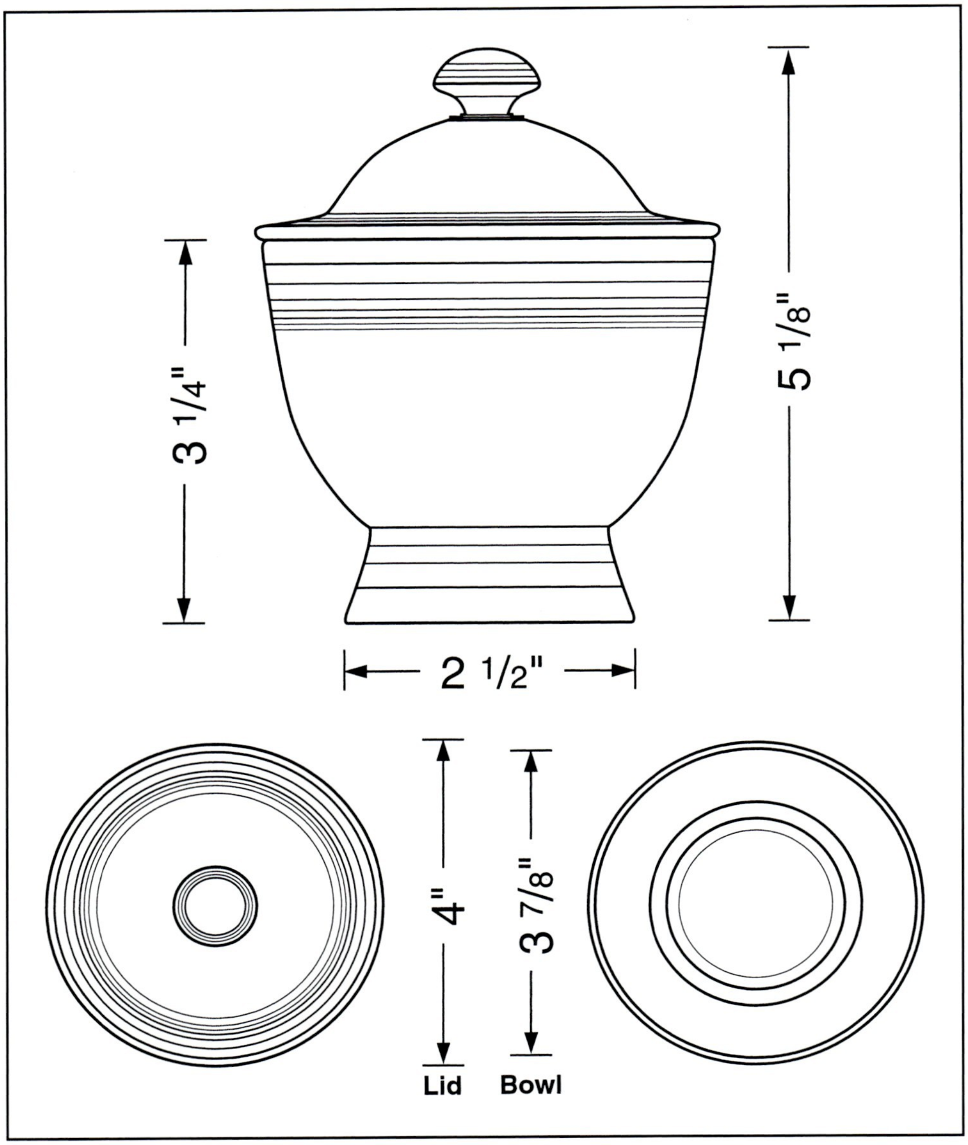

5 1/8"
3 1/4"
2 1/2"
4"
3 7/8"
Lid Bowl

Tea Server

The medium teapot used in the original line since 1937 was also used with Amberstone and Fiesta Ironstone. To fit in, it required a change in the lid and the removal of the impressed mark. The original medium teapot lid was one piece. In order to use the smooth, rounded knob featured on other Ironstone pieces a new lid and a knob had to be made for the teapot.

The teapot is another item made only in Amberstone brown and antique gold. In the gold glaze it was used for both Fiesta Ironstone and Casualstone. Like the coffeepot, these pieces are somewhat difficult to find and usually are among the more costly items to add to a collection.

Fiesta Ironstone Tea Server

Modeling Date	May 1967
Model Number	2947[1]
Revisions	None
Production Began	May 1967*
Discontinued	December 1972*
Length of Production[2]	5.6 Years*

Colors: Amberstone Brown, Antique Gold

*Estimate

[1]Lid and knob only, used on medium teapot from original Fiesta line

[2]Includes Amberstone production

Fiesta Ironstone tea server. $50-59.

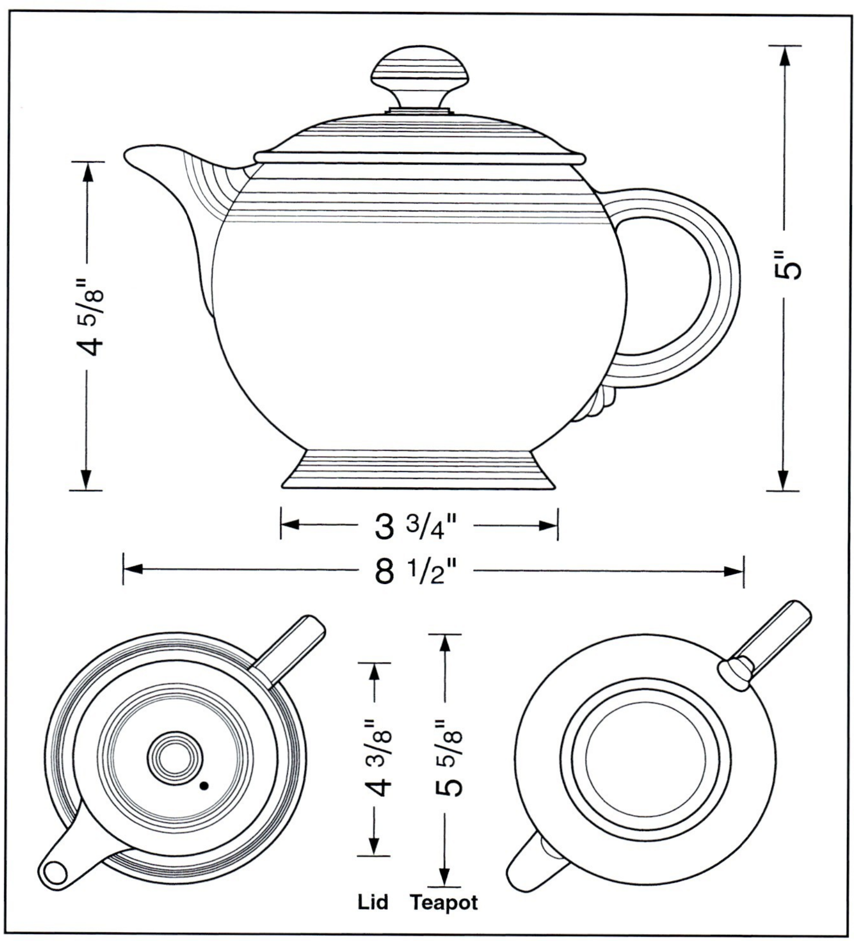

Fiesta Red vs. Fiesta Ironstone Red

One question frequently asked by new collectors is: "How can I tell the difference between original red Fiesta pieces and those made in red for Fiesta Ironstone?" Here's the answer, in a side-by-side comparison of easily confused pieces.

10" plate - Original red dinner plates have two thick rings under the rim. Ironstone red dinner plates have no rings under the rim.

7" plate - Original red salad plates have two thick rings under the rim. Ironstone red salad plates have two thin rings under the rim.

Teacup - Original red cups have the ring handle. Ironstone red cups have a C-shaped handle.

Saucer - Original red saucers have one or two thick rings under the rim. Ironstone red saucers have two thin rings under the rim.

Creamer - Original red creams have the ring handle. Ironstone red creams have a C-shaped handle.

Oval platter - This is the tough one. There were two sizes of red platters in the original line. The first one measures 12-3/4" in length, the second one is 12-1/2". Both should have the "Genuine Fiesta" backstamp. Ironstone red platters are simply unmarked versions of the 12-1/2" platter.

Sauce boat - Original red sauce boats have an impressed mark on the bottom. Ironstone red sauce boats are not marked.

Salt and Pepper shakers - Original red shakers have seven holes, the holes in the salt shaker are larger. Ironstone red shakers have the same size holes, but the pepper has only six, not seven like the salt. It's easier to tell the difference if the shakers are purchased in pairs.

Chapter 5

Post-1986 Fiesta

What's Old Is New Again

Changing times in America and the world marketplace caused the thirteen-year gap in Fiesta production. By January 1, 1973, the day HLC officially retired Fiesta, the shape was considered by many to be "old" and no longer competitive in the market place. The antique gold and turf green colors of Fiesta Ironstone was no longer in vogue and had fallen out of favor with consumers. Foreign competition flooded the market with cheaper products, virtually shutting down domestic pottery productions. It was during this time that many US china companies folded.

By 1986 the baby boomers were now adults setting up homes and raising families. They created many new trends in the market place. Americans adopted a more casual life style. Entertaining more informally in their homes, consumers wanted dinnerware with a fresh look.

Buying the rights in the early 1980s from Russel Wright's family, Bloomingdales began a project to reproduce Russel Wright China. Stuebenville, the original producers of Russel Wright China and no longer in business, was not an option so Bloomingdales approached HLC with their project idea. By 1985 HLC logs show that models of some pieces of the Russel Wright China were under development, but due to the large costs of developing and producing an exclusive line of china for Bloomingdales the Russel Wright China never went into production. Instead recognizing the new market trends, HLC suggested the reintroduction of Fiesta and offered Bloomingdales the opportunity to introduce the new Fiesta line. Fiesta officially made its come back on February 28, 1986. Shortly after is reintroduction, Jonathan Parry received word from Bloomingdales that for the first time in Bloomingdale's history a housewares pattern was registered by three people as their choice in the Bridal Registry. That choice: Fiesta. What's old is new again and Fiesta keeps making history.

The Post-'86 Colors

In 1986 while recognizing changing tastes in the consumer markets, the folks at Homer Laughlin believed the time was right to add Fiesta back into the line up because of it's classic art deco design and "retro" appeal. Much of the dinnerware during this time lacked color and many of the selections produced were white or decorated with pale designs. While appropriate for formal table settings, casual dining sets went lacking. Fiesta with its strong lines and zesty colors filled the need of shoppers and quickly became popular once again.

Choosing colors that had strong market appeal throughout the fashion and housewares industry as well as favored by the public, the first post-'86 colors included white, black, rose, apricot (discontinued in 1998), cobalt blue, yellow and gray. HLC's art director, Jonathan Parry, wanted white, black, and gray as neutral colors within the line, but the HLC management believing that Fiesta equates with "color" over ruled and gray was dropped from the initial color group until its introduction in 1998. HLC added turquoise in 1988, periwinkle blue in 1989, sea mist green in 1991, and persimmon in 1995. In making the final selections, HLC also considered what colors were practical for mass production. There has never been formal test marketing of new hues. After the production colors were initially selected, a list of possible names for each color was complied by the art and sales department. This list was submitted to the CEO's wife, Mrs. Joseph Wells III, who then chose the final name for each new color and continues that tradition today with each addition to the line.

Colors fall in and out of favor with consumers as fashion and homeware color preferences change. For instance, cobalt blue is now more in favor than in past years. Always popular in Midwest markets, it's now popular from coast to coast. Apricot fell out of favor with shoppers when persimmon was introduced. Its sales dropped dramatically, the demand died out and apricot was discontinued. Black has been in limited production and at the time of this writing is expected to be discontinued by HLC. The company offered two explanations - although all Fiesta will scuff and scratch to some degree, black shows these imperfections more than other colors and that by phasing out black the factory's capability to produce other colors will increase.

Since the reintroduction of Fiesta there have been four limited edition colors - lilac (1993-1995), sapphire (1997), chartreuse (1997-1999) and juniper (2000-2001). For HLC, it was a marketing decision to produce certain colors over a restricted time period. By announcing a new limited edition color ahead of production, shoppers can then plan to update their present set of dishes. The understanding is that if they like the new color, it is with the knowledge that there is a limited window of opportunity to make their purchases. By taking limited edition colors in and out of production while maintaining a stable "base" line, consumers can add extra pieces to their present set for a fresh new look. The popularity of this idea can be seen by the surge in department store sales when a new limited edition color is introduced. Another more basic reason for a limited run color is production line space at the factory. HLC simply can't put a new color in without taking another color out.

The discontinuation of lilac, the number one selling color in Dayton Hudson stores at the time, brought a storm of protest to HLC's doorstep. When the stores insisted that lilac be continued, HLC refused to bring it back. HLC optimistically told the store buyers the next limited edition color would be "as hot" as lilac and they were right. Chartreuse was an instant hit and sold well for it's entire two-year run. Today, collectors so highly prize lilac that prices approach those found in vintage ware in many items. Sapphire was produced as a Bloomingdale's exclusive for only one year and is accordingly seen by many as a color that will be of greater value in coming years due to its shorter run. Although HLC's only intention for reintroducing Fiesta was to produce a fine quality dinnerware for everyday casual dinning, post-'86 Fiesta continues to grow in popularity with collectors around the world.

Vintage Fiesta or Post-'86?

A frequently asked question by collectors just starting out is "How can one differentiate between the vintage and the post-'86 Fiesta?" Many colors and shapes of the new ware are close in appearance to the vintage and can confuse new and seasoned collectors alike. Being aware of the differences can save a buyer from spending hundreds of dollars for an item sold at Bloomingdale's for fewer than forty dollars and a seller the embarrassment of advertising a post-86 piece as vintage. Most dealers are honest and will not try to swindle their customers and it's essential for a successful dealer to maintain a good reputation. However, with Fiesta becoming a highly prized collectable, people interested in making a quick buck can easily dupe a collector who is unaware of the differences between the old and the new.

Vintage Fiesta was made from semi-vitrified clay that is different from the vitrified clay used in the today's production. Semi-vitrified clay is more porous making the finished product lighter and more fragile. Because it shrinks more during the firing process, new ware is slightly smaller than the old products made from semi-vitrified material. One method to determine the difference between a vintage piece and its post-'86 counterpart made from an original mold is to measure the item. For example, a 10" vintage vase will be a little bit taller than its new counterpart made from the same mold.

Vintage ware is made from semi-vitrified clay that is 14 percent more absorbent than vitrified clay and hence less structurally dense. Though not to recommend this method (it's not sanitary or tasty), one way to determine the authenticity of a vintage piece that will also get you noticed in an antique shop is turn the piece over and place your tongue on the unglazed area of its foot. If your tongue sticks a bit – it's vintage. It is an odd but decisive way to tell if a piece is old Fiesta.

The Fiesta designs have changed through the years. Knowing when a certain piece was produced is also a good way to know if the article could possibly be vintage. Obviously a post-86 millennium vase is not vintage, but a carafe with a lid would be old. Small yet noticeable changes in a piece can give clues to dating an item.

For example, by looking inside a vintage disk pitcher where the top of the handle meets the body you will notice a small dimple - in the new version the dimple is much bigger. A redesigned post-86 demitasse cup as no pedestal foot unlike its vintage counterpart that clearly "stands proud."

If you're trying to tell if a round candle holder is vintage, look inside the bulb. Vintage holders were dipped and are glazed inside and out. The post-86 round candle holders are sprayed with color and the interiors are usually not fully glazed.

When distinguishing between vintage and post-'86 plates, using only measurements as a guide may be confusing. Although standardized within the line, vintage plates were not always truly uniform in size. One quick way to determine if a plate is vintage or post-86 is to check the base of the plate for sagger pin marks. Vintage plates have a glazed foot so sagger pins were used

Chartreuse Coffeepot - Twenty four chartreuse coffee pots were produced by HLC and auctioned off to benefit the East Liverpool High School Alumni Association. These numbered coffee pots are highly sought after by collectors. Although unseen, in this photo the coffeepot shown has no ELHSAA marking or number on the bottom.

to prevent the glaze from touching other pieces or the sides of the kiln, thus leaving sagger pin marks. Post-'86 plates have a dry foot so they won't have pin marks. Back stamps are different for the vintage and post-86 plates and can also be used to date a plate, but remember that not all vintage pieces including plates were marked.

Since the introduction of post-'86 chartreuse, HLC produces all remakes of vintage Fiesta pieces with a small, embossed "H" on the base of each piece. These items include: the bud vase, 10" medium vase, disk pitcher, juice disk pitcher, salt and pepper shakers, gravy boat, tripod candle holder, round candlestick holder, figure-8 tray with cream and sugar bowl, individual creamer, and the individual sugar bowl excluding the lid (the new individual sugar bowl is made from the vintage marmalade mold - the lid was remodeled to remove the notch). Any piece that was remodeled for production purposes and not produced using the original mold is excluded.

On a final note, the absolute best way to know if any piece is post-'86 or vintage is to know the colors of each era. Doing a bit of homework before shopping can save money, embarrassment, and anguish as you build your collection.

Coffee Server, 36 ounces (Item 493) - Redesigned a month after its introduction at Bloomingdales, the post-'86 coffee server resembling its vintage counterpart is a highly collectable and prized piece. According to HLC, the redesign was necessary because the modern vitrified clay was not compatible with the vintage design. During the firing process, vitrified clay becomes semi-liquid and would collapse on itself in the kiln. The contoured top adds stability to the design, thus preventing the coffee server from warping. The flared finial replaced the Ironstone knob. The pictured coffee server is shown in Fiesta white.

Teapot, 44 ounces (Item 496) - Like the coffee server, the teapot (shown in black) had design changes early on in production. Easy to differentiate from the vintage teapot due to its notable styling, the restyled version was changed after its introduction due to production problems. The very early version, sporting the Ironstone knob, is difficult to find as only very small quantities were produced. The new post-'86 teapot has the flared finial, replacing the Ironstone knob. No records exist to indicate the exact date this change took place.

Presentation Bowl (Item 437) - First referred to as a "tri-footed fruit bowl" in an HLC design log, the presentation bowl is a dazzling piece with its classic Art Deco lines. Six prototypes were modeled before the final design was selected. Shown in persimmon, it measures 11 5/8" across and 2 5/8" tall. The presentation bowl was produced in the coveted raspberry glaze to commemorate the 500-millionth piece of Fiesta produced. This design was produced in all the 1997 colors and was officially retired in 1999. Exclusive in the chartreuse color to the Dayton-Hudson-Marshall Fields stores and in black through the HLC Outlet, these are a collector's favorite.

Bouillon Cup, 6 3/4 ounces (Item 450) - Not part of the original Fiesta line, it was added shortly after its reintroduction into the market. This is a picture of a Rose Bouillon cup.

Cereal Bowl, 5 5/8″ diameter (Item 460) - The cereal bowl holds 14 1/2 ounces and is shown here in chartreuse. The sapphire cereal bowl was an exclusive item at Bloomingdales.

Stacking Cereal Bowl (Item 472) - The chartreuse stacking cereal bowls were a Bloomingdales exclusive. The bowl measures 6 1/2".

Fruit Bowl, 5-3/8″ diameter (Item 459) - Shown in turquoise.

Mixing Bowl – Small, 7 1/2″ 48 ounces (Item 421) - Shown in gray. Medium, 8 1/2″ 64 ounces (Item 422) - Shown in persimmon. Large, 9 1/2″ 70 ounces (Item 482) - Shown in yellow. This popular set is also referred to as nesting bowls. Many collectors have hoped that lids for the bowls and in responding to their customers, HLC has worked on a machine that would fashion lids, but to date the project has been put hold.

Pedestal Bowl, 9 7/8" 64 ounces (Item 765) - When first introduced, the chartreuse version was an exclusive at Macy's Department Stores. HLC logs document four revisions to the base before it was put into production in 1998. It is shown in gray.

Rim Soup Bowl, 9" (Item 451) - Shown in yellow, it is a smaller version of the 12" Fiesta pasta bowl.

Rim Soup Bowl, 12" (Item 462) - This handsomely designed soup bowl gracefully displays strong geometric rings around its top edge. It's also known as a pasta bowl and is shown in chartreuse.

Tripod Bowl, (Item 420) - Not to be confused with the tripod candle holder (also known as the pyramid candlestick holder) HLC produced this diminutive bowl in response to the popularity and rising sales of candles in the US market. Shown in cobalt with the candle that it is frequently sold with, it is a modestly priced and popular item.

Serving Bowl, 2 quart (Item 455); Serving Bowl, 8 1/4" diameter (Item 471); Soup Bowl, 6 7/8" diameter (Item 461) - The 2 quart serving bowl is shown in gray. The serving bowl is shown in white and holds 39 ounces. The soup bowl is shown in persimmon and holds 19 ounces.

Tripod Candle Holder, (Item 489) - Also called a pyramid candlestick holder, collectors raced to get their pair of chartreuse holders when first available in that limited edition color. Also pictured here in cobalt, this classic art deco stylized piece is produced from the original vintage molds. Lilac holders, an exclusive of Bloomingdales, fetch high prices in the collecting market today.

Covered Butter Dish, (Item 494) - Butter didn't always come out of a tub or squirt out of a plastic bottle. Gaining favor among collectors of all types of glass and kitchenware, covered butter dishes are more popular than ever. This butter dish is in periwinkle.

Round Candle Stick Holders, (Item 488) - Pictured here in white and rose, these are also referred to as Fiesta bulbs. The chartreuse round candle stick holders were sold as an exclusive at JCPenney stores. The lilac holders were first offered by China Specialties. This item is made from the original mold and was part of the original post-'86 lineup.

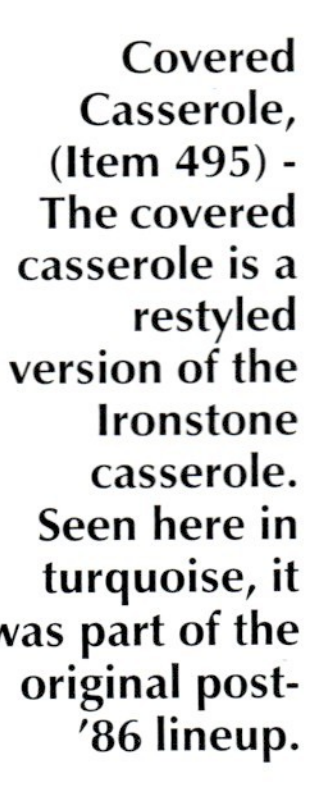

Covered Casserole, (Item 495) - The covered casserole is a restyled version of the Ironstone casserole. Seen here in turquoise, it was part of the original post-'86 lineup.

Carafe, (Item 448) - Even though the Carafe was introduced in 1996, after Lilac was discontinued, there have been a few Lilac Carafes found. Unlike the Vintage Carafe, the restyled Carafe has no lid. The type of clay used in its manufacturing also makes it much less fragile. The Sapphire Blue Carafe was sold only at Bloomingdales. This Carafe is pictured in Chartreuse.

Standard Creamer, (Item 492) - Shown in seamist, the standard creamer was made from the original vintage mold. Its classic design has appealed to collectors for years.

Clock, (Item 473) – Originally an exclusive for JCPenney in 1993 and then discontinued, it was reintroduced in 1996 and sold through general retailers. The chartreuse clocks produced for JCPenney were a fluke. The incident apparently involved the JCPenney computer not receiving data from its programmers that the clock wasn't available in chartreuse. With no chartreuse clocks in inventory their automatic replenishment system generated an order. Since JCPenney orders from HLC via an electronic data interchange, their computer sends an order to the HLC computer system without any human involvement. The HLC computer accepted the order and entered it into production. Factory personnel, believing the order was legitimate, produced and shipped over two hundred clocks in a six-month period before HLC learned of the error. The clock pictured is apricot.

After Dinner Cup with Saucer, (Item 478) - Many collectors enchanted by the small cups with unique stick handle would love to see a matching demitasse pot, but unfortunately HLC has no plans to produce one in the near future. The pictured cup and saucer, first offered by Bloomingdales and China Specialties, is in the highly sought lilac color.

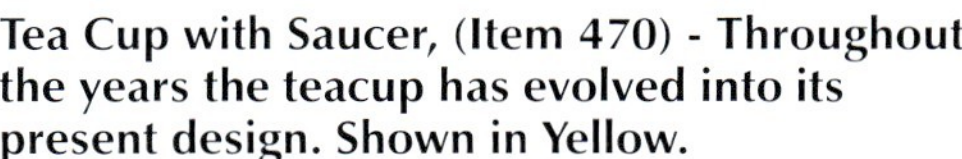

Tea Cup with Saucer, (Item 470) - Throughout the years the teacup has evolved into its present design. Shown in Yellow.

Tom and Jerry "Fiesta" Mug, (Item 453) - Although the body of the mug itself is not made from the original mold, its vintage look is not by accident. HLC logs indicate the handle for this post-'86 piece used the original Tom and Jerry mold. As with most pieces with handles, these are placed on each mug by hand. Shown in juniper.

Pedestal Mug, (Item 424) - The pedestal mug, also known as a latte mug, was HLC's response to the growing popularity of coffeehouses and exotic brews. Consumers in their twenties and early thirties have continued the trend started by their baby boomer parents of a more relaxed life style. This often includes serving guests *vente* lattes during a casual meal at home. This mug is shown in pearl gray.

Napkin Rings, (Item 469) - Shown in periwinkle. Sold in sets of four, the napkin rings are popular with many collectors. When the production of chartreuse was about to end, HLC decided to make a few hundred napkin ring sets in that color that were sold at their outlet store. They had previously been unavailable in that color and are now highly sought.

Large Disk Pitcher, (Item 484) - Made from the original vintage mold, this unrivaled art deco design is distinctively Fiesta. Through the years other manufactures have tried to imitate its sleek lines, but always fell short. Able to hold 67 1/4 ounces, it's available in all the post-'86 colors and found with many popular decal treatments as well. Shown in juniper.

Mini Disk Pitcher, (Item 475) – Essentially an individual creamer with a capacity of 4-¾ ounces, this cute miniature has found its way on to the display shelves of many collectors. Shown here in rose, it is found in all the post-'86 colors except sapphire blue. It is also been produced with a number of many popular decal applications.

Small Disk Pitcher, (Item 485) – Also known as a juice pitcher, this item is made from the original mold. Although never glazed in sapphire, it is available in all other post-'86 colors. Shown here in turquoise, the small pitcher holds 28 ounces. Used by the HLCCA for our exclusive 1930s decal series, it is also produced with other popular decals.

Welled Snack Plate, (Item 760) - Reminiscent of the 1950s hostess party plates used at countless Tupperware parties and church socials, the welled snack tray combines a hint of nostalgia and functional practicality. Shown here is the tray in turquoise and the cup in yellow. It was introduced in 1997.

Plates - 6″ Bread and Butter, (Item 463) - Shown in seamist. 7″ Salad, (Item 464) – Shown in yellow. 9″ Luncheon, (Item 465) – Shown in rose. 10″ Dinner, (Item 466) – Shown in periwinkle. Chop Plate, (Item 467) – Shown here in persimmon. Modeled after the vintage plates, post-'86 Fiesta plate molds were reconstructed making them slightly larger than the original molds to compensate for shrinkage that occurs when vitrified clay is fired. Durable and coated in a lead free glaze, post-'86 Fiesta is found not only gracing the tables of Americans' homes, but is also in popular restaurant chains and quaint cafés. The chop plate is found on the Homer Laughlin China company web site as a "signature plate," this item is 11 3/4″ in diameter.

60th Anniversary Beverage Set - Anticipating the 60th anniversary of Fiesta, factory logs indicates the modeling of this set in June 1995. When released some collectors and dealers grumbled when noticing two retired colors, sapphire and lilac, offered as set color choices. They feared the rising prices of the two then-discontinued colors would fall if HLC reversed their marketing decision not to reintroduce retired colors. Besides sapphire (shown) and lilac, the sets were also produced in turquoise, cobalt, periwinkle, persimmon, and rose. Rose is very hard to locate as only approximately three hundred sets were produced as an exclusive color for a retailer before they dropped their order. It's unknown exactly how many sapphire sets were made, but their production was limited to only 180 days.

Jumbo Cup and Saucer - The jumbo cup and saucer are not truly Fiesta. The pieces, also known as Fiesta Mates, are from HLC's restaurant line. Dipped in Fiesta glazes, they lack the overall styling of the regular Fiesta line. The sapphire blue jumbo cup and saucer shown here along with a standard teacup and saucer were made for Bloomingdales.

Sugar/Creamer/Tray Set, (Item 821) - One of the initial post-'86 pieces and made from the original mold, the sugar bowl and creamer sit on the figure-8 tray. Shown in apricot.

Oval Vegetable Bowl, (Item 409) – Introduced in late 1999, the oval vegetable bowl adds a flattering new dimension to a table setting. Shown in rose.

Relish Tray, (Item 499) - Also known as a utility tray or a corn-on-the-cob tray, this functional item has charm as well versatility. Shown in lilac.

Pizza Tray, (Item 505) - Whether ordering out or making one at home, pizza is a quick and popular meal. Thanks to a hotel customer needing a pizza tray, art director Jonathan Parry designed the Fiesta pizza tray. The hotel version of the pizza tray is produced with a clear glaze. The tray pictured is turquoise.

Sauce Boat, (Item 486) - With its classic design, the sauce boat remains in vogue with HLC customers and collectors alike. Shown here in lilac, this item is also referred to as a gravy boat or server.

Round Serving Tray, (Item 468) - Shown in chartreuse, the round serving tray is also referred to as a cake plate. It is 12" in diameter. One thousand round serving trays in sapphire blue were made and sold at the HCL outlet store around the time sapphire was an exclusive at Bloomingdales.

Goblets, (Item 429) - Home fashion trends aren't the only thing HLC notices when developing new pieces for their lineup. American's eating habits are also scrutinized and while they're becoming more health conscious, they still eat six times more ice cream than any other population in the world. These goblets are great for ice cream sundaes as well as high protein health shakes. The underside of the goblet has the letters "JG" - the initials of Joseph Geisse, the head modeler of the HLC art department. Once a new item is envisioned, a plaster model is created by the modeler after the design is on paper, test pieces are fired, and many refinements to a design might be made before the final plaster model is made. The master mold, used to make production molds, is created using the final plaster model. In this instance, the initials of the modeler stayed throughout the process all the way to production. Shown in yellow.

Two Cup Teapot, (Item 764) - Designed in 1996, the two cup teapot was initially developed for a Fiesta children's tea set that never went into production until a modified versiion was released as My First Fiesta. The two cup teapot in chartreuse was first offered as an exclusive at Profitt Stores. Shown in Periwinkle.

Rangetop Shakers, (Item 756) - Shown in periwinkle, the rangetop shakers are sturdy enough to withstand the wear and tear of everyday use and with many colors to choose from fit into any kitchen's decor. Their larger size and big handles make them more chef-friendly when cooking. Not part of the original post-6 lineup, they were first introduced in 1997.

Standard Sugar Bowl, (Item 498) – This item is made from the original mold used in the production of the vintage marmalade with a modification to the lid, removing its notch, the Standard Sugar Bowl, seen in Cobalt, pairs well with this the Standard Creamer.

Salt and Pepper Shakers, (Item 497) - Shown in juniper, these classic little shakers are another item made from the original mold. Not only a favorite of diehard Fiesta fans, many hobbyists with general shaker collections enjoy the Fiesta versions as well. Although never offered in sapphire, they are available in all other post-'86 colors.

Hostess Tray, (Item 753) - Introduced in 1997, this item is also known as a chip and dip tray. Shown in rose it is 12" in diameter. A separate center bowl, shown in periwinkle, holds the dip while chips are arranged around it on the tray. Perfect when used in combination with the welled snack trays, the hostess tray makes a great centerpiece for any party table.

Millennium I Vase, (Item 425) - Limited to one thousand vases in each color, the millennium I vase continues the Fiesta legacy of innovative and attractive designing. The art department was working on the vase when Bloomingdales representatives visiting the plant first noticed it. Knowing a good thing when they saw it, they negotiated a deal making it a Bloomingdales exclusive. It's contour closely resembles the post-'86 carafe. Affectionately known as a "milli vase" by collectors, the demand for this vase has sent its price soaring on the secondary market. There were also twenty-four black millennium I vases sold at auction to benefit the East Liverpool High School Alumni Association. Each of the black vases were marked and numbered for the 1999 event. Shown here in persimmon.

8" Vase - A newcomer to the post-'86 lineup, this 8" vase shown in persimmon is made from the original vintage mold. Accommodating smaller flower arrangements, it allows post-'86 collectors the opportunity to buy a vintage classic without the vintage price.

Millennium II Vase, (Item 438) - After the success of the millennium I vase, Federated Stores wanted their own exclusive milli vase. The milli II is based on the disk pitcher design. With an unlimited production number hence making it more available and lower priced, the Milli is popular with collectors. The vase was discontinued at the end of 1999. Shown in Cobalt.

Millennium III Vase, (Item 445) - Still wanting a new vase for their own general release, HLC designed the millennium III. Resembling a vintage vase in the art department's morgue, the appealing design was updated for 1999. Shown here in seamist green. It was produced without a quantity limit and was both easily attainable and modestly priced. FTD Florists ordered a large number of milli III vases in chartreuse just before that color was discontinued. China Specialties produced a Sun Porch decal version of the vase and the factory itself offered a rose-decaled treatment sold exclusively at the HLC outlet store.

Oval Platters – Large, (Item 0458). Medium, (Item 0457). Small, (Item 0456) - The large oval platter, shown here in gray, is 13 5/8″ in diameter. The medium tray, shown in cobalt, is 11 5/8″ in diameter, and the small tray is 9 5/8″ in diameter. These gorgeous platters are durable and easily withstand everyday use.

Spoon Rest - This is the plaster cast of the new Fiesta spoon rest. Its exquisite art deco lines make this a post-'86 classic. The finished product, to be introduced through Linens and Things, is planned for a year 2000 release.

Pie Baker, (Item 487) - The pie baker or pie plate is 10-1/4″ in diameter. Shown in Yellow. Yes, it is safe to bake a pie in the dish and the finish is durable so the pie can be cut with a regular knife. The chartreuse pie baker was an exclusive for Betty Crocker. This item was not produced in sapphire.

Millennium Candle Sticks, (Item 430) - In preparation for the new millennium, Bloomingdales asked HLC to develop these tapered millennium candle sticks. Due to advance advertising, these holders were popular even before they became available to customers. With U.S. candle sales rising, HLC and Bloomingdales believed this item would be an overwhelming success and they were right. Shown in chartreuse.

Stacking Set - Based on the vintage stacking set this prototype was never produced, but may be at a later date.

Tumbler, (Item 446) - Available individually or found in sets of four with the disk pitcher sets, the tumbler has been produced in all post-'86 colors and is shown in turquoise. It is also found in various decaled versions.

Sugar Caddy - This popular item is from the HLC Fiesta Mates line. The caddy is taken from a restaurant line then dipped in a Fiesta glaze. At the end of chartreuse production, several hundred chartreuse caddies and napkin rings were made and sold exclusively at the HLC outlet store. Shown is the sugar caddy in black.

New Trial Glaze Colors - Before Fiesta was reinstated, the art department at HLC prepared these test glazes. A few test pieces were displayed at the Chicago trade show in 1985 as a way to get consumer reaction to some of the new colors under consideration.

Medium vase, (Item 491) – One of the most well known Fiesta items, the medium vase is based on the vintage 10" vase. It is available in all post-'86 colors. The sapphire medium vase was produced for Bloomingdales. After the vase was produced and during their sapphire exclusive time period, Bloomingdale's entered into an agreement with a San Francisco antiques dealer "Dishes Delmar" to sell them the entire production of one item. The dealer purchased one thousand sapphire vases. HLC produced several hundred additional sapphire medium vases and sold them through their outlet store during the late fall of 1996.

The Juniper Assortment - After much secrecy, HLC officially unveiled their new limited edition color at the Chicago Home Show. Juniper, released in late 1999 to replace the outgoing chartreuse, will be produced through the year 2001. Members of the HLCCA got a sneak preview when new juniper items graced the cover of their association's publication, "The Dish" in November 1999. Juniper instantly became a hit with collectors.

Post-'86 Decal Collections

Collectors have a wider variety of colorful and exciting products to choose from through offerings of post-86 Fiesta items with decals. The decals, designed by the HLC art department or other graphic design companies, are sometimes added by businesses for promotional campaigns while others customize Fiesta items and sell them as exclusives. For example, the Disney Channel had a Mickey Mouse disk pitcher made as an incentive for Disney Channel employees. Approximately eleven hundred pitchers were produced and these are now a highly sought item on the secondary market.

In 1993, Warner Brothers entered into the Fiesta decaled market with its introduction of Loony Tunes tableware. During production, decals designed by Warner Brothers are applied to post-86 Fiesta items with a special backing placed on the back of each design. This prevents the color of the glaze from showing through the decal and distorting the image. These items are made with an inglaze decal and are fired twice. After the ware is produced, the decal is added and the pieces refired at cone 4 (about 2000 degrees Fharenheight). The decal sinks into the glaze giving the final product a smooth feeling. The decal won't scratch off and makes the items dishwasher and microwave safe. Warner Brother Loony Tunes products will never be found at a HLC warehouse sale or the Outlet store as they are produced strictly for Warner Brothers and for sale through their catalog or in their flag ship store in New York City.

Other popular Fiesta items are produced for China Specialties. Embraced by many collectors, the Moon Over Miami and the Sunporch decals are produced in limited numbers. They are available at an antique mall close to the HLC factory and to subscribers of the Fiesta Collectors Quarterly newsletter. Unlike the inglaze decal used for Warner Brothers, an overglaze decal is used for China Specialties items. Similar to the in-glaze decal, an overglazed decal is placed on a fired Fiesta piece and then is refired. However, the refiring takes place at approximately 900-1000 degrees Fharenheight and the decal doesn't sink into the glaze. It sits on top of the glaze and can be felt as one runs a finger over it. Consequently, the decal can scratch off and each item is labeled not to be used in the preparation or serving of food. Except for the counter display signs offered by China Specialties, the decals are made by an outside company and are added to the items after they leave HLC.

Items produced for Mega China are also popular items among collectors. General decal ideas are submitted by the company and then designed by the HLC art department and fitted to the Fiesta items. They are fired using the in-glaze process. All items are dishwasher safe and may be used in the microwave.

All other Fiesta decal pieces produced by HLC are made using in-glaze decals. This includes items such as HLCCA's juice pitcher series, FCoA exclusives, and all decaled post-86 Fiesta tableware items in major department stores and outlets.

The 1930 and 1931 HLCCA juice pitcher exclusive to members.

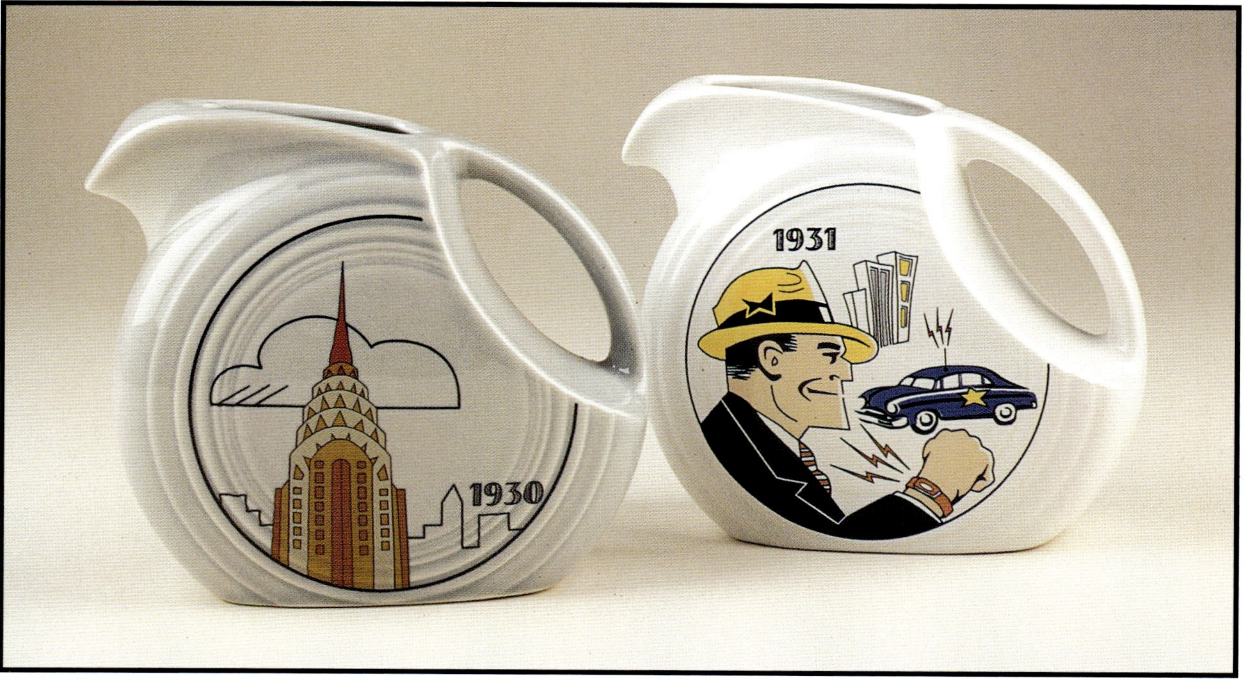

A sampling of Warner Brothers decorations.

HLCCA awards.

Fiesta Club of America handled platter. $30-40.

The Raspberry Bowl

In November of 1997, Homer Laughlin China produced the 500-millionth piece of Fiesta. A special commemorative piece produced to celebrate this historic occasion in December of 1997, the raspberry presentation bowl made its appearance. Unique because of the glaze raspberry, a glaze with a rich burgundy hue, will never be used by HLC again. Limiting the quantity to just 500, each commemorative piece is individually numbered. While fifteen pieces were sold at public auctions, benefiting charities selected by HLC management, the remainder of the bowls were distributed to company share holders and members of the Wells and Aaron families. Under tight security, all damaged Raspberry Bowls were destroyed and buried in a secured, unpublicized area. How sought after are these bowls? At the Fourth Annual East Liverpool Alumni Association Pottery Auction, held in June of 1998, five bowls alone netted $23,900!

The commemorative raspberry presentation bowl.

A detail of the marking on the raspberry presentation bowl.

Rare Color and Shape Combinations

Many collectors ask how an item such as a lilac carafe or a sapphire bud vase comes into existence. By HLC production records they're not supposed to exist. Interestingly enough these marvelous collector pieces are the result of "just another day" in the art department at HLC. The carafe was first documented in the HLC Art Department journal, January 8, 1996 and was introduced to shoppers later that same year. While phasing out lilac, the art department needed to run production tests on the new carafe. A new design that looks good on paper may not be practical in production. Unforeseen problems such as warping and cracking in the firing process can arise making further design modifications necessary. During this test period, the carafe was glazed with the color of the particular test day and in some cases this meant the lilac color. By the time the carafe was fully developed and entered the market place lilac had been discontinued leaving a few elusive lilac versions for the lucky collectors.

In the case of the sapphire bud vase it is the same scenario, but in reverse. Bloomingdales wanted an exclusive color for its stores and the art department developed a variety of hues, experimenting with different shades of blue. When the company decided on its final glaze selection - sapphire blue - the testing continued. A number of greenware pieces in many sizes and shapes were randomly taken off the assembly line and glazed in the new sapphire blue. The art department assesses all new glazes and looks for any possible manufacturing problems before it is used in the factory. The sapphire bud vase, like the lilac carafe, was a test piece. The art department routinely destroys test pieces, but some do slip through the cracks. How they make into the hands of eager collectors is another mystery waiting to be solved.

Fiesta carafe in lilac.

Fiesta Mates

Fiesta Mates are items found generally within one of HLC's restaurant lines that are then dipped in Fiesta glazes. The sugar caddy, jumbo cup and saucer, utility tray, and the Fiesta Mates bowl are so popular with Fiesta fans, they are listed on both the Fiesta Mates and Fiesta piece listings at HLC. Fiesta Mates aren't marked with the Fiesta backstamp. There are two different markings that can be found on Fiesta Mates - the HLC inkstamp and the raised HLC mold marking. In addition to the items mentioned above, the Fiesta Mates selection includes the colonial teapot, baker, Denver mug, after-dinner cup and saucer, tower mug, ramekin, small pedestal bowl, small creamers, and the skillet. Like the sapphire color in general, the sapphire jumbo cup and saucer were exclusives for Bloomingdales.

Licensed Fiesta Products

For those that can't get enough Fiesta, HLC has licensed fifteen companies to produce everything from ice crushers to toasters to door pulls sporting the Fiesta retro style. It all started when Jonathan Parry, the Art Director of HLC and Dave Conley, Director of Marketing and Sales put their heads together and compiled a list of kitchen items they would like to see produced with this Fiesta "flair." After narrowing down the list, HLC contacted manufactures that could create the items with both good quality and practicality factoring heavily in their decisions. The manufactures chosen for the project included Metrokane of New York and two California-based companies, Metro Marketing and Creative Imaginations.

Mertrokane, the maker of the Retro Ice Crusher, also produces the Mighty OJ Manual Juicer. The design of the juicer is a classic, earning it a spot in the Museum of Modern Art in 1984, and was updated for use with the Fiesta line. Both the juicer and the ice crusher come in three Fiesta colors: turquoise, persimmon and yellow. The Fiesta name is engraved on each item.

Creative Imaginations is the maker the Fiesta towel hooks, miniatures, ornaments, thumb tacks, message boards, drawer pulls and scrapbook stickers. Each of the products went into production only after being approved by Mr. Parry. Any product produced using the Fiesta image must meet quality and product concept standards set by HLC.

Working with Mr. Parry, Metro Marketing developed Fiesta Serve Ware, a line of enamel-on-steel cookware. Sold at Bloomingdales, the line includes a 12" 4-quart covered casserole, 7-quart covered dutch oven, a colander, an oval roaster, a set of four bowls with plastic covers, and a thermal gravy server. They come in seven popular Fiesta colors: chartreuse, cobalt, periwinkle, persimmon, yellow, turquoise, and white.

Other popular Fiesta licensed products include: table linens, a teakettle, candles, refrigerator magnets, kitchen timers, flatware, cutlery, picture frames, glassware, and thermal coffee pots.

Fiesta bud vase in sapphire.

Chapter 6

The Kitchen Kraft mark.

Fiesta Kitchen Kraft

There are few records at Homer Laughlin to document the beginnings of the Kitchen Kraft line. The modeling log does contain details of each item proposed, but information about the line itself is not available. Even Frederick Rhead's personal journal for 1937 is missing. The material presented here was compiled from trade journal ads, the HLC modeling log, HLC price lists, and wholesale catalogs.

The Kitchen Kraft line was designed to augment and update the shapes of OvenServe, which had been in production since 1933. Some items were completely new, such as the covered refrigerator bowls, others replaced items already in production. The series of nearly 20 shapes was modeled during March, April, and May 1937. Because of its relationship with OvenServe, the new line was called "Kitchen Kraft OvenServe."

Originally it was produced only in white or ivory with decals. The hollowware did not have an impressed mark, but was left plain for the "Kitchen Kraft OvenServe" backstamp. HLC advertised the new shapes in trade journals beginning in July 1937. The ads touted the strength and up-to-date shapes: "Kitchen Kraft OvenServe is distinguished by the same sturdiness, durability and utility which mark the regular OvenServe line... But in Kitchen Kraft, we offer a new, graceful, modern shape, calculated to appeal instantly to discriminating purchasers."

The Kitchen Kraft shapes seem to have been in production for about 15 years (1937-1952). After the first six months J. M. Wells, HLC's general manager, decided to offer the Kitchen Kraft shapes in four of the Fiesta colors. An inscribed mark was designed specifically for this new line. A modeling log entry in December 1937 documents its first use: "KK casserole, Fiesta writing." The same mark was used on all items that would normally be marked. This newest incarnation was named Fiesta Kitchen Kraft.

The colored ware was introduced at the Chicago and Pittsburgh national housewares shows in January 1938. Advertising to the trade was heavy with praise: *"Now... the parade of Color invades the kitchen, too! In Fiesta Kitchen Kraft, Homer Laughlin offers to the American housewife a ware that combines rich, colorful beauty with a high degree of practical utility... Customers have four lovely colors to choose from... Green, Yellow, Blue and Red... all brilliant and attractive, making possible numerous appealing color combinations."*

The Mexicana decoration on a Kitchen Kraft 9" underplate.

Items in Fiesta Kitchen Kraft

Fiesta Kitchen Kraft was made for a period of about six years. Price lists were made for the line and included 21 items for sale:

Fiesta Kitchen Kraft Items

Cake plate	Mixing bowl, 10"
Cake server	Pie plate, 9.5"
Casserole, covered, 7 1/2"	Plate, 6" (Fiesta)
Casserole, covered, 8 1/2"	Plate, 9" (Fiesta)
Casserole, covered, individual	Refrigerator set, body
Jar, covered, large	Refrigerator set, cover
Jar, covered, medium	Salad fork
Jar, covered, small	Salad spoon
Jug, covered	Shaker, pepper
Mixing bowl, 6"	Shaker, salt
Mixing bowl, 8"	

Paper label, "guaranteed fiesta Kitchen Kraft USA.

In addition to being sold as a separate line, some Fiesta Kitchen Kraft items were used in the promotional campaign of the early 1940s and offered in combination with Fiesta items at special prices.

Items Of Special Interest

The color illustration on Fiesta Kitchen Kraft price lists shows 6" and 9" plates that were to be used under casseroles on the dinner table. They have a moderately wide, plain rim and a shallow well. Both sizes of plates were offered in the original Kitchen Kraft OvenServe line with white or ivory glaze and decals. Those plates do look like the ones illustrated on the Fiesta Kitchen Kraft price lists. However, there is no mention of plates in the HLC records where all of the other Kitchen Kraft items are listed. More than likely they were borrowed from HLC's Brittany line.

Apparently the plan was to glaze them in the four Fiesta colors, like the other items from Kitchen Kraft OvenServe. Current evidence indicates the plates were never produced in solid colors. In fact, the Fiesta Kitchen Kraft price lists include the word "Fiesta" after each plate, likely indicating that normal Fiesta 6" and 9" plates were sold instead.

For years collectors have included two other items with Fiesta Kitchen Kraft that were not designated as part of the line. A 10" version of the pie plate and a plain 13" platter were made for the Royal Metal Manufacturing Company of Chicago in 1936. Even though they never appeared on Fiesta Kitchen Kraft price lists, they were apparently used for Kitchen Kraft OvenServe with decals. The shape of the Royal Metal pie plate was copied and made in a slightly smaller size for Kitchen Kraft. Details for the pie plate and platter are given at the end of this section.

Another Royal Metal item that resembles Fiesta Kitchen Kraft, but was not part of the line, is a covered 7-1/2" casserole. This piece was designed during the time when most of the Kitchen Kraft items were modeled (May 1937) and closely copies the shape of the standard Kitchen Kraft casserole. Sometimes found in the original metal frame, these casseroles were glazed in the Fiesta colors. They are unmarked and have a slanted rim, which is noticeably different from the flat rim of the Kitchen Kraft casseroles. The normal lids for this piece have a smaller knob than the Kitchen Kraft lids, but lids with large knobs have also been found on this casserole.

There was one thing created for Kitchen Kraft that was made a standard item in the Fiesta line. Frederick Rhead wanted this new kitchenware to have a "salad nappie" that could be sold with a ceramic spoon and fork. Soon after it was modeled, HLC management decided the new bowl should a part of the Fiesta line. Although the smooth inside of the bowl had the familiar ring patterns of Fiesta added, the relationship to other Kitchen Kraft bowls is still evident. The double rings under the rim and smooth sides correspond with those features on both the casseroles and mixing bowls of Kitchen Kraft. Collectors today know it as the 11 3/4" fruit bowl.

Dates of production shown below for Kitchen Kraft in Fiesta colors were determined from price lists and the assumption that this line of colored ware was not produced after the red glaze was discontinued in early 1944. The dates do not apply to Kitchen Kraft with decals. Generally, the information provided for each piece is confined to the colored ware only.

The Fiesta 11 3/4" fruit bowl, left, was originally designed for Kitchen Kraft.

The Royal Metal casserole, pie plate and oval platter.

Royal Metal casserole with holder.

Mixing Bowls

Of all items in the Kitchen Kraft line the mixing bowls were made for the longest time. The bowl shapes had slight modifications over the years and were still being produced into the 1970s. It isn't known if production was continuous. The bowls were used for several lines of solid color ware including Fiesta Kitchen Kraft, Harlequin, Jubilee, and Rhythm.

The mixing bowls were made in three sizes determined by the diameter: six inches, eight inches, and ten inches. The Fiesta Kitchen Kraft bowls featured the impressed mark created for the line. Bowls glazed for other colored lines were unmarked and were also used for Kitchen Kraft with decals. Additionally, a special paper label was applied to the Fiesta Kitchen Kraft ware.

The bowls were jiggered and have very little in the way of decoration. The two "stair-stepped" rings under the rim are a distinctive feature that is shared with the larger casseroles. The design is repeated at the base of the bowl above the prominent foot. Unlike those made for Fiesta the Kitchen Kraft mixing bowls were smooth inside; there is no banding or ring pattern. The mixing bowls, like other items in the line, were glazed in Fiesta red, blue, green, and yellow.

Many Fiesta Kitchen Kraft items are hard to find. The mixing bowls certainly fall into that category. No one size is more available than any other, but the larger ones are valued higher than the small ones. Color shouldn't make any difference in the value, but red and cobalt do seem to command a higher price probably due to popularity among collectors.

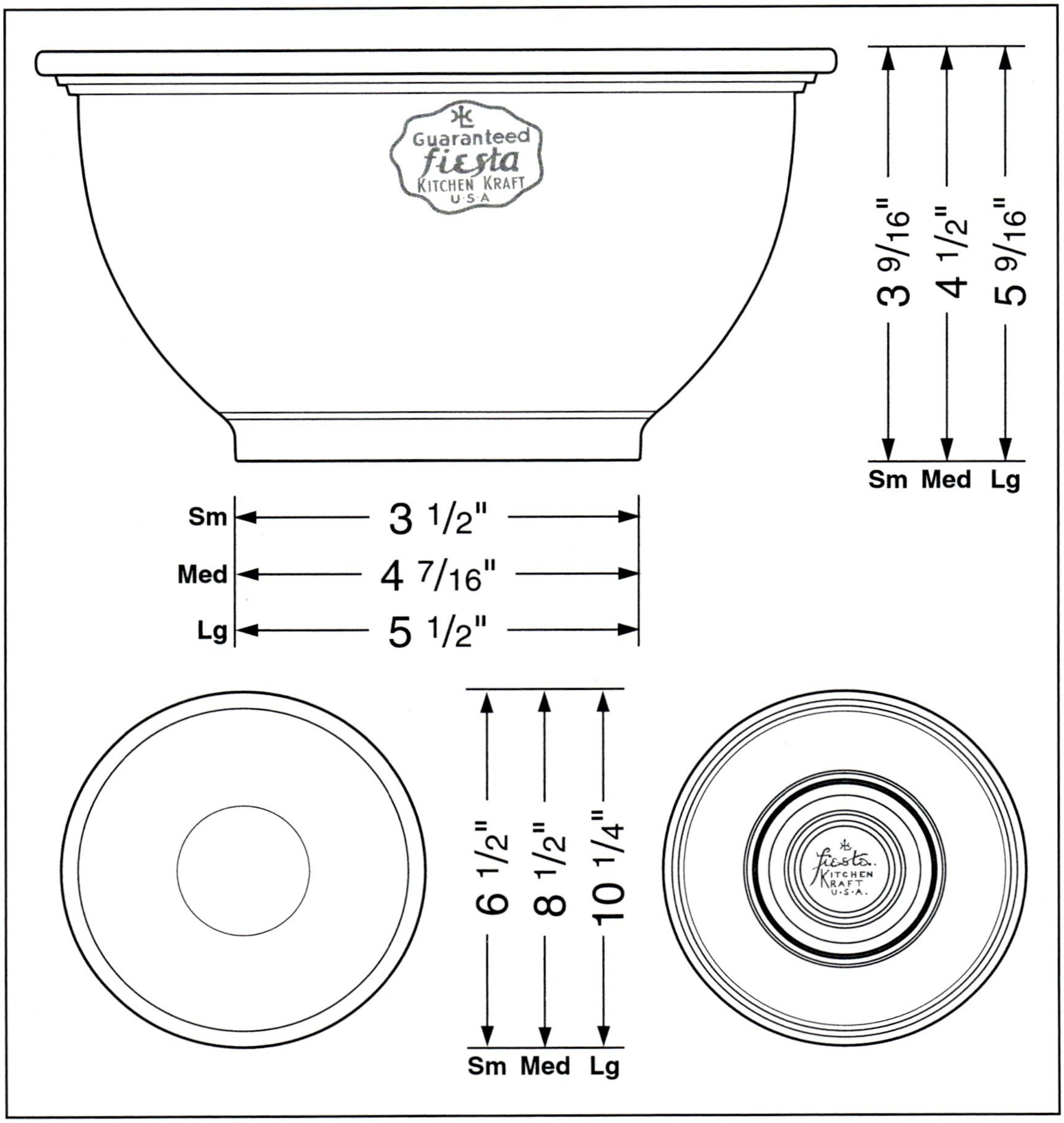

Guaranteed
fiesta
KITCHEN KRAFT
U·S·A

3 9/16" 4 1/2" 5 9/16"
Sm Med Lg

Sm 3 1/2"
Med 4 7/16"
Lg 5 1/2"

6 1/2" 8 1/2" 10 1/4"
Sm Med Lg

fiesta
KITCHEN
KRAFT
U·S·A·

The Fiesta Kitchen Kraft mixing bowls.

Kitchen Kraft 6" Mixing Bowl

Modeling Date .... April 1937
Model Number 812
Revision .... May 1945, 1956[1]
Production Began .... December 1937*
First Price List .... January 1, 1938
Last Price List .... October 1, 1942
Discontinued .... Early 1944*
Length of Production[2] .... 6 Years*
Colors: Red[3], Cobalt, Green, Yellow, Spruce[3], Shell Pink[4], Forest[5]
*Estimate
[1]Reason for revision not known
[2]Kitchen Kraft in original Fiesta colors
[3]Used on unmarked bowl for Harlequin
[4]Promotional item for HLC's Jubilee (unmarked)
[5]Promotional item for HLC's Rhythm (unmarked)

Kitchen Kraft 8" Mixing Bowl

Modeling Date .... April 1937
Model Number 811
First Revision .... October 1940, 1508[1]
Second Revision .... May 1945, 1955[2]
Third Revision .... July 1945, 1964[2]
Production Began .... December 1937*
First Price List .... January 1, 1938
Last Price List .... October 1, 1942
Discontinued .... Early 1944*
Length of Production[3] .... 6 Years*
Colors: Red, Cobalt, Green, Yellow, Harlequin Yellow[4], Blue[5], Celadon Green[6]
*Estimate
[1]First revision may not have been produced
[2]Reason for revision not known
[3]Kitchen Kraft in original Fiesta colors
[4]Promotional item for HLC's Rhythm (unmarked)
[5]Used on unmarked bowl for Harlequin
[6]Promotional item for HLC's Jubilee (unmarked)

Kitchen Kraft 10" Mixing Bowl

Modeling Date .... April 1937
Model Number 806
Revision .... April 1945, 1951[1]
Production Began .... December 1937*
First Price List .... January 1, 1938
Last Price List .... October 1, 1942
Discontinued .... Early 1944*
Length of Production[2] .... 6 Years*
Colors: Red, Cobalt, Green, Yellow, Chartreuse[3], Harlequin Yellow[4], Mist Gray[5]
*Estimate
[1]Reason for revision not known
[2]Kitchen Kraft in original Fiesta colors
[3]Promotional item for HLC's Rhythm (unmarked)
[4]Used on unmarked bowl for Harlequin
[5]Promotional item for HLC's Jubilee (unmarked)

Cake Plate

In keeping with the "modern" style of the Kitchen Kraft line, the cake plate is severely devoid of decoration. It features only a single ring around the outside forming a slightly depressed rim. This is one of the Fiesta Kitchen Kraft items that were marked only with a paper label. A few have been found with a Fiesta backstamp, but the cake plate was not normally marked.

Like all plates, this one was made on the jigger machine. There are no known revisions or variations of the design. Unlike much of the ware in the Fiesta Kitchen Kraft line, this item is fairly easy to find in all four colors.

Kitchen Kraft Cake Plate

Modeling Date	May 1937
Model Number	838
Revisions	None
Production Began	December 1937*
First Price List	January 1, 1938
Last Price List	October 1, 1942
Discontinued	Early 1944*
Length of Production[1]	6 Years*

Colors: Red, Cobalt, Green, Yellow

*Estimate

[1]Kitchen Kraft in original Fiesta colors

The Fiesta Kitchen Kraft cake plates. Cobalt, $63-67; Red, $60-63; Yellow, $49-52; Green, $48-51.

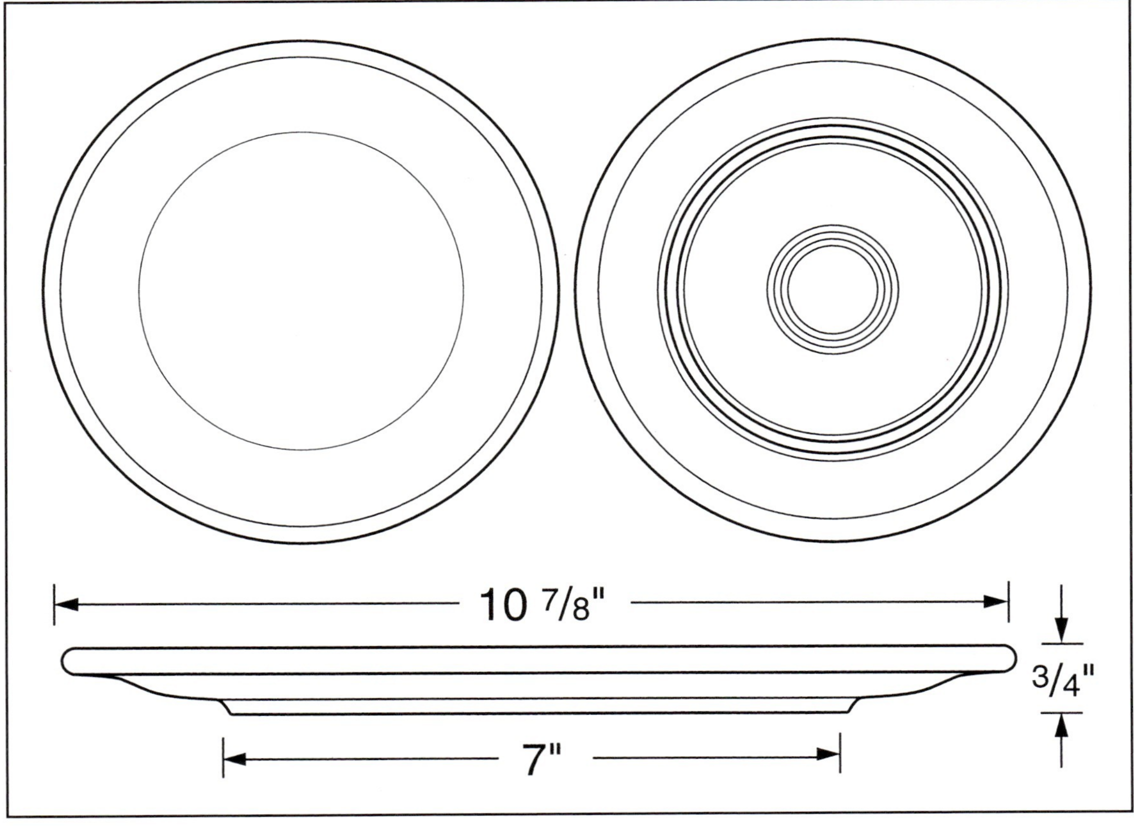

The Fiesta Kitchen Kraft covered casseroles.

Covered Casseroles

Casseroles were always a staple item in oven-to-table ware and Kitchen Kraft OvenServe was no exception. Three sizes were designed for the line and all three were also used for Fiesta Kitchen Kraft. They were given names based loosely on their size. The 8-1/2" and 7 1/2" casseroles are pretty accurately named, based on their diameters. The smallest casserole was at one time during development called a "bean pot," but by the time the line was in production, it was named the individual casserole.

The large casserole was the first item designed for Kitchen Kraft in March 1937. It went through several revisions before the final size and shape was approved. The 7-1/2" model was copied from the larger one, but the smallest had an entirely different look. All of the casseroles had "inside lids" meaning the lid fit within the rim of the bowl and did not overhang the outside edge like casseroles for Fiesta and Harlequin.

These covered bowls were sold individually with a matching color lid. However, during the promotional campaign of the early 1940s, the 8-1/2" model was sold in green with a red lid accompanied by a yellow 9" Fiesta Kitchen Kraft pie plate in a "Kitchen Set." The small casserole was sometimes sold with the salt and pepper shakers as a "range set" and assumed the role of the grease jar.

The two larger casseroles were made by jiggering, as were their covers. The lids had hand finished knobs and the space where the fingers grip the handle can vary in depth and shape. The small casserole has a reverse curve and was probably made by the slip casting method, but may have been hand-shaped after jiggering. They often will show a slight variation in outline from piece to piece.

All of the casseroles made for Fiesta Kitchen Kraft feature the impressed mark. Sometimes the same molds were mistakenly used for the regular Kitchen Kraft line and the impressed mark will appear on ware with decals. Paper labels were often applied to casserole lids.

The two larger casseroles are probably the most available of all items of Fiesta Kitchen Kraft. They tend to be valued according to size and color with the larger one in red garnering the highest prices. The individual casseroles are harder to find and accordingly highly valued.

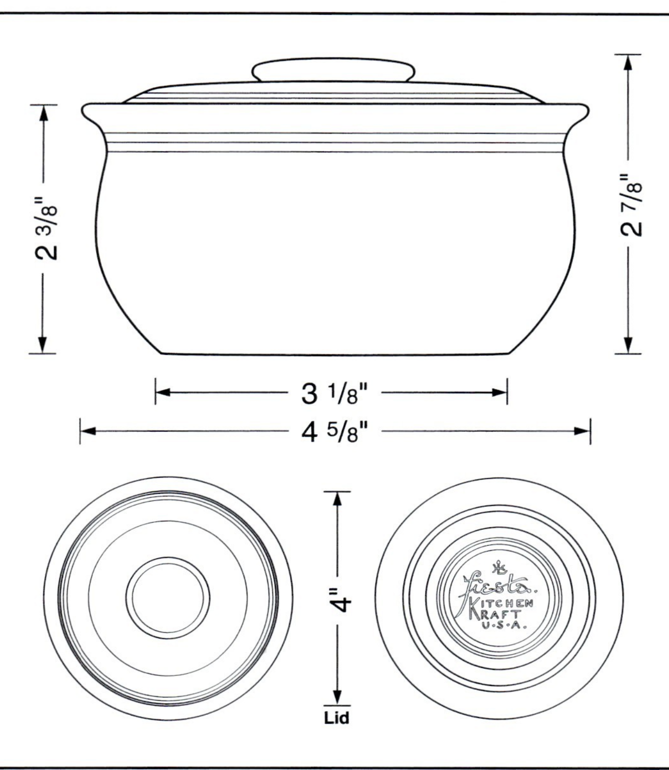

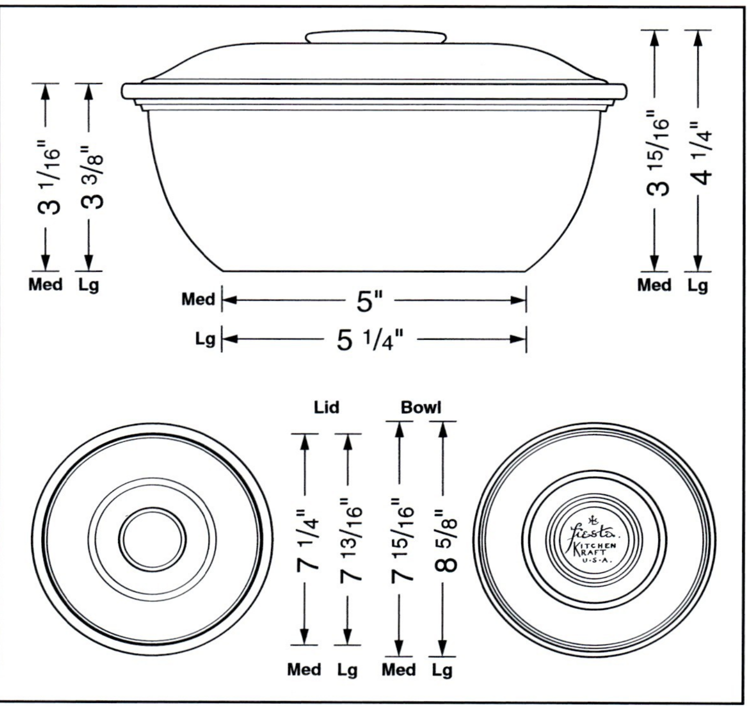

Kitchen Kraft Individual Casserole

Modeling Date	April 1937
Model Number	820[1]
Revision	May 1937, 831[2]
Revision	June 1937, 846[3]
Production Began	December 1937*
First Price List	January 1, 1938
Last Price List	October 1, 1942
Discontinued	Early 1944*
Length of Production[4]	6 Years*

Colors: Red, Cobalt, Green, Yellow

*Estimate

[1]First model, not produced

[2]Casserole revised larger

[3]New cover for revised casserole

[4]Kitchen Kraft in original Fiesta colors

Kitchen Kraft 7 1/2" Casserole

Modeling Date	April 1937
Model Number	815
First Revision	May 1937, 823[1]
Second Revision	July 1939, 1283[2]
Production Began	December 1937*
First Price List	January 1, 1938
Last Price List	October 1, 1942
Discontinued	Early 1944*
Length of Production[3]	6 Years*

Colors: Red, Cobalt, Green, Yellow

*Estimate

[1]Wide cover, not produced

[2]Cover rim flattened

[3]Kitchen Kraft in original Fiesta colors

Kitchen Kraft 8 1/2" Casserole

Modeling Date	March 1937
Model Number	799[1], 803[2]
First Revision	April 1937, 817[3]
Second Revision	April 1937, 819[4]
Production Began	December 1937*
First Price List	January 1, 1938
Last Price List	October 1, 1942
Discontinued	Early 1944*
Length of Production[5]	6 Years*

Colors: Red, Cobalt, Green, Yellow

*Estimate

[1]First model not produced

[2]New lid for first model

[3]Shape revised

[4]Same shape as 817, but smaller

[5]Kitchen Kraft in original Fiesta colors

Covered Jars

The names for these ball-shaped jars come from the Fiesta Kitchen Kraft price lists: small, medium, and large. There was no indication of what they might be used for and apparently, the buyer was left to make that determination for herself. However, in the HLC modeling log the first model was called a "cookie jar." That name is sometimes used today when these items are being sold. One early Forties wholesale catalog also used that term for the larger jar. Specific names for the two smaller jars were not given.

The Fiesta Kitchen Kraft covered jars.

For collectors unfamiliar with them, the sizes can be easily determined by measuring the height. Some have suggested using the jar circumference as a guide, but that's impractical when searching the crowded shelves of antique shops. The largest jar is approximately 7" tall, the medium sized one is about 6" tall, and the smallest one is just shy of 4 3/4" tall. They are actually not at all difficult to tell apart, even without measuring.

A few versions of the large jar were tried before the final shape was decided upon and copied for the two smaller ones. Some of the models even had side handles, which somehow seem appropriate on a cookie jar, but apparently looked out of place with the smooth shapes Frederick Rhead had designed for the other items in the line. The plain ball shape was approved and used for all three sizes. It was later copied for the salt and pepper shakers.

There are no modeling log entries documenting the various changes made to the lids, but sometime during production of the Fiesta Kitchen Kraft covered jars the knobs of the covers were modified. The earliest versions had straight sides, like the covered jug lids, and were very difficult to grasp. Later versions are smaller and were finished by hand, the knob being undercut and smoothed to create a place for fingers to grip when lifting the lid. The look and shape of the handle can vary slightly due to the hand finishing.

The jars were slip cast and the lids appear to be jiggered. They were marked with both an impressed logo and with paper labels. All sizes of the covered jars are difficult to find in Fiesta colors. The two larger jars are usually valued slightly more than the smaller one, but all are scarce. Collectors can expect to use a sizable chunk of their collecting budget for a single jar in excellent condition, no matter what size or color it is.

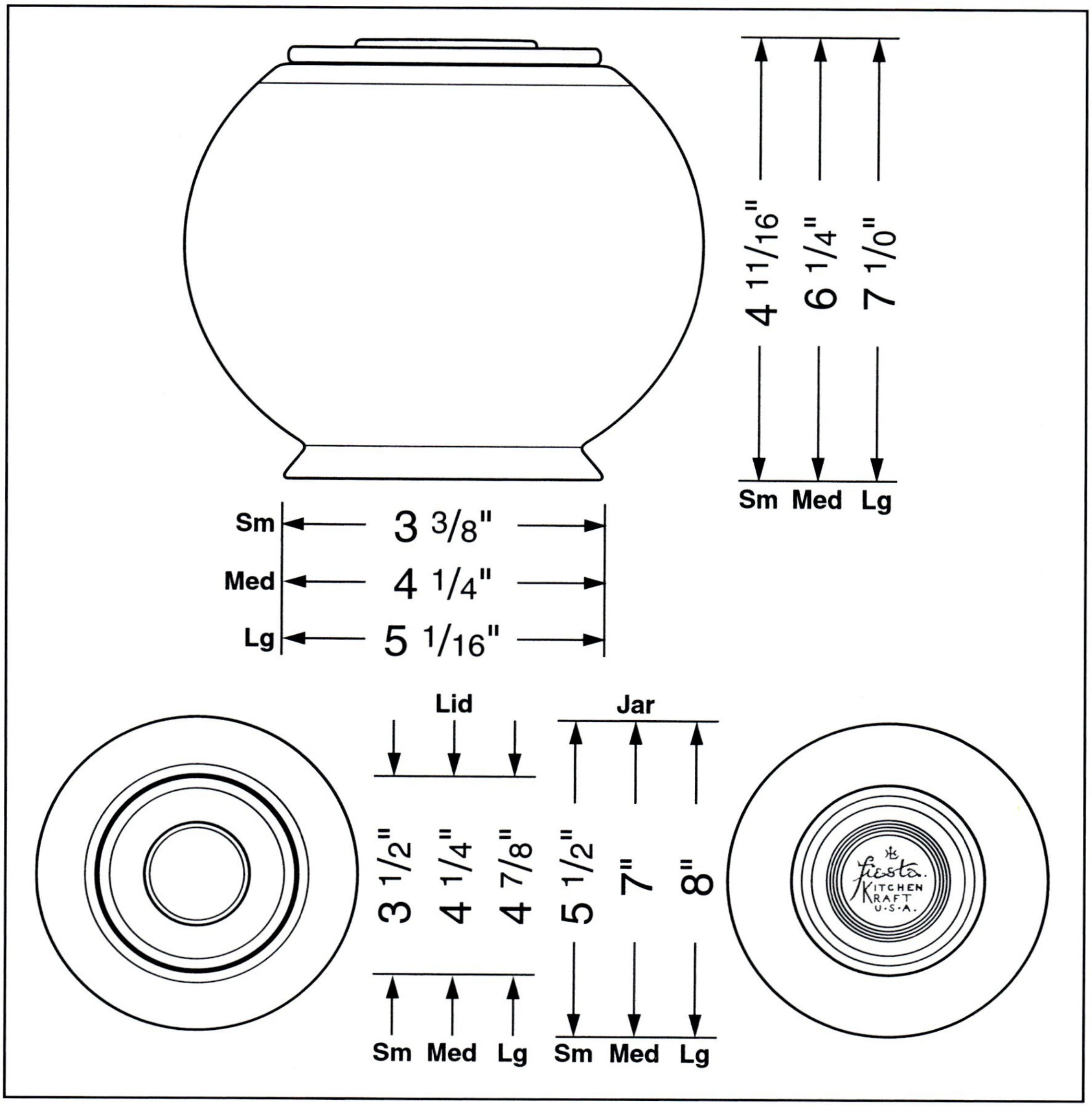

Kitchen Kraft Small Covered Jar	
Modeling Date	May 1937
Model Number	827
Revisions	None
Production Began	December 1937*
First Price List	January 1, 1938
Last Price List	October 1, 1942
Discontinued	Early 1944*
Length of Production[1]	6 Years*

Colors: Red, Cobalt, Green, Yellow
*Estimate
[1]Kitchen Kraft in original Fiesta colors

Kitchen Kraft Medium Covered Jar	
Modeling Date	May 1937
Model Number	826
Revisions	None
Production Began	December 1937*
First Price List	January 1, 1938
Last Price List	October 1, 1942
Discontinued	Early 1944*
Length of Production[1]	6 Years*

Colors: Red, Cobalt, Green, Yellow
*Estimate
[1]Kitchen Kraft in original Fiesta colors

Kitchen Kraft Large Covered Jar	
Modeling Date	April 1937
Model Number	813
First Revision	April 1937, 816[1]
Second Revision	May 1937, 821[1]
Production Began	December 1937*
First Price List	January 1, 1938
Last Price List	October 1, 1942
Discontinued	Early 1944*
Length of Production[2]	6 Years*

Colors: Red, Cobalt, Green, Yellow
*Estimate
[1]Both revisions had side handles; neither was produced
[2]Kitchen Kraft in original Fiesta colors

Covered Jug

The modeling and production history of this item is very confusing. There were no less than six versions, the last one created in 1951. For Fiesta Kitchen Kraft, two sizes were made. They can be distinguished by measuring the height. At the spout, the larger one is 5 3/4" and the smaller jug is 5 3/8". The lid is not included in these measurements.

There is a distinct difference in the lids for the two sizes of the jug as well. The cover for the large jug has a single-step flange that fits into the opening of the jug. The flange is 3/8" deep. The smaller jug has a two-step flange that is 5/8" deep. The lid for the smaller jug is thicker overall and heavier than the one for the large jug. Both have a straight-sided knob that is difficult to grasp. It is surprising that the lid was never redesigned during all the changes.

The original jug was model 824, created in May 1937. It is listed in the HLC modeling log as having a two-quart capacity (64 ounces). Another model, made a few days later, is labeled "covered jug, small." This would seem to indicate that the first model was the "large" version and that is how the jug was eventually listed on Fiesta Kitchen Kraft price lists, "Jug, covered, large." The smaller model was not produced and its exact size is not known, but the difference was apparently significant.

The size difference between the two covered jugs.

The Fiesta Kitchen Kraft covered jugs.

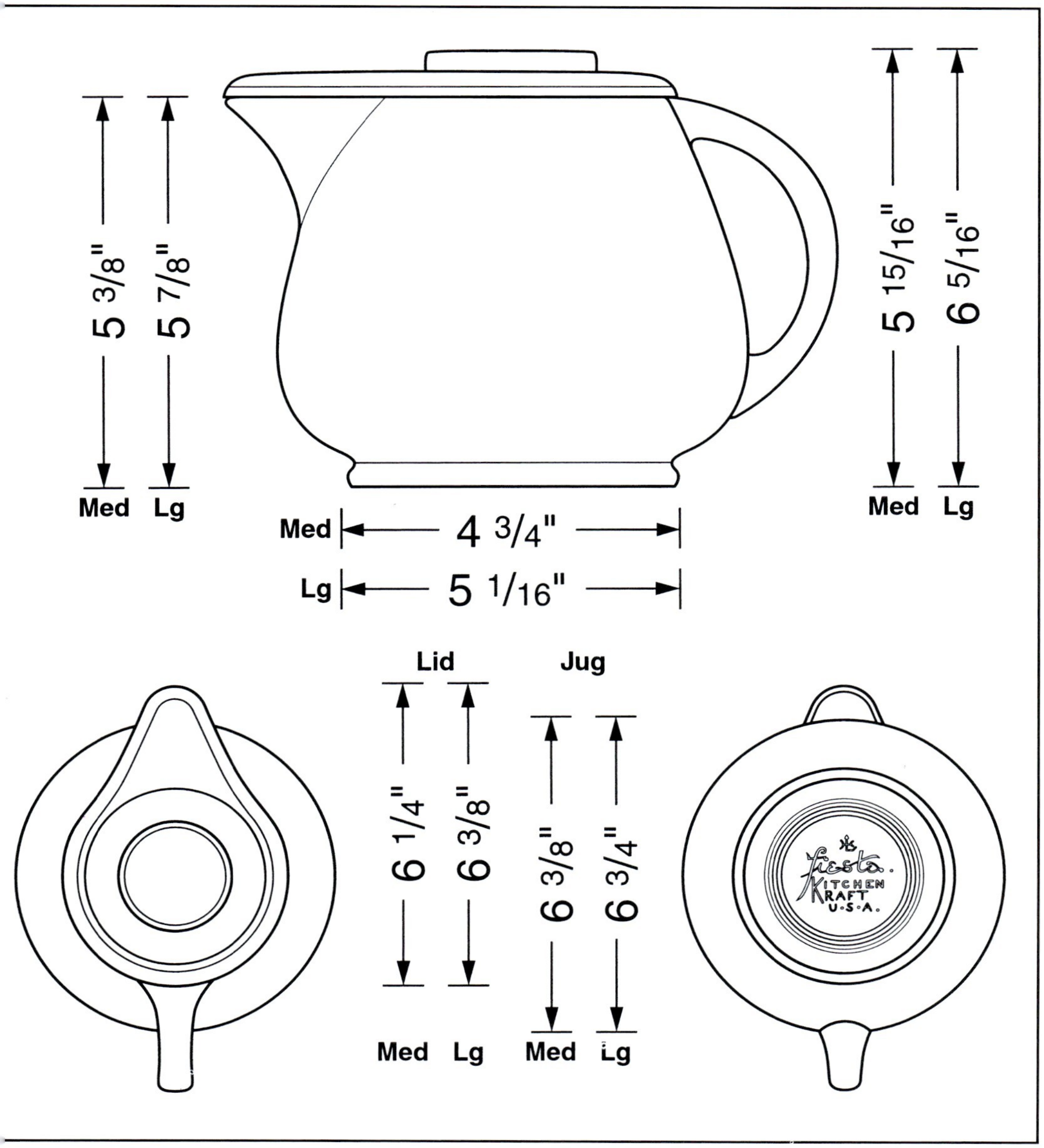

5 3/8" Med
5 7/8" Lg
Med 4 3/4"
Lg 5 1/16"
5 15/16" Med
6 5/16" Lg
Lid
6 1/4" Med
6 3/8" Lg
Jug
6 3/8" Med
6 3/4" Lg
Fiesta KITCHEN KRAFT U.S.A.

In July 1937 the log entry for another version (model 882) says, "Jug, K.K., #824 made smaller." A note dated July 28, 1937, found in another HLC document, says, "J.M.W. released new model K.K. covered jug model no. 882 to replace model no. 824." July 1937 is the time when Kitchen Kraft was first being advertised in pottery trade journals. It is not clear if the first model was actually produced or if this revision was made before the start of production.

The capacity of model 882 is given as "24s", which is approximately four pints, or two quarts. This is the same volume as model 824, so the exact difference between the two is unknown. Few items in the colored glaze lines made by HLC bear the archaic size indicators such as 24s. One exception is the Harlequin 36s bowl.

In January 1938, just after Fiesta Kitchen Kraft was put on the market, another revision was made. This one, model 1038, had a capacity of 67 1/2 ounces. The next month another revision was recorded. It had a capacity of 61 ounces and is the size of the smaller of the Fiesta Kitchen Kraft jugs found today. Model 1038 was apparently not produced. A February 18, 1938 note in HLC records says, "Released K.K. covered jug model 1043 replacing model no. 824 which was too large." This seems odd because 824 had already been replaced, in July 1937, with model 882.

Whichever model was in production between July 1937 and February 1938 (824 or 882) it was the larger of the two sizes of covered jug in the Fiesta Kitchen Kraft line. Of course, the colored glazes were not used on this shape until production of Fiesta Kitchen Kraft began in late 1937. This means that the larger jug should be less common, having a production run of only a few months until the smaller model replaced it in February 1938. It is possible, however, that the larger size continued in production after that date until the molds wore out and were replaced with the new, smaller design. There is no documentation to indicate any specific scenario.

Like all holloware, the covered jug was slip cast and finished by hand. It bears the "Fiesta Kitchen Kraft" impressed mark on the bottom. The size of the jug has no bearing on the value, which tends to be quite high and due to their scarcity, examples of this piece in any color are usually highly valued.

Kitchen Kraft Covered Jug

Modeling Date .... May 1937
Model Number .... 824[1]
First Revision .... May 1937, 833[2]
Second Revision .... June 1937, 854[3]
Third Revision .... July 1937, 882[4]
Fourth Revision .... January 1938, 1038[5]
Fifth Revision .... February 1938, 1043[6]
Sixth Revision .... March 1951, 2249[7], 2254[7]
Production Began .... December 1937*
First Price List .... January 1, 1938
Last Price List .... October 1, 1942
Discontinued .... Early 1944*
Length of Production[8] .... 6 Years*
Colors: Red, Cobalt, Green, Yellow
*Estimate
[1]Original 2 qt. (64 oz.) capacity
[2]Revised smaller, not produced
[3]Cover for #824 revised
[4]#824 "made smaller", 24s size
[5]Revised to 67 1/2 oz. capacity
[6]Revised to 61 oz. capacity
[7]Revised to 63 oz. capacity, 2254 is new cover
[8]Kitchen Kraft in original Fiesta colors

Kitchen Kraft 9 1/2" Pie Plate

This plain, unmarked pie baker can easily be confused with similar items from other manufacturers. Knowledge of the colors, and the fact that the plate has a fairly wide rim and a completely glazed bottom, will help collectors tell them from the competition. Like other items in the Kitchen Kraft line, there is very little decoration. A slight indentation under the rim is the only distinguishing feature.

The HLC modeling log indicates that the shape of this pie plate was copied from an existing pie plate made for the Royal Metal Manufacturing Co. in 1936. The Royal Metal piece was designated a 10" plate, but actually measured 10 1/4 inches. The Kitchen Kraft copy measured 9 3/4", but was listed as 9 1/2" on official price lists. Today collectors use various names for the two pie bakers. They are often called the "nine inch" and "ten inch" pie plates. Some will be more precise and say "9 1/2 inch" and "10 1/2 inch." Others will use "small" and "large" to describe them.

The Fiesta Kitchen Kraft 9 1/2" pie plate. Cobalt, $44-46; Red, $37-40; Yellow, $31-34; Green, $36-39.

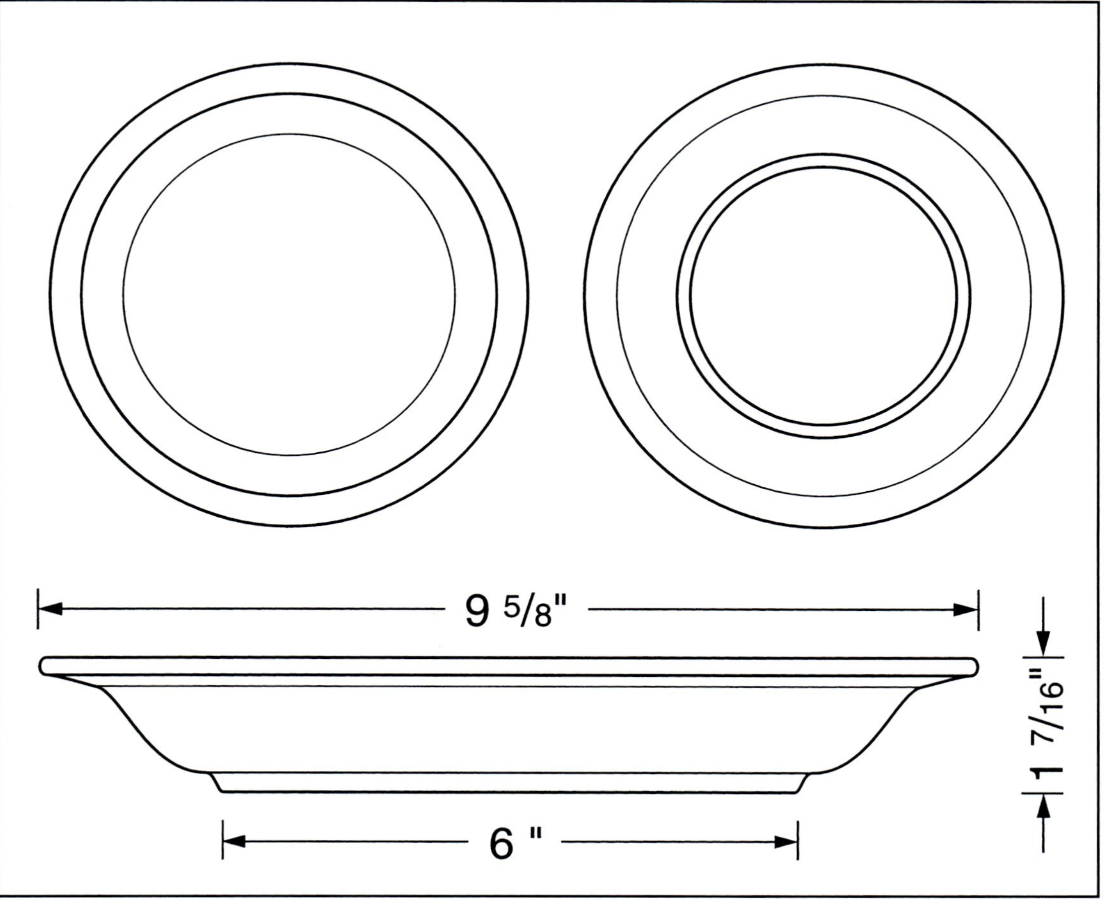

Apparently both sizes were used for Kitchen Kraft with decals, but only the 9 1/2" version appeared on Fiesta Kitchen Kraft price lists. Because they are fairly easy to find, the 10" size may have been made in a large quantity using the Fiesta glazes. However, known Fiesta Kitchen Kraft price lists and wholesale catalog listings do not include this size as part of the line. See the entry below for the Royal Metal Manufacturing 10" pie plate.

In addition to being offered separately as part of the Fiesta Kitchen Kraft line, the 9" pie plate was combined with the large casserole and sold as a set during the early 1940s promotional campaign. See the section on *Special Promotional Campaign* elsewhere in the book.

These jiggered items were marked only with a paper label. The nine-inch pie plate seems somewhat difficult to find, but all four colors can be located with a little effort. Usually found without their original labels, of course, they may not be identified correctly as HLC ware and can be purchased at reasonable prices.

Kitchen Kraft 9 1/2" Pie Plate

Modeling Date	April 1937
Model Number	809[1]
First Revision	February 1939, 1204[2]
Production Began	December 1937*
First Price List	January 1, 1938
Last Price List	October 1, 1942
Discontinued	Early 1944*
Length of Production[3]	6 Years*

Colors: Red, Cobalt, Green, Yellow

*Estimate

[1]Based on shape of model 602, see Royal Metal pie plate

[2]Narrowed rim, shallower well

[3]Kitchen Kraft in original Fiesta colors

Refrigerator Body and Cover

In March, 1937, Frederick Rhead designed a straight-sided storage bowl with a flat lid for the Jewel Tea Company, but it was not put into production. For Kitchen Kraft, in May, 1937, he created two versions of a refrigerator bowl. One had lug handles, the other did not. Neither version was produced. A few weeks later he decided to use a slightly modified version of the Jewel Tea covered bowl for the new kitchen line. Collectors today know it as the "refrigerator unit" or "stacking set" when the lid is applied.

According to Fiesta Kitchen Kraft price lists, the parts for the storage set were sold separately. So any combination of colors or number of bowls in the set can be considered "original." For the promotional campaign of the early 1940s, a set consisted of three bowls in mixed colors, one each in green, yellow, and cobalt, and a lid in Fiesta red.

The bowls and lids were made by jiggering. The bowls bear the inscribed Fiesta Kitchen Kraft mark and many also had a paper label applied. The lids were marked only with the label. This shape was also used for the regular Kitchen Kraft line where it was glazed in white or ivory and sported a variety of decals. A few ivory sets without decals have turned up over the years, but they are very difficult to find and always command high prices. Even in the normal Fiesta Kitchen Kraft colors the parts for the refrigerator storage sets are somewhat difficult to find and a mixed-color, three-bowl set with a lid is a highly valued find.

Complete Fiesta Kitchen Kraft refrigerator units.

Kitchen Kraft Refrigerator Body and Cover	
Modeling Date	May 1937
Model Number	828[1]
First Revision	May 1937, 829[2]
Second Revision	June 1937, 848[3]
Production Began	December 1937*
First Price List	January 1, 1938
Last Price List	October 1, 1942
Discontinued	Early 1944*
Length of Production[4]	6 Years*

Colors: Red, Cobalt, Green, Yellow, Ivory

*Estimate

[1]First model not produced

[2]Same with lug handles, not produced

[3]Based on earlier design for Jewel Tea Co. (#781)

[4]Kitchen Kraft in original Fiesta colors

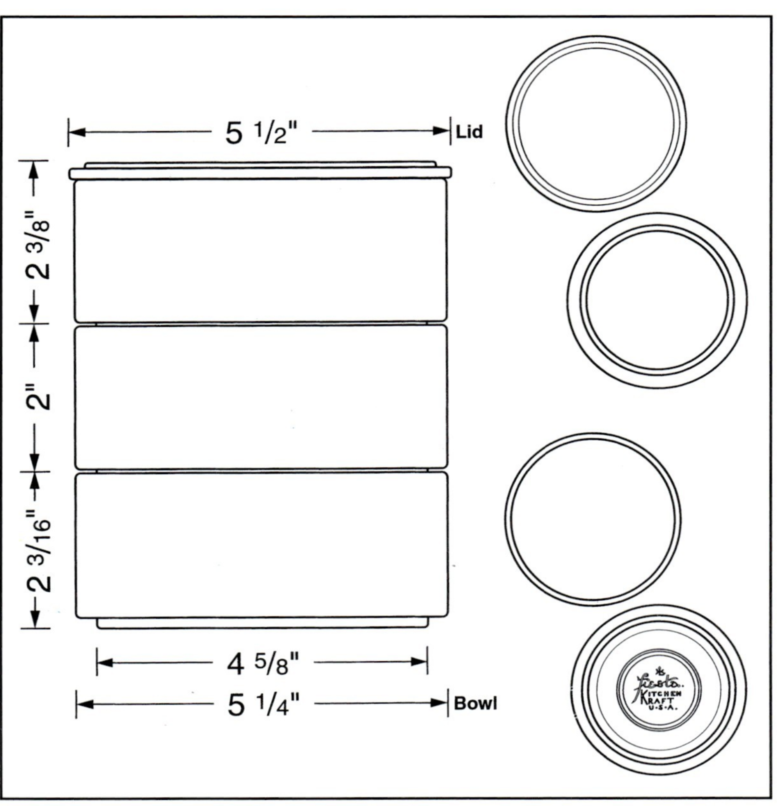

Salt and Pepper Shakers

There were two sets of salt and pepper shakers designed for Kitchen Kraft. The HLC modeling log entry for the set that was not produced said, "same as O.S., but without modeled embossed sprig per D.T." A range top shaker was designed for OvenServe in May 1934, but there is no evidence that it was ever produced. That shaker may be the one referred to in the log. For Kitchen Kraft, the shaker shape approved for production looked like the ball-shaped covered jars and also resembled the smaller Fiesta shaker.

The shakers were slip cast pieces with hand-created holes in a hexagonal pattern. The salt shaker has larger holes than the pepper, but the pattern size is the same. Like many other Kitchen Kraft items, the shakers can also be found in ivory or white with a variety of decals. They were marked only with a paper label.

Fiesta Kitchen Kraft shakers are somewhat difficult to find and moderately valued when located as a pair.

Kitchen Kraft Salt and Pepper Shaker	
Modeling Date	June 1937
Model Number	842
Revisions	None
Production Began	December 1937*
First Price List	January 1, 1938
Last Price List	October 1, 1942
Discontinued	Early 1944*
Length of Production[1]	6 Years*

Colors: Red, Cobalt, Green, Yellow

*Estimate

[1]Kitchen Kraft in original Fiesta colors

Fiesta Kitchen Kraft shakers. (Priced per pair) Cobalt, $80-87; Red, $76-83; Yellow, $77-83; Green, $69-76.

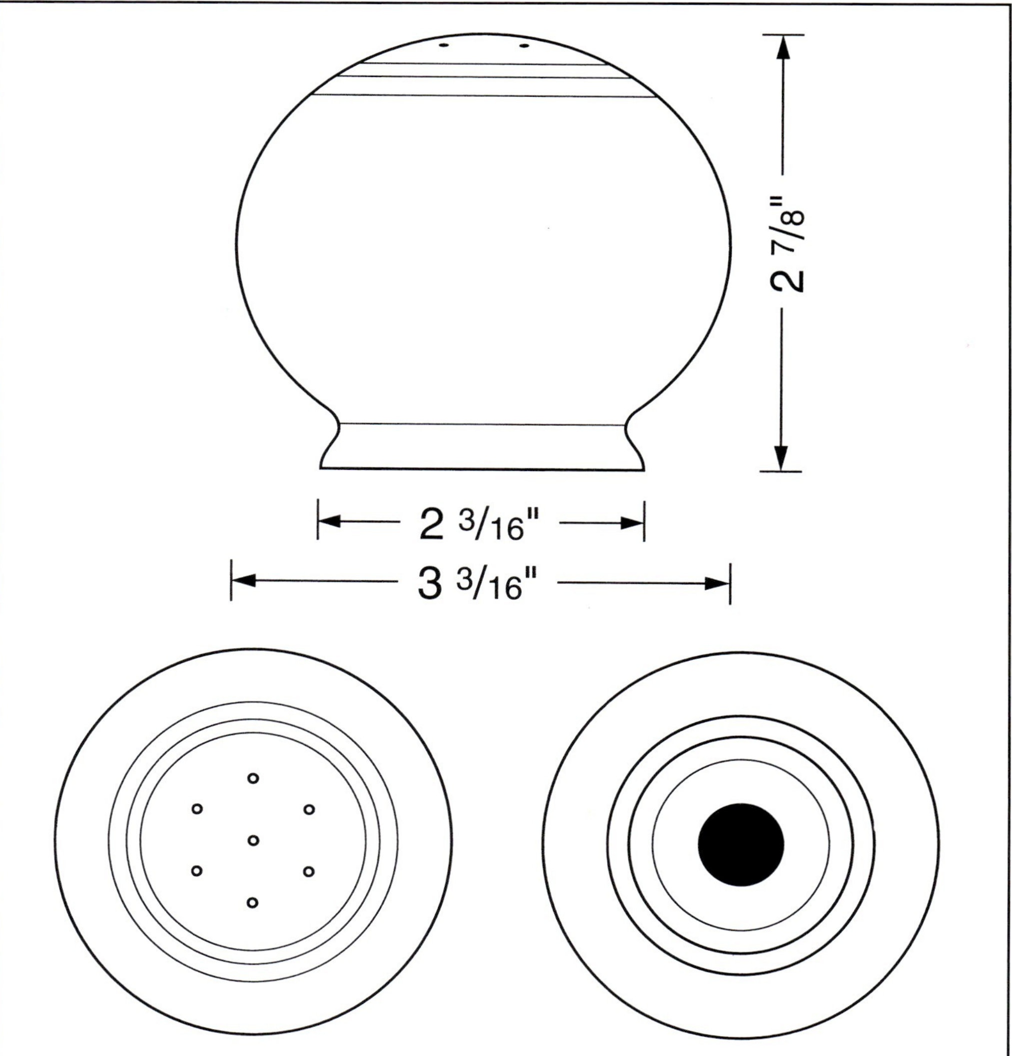

Fork, Spoon, and Cake/Pie Server

More than a year after the introduction of the original OvenServe line in 1933, Frederick Rhead designed a cake/pie server and spoon for that line. They were glazed in ivory or white and had decals applied. It wasn't until the Kitchen Kraft line was created in 1937 that a fork was added to the group of OvenServe utensils. Rhead intended the new fork and existing spoon to be used with the "salad nappie" he designed for Kitchen Kraft.

It didn't turn out the way he expected. The salad nappie was moved by HLC management to the regular Fiesta line and became the 11 3/4" fruit bowl. The fork, spoon, and cake server were then sold separately as part of Fiesta Kitchen Kraft and glazed in the four Fiesta colors. Some received the ivory or white glaze and decals to accompany the Harmony sets (see below).

All the utensils were slip cast pieces. They were unmarked except for the Kitchen Kraft or Fiesta Kitchen Kraft paper label. The only variation occurs with the spoon. A longer model, with a narrower bowl, was produced soon after the original in 1934. The hard-to-find long spoon was not part of Fiesta Kitchen Kraft and is known only in the ivory glaze.

With a little effort, these items can be found in all four colors. A few will have the paper label intact and those that do tend to be more highly valued than those without.

Fiesta Kitchen Kraft utensils.

Kitchen Kraft Salad Fork

Modeling Date	June 1937
Model Number	843
Revisions	None
Production Began	December 1937*
First Price List	January 1, 1938
Last Price List	October 1, 1942
Discontinued	Early 1944*
Length of Production[1]	6 Years*

Colors: Red, Cobalt, Green, Yellow
*Estimate
[1]Kitchen Kraft in original Fiesta colors

Kitchen Kraft Salad Spoon

Modeling Date	September 1934
Model Number	269[1]
First Revision	October 1934, 274[2]
Second Revision	December 1934, 294[3]
Production Began	December 1937*
First Price List	January 1, 1938
Last Price List	October 1, 1942
Discontinued	Early 1944*
Length of Production[4]	6 Years*

Colors: Red, Cobalt, Green, Yellow, Others[5]
*Estimate
[1]Short handled model
[2]Long handled model, not produced
[3]Long handled model with narrowed bowl
[4]Kitchen Kraft in original Fiesta colors
[5]OvenServe Orange, Ivory, White

Kitchen Kraft Cake Server

Modeling Date	September 1934
Model Number	270
Revisions	None
Production Began	December 1937*
First Price List	January 1, 1938
Last Price List	October 1, 1942
Discontinued	Early 1944*
Length of Production[1]	6 Years*

Colors: Red, Cobalt, Green, Yellow, Others[2]
*Estimate
[1]Kitchen Kraft in original Fiesta colors
[2]OvenServe Orange, Ivory, White

The long spoon compared to the standard (shorter) spoon.

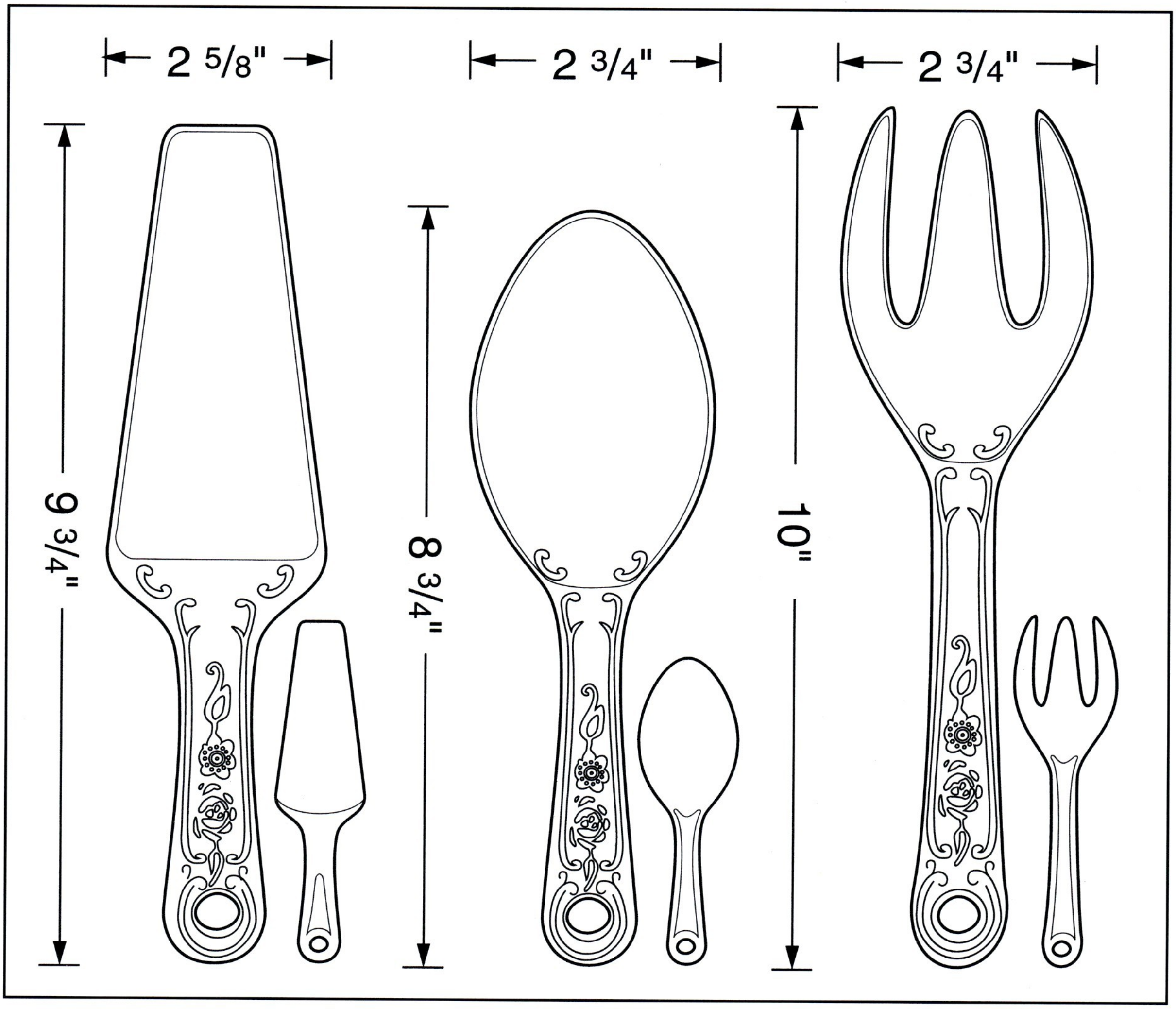

2 5/8"
9 3/4"
2 3/4"
8 3/4"
2 3/4"
10"

Other Shapes and Colors

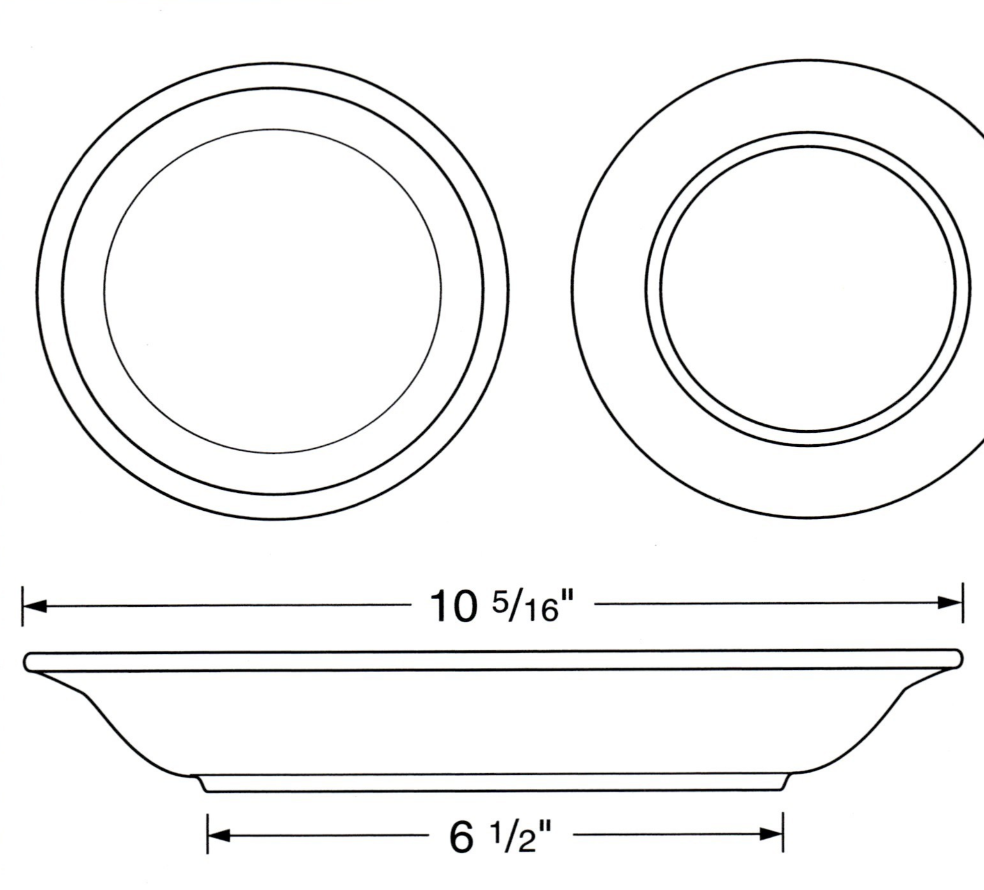

Royal Metal Manufacturing Co.

The Royal Metal Manufacturing Company of Chicago made many different metal items—everything from furniture to kitchenware. During the 1930s, the company was a frequent buyer of ware created by Homer Laughlin to fit in the company's metal frames. Of interest to Fiesta and Harlequin collectors are four items known to have been glazed in colors from those lines. Three of the pieces, a casserole, a pie plate, and an oval platter, were all designed in May 1936. The 1936 casserole is covered in the section on Fiesta promotional items elsewhere in this book. The second casserole, which is very similar to the Kitchen Kraft design, was discussed in the introduction above. Because of their similar designs, the pie plate and platter are often associated with Kitchen Kraft. Details on these two items are provided here.

Royal Metal Manufacturing 10" Pie Plate

One could consider the 10" pie plate to be the original piece of Kitchen Kraft. It was the first of three items made for the Royal Metal Manufacturing Co. by HLC in 1936. In a June 29th journal entry, Frederick Rhead associated ware for Royal Metal with Fiesta. This is interpreted to mean that they were to be glazed in the Fiesta colors. The glazes for Harlequin were selected by the end of the year and soon the Royal Metal pie plate was produced in those colors as well.

The distribution method for Royal Metal items is not fully understood. Our researchers found no trade journal ads for HLC ware in metal frames, nor were any wholesale catalogs or HLC price lists located that offered it. Royal Metal is known to have used paper labels with the trade name "RoyalChrome". Perhaps the company had its own distribution system or maybe the ware was sold by Homer Laughlin through other channels.

The very plain pie bakers were made on the jigger machine and had no identifying marks except for the label. They are not too difficult to locate in the Fiesta glazes. Few of these pie plates are found today with the original metal frame or paper label. Those in Harlequin colors are valued at five or six times the ones in Fiesta glazes.

Royal Metal Mfg. 10" Pie Plate

Modeling Date	May 1936
Model Number	602
Revisions	None
Production Began	July 1936*
First Price List	None[1]
Last Price List	None[1]
Discontinued	Early 1944*
Length of Production[2]	7.5 Years*

Colors: Red, Cobalt, Green, Yellow, Harlequin yellow, blue, spruce, maroon

*Estimate

[1]Not found on any price list

[2]Includes all available colors

Royal Metal Manufacturing 10" pie plate. Cobalt, 44-46; Red, $43-45; Yellow, $34-39; Green, $41-44.

Royal Metal Manufacturing oval platter with holder and label. Platter is Harlequin yellow.

Royal Metal Manufacturing Oval Platter

The second item created for Royal Metal in 1936 was an undecorated 13" oval platter. Like the 10" pie plate, it was glazed in the Fiesta colors when first produced, then later in the Harlequin colors. It was also made to fit in a metal frame.

A revision to the original shape was made in June 1936. Curiously, the revision was not put into production until June 1937. This was when the majority of Kitchen Kraft OvenServe was in production. It is believed the revised platter was an addition to that line and it was glazed in white or ivory with decal decoration.

These platters were made on the ram press. They were marked only with a paper label. Those in Fiesta glazes are fairly easy to find, but the ones in Harlequin colors require much more searching and are valued quite a bit higher.

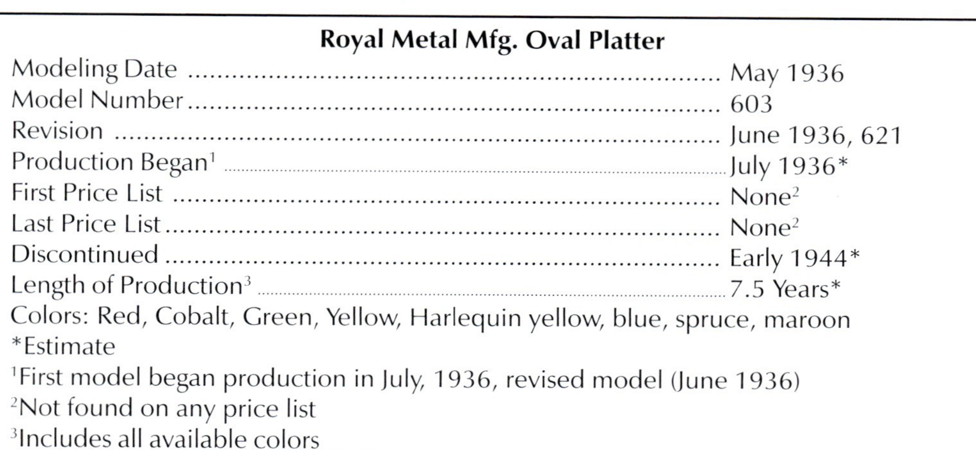

Royal Metal Mfg. Oval Platter

Modeling Date	May 1936
Model Number	603
Revision	June 1936, 621
Production Began[1]	July 1936*
First Price List	None[2]
Last Price List	None[2]
Discontinued	Early 1944*
Length of Production[3]	7.5 Years*

Colors: Red, Cobalt, Green, Yellow, Harlequin yellow, blue, spruce, maroon

*Estimate

[1]First model began production in July, 1936, revised model (June 1936)

[2]Not found on any price list

[3]Includes all available colors

Royal Metal Manufacturing oval platter. Cobalt, $64-74; Red, $77-82; Yellow, $67-70; Green $55-60.

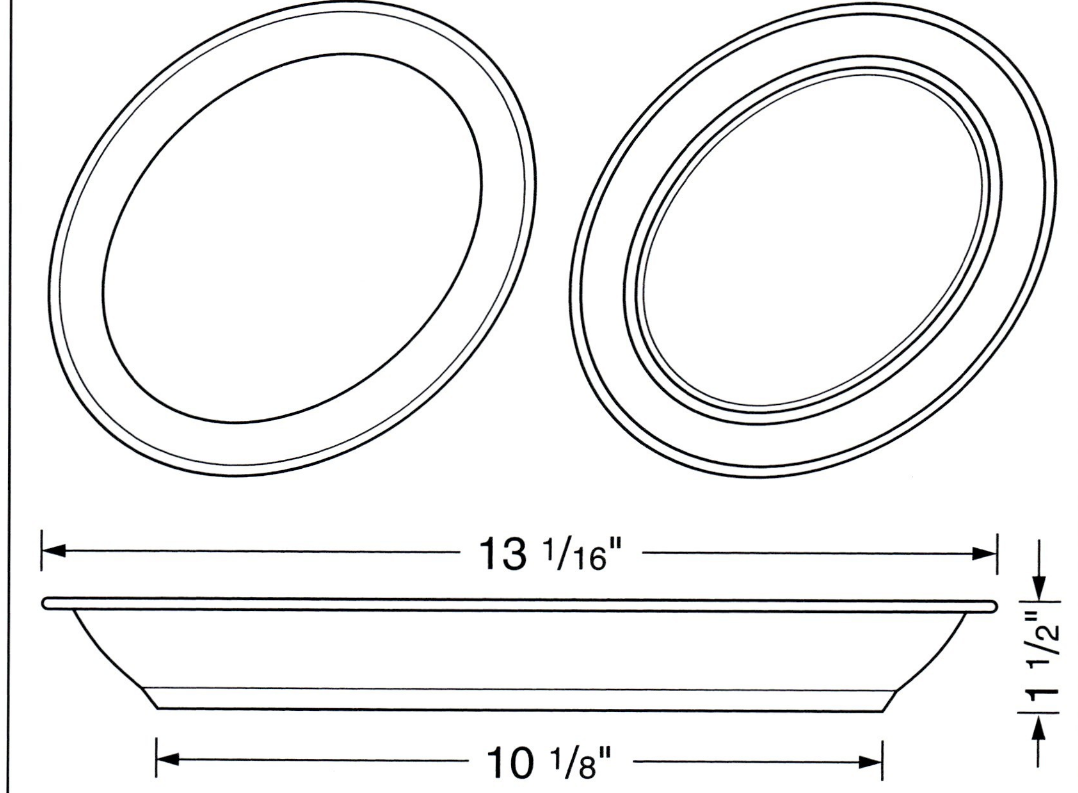

Mixing Bowls for Harlequin

The Kitchen Kraft mixing bowls apparently proved to be useful and popular so HLC management decided to use them for other lines. They were offered in the Harlequin glazes, but limited to certain colors for each size. It is not known if Woolworth's sold the Harlequin colored bowls, but apparently they were also sold by HLC directly. They may also have been used for a sales promotion.

The largest mixing bowl was available in Harlequin yellow, the 8" bowl came in Harlequin blue, and the smallest in spruce green or Fiesta red. The bowls were not marked with an inscribed logo, but may have had paper labels.

Collectors will have a much harder time finding these bowls than those glazed in the Fiesta colors and prices are comparatively higher.

Kitchen Kraft mixing bowls for Harlequin. 6" Red, $91-94; 6" Spruce, $91-94; 8" Blue, $115-125; 10" Yellow, $130-135.

Mixing Bowls for Jubilee and Rhythm

The same three bowl set can also be found in glazes used for HLC's Jubilee and Rhythm lines. Jubilee was designed in 1947 by Don Schreckengost to commemorate the 75th anniversary of the company. It was made in four pastel colors: shell pink, mist gray, cream beige, and celedon green.

Collectors believe the Kitchen Kraft mixing bowl set was offered in Jubilee colors as part of a sales promotion. The colors used were shell pink on the 6" bowl, celedon green on the 8" bowl, and mist gray on the 10" bowl.

These sets are not easy to find, but they have been found in sufficient quantity that a rumor about the large bowl can be laid to rest. Contrary to previous statements, more than one 10" bowl is known. Collectively the authors and editors of this book have seen, or know of, at least fifteen of them in the past two years alone. Values for the set, including the gray bowl, tend to be about the same as for those in Harlequin colors.

The Kitchen Kraft bowls can also be found in Rhythm colors. In 1951, Homer Laughlin began making Rhythm in solid colors, which was also designed by Mr. Schreckengost. Very likely, this was another sales promotion because the bowls are found in only one color per size: 6" in forest green, 8" in Harlequin yellow, and 10" in chartreuse. The bowls were not marked.

The mixing bowl set in Rhythm colors are even harder to find than those in Jubilee colors and the values for them tend to be a bit higher as a result of their scarcity.

Casseroles for Serenade

In June 1939 Frederick Rhead noted in his journal: "Royal Metal and Seller [M. Seller Co. of San Francisco, HLC's West Coast distributor] Fiesta K.K. casserole body 7-1/2" to be made with Serenade mark in glazes in following colors: pink, yellow, blue and Swing glaze. Casserole cover 7-1/2" (no mark) in Serenade all colors for Seller. 4 reg. colors. Few bodies in green for Seller. Fiesta mark taken off. Serenade mark on body. Watch glass cover, slightly adjust [jiggering] tool. Casserole body must fit on glass cover and reg. K.K. cover."

The new casseroles were released to production on June 23, 1939. A few days later Rhead wrote, "J.M.W. up on Royal Metal 'Serenade' casseroles. Samples… are a little tight for Pyrex cover. Explained that first samples were tight but had already specified to G.P. [Guy Pittenger, HLC Plant #4 supervisor] on release what should be done with tool."

Collectors of HLC's Serenade have found Kitchen Kraft casseroles with the inscribed Serenade mark in several colors, but most have been missing the cover. These two entries in Frederick Rhead's journal help explain why. There were two groups of Serenade-marked 7 1/2" Kitchen Kraft casseroles. One was made for the Royal Metal Manufacturing Co. of Chicago. The Royal casseroles were glazed in Serenade's pastel pink, blue, and yellow plus the white glaze used for Swing. A cover made of ovenproof Pyrex® glass was used on this group. The second group was made for the M. Seller Company and distributed on the West Coast. Casseroles in this group were made in Serenade's four regular colors, as well as some in Fiesta green, and had the usual Kitchen Kraft lids.

There is no information on what the glass covers looked like or how long the Serenade casseroles were produced. Values tend to be reasonable for the bowls without covers and slightly higher than Fiesta Kitchen Kraft casseroles for those with lids.

Fiesta Harmony Lines

As mentioned in the introduction to the Fiesta section, HLC offered "Harmony" sets in mid-1936. The sets consisted of a service for eight made of Fiesta and Nautilus shapes. The Nautilus pieces featured color coordinated decals. Soon after the Kitchen Kraft line was introduced, several items were decorated in the Harmony service decals in order to provide kitchenware that matched the dinnerware sets.

Exact lists of items have not been located, but collectors report that most pieces in the Kitchen Kraft line were decorated in this manner. Items known to have the Harmony decals are: casseroles, covered jars, covered jug, salt and pepper shakers, spoon, fork, cake knife, cake plate, and pie plate.

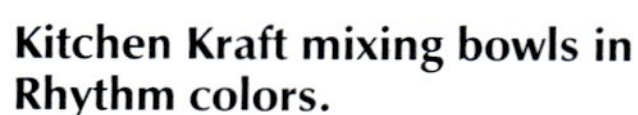

Kitchen Kraft mixing bowls in Rhythm colors.

Chapter 7

Harlequin

Creation and Evolution of Harlequin

In the late 1930s, influenced by the popularity of the new solid color dinnerware lines, including Fiesta, Homer Laughlin teamed up with F. W. Woolworth on a new dinnerware line. Woolworth dominated the inexpensive china market through the company's nationwide chain of five-and-ten-cent stores. Both firms wished to introduce solid-colored dinnerware into this market.

In late 1936, Woolworth introduced Harlequin, a limited line of colored glazed dinnerware. It was a basic line consisting of 16 shapes in four colors; maroon (called "red" at the time), blue, spruce green (called simply "green" at the time), and yellow. It is uncertain who named the line, but Harlequin proved to be Woolworth's best selling dinnerware line of all time. The dishes were in stores for the next 28 years.

In the early summer of 1936, Frederick Rhead, the art director at Homer Laughlin, was busy developing shapes for the new inexpensive line. At the same time, Dr. A. V. Bleininger was also working on new glazes. Bleininger and H.W. Themicke were the chief chemists at Homer Laughlin. They were responsible for both the Fiesta and Harlequin glazes. From notes in company records and Rhead's personal journals, it appears that the glaze development was a difficult task. Progress on the new shapes and glazes was reported to J. M. Wells, president of the company. The following is a letter to Bleininger from Rhead in July ,1936.

July 10th 1936
Dr. A. V. Bleininger
H. L. Co.
Newell, W. Va.

Dear Dr. Bleininger:

Mr. J.M. Wells phoned today from New York with regard to the Woolworth selection for the new colored glaze line.

Shape: Plates No's 15 and 22. This is the plain shape (model No 613) with the lines turned inside the verge.

Glazes : Blue No 2247. Pink No 2332. Green No 2342-A (Alternate: 2337-A). and Vellum.

INSTRUCTIONS WITH REGARD TO FURTHER SAMPLES:

We are to proceed at once to get out further seven inch plates in above shape and colors at the earliest possible moment. These samples are to be sent to the west coast branches (J.M.W. will be back before the samples are out and will furnish shipping instructions).

Model 613 is to be released to Guy Pittenger and drawings are to be made of the regular Woolworth items in this line.

Status of development to date (July 13th 1936):

Model 613 has been released and further samples are being made in both talc and ivory bodies.

We have some three dozen plates in talc body available for the green, pink and blue. Ivory samples will be out this week.

Drawings have been made for the tea and J.M.W will make selection of type because this will determine character of hollow ware and other items.

F.H.R.

It is evident that all three men were involved in the development. By early August, as glazes were being tested, Wells requested a "strong pink" and asked for yellow samples as well. It is apparent that in records the terms "rose," "pink," and "crimson" are referring to the color today's collectors know as "maroon."

Wells selected "Pink #2369" but there were problems with the samples. Rhead writes in his notes: "Various Woolworth glazes out - green and blue ok but pink is dark and rather dirty in color. Yellow very uneven." When he discussed this with both Bleininger and Themicke, they agreed they would put more time in on the maroon. Bleininger claimed the problems were from " bad dipping." Rhead wanted the glaze as "opaque as possible and practical." On September 2, with the glaze problems abating, Rhead asked Wells to review the samples. Over the subsequent three weeks the line was sent into production. By September 21, it had acquired the name "Harlequin."

On September 28, 1936, Bleininger expressed some concerns over Harlequin (and possibly Riviera) hurting the sales of Fiesta, but Wells felt that the ten percent to fifteen percent price difference placed them in separate categories. Rhead's journal documents him at the #4 plant on November 4 "to see Harlequin coming from the kiln." He was still not quite satisfied with the glazes, remarking, "blue and yellow seem ok but rose [maroon] and green [spruce] appear light and streaked." He believed they should be dipped heavier. When he spoke to Bleininger about the lightness of the "green and crimson," Bleininger replied, "there are fifteen dippers and that some of them are no good. We can't get enough good dippers!" The problems must have been solved since Harlequin was in the stores by the end of 1936.

Harlequin, like Fiesta, had wonderful lines inspired by the Art Deco and streamlined movements. However, in contrast to Fiesta, whose shape is based on concentric circles, Harlequin is all about sharp angles. Hollow pieces had conical bodies and triangular handles. Flat pieces were decorated with a series of rings just in from the edge.

There is very little information available to researchers about Harlequin, especially when compared with the data available on other lines. Dated price lists for other lines allow the researcher to track the introduction and discontinuance of shapes and colors. Unfortunately, with one exception, such lists do not exist for Harlequin. Since the line was produced for a single client, there was no reason to prepare the price lists that normally went to wholesalers and jobbers. Researchers are forced to rely on Rhead's journals and the model logs at Homer Laughlin, both of which do a good job of documenting the initial creation and introduction of the line. But documentation on changes in later years is woefully lacking. Researchers can only make estimates of the introduction and discontinuance of colors and pieces based on fragmentary evidence and documented events in other lines at the factory.

According to the earliest company records, the Harlequin line at its introduction consisted of: 10" dinner plate, 9" luncheon plate, 8" soup plate (now known as a deep plate), 7" salad plate, 6" dessert plate, covered casserole, covered sugar bowl, creamer (the version with a high lip), 9" baker (oval vegetable), 11" platter, teacup and saucer, salt and pepper shakers, 9" nappy (round vegetable), double eggcup, and a fruit bowl.

By 1938 Harlequin had enjoyed enough success that the line was expanded. The line almost doubled in size to include the ball jug, covered butter, cream soup, marmalade, novelty creamer, nut dish, 22-ounce jug, 13" platter, regular ashtray, sauce boat, single eggcup, teapot, and tumbler. The line was expanded yet again in 1939 with the addition of the animals, basketweave ashtray, saucer ashtray, individual creamer, individual salad bowl, and the after dinner (or demitasse) cup and saucer. The final expansion in 1940 introduced the relish tray, syrup, candleholders, 36s bowl, and the 36s oatmeal bowl.

As mentioned above, the original four Harlequin colors introduced in 1936 were maroon, spruce green, yellow, and blue. Over the years, collectors have come to call this blue "mauve blue." Homer Laughlin never used this name. The Harlequin yellow is much brighter than the yellow glaze used on Fiesta and has the distinction of being the only color that was in production for the entire life of the line.

As the line grew, so did the color assortment. In late 1939 and the early 1940s, four new colors were introduced. The names of the time were salmon, tangerine, and turquoise. Today's collectors know the first two better as rose and red. Use of these three colors for Harlequin began in late 1939. Between late 1941and early 1942 the fourth forties color, light green, was added. Collectors refer to these as the "forties colors."About the same time, the original colors of maroon and spruce were dropped from production. There apparently was some overlap in the production of all these colors.

It was at this time that the line saw some of its first cuts. The single eggcup, marmalade, syrup, saucer ashtray, and candleholders were the first pieces to be dropped. Since the introduction of light green coincided with the discontinuation of these shapes, they are extremely scarce or nonexistent in that color. It is probable that only a few, if any, were dipped in light green.

Because of restrictions on the civilian use of uranium during World War II, the red glaze, which contains that mineral was dropped from production in 1943. The number of pieces in the line was further reduced between 1944 and 1945. This cut would include the butter dish, relish tray, oval baker, regular ashtray, and tumbler. The nut dish and individual creamer are slightly harder to find in light green, so it is possible that they were dropped a bit earlier.

As fashions changed, more changes would occur in the color assortment. Sometime between 1950 and 1952, the "fifties colors" were introduced. These were three new colors, gray, chartreuse, and forest green. Light green and blue disappeared from the line. The only price information available from this time is a 1956 Woolworth Christmas catalog. In it, a 16-piece starter set for four is $3.98, all open-stock items are priced from 19 to 89 cents.

The final color assortment was introduced in 1959. It consisted of yellow and turquoise, red, and a new green, now known as medium green.

Harlequin Colors

Original	maroon, spruce green, yellow, blue
Forties	red, rose, turquoise, light green
Fifties	gray, chartreuse, forest green, medium green

In the early 1960s, sales of Harlequin were slowing. It is likely that the sale of open stock ended about this time or perhaps earlier. In the psychedelic 1960s, popularity of solid-color Harlequin inexplicably diminished, and Woolworth phased out sales around 1965.

Basketweave ashtrays in forest and gray. Forest, $65-78; Gray, $62-71.

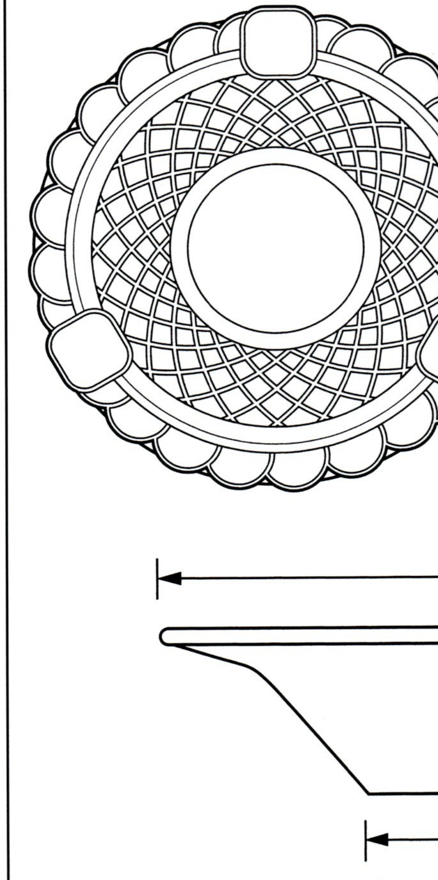

Basketweave ashtrays in the forties colors. Rose, $43-37; Green, $66-84; Turquoise, $44-48; Red, $49-56.

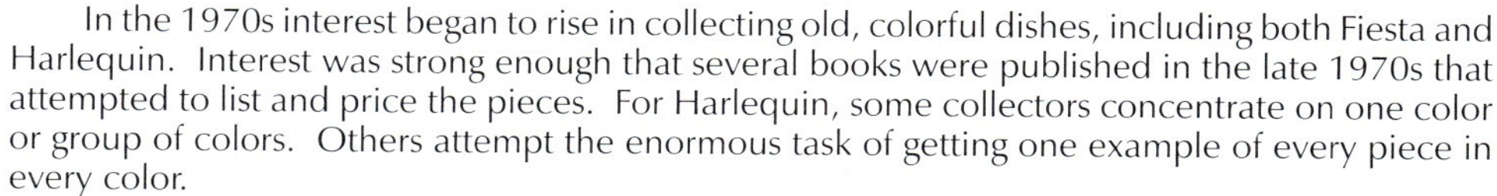

Collecting Harlequin

In the 1970s interest began to rise in collecting old, colorful dishes, including both Fiesta and Harlequin. Interest was strong enough that several books were published in the late 1970s that attempted to list and price the pieces. For Harlequin, some collectors concentrate on one color or group of colors. Others attempt the enormous task of getting one example of every piece in every color.

Collectors have learned that the last color introduced, medium green, is generally the most difficult to find. Pieces of medium green Harlequin fall into three categories, scarce, very scarce, and very, very rare. In general, most medium green Harlequin is much harder to find than medium green Fiesta.

Medium green Harlequin 9″ plates, 7″ plates, fruit bowls, teacups and saucers, and 36s oatmeal bowls are scarce but can be found. The 11″ platter, 13″ platter, sugar bowl, regular creamer, sauceboat, 36s bowl, 10″ plate, 6″ plate, and 9″ nappy are very scarce and difficult to find. The covered casserole, novelty creamer, salt and pepper shakers, double eggcup, demitasse cup and saucer, large cup, 22-ounce jug, and cream soup bowl are very, very rare. Fewer than ten examples of each have been reported of the ball jug, novelty creamer, teapot, and casserole. The rarity of these pieces undoubtedly exceeds that of the renowned Fiesta medium green cream soup. It seems unlikely that these were ever part of regular production. Harlequin was phased out around the time that medium green was in production. Woolworth probably dropped open stock about this time, so very few, if any, serving pieces were ordered. It has been conjectured that last four items were color samples, made when the color was being tested.

Over the years, collectors have discovered Harlequin pieces in nonstandard glazes. Several pieces have been reported in ivory, a standard Fiesta color, but never a standard Harlequin color. A few ivory pieces (either ivory bodies or ivory glaze) are mentioned in the model log and in Rheads' journal. It seems plausible that the ivory Harlequin pieces were made as samples. The 10″ plate, 7″ plate, tumbler, novelty creamer, syrup, and saucer ashtray have been found in ivory. However they came to be, ivory pieces are very rare and command appropriate prices when they come on the market.

In the last year or so several of the teacups have been found in sky blue glaze. Possibly these cups are from a color test. A few plates have been reported in this color as well.

Items Available in Harlequin

Ashtrays

Unlike Fiesta, which had a single ashtray shape, Harlequin had three ashtrays. Starting in 1938, an ashtray shape, in one form or another, was part of the Harlequin line. While not commonly a part of today's dinnerware lines, ashtrays were common in the 1930s and 1940s

Basketweave Ashtray

Rhead modeled the basketweave ashtray after the Japanese Marutomo ware ashtray, but removed the floral design. This shape is model #1309, released to production on September12, 1939. Kraft created the original models for all the Harlequin ashtrays. It is available in all twelve colors but is extremely rare in medium green.

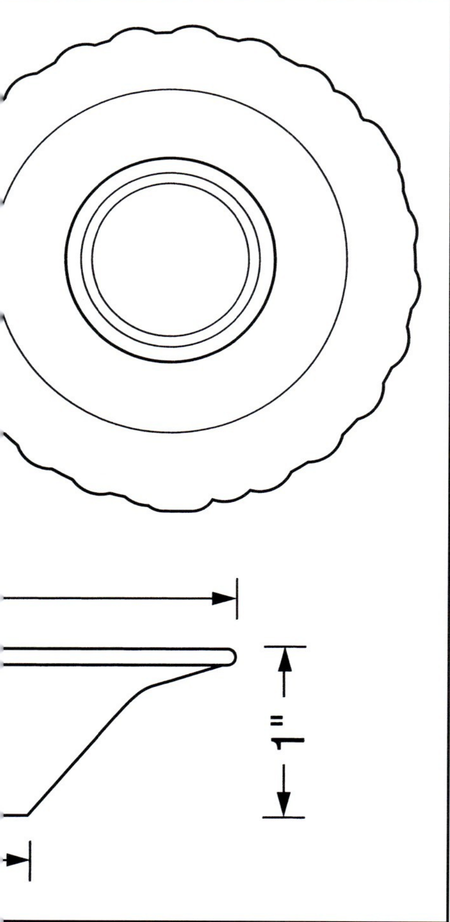

Harlequin Basketweave Ashtray	
Modeling Date	1938
Model Number	1309
Revision	none
Production Began	September 1939
Discontinued	1959
Length of Production	21 Years
Colors: All	

Basketweave ashtrays in the colors available at shape introduction. Maroon, $53-61; Blue, $41-45; Spruce, $54-65; Yellow, $36-39.

Regular Ashtray

The regular ashtray is model #1025. It is referred to in the log as "Ashtray, Harlequin Shape" and is the little sister to the Fiesta ashtray. The Fiesta ashtray is 5 1/2" in diameter while the Harlequin one is 5 9/16". They can be easily confused. The regular ashtray was discontinued early and is available in the original and forties colors, with rose and light green being scarce.

Harlequin Regular Ashtray	
Modeling Date	January 1938
Model Number	1025
Revision	None
Production Began	January 1938
Discontinued	c.1945
Length of Production	8Yyears

Colors: Maroon, Yellow, Spruce, Blue, Red, Turquoise, Rose and Light Green

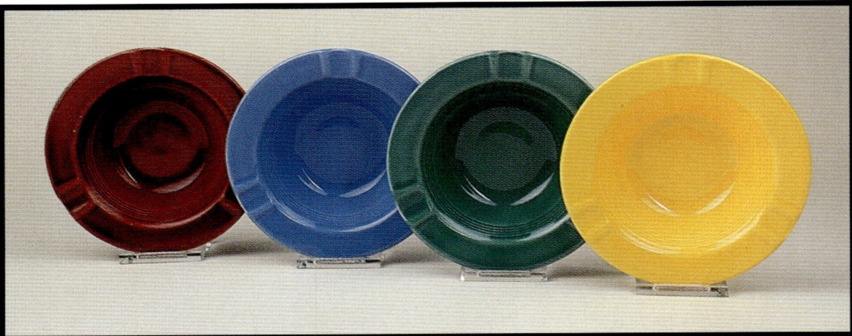

Regular ashtrays in colors available at shape introduction. Maroon, $68-76; Blue, $48-54; Spruce, $60-69; Yellow, $38-46.

Regular ashtrays in green, $105-150; red $63-71; turquoise, $39-45.

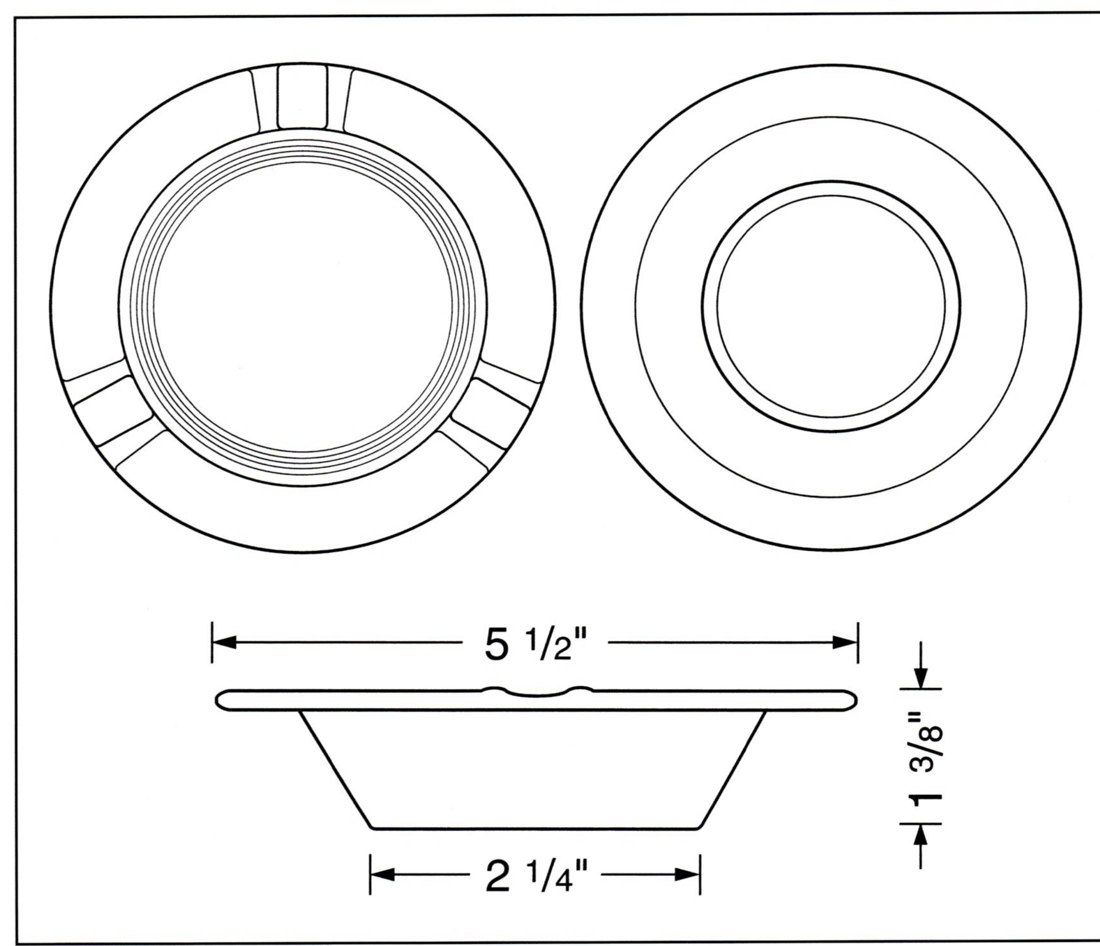

Saucer ashtrays in the original colors. Marron, $85-93; Blue, $72-80; Spruce, $83-91; Yellow, $62-68.

Saucer Ashtray

The saucer ashtray is a novelty item. The saucer has a small ashtray built into the side where one would traditionally rest a spoon. There are two log entries for this item, #1313 and #1335. #1313, done in August 1939, is shown devoid of rings and is simply listed as "Saucer Ashtray." A month later it was redone with rings as #1335 and listed as "Saucer, Harlequin Ashtray." It is not clear for which line, if any, the initial design was intended. The second version, with rings, was definitely Harlequin. These novelty ashtrays appear to have been discontinued about 1942, earlier than the regular ashtray. The saucer ashtrays are not easy to find in any color. The shape seems to have been dropped early enough that they were not regularly made in light green and rose, but a few in each color have been reported. Examples have been reported in ivory, a color not normally used for Harlequin. The saucer ashtrays are hard to find in mint condition. It seems that when these were used, they were well used.

Harlequin Saucer Ashtray	
Modeling Date	August 1939
Model Number	1335
Revision	September 1939
Production Began	September 1939
Discontinued	c.1942
Length of Production	5 Years
Colors: Maroon, Yellow, Spruce, Blue, Red, Turquoise, Rose and Light Green	

Saucer ashtrays in turquoise, $65-72 and red, $83-90.

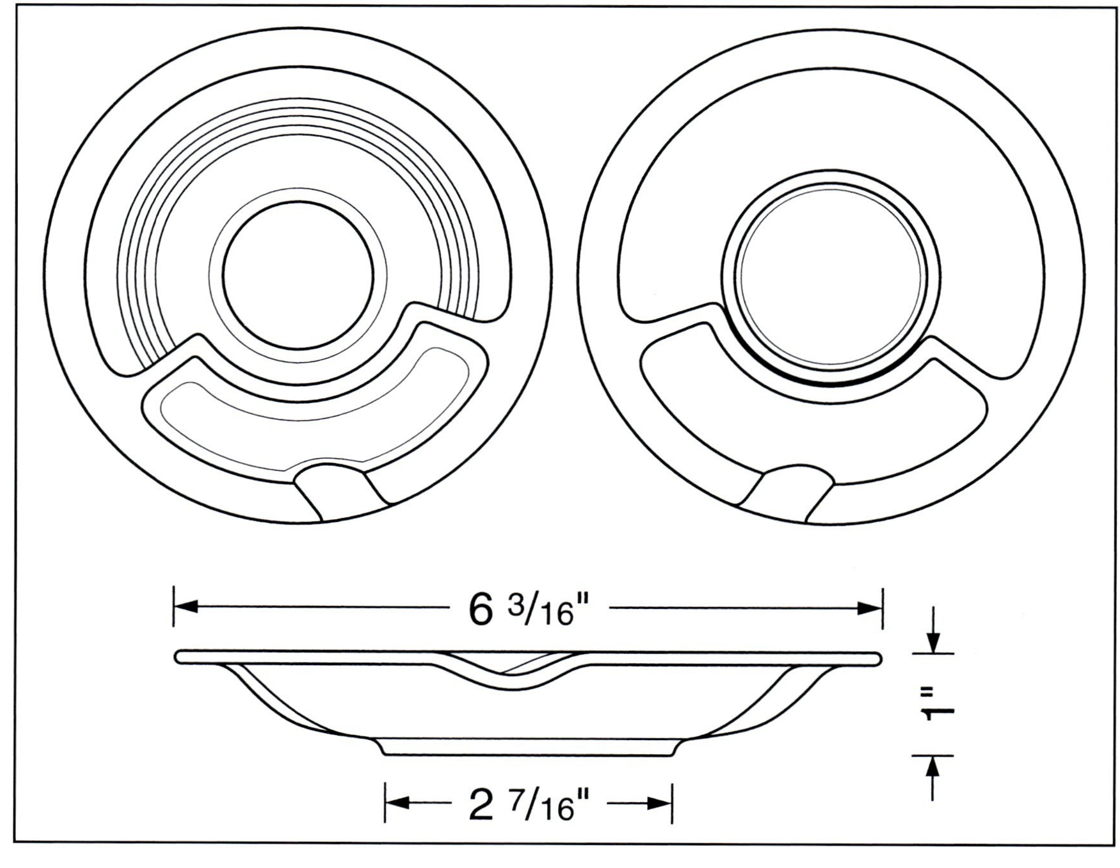

Bowls

Bowls were an integral part of the Harlequin line. Eight different bowls meant a bowl for everything.

36s Bowl

The 36s bowl was the last piece added to the regular Harlequin line and the last Harlequin shape designed by Rhead. A short note in Rhead's journal of October 31, 1940, says "JMW-36's Harlequin bowl." The model log entries dated November, 1940, show two illustrations: a prototype #1516 and the produced model #1517. #1516 was the same shape as the cream soup and follows its design perfectly. However, #1517, the shape collectors know as the 36s bowl, was the version released to production: Rhead's journal on November 27, 1940 notes "release for Woolworth's-Harlequin Bowl model #1517." This curved bowl does not demonstrate the normal angular geometry of Harlequin. It holds 16 ounces comfortably and 18 ounces to the rim. While it is found in all twelve colors, it is hard to find in maroon and spruce because it was introduced shortly before those colors were dropped in late 1940. Those two colors are more difficult to find than the medium green version.

36s bowl in medium green, $165-185.

Harlequin 36s Bowl	
Modeling Date	October, 1940
Model Number	1517
Revision	None
Production Began	November, 1940
Discontinued	1959
Length of Production	19 Years
Colors: All	

36s bowls in colors available at shape introduction. Maroon, $105-130; Blue, $45-52; Spruce, $82-105; Yellow, $27-29.

36s bowls in the fifties colors. Chartreuse, $42-46; Forest, $45-48; Gray, $41-46.

36s bowls in the forties colors. Rose, $35-38; Green, $42-44; Turquoise, $26-27; Red, $41-44.

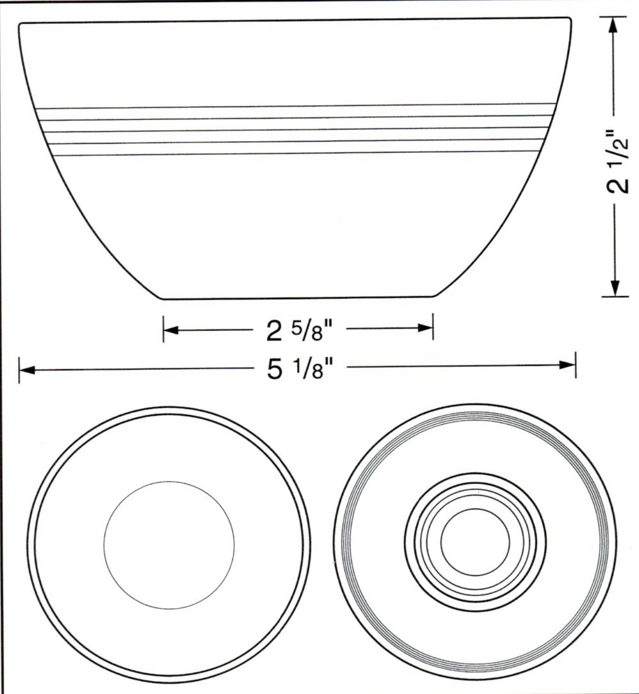

36s Oatmeal Bowl

It appears the 36s oatmeal bowl was designed a full year before it was put into production. It first appears in Rhead's journal on March 24, 1939, when he states, "oatmeal to have same rim as fruit" It is model # 1388. Rhead's journal shows it was released to production on May 23, 1940, when Rhead wrote, "Release Harlequin Relish tray and Oatmeal Harlequin to Finley". This smaller bowl is shaped exactly like the fruit bowl and nappy. It is found in all twelve colors but is hard to find in the fifties colors and, for some reason, seems very hard to find in red. As with the 36s, it is very rare in spruce and maroon.

Harlequin 36s Oatmeal Bowl

Modeling Date	April 1940
Model Number	1388
Revision	None
Production Began	May, 1940
Discontinued	1959
Length of Production	19 Years
Colors: All	

36s oatmeal bowls in original colors. Maroon, $84-120; Blue, $21-22; Spruce $73-99; Yellow, $16-18.

36s oatmeal bowls in the fifties colors. Chartreuse, $23-27; Forest, $29-31; Gray, $25-29.

36s oatmeal bowls in the forties colors. Rose, $18-20; Green, $24-26; Turquoise, $16-17; Red, $18-20.

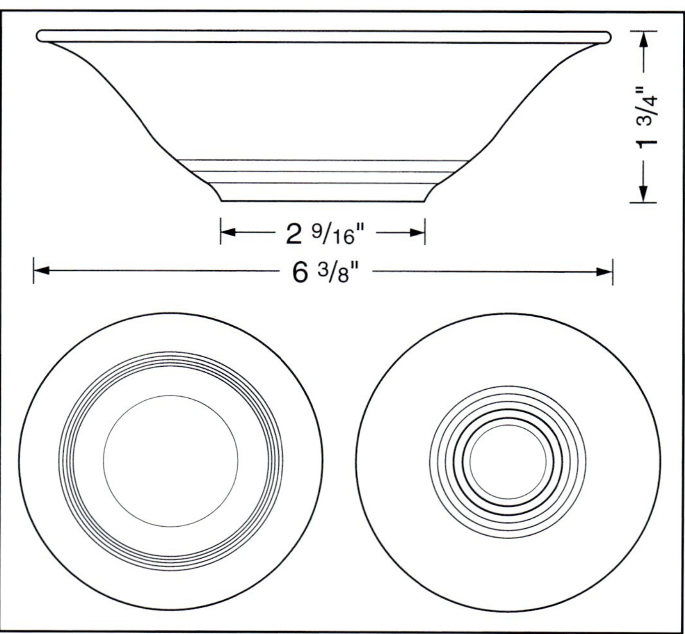

36s oatmeal bowl in medium green, $74-91.

Cream Soup Bowl

Model # 1045, the cream soup bowl, was added to the line in the early expansion with a production release date of March 5, 1938. The bowl is formed with the classic Harlequin geometry of straight sides and angular handles. It measures 4 7/8″ in diameter by 1 7/8″ in height. Although handled bowls are unpopular by today's standards, it is a graceful piece that really embodies the Harlequin style with the handles on each side. It was available in all twelve colors, but is getting hard to find in the fifties colors. The medium green Harlequin cream soup is extremely rare, probably because the shape was phased out just as medium green was introduced.

Harlequin Cream Soup Bowl

Modeling Date	February 1938
Model Number	1045
Revision	None
Production Began	March, 1938
Discontinued	1959
Length of Production	21 Years
Colors: All	

Cream soup bowls in colors available at shape introduction. Maroon, $36-39; Blue, $29-31; Spruce, $34-36; Yellow, $23-26.

Cream soup bowls in the fifties colors. Chartreuse, $33-37; Forest, $34-37; Gray, $34-36.

Cream soup bowls in the forties colors. Rose, $26-30; Green, $33-34; Turquoise, $23-24; Red, $33-35.

2 7/8"
6 3/4"
4 7/8"

Cream soup bowl in medium green, $1465-1635.

Fruit bowls in colors available at shape introduction. Marron, $12-14; Blue, $10-12; Spruce, $12-13; Yellow, $9-10.

Fruit Bowl

The fruit bowl, model #655, was originally introduced in a six-inch diameter version. The log describes it as "fruit rolled top, same design as above [the item above was the nappy]." It was released to production September 11, 1936. By April 1937 it seems to have been remodeled. A new shape, model #795, is described as being 5 11/16" in diameter. It is available in all twelve colors with the fifties colors being somewhat scarce.

Harlequin Fruit Bowl	
Modeling Date	July 1936
Model Number	655
Revision	1937, 1940
Production Began	September 1936
Discontinued	1959
Length of Production	24 Years
Colors: All	

Fruit bowls in forties colors. Rose, $10-11; Green, $12-13; Red, $13-16; Turquoise, $9-10.

Fruit bowls in fifties colors. Chartreuse, $12-13; Forest, $12-14; Gray, $10-12.

Fruit bowl in medium green, $32-35.

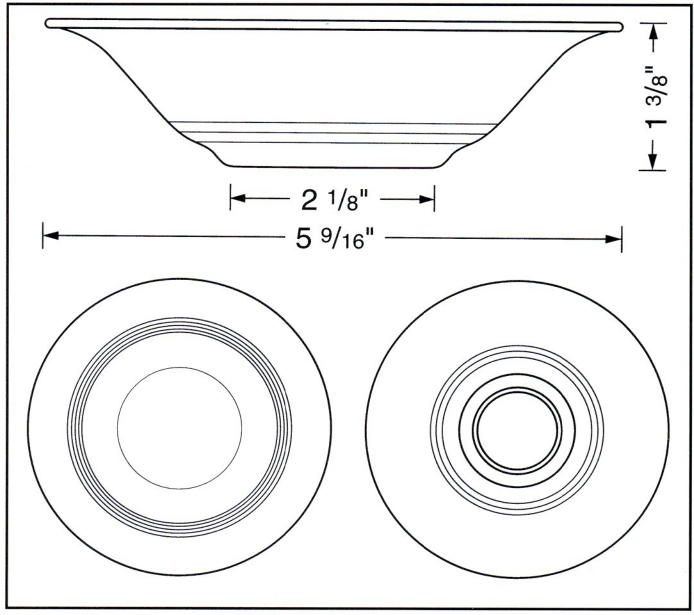

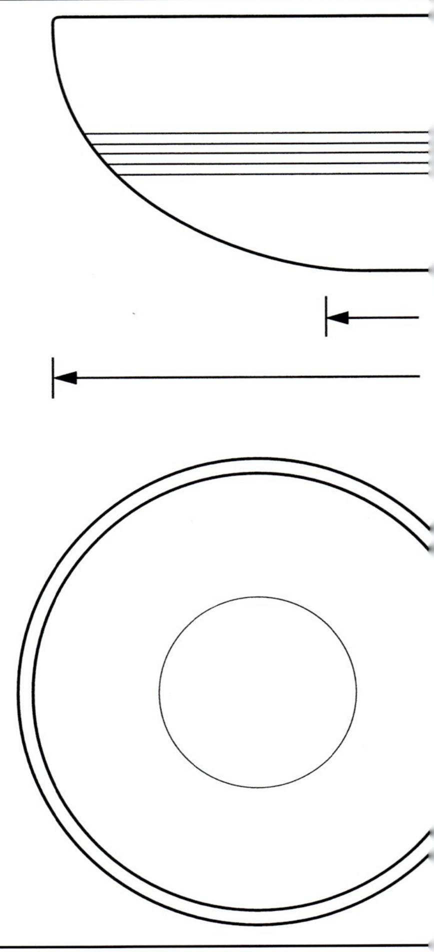

Individual Salad Bowl

Although originally designed for Fiesta, the individual salad bowl was modified and added in the first expansion of the Harlequin line. Its generous size, 7 1/2" by 2 1/8", made it a very useful bowl and a welcome addition to the line. Although it was made in all twelve colors, its later introduction makes it hard to find in maroon and spruce. This is one of the few pieces not found in Rhead's journals.

New information indicates that the Harlequin individual salad may have been remodeled in 1959. In that year, an individual salad bowl was added to the Fiesta line. It is model #2552 and is listed as "Harlequin / Fiesta Bowl." It may be that for ease of production, this shape was made without inside rings for Harlequin and with inside rings for Fiesta. This could explain why these "Fiesta" bowls have been found without inside rings in red, turquoise, medium green, and Harlequin yellow—the Harlequin colors of that period. It would also explain the rarity of the Harlequin individual salad in medium green. Many collectors believe that next to the medium green cream soup bowl, the individual salad in medium green is the scarcest Harlequin bowl.

Harlequin Individual Salad Bowl

Modeling Date	September 1939
Model Number	1326
Revision	1959
Production Began	November 1039
Discontinued	1959
Length of Production	20 Years
Colors: All	

Individual salad in colors avaialble at shape introduction. Maroon, $48-53; Blue, $31-33; Spruce, $33-40; Yellow, $29-32.

Individual salad in fifties colors. Chartreuse, $38-41; Forest, $43-48; Gray, $42-47.

Individual salad in forties colors. Rose, $22-24; Green, $31-35; Red, $40-45; Turquoise, $18-20.

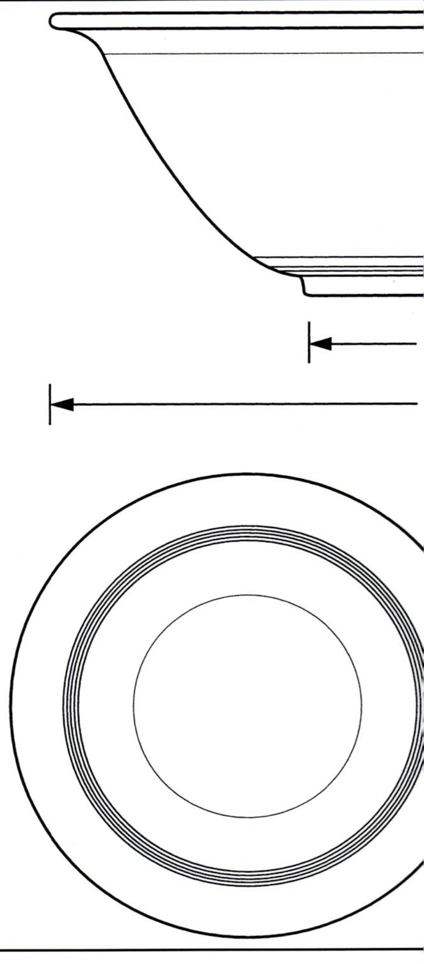

Individual salad in medium green, $145-170.

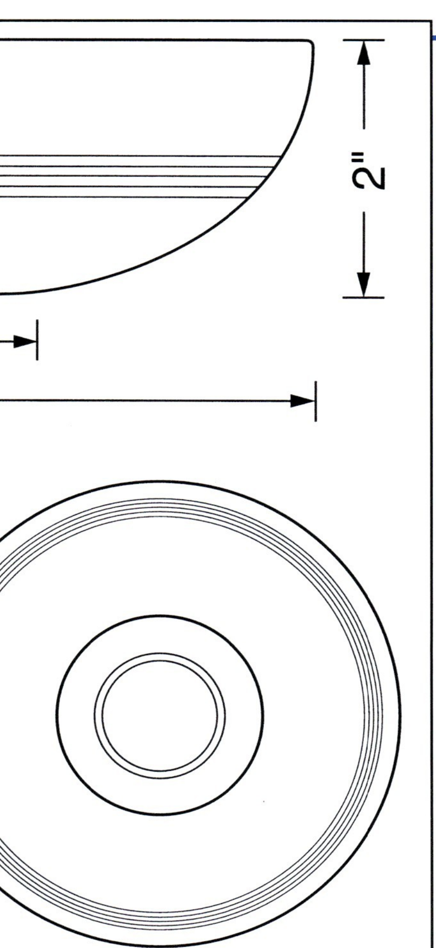

Nappy

The large size of the nappy makes it a very practical and attractive serving bowl for the table. Part of the original assortment, the nappy #654 was described as "Nappie,-rolled top, modeled lines inside". It was modeled by Bill Berrisford in July 1936 and was sent into production on September 11, 1936. It is 9" across and can be found in all twelve colors. It is one of two serving bowls in the line.

Harlequin Nappy	
Modeling Date	July 1936
Model Number	654
Revision	None
Production Began	September 1939
Discontinued	1959
Length of Production	20 Years
Colors: All	

Nappy in colors original to shape at introduction. Maroon, $44-49; Blue, $34-37; Spruce, $47-51; Yellow, $30-31.

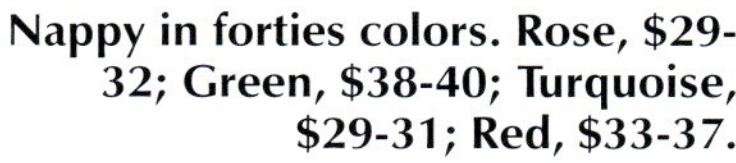

Nappy in forties colors. Rose, $29-32; Green, $38-40; Turquoise, $29-31; Red, $33-37.

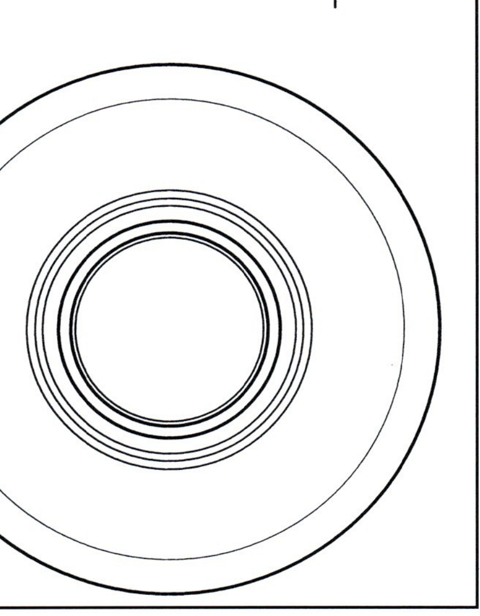

Nappy in fifties colors. Chartreuse, $41-45; Forest, $42-46; Gray, $41-45.

Nappy in medium green, $110-120.

Oval Baker

Many collectors believe that the oval baker was not original to the Harlequin line; however, according to the model log, the baker #679 was released to production at the same time as the other initial pieces of the line in September 1936. It is described as "baker-Woolworth same design as nappie #654" and was also modeled by Arthur Kraft. It is a shorter, oval version of the nappy. The baker was discontinued before the introduction of the fifties colors and therefore only available in the original and forties colors. Collectors report it being difficult to locate in red.

Harlequin Oval Baker

Modeling Date .... September 1936
Model Number 679
Revision .... None
Production Began .... September, 1936
Discontinued 1945
Length of Production .... 9 Years
Colors: Maroon, Yellow, Spruce, Blue, Red, Turquoise, Rose and Light Green

Above: **Oval baker in colors available at shape introduction. Maroon, $35-39; Blue, $31-33; Spruce, $40-43; Yellow, $27-29.**

Above right: **Oval baker in all the forties colors. Rose, $33-36; Green, $40-42; Turquoise, $30-33; Red, $35-37.**

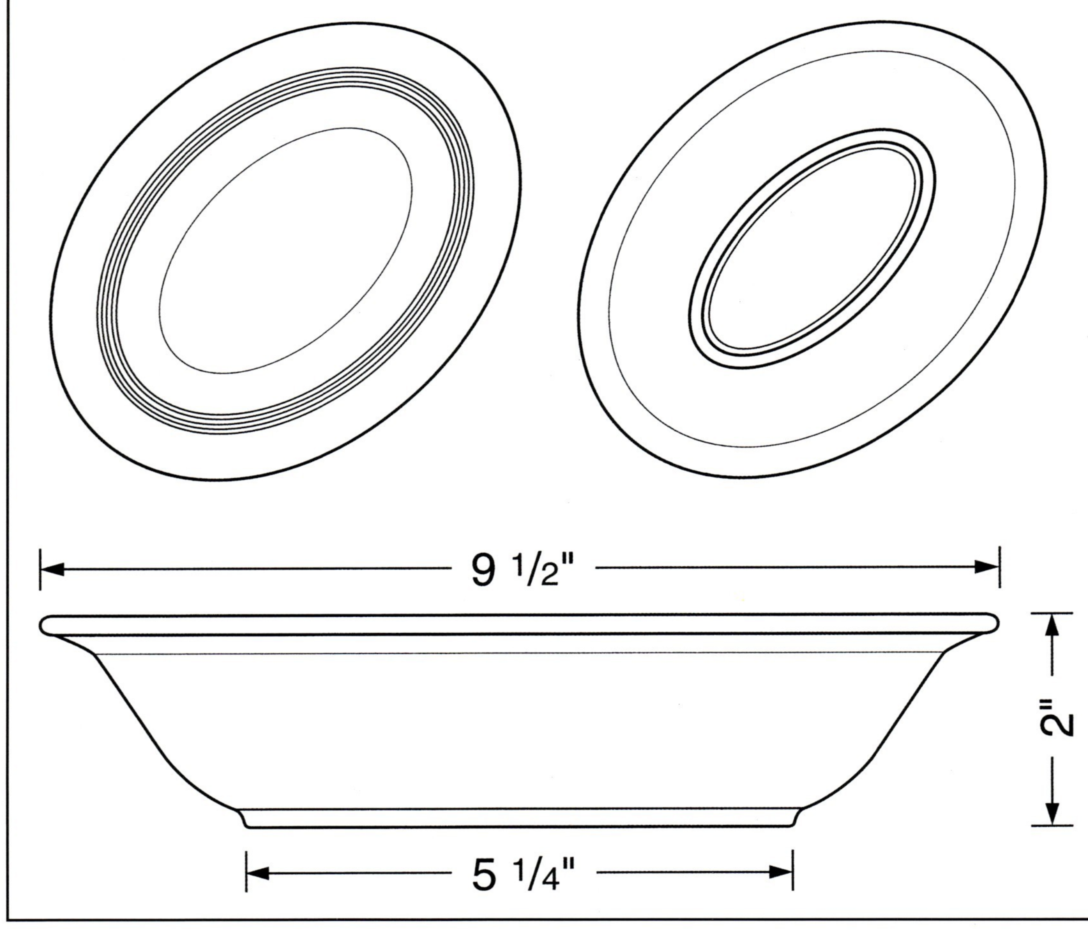

Harlequin butter dish in all colors available at the introduction of the shape. **Maroon, $150-160; Spruce, $140-145; Blue, $125-135; Yellow, $100-110.**

Butter Dish

The Harlequin butter dish shape was borrowed from a line called Jade, which was developed in the early 1930s. In entries from May1938, Rhead writes "see about jade butter (Harlequin)" and "to make 1 dozen covered butters-jade for Harlequin." This dozen were most likely intended to be samples. The Harlequin butter holds a half pound of butter. At the time, butter was sold in large half-pound slabs; today's slender sticks of butter came later. The dish lacks the Harlequin geometric styling but in matching glazes it blends nicely. It was discontinued before the 1950s, so it is only found in the original and forties colors. This butter was also sold for use with Riviera and Fiesta and is therefore found in cobalt, ivory, and Fiesta yellow.

Butter Dish	
Modeling Date	May 1938
Model Number	Not Available
Revision	None
Production Began	June 1938
Discontinued	Mid- to Late '40s
Length of Production	about 10 Years
Colors: Maroon, Yellow, Spruce, Blue, Red, Turquoise, Rose and Light Green	

Butter dish in the forties colors. Rose, $160-175; Green, $165-196; Turquoise, $105-110; Red $140-150.

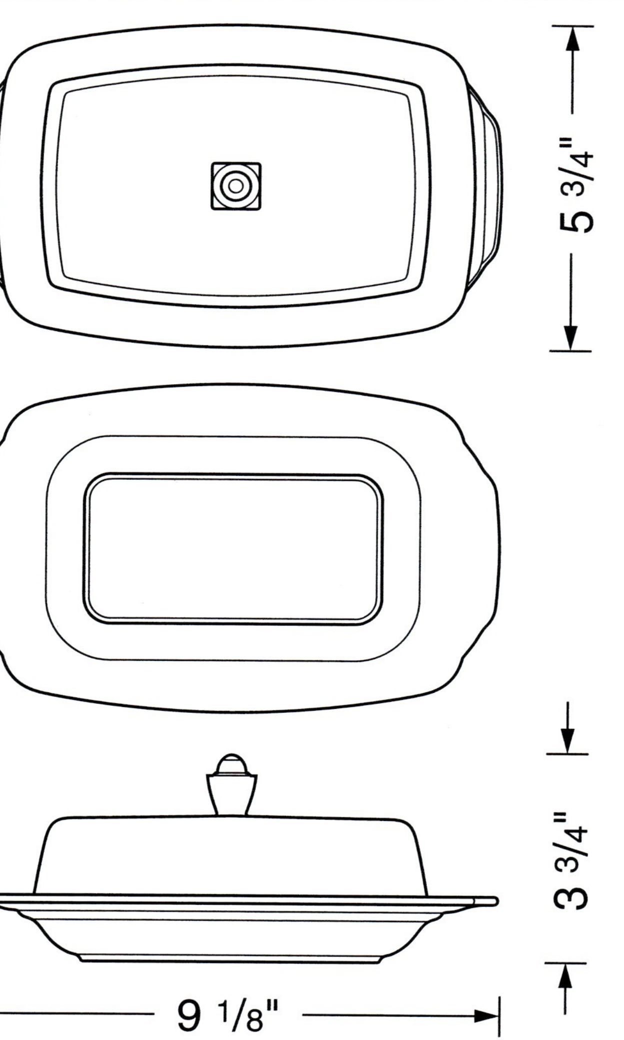

Candleholders

If it is the Art Deco and Streamlined Modern influence that attracts a collector to Harlequin, then the candleholders will be a must have for any collection. Telescoping is a common theme in Art Deco styling and is well represented in this piece.

Rhead was working on the candleholders in March 1940. The model log shows only three sketches, but the way they are numbered indicates that others may have been done. Numbers 1381, 1382, and 1383 are referred to as 1A, 2A, and 3B, respectively. Rhead notes that he sent samples to Wells on April 3, 1940 as indicated by his journal entry, "candlesticks (Harlequin) to JMW for Woolworths", and then on April 16, 1940, he writes "candlestick 1A #1381 release. OK".

The candleholders were made for only two years and are hard to find in any of the original or forties colors. The candleholders were discontinued at approximately the same time light green was added, so it is unclear whether light green candleholders were ever a standard production item. However, at least one pair has found its way into a collection. It is a shame that such a beautiful piece was so short-lived.

An assortment of the rare candleholders. (Pair) Maroon, $365-390; Red, $$300-310; Yellow, $265-285; Spruce, $335-370; Blue, $315-360.

Harlequin Candleholders

Modeling Date	April 1940
Model Number	1381
Revision	None
Production Began	May 16, 1940
Discontinued	c.1942
Length of Production	2 Years

Colors: Maroon, Yellow, Spruce, Blue, Tangerine, Turquoise, Rose and Light Green

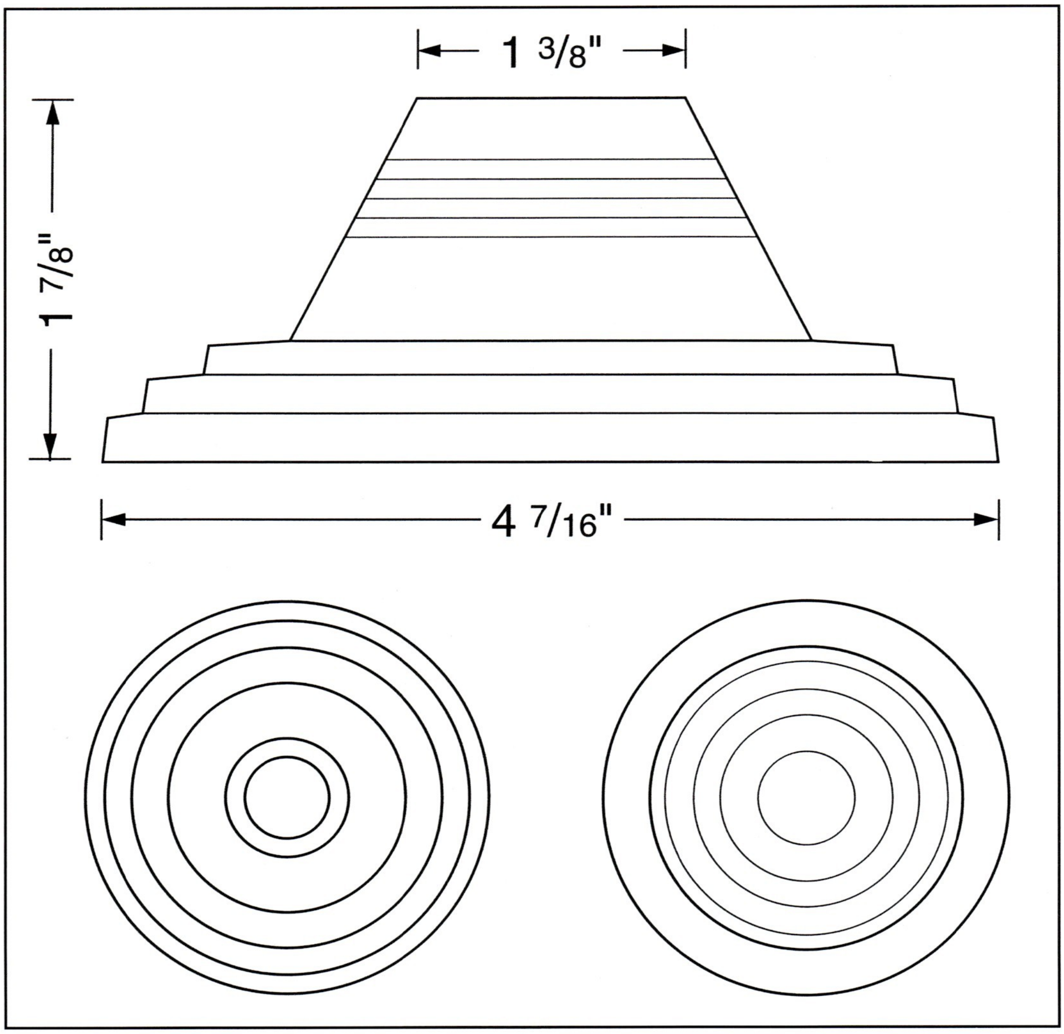

1 3/8"

1 7/8"

4 7/16"

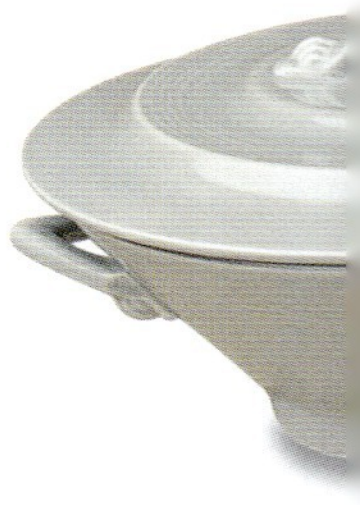

Casserole with Lid

The covered casserole incorporates all the elements essential to the Harlequin design. It has all the angles covered. Cones, circles, and triangles are all evident. In a journal entry dated Sunday, July 19, 1936, Rhead notes, "all day on Woolworth colored glaze casserole." The model log shows a preliminary drawing , #659, that has round handles and curved sides and also model #661, described as "strait[sic] sided casserole Woolworth." The latter model is the shape sent into production. There are no more illustrations in the log, but at least two more models were made, #663, described as "casserole, straight sides but without foot" and #665 "casserole curved side without foot". The casserole holds four liquid cups comfortably and five cups to the rim. It is found in all twelve colors, with the fifties colors harder to find. The medium green covered casserole is a great rarity. Fewer than five have been reported. It is likely that it was not regularly produced in this color and that the existing examples may be no more than a test run.

Harlequin Casserole with Lid	
Modeling Date	August 1936
Model Number	661
Revision	None
Production Began	September 11, 1936
Discontinued	1959
Length of Production	23 Years
Colors: All	

The covered casserole in the colors available at the shape introduction. Maroon, $145-160; Blue, $125-140; Spruce, $165-175; Yellow, $105-115.

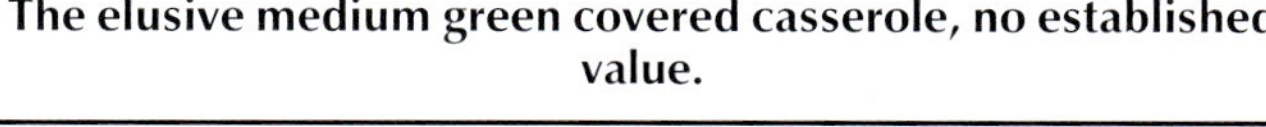

The elusive medium green covered casserole, no established value.

Covered casserole in the fories colors. Rose, $105-115; Green, $160-165; Turquoise, $100-110; Red, $120-130.

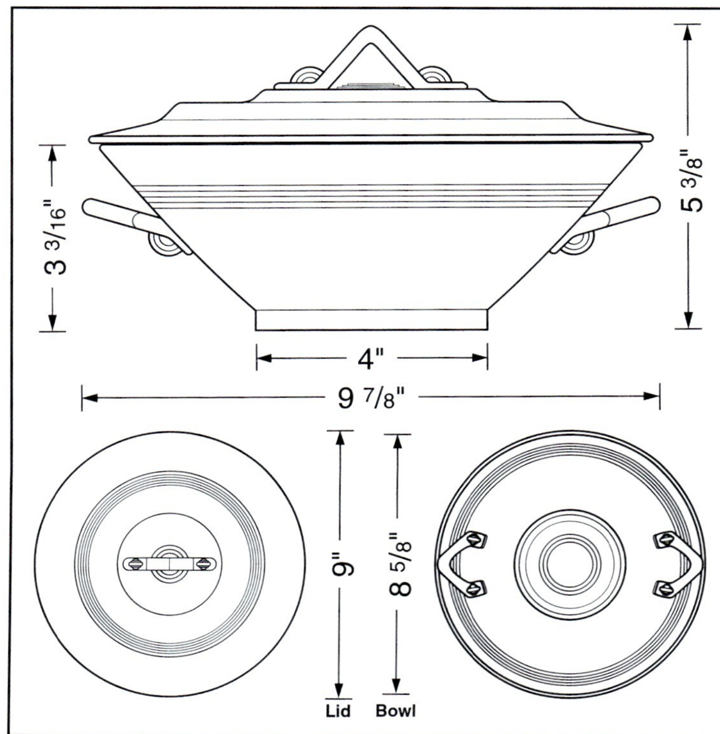

Covered casserole in the fifties colors. Chartreuse, $160-190; Forest, $250-320; Gray, $140-155.

Creamers

The creamer was one of the few pieces that was remodeled (from regular to high-lip) during its lifetime. In addition to the regular creamer, a novelty creamer was also sold with the line. The third creamer, highly sought out by Harlequin collectors, is the individual or toy creamer.

High-Lip & Regular Creamer

The original Harlequin creamer is known to today's collectors as the high-lip creamer. It is found in two versions, the narrow lip and the wide lip. The model log lists "#668 cream, straight sides with lines, Woolworth." There is no sketch, but the creamer shown in the earliest brochure is the narrow-lip version. In his journal on February 9, 1937, Rhead states "Letter for Woolworths: The Harlequin creamer: The new spout pours all right but they want it more graceful. To work on new adjustment". It is not clear which version, narrow or wide, came first. Both versions of the high-lip creamer are rare and only available in the original four colors. The next mention of a creamer in the model log is from November 1942, "#1850 cream with foot same as [sugar]." It is clear from the model log that this number was given to a new model because redesigned shapes were needed for a new patent jigger. There is no clear mention of an original model number for the regular creamer. It may be #775, modeled in February 1937.

The regular creamer is readily available in all the original four colors, so it is clear that it was produced prior to 1942. Perhaps it went into production when the high-lip version was retired sometime in 1938. It may be that the narrow high lip was changed to the wide high lip and to make it more "graceful." And finally it was remodeled to the regular version. The regular version is truly the most graceful of the creamers. The edge wraps into the bowl and directs the cream directly to the spout, something that was lacking in the earlier models. The regular creamer can be found in all twelve colors, and, with the exception of medium green, spruce and maroon are probably the hardest to find.

Regular creamer in the fifties colors. Chartreuse, $21-23; Forest, $26-28; Gray, $19-22.

Harlequin High-Lip Creamer	
Modeling Date	August 1936
Model Number	668
Revision	1937
Production Began	September 17, 1936
Discontinued	c.1938
Length of Production	2 Years
Colors: Maroon, Yellow, Spruce, and Blue	

Harlequin Regular Creamer	
Modeling Date	1938
Model Number	Not Available
Revision	None
Production Began	1938
Discontinued	1959
Length of Production	21 Years
Colors: All	

Medium green Harlequin regular creamer, $73-79.

Regular Halrequin creamer in the colors available at introduction. Maroon, $23-25; Blue, $19-21; Spruce, $25-27; Yellow, $12-13.

Regular creamer in the forties colors. Rose, $17-19; Green, $22-23; Turquoise, $13-14; Red, $22-23.

The two style of high-lip creamers. Spruce, $175-195; Yellow, $175-195.

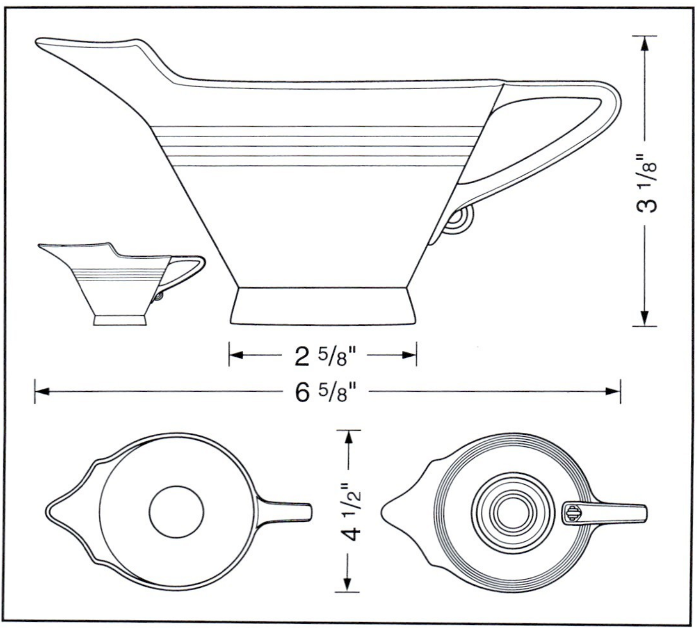

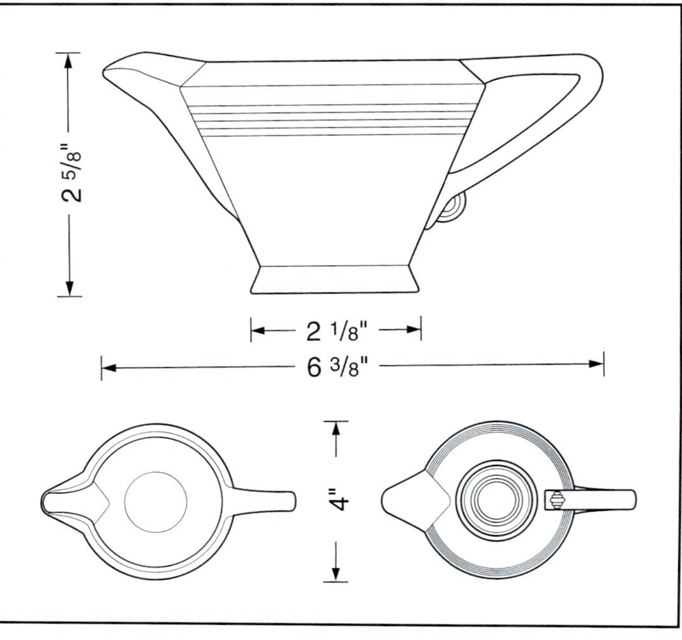

Novelty Creamer

The novelty creamer is a miniature version of the ball jug. It is unclear whether this was to be used as a creamer or sold as a novelty miniature. The shape is model #1164, described as "cream ball round 10.5 ozs cap." A preceding sketch in the model log, #1163, is called "cream ball oval" and was done at the same time in November1940. Rhead's journal notes that "JMW [Wells] released small ball jug model 1164 on 12/12/38." It appears these were not designed for the Harlequin line. An entry dated January 5, 1939, states "small jug for Woolworth to be H". It is not certain if the "H" refers to Harlequin, but since these were sold with the line it is a reasonable deduction. It is hard to believe these could have been made for another line. The model log shows sketches of several different versions. The rings around the "ball" of the jug were most likely not added until it was decided to include the shape in the Harlequin line. The novelty creamer is found in all twelve colors. While it was once thought that these were not made in medium green, one or two have been reported and are considered extremely rare.

Harlequin Novelty Creamer

Modeling Date	November 1938
Model Number	1164
Revision	None
Production Began	December 1938
Discontinued	1959
Length of Production	21 Years
Colors: All	

Novelty creamers in the fifties colors. Chartreuse, $64-75; Forest, $64-73; Gray, $62-72.

Novelty creamers in colors original to the shape. Maroon, $49-53; Blue, $39-42; Spruce, $46-54; Yellow, $29-31.

Novelty creamers in the forties colors. Rose, $36-38; Green, $45-51; Turquoise, $29-31; Red, $38-41.

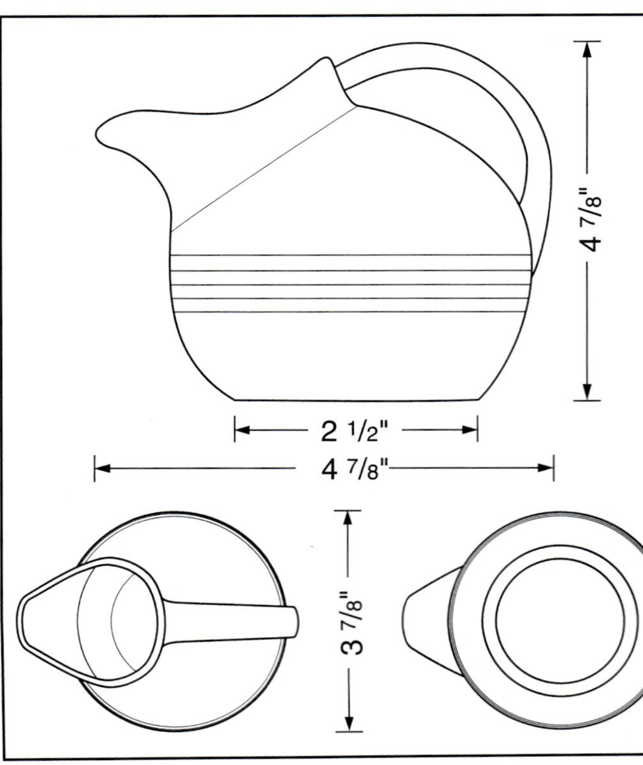

Individual / Toy Creamer

Many non-Harlequin collectors collect these tiny toy creamers since they fall into the "miniatures" category. While they may be cute, they are most likely not really part of the Harlequin line. The shape is model #1181. The journal entry from January 28, 1939, states, "Sent to Woolworth 2 samples of small jug #1181. Sketches were submitted to Wm. Lindquist on Dec.29, 1938." The description in the model log for the same piece states "Jug, (ind). Woolworth toy cream." The tiny creamer was released to production on February 2, 1939. The name "Harlequin" has never been found in a mention of this piece. It was dipped in Harlequin glazes and sold at Woolworth, and thus it has come to be called "Harelquin" by today's collectors and is found in most collections of the line. The "Toy Creamer" is found in the original and forties colors. It was dropped in the early 1940s, which explains why it is rare in rose and light green.

Harlequin Individual Creamer

Modeling Date	January 1939
Model Number	1181
Revision	None
Production Began	February 1939
Discontinued	c.1942
Length of Production	3 Years

Colors: Maroon, Yellow, Spruce, Blue, Red, Turquoise, Rose and Light Green

Individual creamer in colors original to the shape. Rhead referred to this as a toy creamer. Maroon, $34-35; Blue, $27-29; Spruce, $24-28; Yellow, $23-25.

Individual creamer in the forties colors. Rose, $44-54; Green, $88-98; Turquoise, $30-40; Red, $26-28.

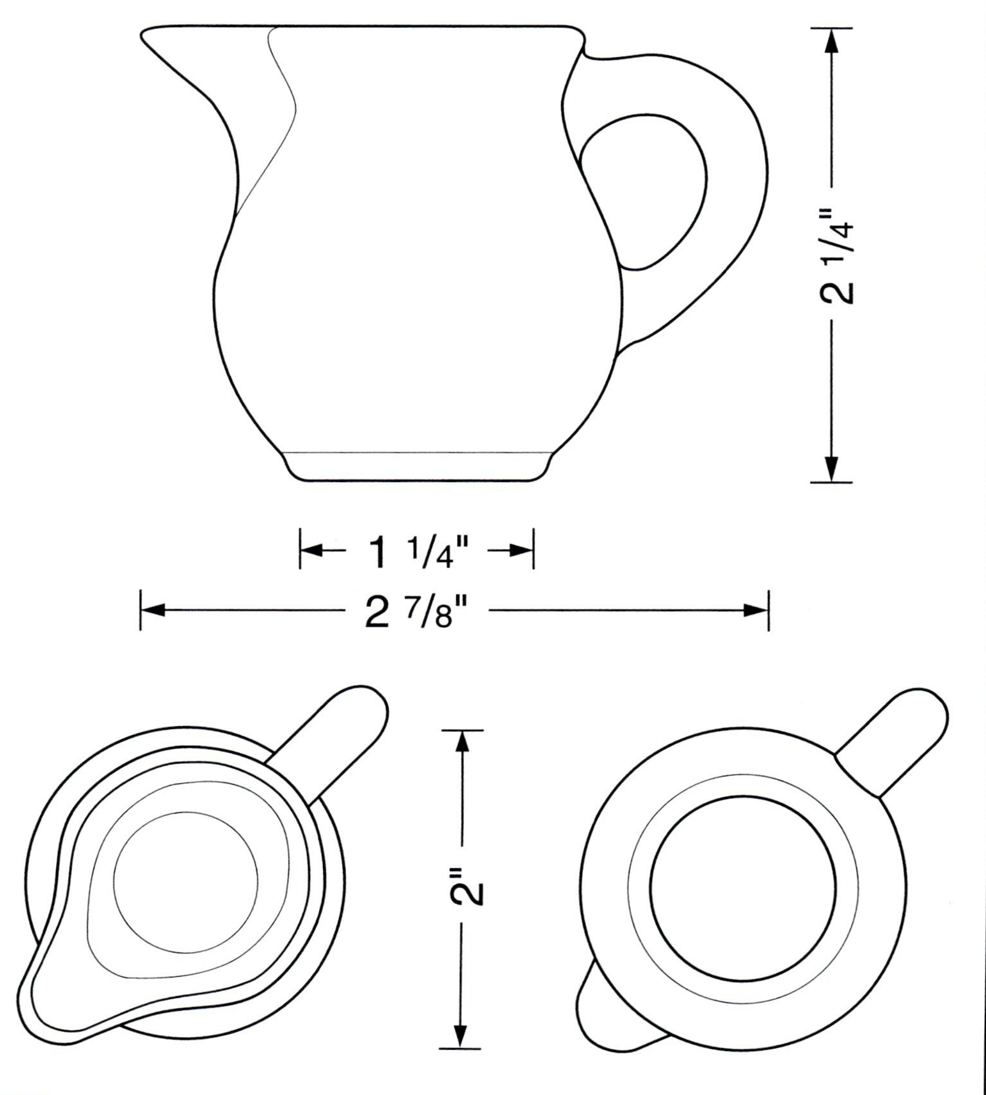

Cups

Demitasse Cup and Saucer

The initial design of the demitasse or A.D. (for "after dinner") cup and saucer is somewhat of a mystery. The model log indicates that the cup and handle is #934; the saucer, #935. They were modeled by Arthur Kraft and described as "R .Cup, A.D.+ Hand, Harlequin Shape" and "R. Saucer, A.D." Both appear to have a September 30, 1937 release date. #1320 is "Hand. for Harlequin A.D. cup, 934." This later shape is dated September1939. It is probably safe to assume that the demitasse set was released in the wave of October 1939. It can be found in all twelve colors but is scarce in the fifties colors and very rare in medium green. Most collectors agree that the demitasse cups are easier to find than the saucers.

Harlequin Demitasse Cup & Saucer	
Modeling Date	September 1937
Model Number	934 (cup), 935 (saucer)
Revision	None
Production Began	September 1939
Discontinued	1959
Length of Production	20 Years
Colors: All	

Demitasse cup and saucer in colors original to the shape. See Appendix E for pricing. Cup and saucer priced separately.

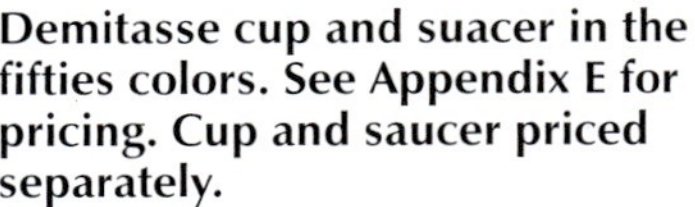

Demitasse cup and suacer in the fifties colors. See Appendix E for pricing. Cup and saucer priced separately.

Demitasse cup and saucer in colors added in the 1940s. See Appendix E for pricing. Cup and saucer priced separately.

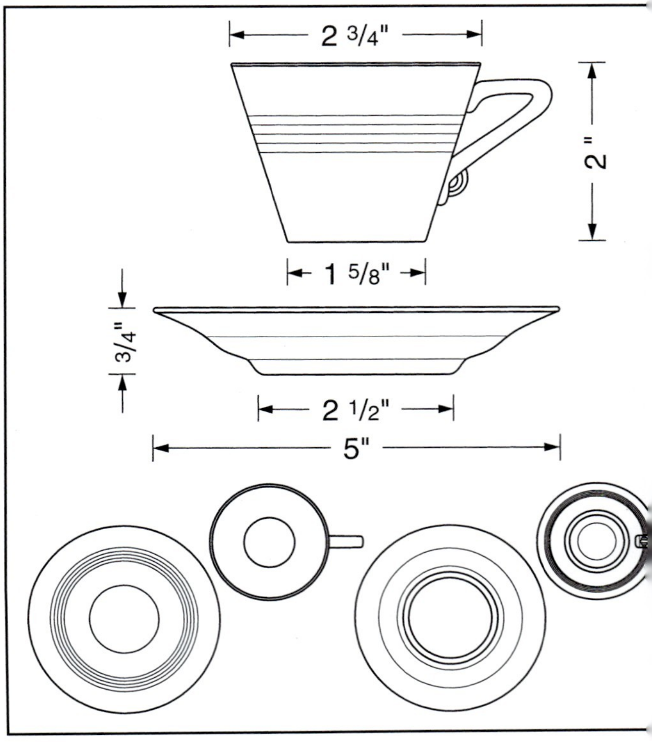

Large Cup

It is not clear if the large cup was sold as a part of the Harlequin line. It is large, by even today's standards. It holds a whopping eleven ounces. By comparison, the Harlequin teacup holds a mere seven ounces; the contemporary Fiesta mug, nine ounces. The large cup was created by combining an Epicure cup body with a large Harlequin handle. The Epicure was a line designed in the early 1950s by Don Schreckengost. The model log shows #2411, dated May 23,1955, as "Harlequin H'dle for Epicure cup." The standard handle apparently was not big enough for the large cup body. The next entry is #2412, dated June 3, 1955, "Larger Harlequin Handle for Epicure cup." The large cup is found in chartreuse, dark green, rose, turquoise, yellow, and medium green. All are scarce. Even though gray was a standard 1950s Harlequin production color, these have not been found in gray. That omission suggests that they were not marketed as Harlequin, but perhaps created for some other purpose.

In the past some collectors have mistakenly called this large cup the "Harlequin tankard." This confusion arises because some time ago factory records were found that showed a "Harlequin tankard" in a list of items dropped before 1952. The large cup was not on any Harlequin list so it was assumed that it must be the discontinued "tankard." But this conjecture had a problem, since the large cup was only found in fifties colors, and the records indicated that the tankard was dropped before the introduction of these colors. The model log confirmed that the large cup was designed in 1955. Further research has found that "tankard" probably refers to the shape also called the "tumbler." In Rhead's journal, there is an entry referring to the "Newberry handled tankard," model #1194. It is clear this was the Riviera handled tumbler. Riviera was a solid color line sold at the Newberry five-and-ten-cent stores. It seems that Rhead occasionally referred to the tumblers as "tankards." It is most likely that the discontinued "Harlequin tankard" was in fact the Harlequin tumbler, not the large cup.

Harlequin Large Cup

Modeling Date	May 1955
Model Number	2411 or 2412
Revision	None
Production Began	Not Available
Discontinued	c.1959
Length of Production	4 Years

Colors: Yellow, Turquoise, Chartreuse, Rose, Dark Green, and Medium Green

The large cup in rose, $240-265, yellow, $230-255, and chartreuse, $240-265.

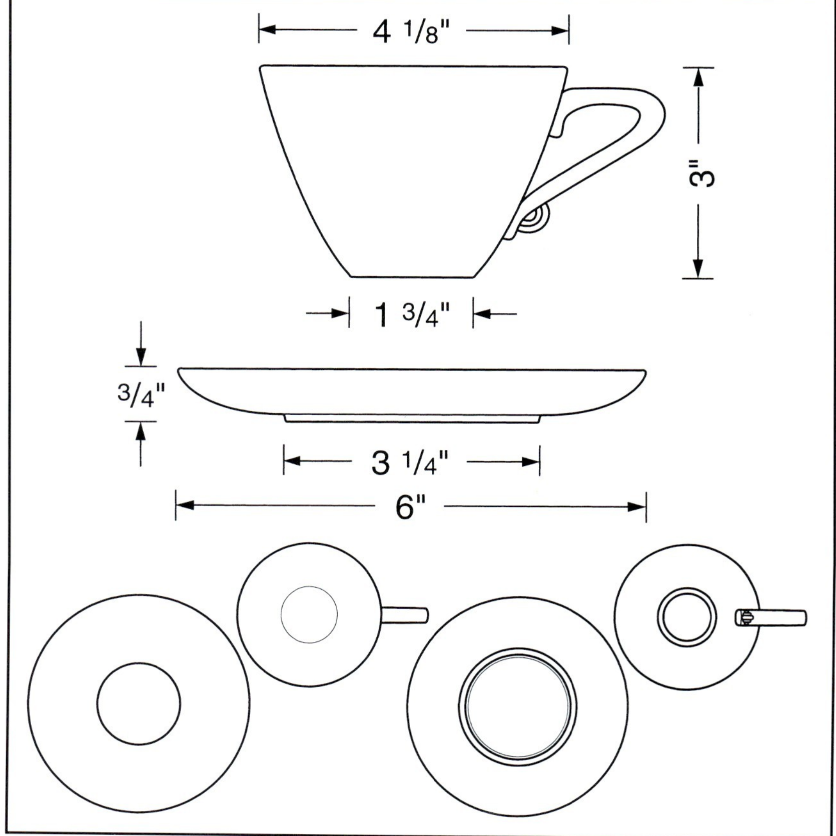

Teacup and Saucer

The teacup exemplifies the Harlequin design. After Rhead designed the plate, he started on the teacup. All the other Harlequin hollowware designs stem from the cup. On July 3, 1936, Rhead notes that he "worked on new cups and glazed ware for Woolworths." The sketches for #649 show a convex shape with a rounded handle described as "teacup convex with lines in center." #651 is the classic Harlequin shape, listed as "teacup strait[sic] side lines in center." Both sketches are dated August 1936. The model log entry for#651 also depicts a variety of cup handles, labeled A, B, and C. On September 11, 1936, the log indicates the release for model # 651 with handle C.

The saucer, #650, is simply described as "Saucer for [649],flat rim." It was sent to production on September 11, 1936 as well. Both pieces are readily available in all twelve colors.

The medium green Harlequin teacup and saucer. See Appendix E for pricing. Cup and saucer priced separately.

Harlequin Teacup & Saucer

Modeling Date	July 1936
Model Number	651 (cup), 650 (saucer)
Revision	None
Production Began	September 1936
Discontinued	1959
Length of Production	23 Years
Colors: All	

Teacups and saucers in original colors. See Appendix E for pricing. Cup and saucer priced separately.

The forties colors on the teacup and saucer. See Appendix E for pricing. Cup and saucer priced separately.

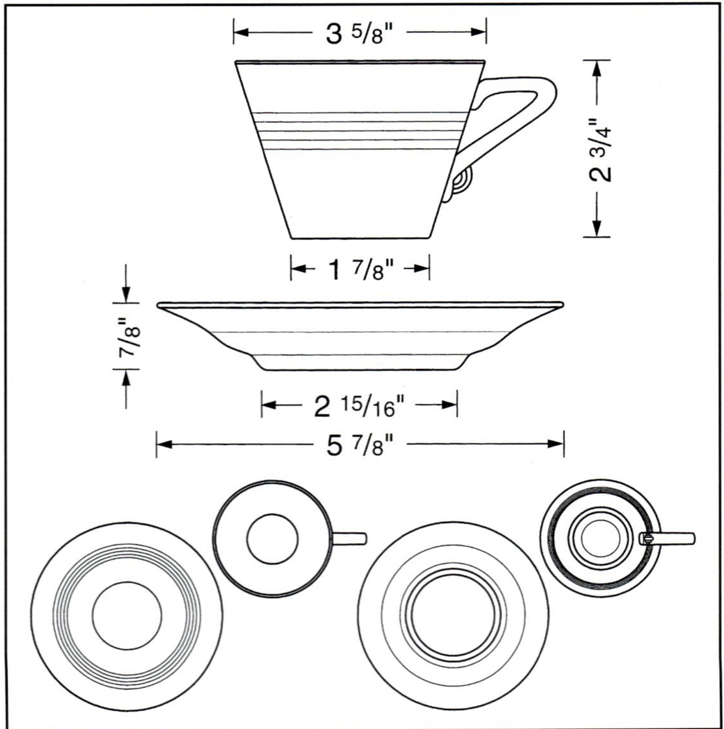

Teacups and saucers in the fifties colors. See Appendix E for pricing. Cup and saucer priced separately.

Double eggcups in original colors to the line. Maroon, $33-35; Spruce, $29-33; Blue, $25-26; Yellow, $26-29.

Eggcups

Double Eggcup

The double eggcup was one of the earliest pieces Rhead designed for "Woolworth's color glazed dinnerware line," probably before the line had acquired a name. It is #682, dated September1936. It was in production for the entire life of the line. It is designed either to hold boiled eggs on the small end or poached eggs in the large end. Today's collectors talk of many new ways to use them from sake cups to votive candleholders and individual flower vases. It is found in all twelve colors with the fifties colors being somewhat hard to find. Dark green seems to be more scarce than the other fifties colors. Medium green double eggcups are quite rare.

Harlequin Double Egg Cup	
Modeling Date	September 1936
Model Number	682
Revision	None
Production Began	September 1936
Discontinued	1959
Length of Production	23 Years
Colors: All	

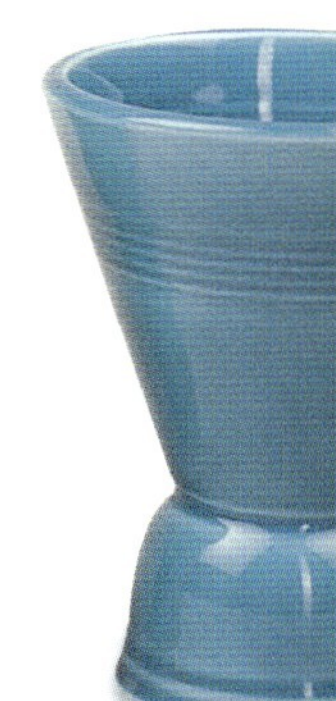

Double eggcups in the forties colors. Rose, $25-28; Red, $31-33; Green, $29-29; Turquoise, $22-24.

Double eggcups in the fifties colors. Forest, $46-57; Gray, $38-43; Chartreuse, $39-46.

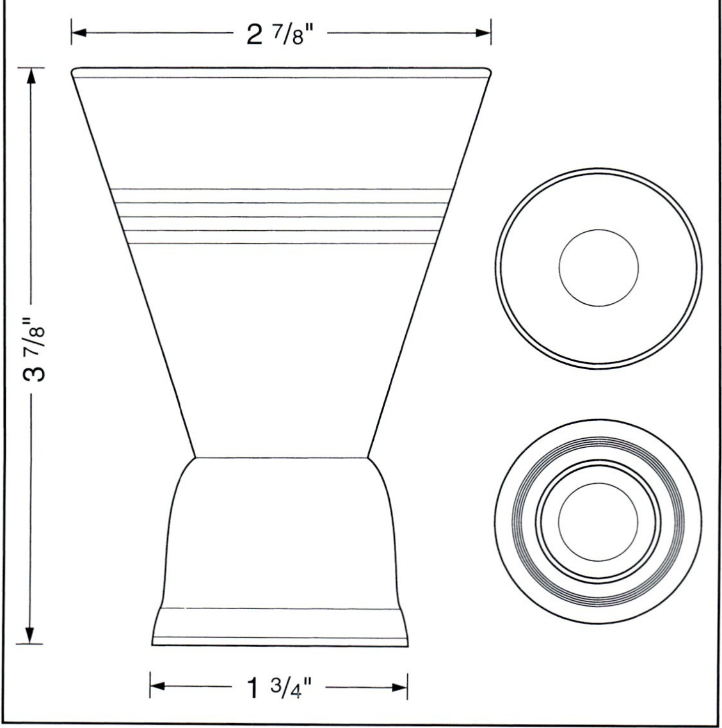

Single Eggcup

These little eggcups are one of the few pieces not decorated with the usual Harlequin rings. The only information available is found in the model log, which shows #1032 as "egg cup. Ivory body." Berrisford made the model in January 1938 and it was in approved for production March 5, 1938. While these were dipped in Harlequin glazes, it is likely that they were not marketed as part of the Harlequin line. They are not called Harlequin in company records. It does seem unnecessary to have two eggcups in one line (although this is a line that has eight different bowls). These were short-lived and discontinued by the early 1940s. They were dipped in the original and forties colors but are rare in rose and light green with only a few reported.

Harlequin Single Egg Cup

Modeling Date	January 1938
Model Number	1032
Revision	None
Production Began	March 1938
Discontinued	c.1942
Length of Production	4 Years

Colors: Maroon, Yellow, Spruce, Blue, Red, Turquoise, Rose and Light Green

The original four colors for the single eggcup. Maroon, $37-38; Spruce, $33-37; Blue, $32-35; Yellow, $27-29.

Single eggcups in the forties colors. Rose, $35-42; Red, $34-36; Green, $220-380; Turquoise, $29-31.

Marmalade

The Marmalade #1040 is a scarce piece favored by many collectors. It was added in the early expansion. The model log calls it "Marmalade Jar Harlequin 9+3/4 oz capacity". It was modeled in February 1938 and released the next month. They are found in the original and forties colors and like many other items, are hard to find in rose and very hard to find in light green. The marmalade relates to the teapot the way the sugar relates to the casserole. If you were to add a spout and handle it would closely resemble the teapot.

Harlequin Marmalade

Modeling Date	February 1938
Model Number	1040
Revision	None
Production Began	March 1938
Discontinued	c.1942
Length of Production	4 Years

Colors: Maroon, Yellow, Spruce, Blue, Red, Turquoise, Rose and Light Green

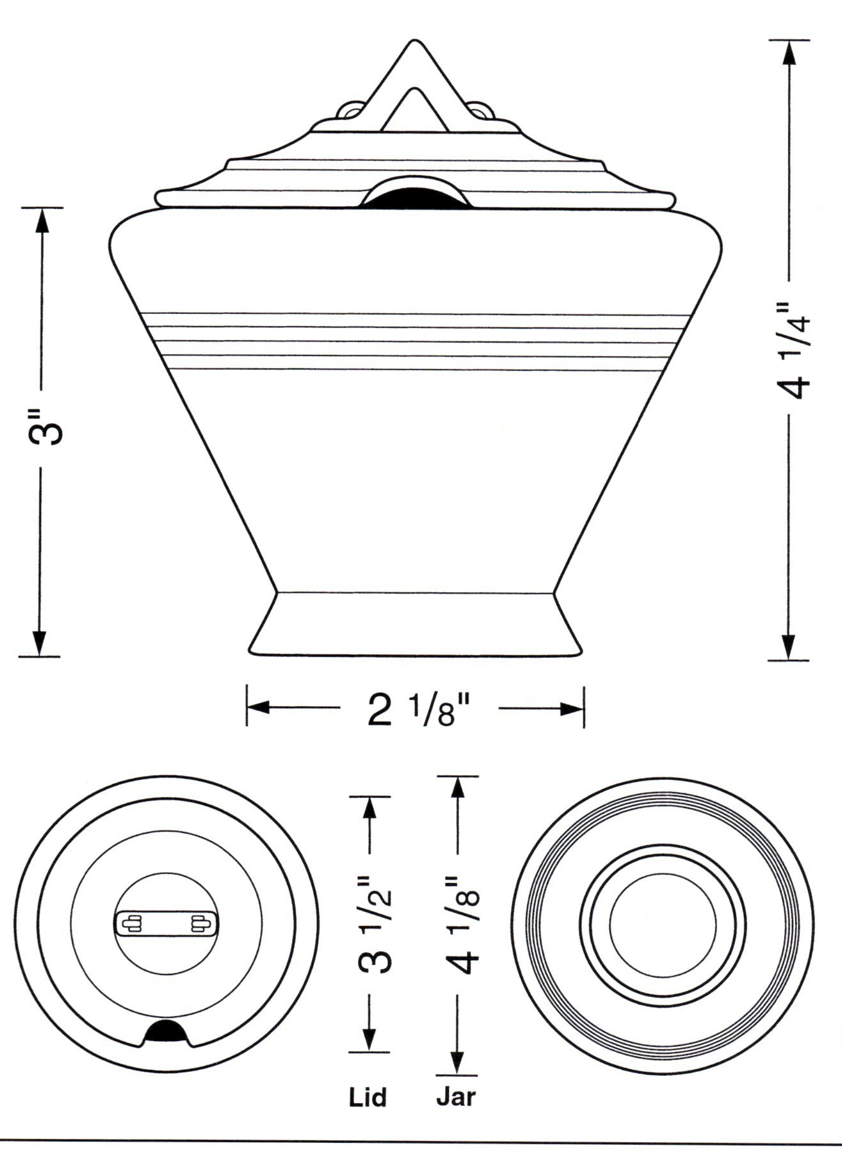

Marmalades in the original colors to the shape. Maroon, $335-355; Blue, $265-300; Spruce, $325-380; Yellow, $210-230.

The four forties colors of marmalades. Rose, $270-305; Green, $420-670; Turquoise, $235-255; Red, $285-300.

Basketweave Nut Dish

In the model log, the nut dish is described as "ash tray, copy of Japanese tray. Nut Bowl" with the note, "indi-no 1," inserted above. It appears this may have been intended as an individual ashtray, but marketed as a nut dish instead. Like the basketweave ashtray, the shape is copied from a similar Japanese Marutomo ware dish. It was released on March 15, 1938. They were in production only a short time, but production must have been very large, as these are not difficult to find in most colors today. They were dipped in the original and forties colors. Rose and light green are scarce. Collectors have found other uses for them as well. Some of the popular uses are as salt cellars, sauce dishes for Chinese food, butter pats, and candy dishes.

Harlequin Basketweave Nut Dish	
Modeling Date	February 1938
Model Number	1039
Revision	None
Production Began	March 1938
Discontinued	c.1943
Length of Production	5 Years

Colors: Maroon, Yellow, Spruce, Blue, Tangerine, Turquoise, Rose and Light Green

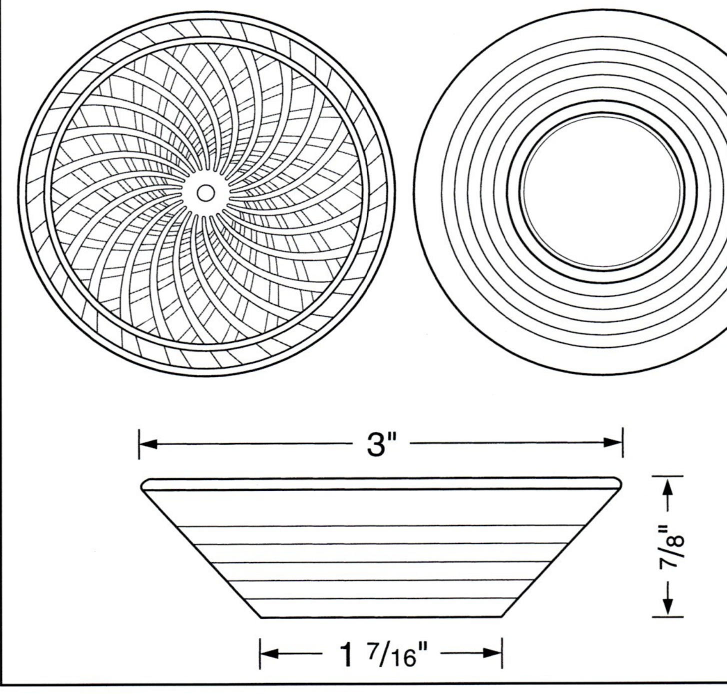

The original colors of the basketweave nutdish. Maroon, $21-23; Blue, $18-20; Spruce, $22-23; Yellow, $16-17.

Basketweave nutdish in the forties colors. Turquoise, $12-13; Green, $105-110; Rose, $42-50; Red, $19-21.

The 22-ounce jug in the original colors. Maroon, $76-84; Blue, $58-63; Spruce, $80-89; Yellow, $38-40.

Pitchers

22-ounce Jug

It is unclear exactly when the 22-ounce jug joined the line. It is first found in the model log as #773, "Jug-called Jug 48s, Harlequin." It was to be released on March 5, 1937. However, the model log is unclear on this piece. It is possible that #773 was the regular creamer. A later entry, #1066, listed as "Jug Harlequin 22 1/2 oz capacity" shows a release date of May 10, 1938. From its accompanying sketch, it is clear that this was the 22-ounce jug that collectors know today. It has been suggested that this jug would have been used for milk or heavy cream on the breakfast table. It is a favorite among collectors. It was made in all colors but is hard to find in maroon and spruce, rare in the fifties colors, and extremely rare in medium green.

Harlequin 22-ounce Jug

Modeling Date	April 1938
Model Number	1066
Revision	None
Production Began	May 1938
Discontinued	1959
Length of Production	21 Years
Colors: All	

The fifties colors of the 22-ounce jug. Gray, $83-89; Forest, $86-93; Chartreuse, $75-85.

22-ounce jug in the forties colors. Rose, $58-65; Green, $76-78; Turquoise, $49-53; Red, $72-75.

The medium green 22-ounce jug, $1445-1555.

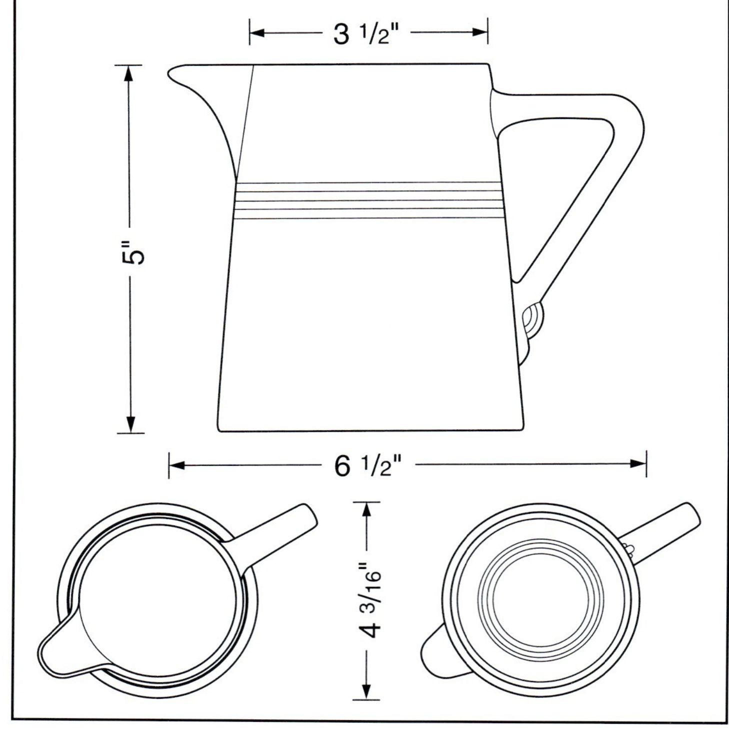

Service Water Pitcher

The service water pitcher is also known as the "ball jug." The shape may have originally been intended for the Fiesta line. The first entry in the model log from March 1937 is #791 "Fiesta water Jug 2qt capacity." It is similar in size and shape to the Harlequin jug. The next sketch is dated three months later, July 1937, and labeled #880 "Service Jug as Hall China." It has the rings around the base and is unmistakably the Harlequin ball jug. It is notable that the piece is not specifically called Harlequin and that it was obviously based on a jug produced by Hall China, across the Ohio River in East Liverpool, Ohio. Most collectors have probably seen the slightly smaller Hall pitcher. The ball jug was made in all twelve colors. It is readily available in the earlier colors, but hard to find in the fifties colors. Dark green is particularly scarce. Less than ten medium green ball jugs have been reported.

Service water pitcher, Medium Green, $2500-3200.

Harlequin Service Water Pitcher

Modeling Date	July 1937
Model Number	880
Revision	None
Production Began	1938
Discontinued	1959
Length of Production	21 Years
Colors: All	

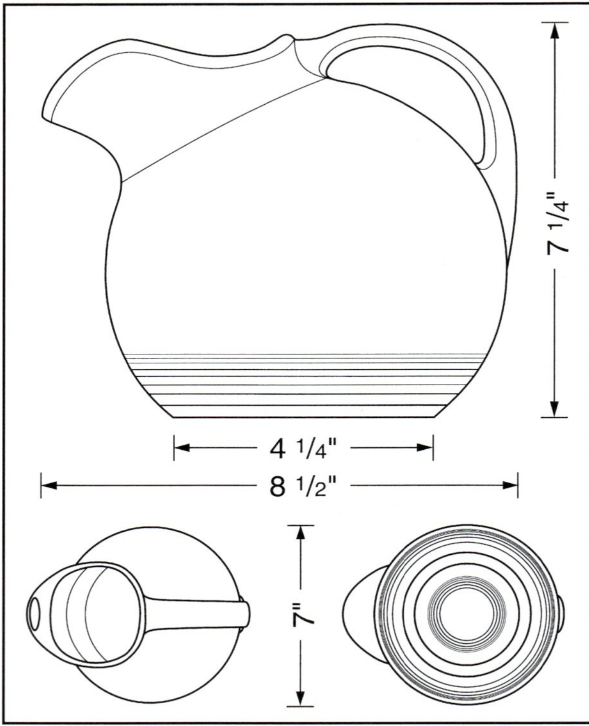

Service water pitchers: Blue, $67-73, Maroon, $110-115, Spruce, $91-98, Yellow, $68-70.

Service water pitchers: Gray, $115-125, Forest, $145-150, Chartreuse, $110-125.

Service water pitchers: Turquoise, $68-70, Rose, $80-84, Green, $ 97-100, Red, $86-89.

Plates

10″, 9″, 7″, 6″ Plates

The plate is how it all started for Harlequin. In June 1936, Rhead was working on "a colored glaze line for Woolworth". The model log from June 1936 shows #613, "plate-embossed lines on ball;" #614, "plate – embossed lines on ball with 8 panels;" and #616, "plate-similar decoration as Fiesta, but on ball-not on edge." On July 2, 1936, Rhead notes "Woolworth Plates in kiln". Of course these were the samples that were to be sent to the various department heads and client representatives. The first plate sent to production was the 10″ dinner plate, #657. It was modeled in August and released September 11, 1936. It was followed by the 7″ plate, #672, and the 6″plate #674. Both of these were released on September 21, 1936. Although a release date is not given for the 9″ plate, it was in the original line and probably also went into production in September 1936.

The 10″, 9″, 7″, 6″plates are available in all twelve colors. The 6″, 7″, and 9″ plates are readily available in all colors, with the exception of medium green, which is hard to find. The 10″ plates are difficult to find in the original and forties colors and rare in the fifties colors. A collector should expect to look a long time for medium green 10" plates; they are very rare.

Harlequin 10″ Plate	
Modeling Date	August 1936
Model Number	657
Revision	None
Production Began	September 1936
Discontinued	1959
Length of Production	23 Years
Colors: All	

Harlequin 9″ Plate	
Modeling Date	June 1936
Model Number	616
Revision	None
Production Began	September 1936
Discontinued	1959
Length of Production	23 Years
Colors: All	

10" plates in the original colors. Maroon, $42-44; Blue, $29-30; Spruce, $40-43; Yellow, $25-28.

9" plates in the forties colors. Rose, $10-11; Green, $15-16; Red, $14-15; Turquoise, $10-11.

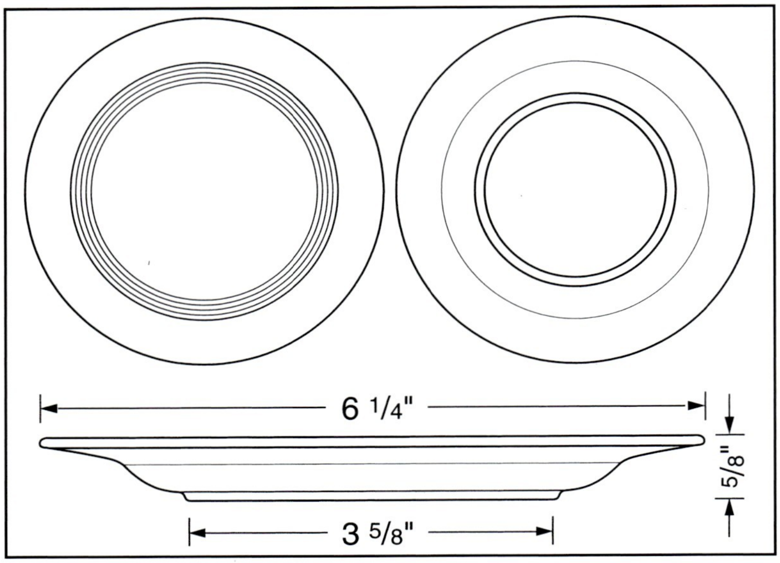

6 1/4"
5/8"
3 5/8"

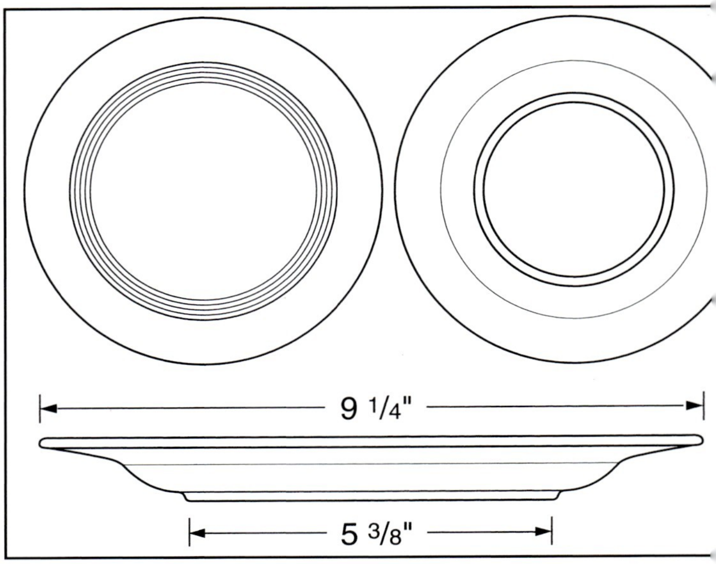

9 1/4"
5 3/8"

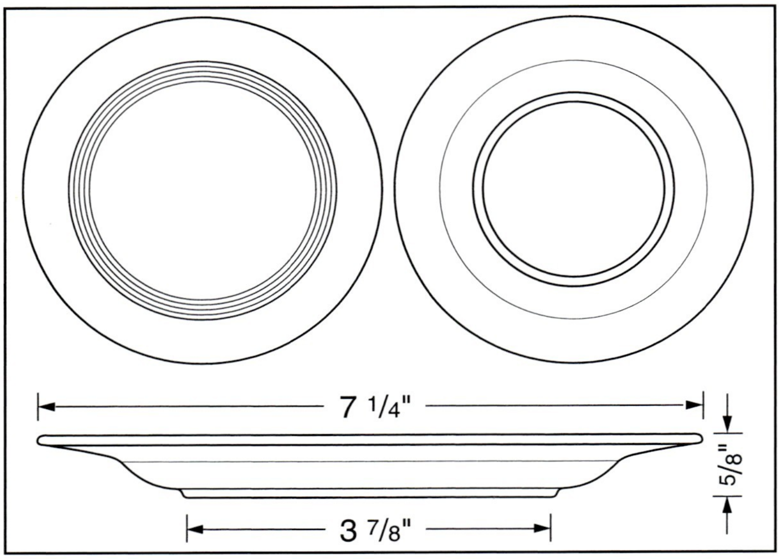

7 1/4"
5/8"
3 7/8"

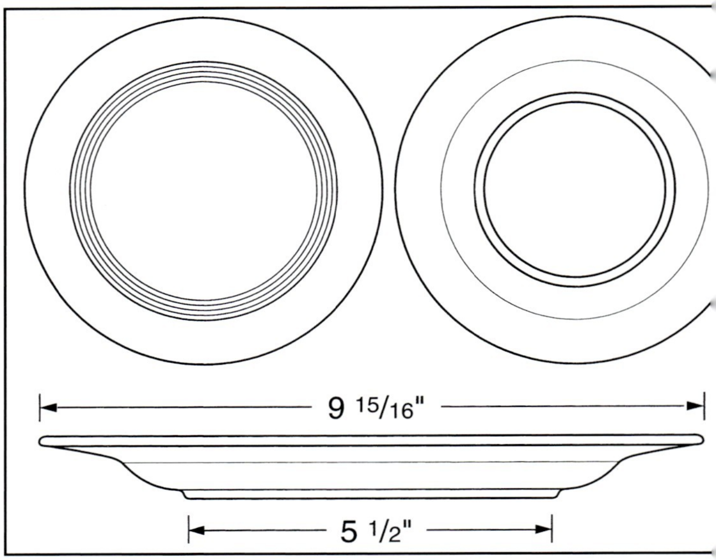

9 15/16"
5 1/2"

Harlequin 7″ Plate

Modeling Date	September 1936
Model Number	672
Revision	None
Production Began	September 1936
Discontinued	1959
Length of Production	23 Years
Colors: All	

Harlequin 6″ Plate

Modeling Date	August 1936
Model Number	674
Revision	None
Production Began	September 1936
Discontinued	1959
Length of Production	23 Years
Colors: All	

Medium green 6" plate, $22-26.

7" plates in the fifites colors. Chartreuse, $9-11; Gray, $6-7; Forest, $10-11.

Deep Plate

The deep plate, #658, was the first sizable bowl in the line other than serving bowls. It probably doubled as a cereal or salad bowl until pieces were available for those functions. It is found in all twelve colors. Medium green and dark green are hard to find and, surprisingly, so is light green.

Harlequin Deep Plate

Modeling Date	August 1936
Model Number	658
Revision	None
Production Began	September 1936
Discontinued	1959
Length of Production	23 Years
Colors: All	

Deep plate in Harlequin original colors. Maroon, $33-37; Blue, $26-28; Spruce, $28-32; Yellow, $18-20.

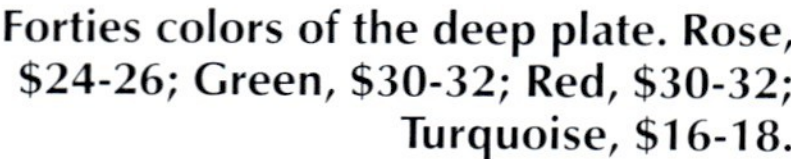

Forties colors of the deep plate. Rose, $24-26; Green, $30-32; Red, $30-32; Turquoise, $16-18.

Deep plate in the fifties colors. Forest, $39-41; Gray, $29-33; Chartreuse, $29-33.

Medium green deep plate, $105-120.

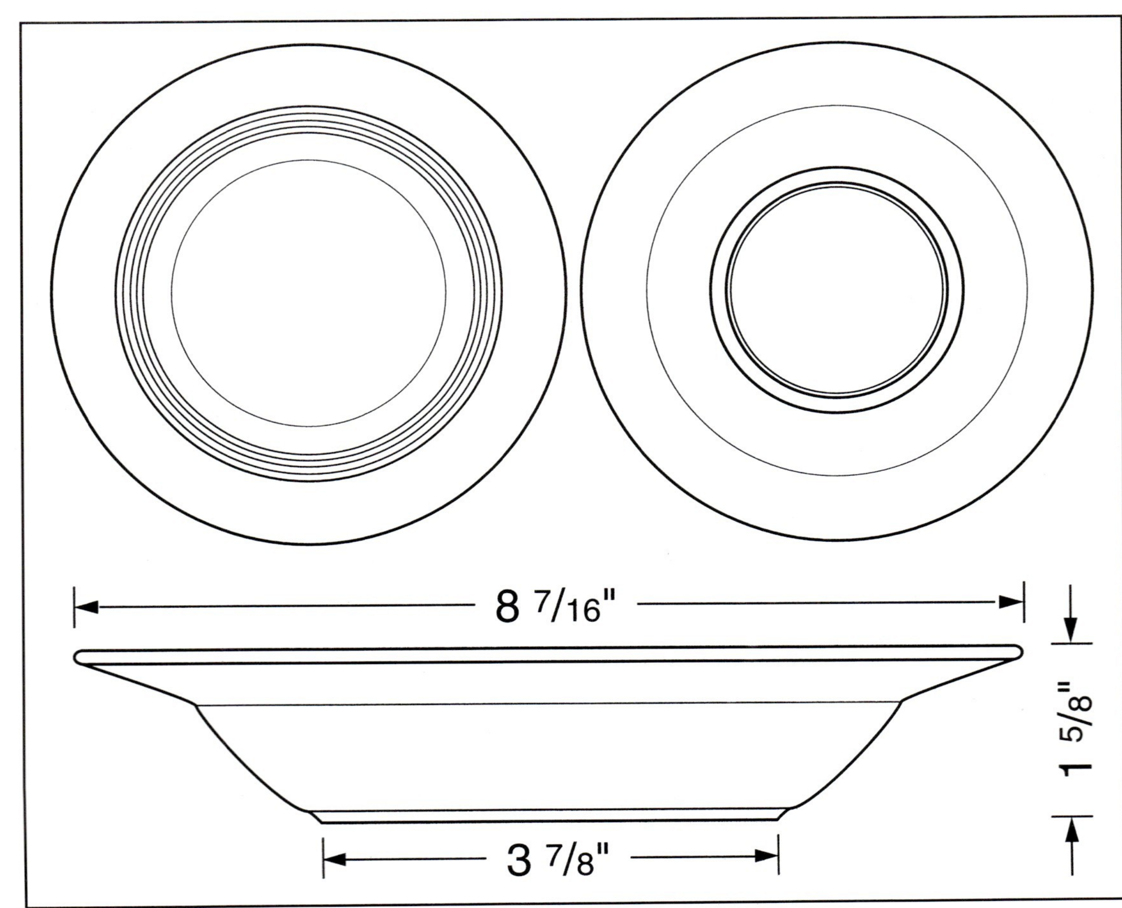

Harlequin 11" platter in original colors. Maroon, $30-33; Blue, $24-26; Spruce, $28-31; Yellow, $20-22.

Platters

11″ Platter

The 11″ platter was original to the line. Rhead designed it as an oval version of the plate. It was a successful piece, and a 13″ version was later added. The 11″ platter was model #675, released on September 24, 1936. It was available the entire run and is found in all twelve colors. Medium green and the fifties colors, dark green in particular, are the hardest to find. Some believe that the 11″ platter in dark green is harder to find than the medium green version.

Harlequin 11″ Platter	
Modeling Date	September 1936
Model Number	675
Revision	None
Production Began	September 1936
Discontinued	1959
Length of Production	23 Years
Colors: All	

Eleven-inch platter in colors added in the 1940s. Rose, $22-24; Green, $27-29; Red, $26-28; Turquoise, $18-19.

Fifties colors for the 11" platter. Chartreuse, $25-28; Gray, $27-30; Forest, $32-34.

Medium green 11" plattter, $265-305.

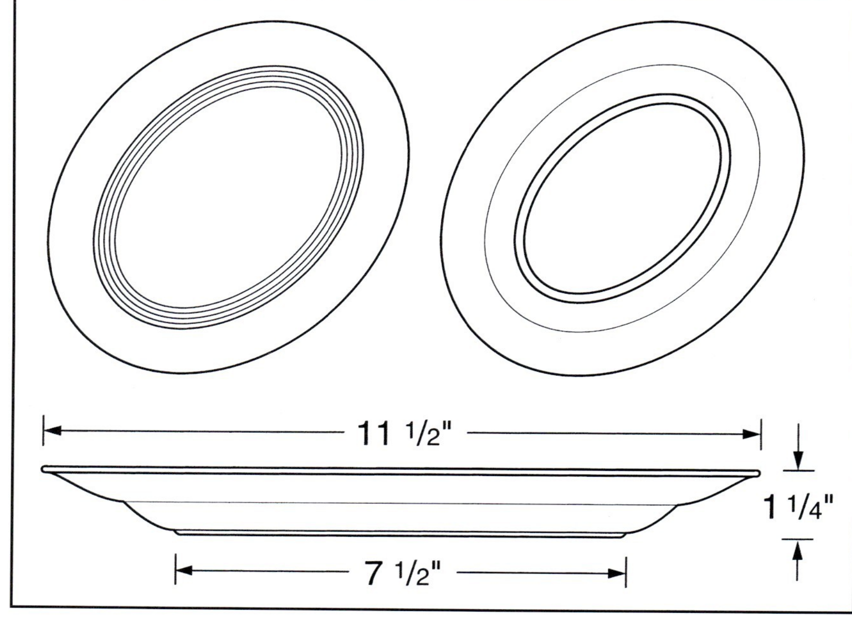

13″ Platter

The 13″ platter, added in March 1938, is a bit harder to find than its 11″ counterpart. It is a huge platter, large enough to hold a medium-sized turkey. It was a part of the line until the end so can be found in all twelve colors, but is hard to find in the fifties colors and medium green.

Harlequin 13″ Platter

Modeling Date	January 1938
Model Number	1029
Revision	None
Production Began	March 1938
Discontinued	1959
Length of Production	21 Years
Colors: All	

Forties colors of the 13" platter. Rose, $32-35; Green, $33-35; Red, $38-41; Turquoise, $22-25.

Thirteen inch platter in original Harlequin colors. Maroon, $37-41; Blue, $31-35, Spruce, $37-41; Yellow, $26-29.

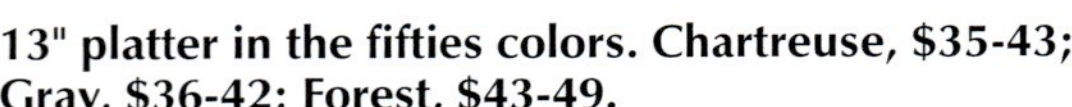

13" platter in the fifties colors. Chartreuse, $35-43; Gray, $36-42; Forest, $43-49.

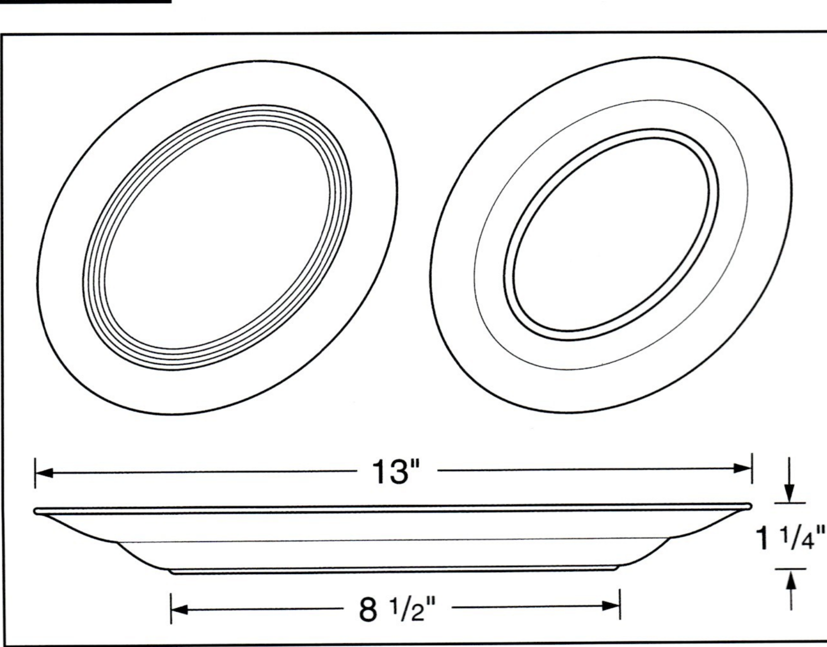

Relish Tray

The relish tray is an exceedingly functional piece, especially when compared with the Fiesta relish, whose inserts are too small to hold much. At first glance, it seems to be devoid of any Harlequin styling, but the sections are triangular and the base has rings on the rim.. On March 23,1940, Rhead writes, "Relish tray same size as fiesta but center a little larger." On April 3, he adds "Harlequin relish tray to JMW for Woolworth sketch". The model was made on April 8, 1940. It was given to Wells on April 25 for his approval, and on May 23 the relish tray #1386 was released into production. The Harlequin base is very similar to the Fiesta relish base, but the ring pattern differs slightly. A Harlequin relish base is only found in turquoise and is unmarked; Fiesta bases are marked. The pie-shaped inserts are usually found in maroon, blue, yellow, and red. Rose and turquoise inserts have been found, but are rare.

Harlequin Relish Tray

Modeling Date	March 1940
Model Number	1386
Revision	None
Production Began	May 1940
Discontinued	c.1945
Length of Production	5 Years

Colors: Base: Turquoise, Inserts: Maroon, Blue, Yellow, Red, Rose, and Turquoise

Harlequin relish tray in standard colors.

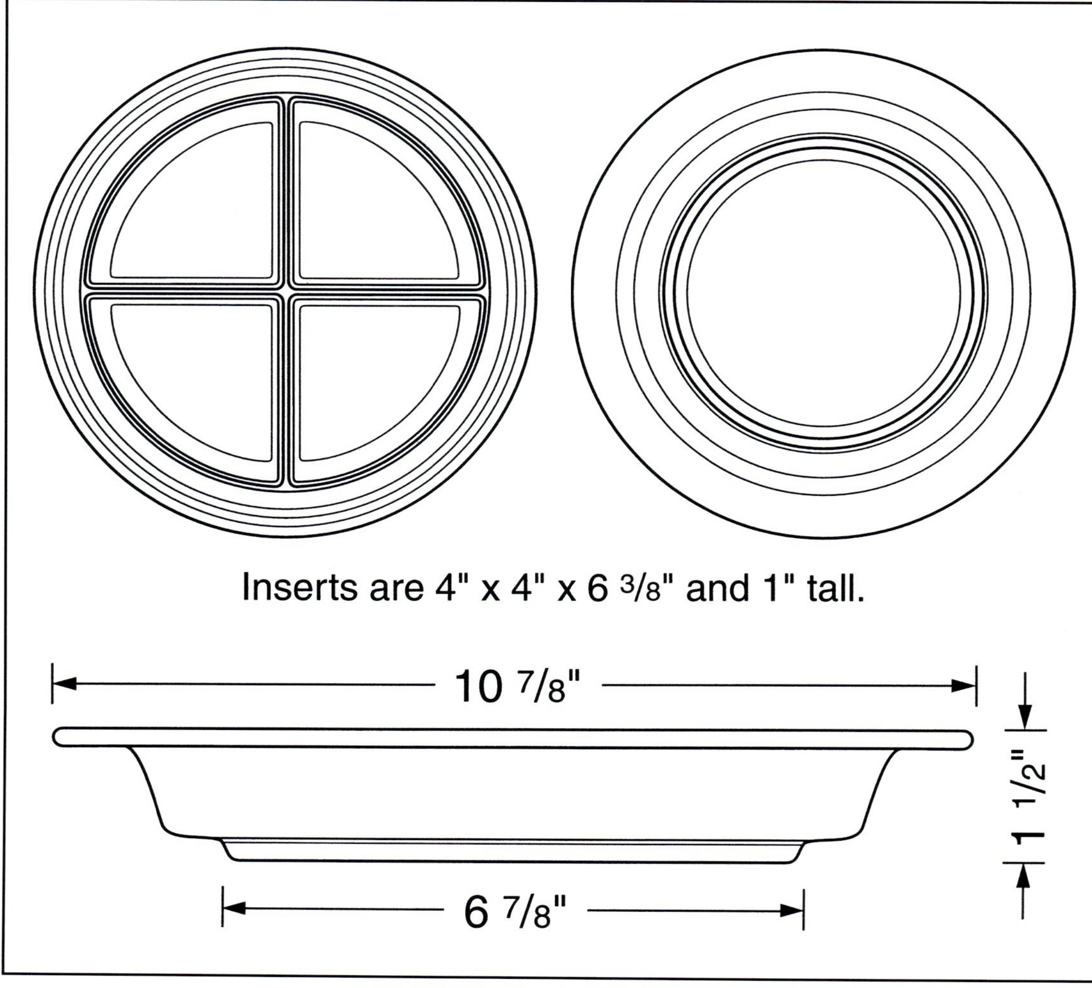

Sauceboat

The sauceboat is a great Harlequin shape. Its extended angular handle really adds to its streamlined appeal. Released to production on May 10, 1938, It was added to the line in the first expansion; the model log lists it as #1067 "Boat, Harlequin." The sauceboat holds 15 1/2 ounces. They were produced in all twelve colors, with the fifties colors being hard to find and medium green very scarce.

Medium green sauce boat, $375-450.

Harlequin Sauceboat	
Modeling Date	April 1938
Model Number	1067
Revision	None
Production Began	May 1938
Discontinued	1959
Length of Production	21 Years
Colors: All	

Sauce boat in colors original to the Harlequin line. Maroon, $41-44; Blue, $30-33; Spruce, $41-44; Yellow, $23-25.

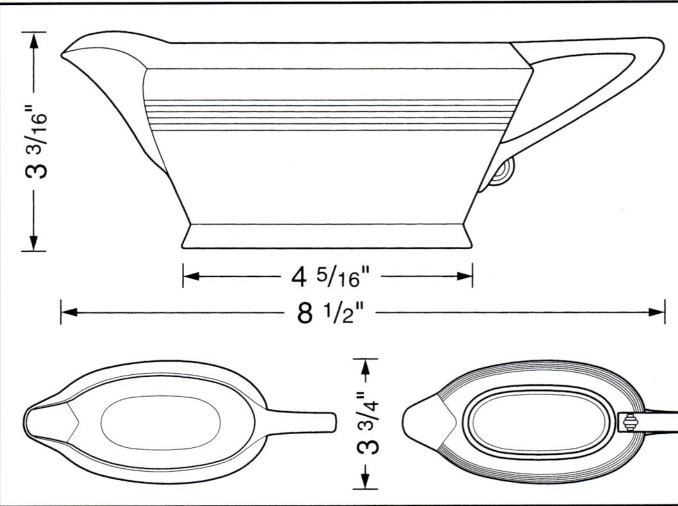

Sauce boat in colors added in the 1940s. Rose, $22-24; Green, $34-36; Turquoise, $21-22; Red, $30-32.

Sauce boat in the 1950s colors. Chartreuse, $39-44; Forest, $45-50; Gray, $43-51.

Salt and Pepper Shakers

Rhead designed the shakers very early when the line was still unnamed. The shaker, #683, went into production in September 1936, and was made for the full run of the line. They are found in all twelve colors. They are somewhat scarce in all of the fifties colors. They are very rare in medium green. The shakers come with cork stoppers, which are frequently found inside the shakers or missing all together.

Harlequin Salt & Pepper Shakers	
Modeling Date	September 1936
Model Number	683
Revision	None
Production Began	September 1936
Discontinued	1959
Length of Production	23 Years
Colors: All	

Salt and pepper shakers in medium green, $240-270 pair.

Salt and pepper shakers in original colors. (Pair) Maroon, $28-31, Blue, $24-28; Spruce, $33-36; Yellow, $17-19.

The salt and pepper shakes in colors added in the 1950s. (Pair) Forest, $35-40; Gray, $31-36; Chartreuse, $33-39.

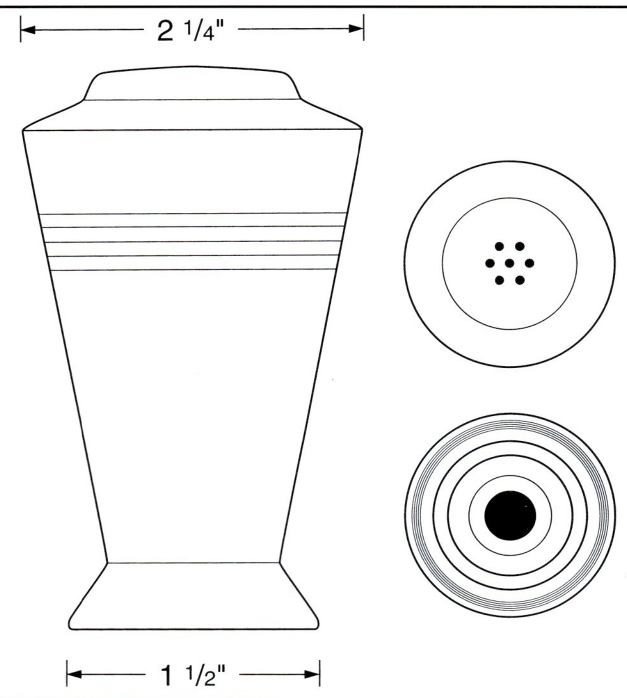

The forties colors of the salt and pepper shakers. (Pair) Rose, $22-24; Green, $26-28; Turquoise, $16-19; Red, $31-33.

Sugar Bowl with Lid

The sugar bowl was the eighth piece designed in the original assortment. The model was executed by Arthur Kraft. It went through several changes in the course of production. The original sketch, #662, dated August 1936, shows a convex body shape, similar to the 36s bowl. In keeping with that body shape, the handles and finial were curved. By the time the piece went into production, the shape had been altered to # 669, which resembled a miniature casserole with straight sides and the familiar triangular handles and finial. The sugar bowl base appears to have been modified a few more times during its 27 years. The first base had a slightly flared foot and three rings on the inside bottom of the bowl. At some point, the inside rings were omitted while the foot became straighter and slightly taller. An October 19,1938 reference in Rhead's journal states, "Harlequin jigged sugar-drawing for turned model." This could have been when the inside rings were omitted. The last reference to a sugar bowl in the model log comes in 1942; perhaps this is when yet another change took place. By the time the fifties colors were introduced the flared foot was back, but the bottom inside rings did not return. The covered sugar bowl can be found in all twelve Harlequin colors. Medium green sugar bowls are very rare.

Harlequin Sugar Bowl	
Modeling Date	September 1936
Model Number	669
Revision	1938, 1942
Production Began	September 1936
Discontinued	1959
Length of Production	23 Years
Colors: All	

Above: **Covered sugar bowl in original colors. Maroon, $36-39; Blue, $25-27; Spruce, $41-44; Yellow, $16-18.**

Above center: **Sugar bowl with lid in colors added in the 1940s. Rose, $22-24; Green $36-39; Turquoise, $18-20; Red, $31-35.**

Above right: **Covered sugar in the fifties colors. Chartreuse, $32-38; Forest, $42-45; Gray, $32-34.**

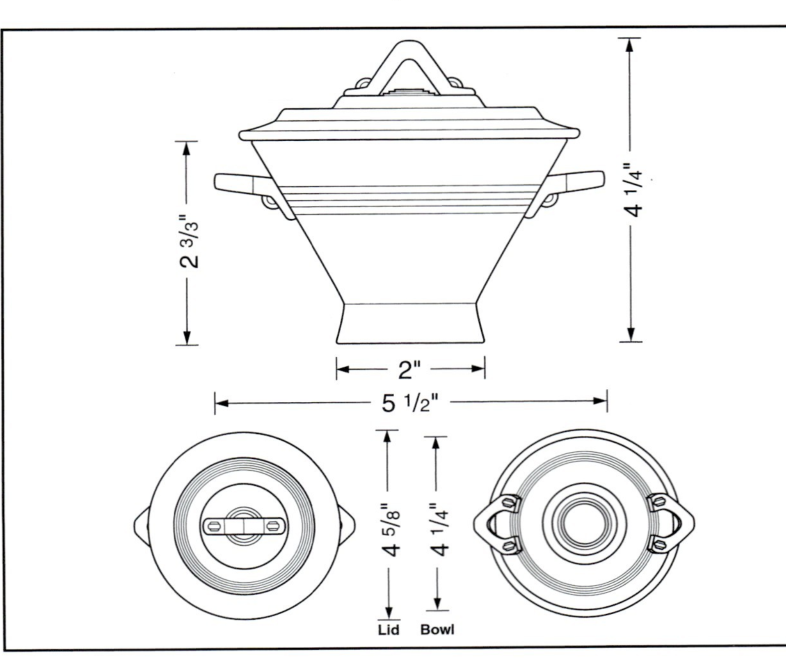

Medium green covered sugar, $115-135.

Harlequin syrup in a variety of colors.

Syrup

The Harlequin syrup is a wonderful addition to any collection but not easy to come by. Rhead designed the shape to match the size of the lid for the Fiesta syrup. He writes on November 25, 1940, "Drawing new shape drip cut-server for Woolworths. Same size and to fit same top. Get drawings right away". One month later on December 29, 1939, he notes "Woolworths drip-cut jar, see Al Kraft". #1353 was modeled by Bill Berrisford and has a release date of January 29, 1940. It is likely that the syrup was in production for as short as 18 months. It is found only in yellow, blue, spruce, and red. It is not clear why these were made in spruce and red, but not in maroon, turquoise, or light green. If turquoise and light green were added late in 1941, it could explain why the syrup is not found in these colors. However, it does not explain why it was not dipped in maroon, which was in production at least until the end of 1940 when the 36s bowl was added to the line. Unconfirmed rumors have reported the discovery of the Harlequin syrup in turquoise and light green. There has been at least one example reported in ivory, not a standard color for Harlequin. The plastic top used on the Harlequin syrup was produced by the Drip-cut Company. This firm produced syrup lids for many kitchenware makers, so similar lids in non-Harlequin or Fiesta colors can be found on other glass syrup jars. The plastic tops tend to fade over time from age, so it is not unusual to find a syrup with a faded top that no longer matches the jar.

Harlequin Syrup

Modeling Date .... November 1939
Model Number 1353
Revision .... None
Production Began .... January 1940
Discontinued c.1942
Length of Production .... 2 Years
Colors: Yellow, Blue, Spruce, and Red

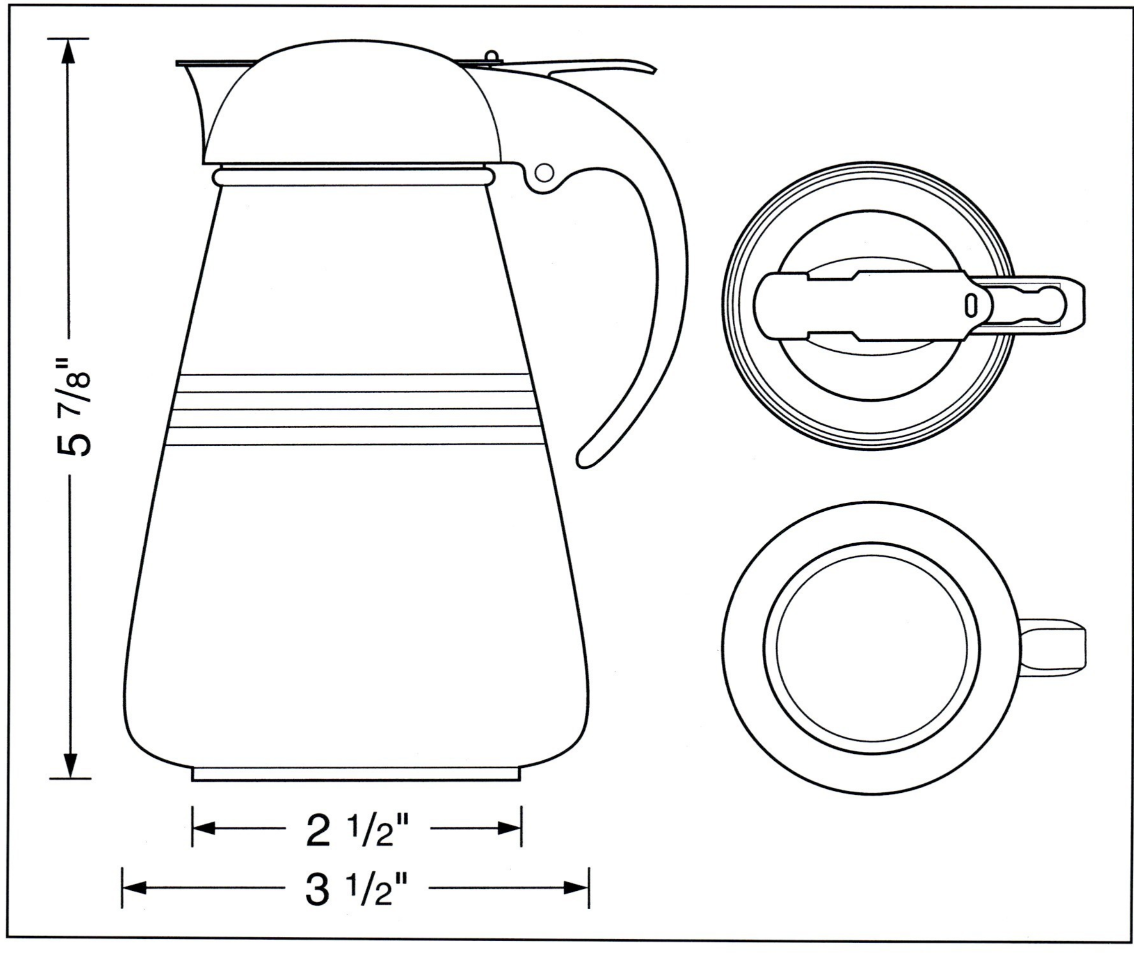

Teapot With Lid

Today collectors favor the teapot for many reasons. It has all the best elements of Harlequin design: the rings, the conical body, the triangle handle, and finial. There is not much information on the teapot in the factory records. It was introduced as part of the first expansion in late 1938. The model log lists it as #1044, "tea pot, Harlequin shape 34.5 ozs cap". Kraft was the modeler. It was released on March 5,1938. The teapot is found in all twelve colors, but examples in the fifties colors are hard to find. Medium green teapots are rare.

Medium green Harlequin teapot, $1365-1870.

Harlequin Teapot

Modeling Date	February 1938
Model Number	1044
Revision	None
Production Began	March 1938
Discontinued	1959
Length of Production	21 Years
Colors: All	

Above: Original colors for the Harlequin teapot. Maroon, $140-160; Blue, $125-135; Spruce, $160-170; Yellow, $95-105.

Above right: Tea server in the forties colors. Rose, $135-150; Green $120-135; Turquoise, $96-105; Red, $135-145.

Teapot in the colors added in the 1950s. Chartreuse, $150-160; Forest, $170-185; Gray, $155-170.

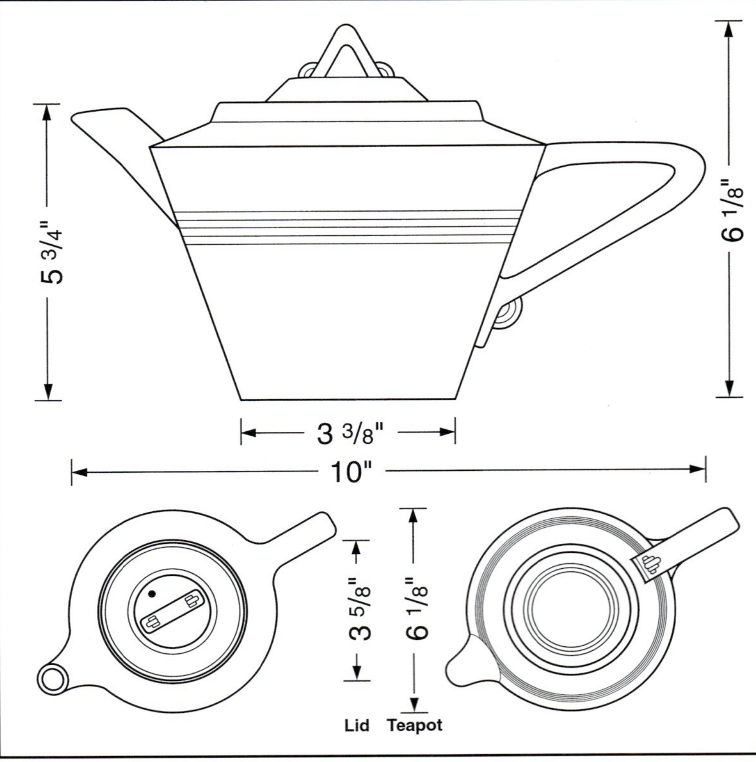

Tumbler

Once thought to be in the original line, it is clear the tumbler was added in the first expansion. Designs were first worked on in December 1937. The log shows #1019 "mug-Harlequin 11 1/2 ozs cap." Apparently Rhead or Wells was not satisfied, and it was remodeled in January 1938. The log lists model #1031, "mug–Harlequin smaller shape than 1019." The tumbler was released to production January 27, 1938. While it was dropped from the line before the fifties colors were added, it is readily available in the original and forties colors. An ivory tumbler, possibly a trial piece, has been reported.

Collectors have found the Harlequin tumblers in light green with an automobile decal. These were reportedly made for "Pearl China," and may not have been decorated by Homer Laughlin. They are not as rare as once thought.

Harlequin Tumbler	
Modeling Date	December 1937
Model Number	1031
Revision	None
Production Began	January 1938
Discontinued	c.1950
Length of Production	12 Years

Colors: Maroon, Yellow, Spruce, Blue, Red, Turquoise, Rose and Light Green

Tumblers in the original assortment of colors. Maroon, $61-65; Spruce, $56-59; Blue, $52-56; Yellow, $47-51.

The tumbers in the forties colors. Rose, $58-66; Red, $55-58; Green, $48-56; Turquoise, $41-42.

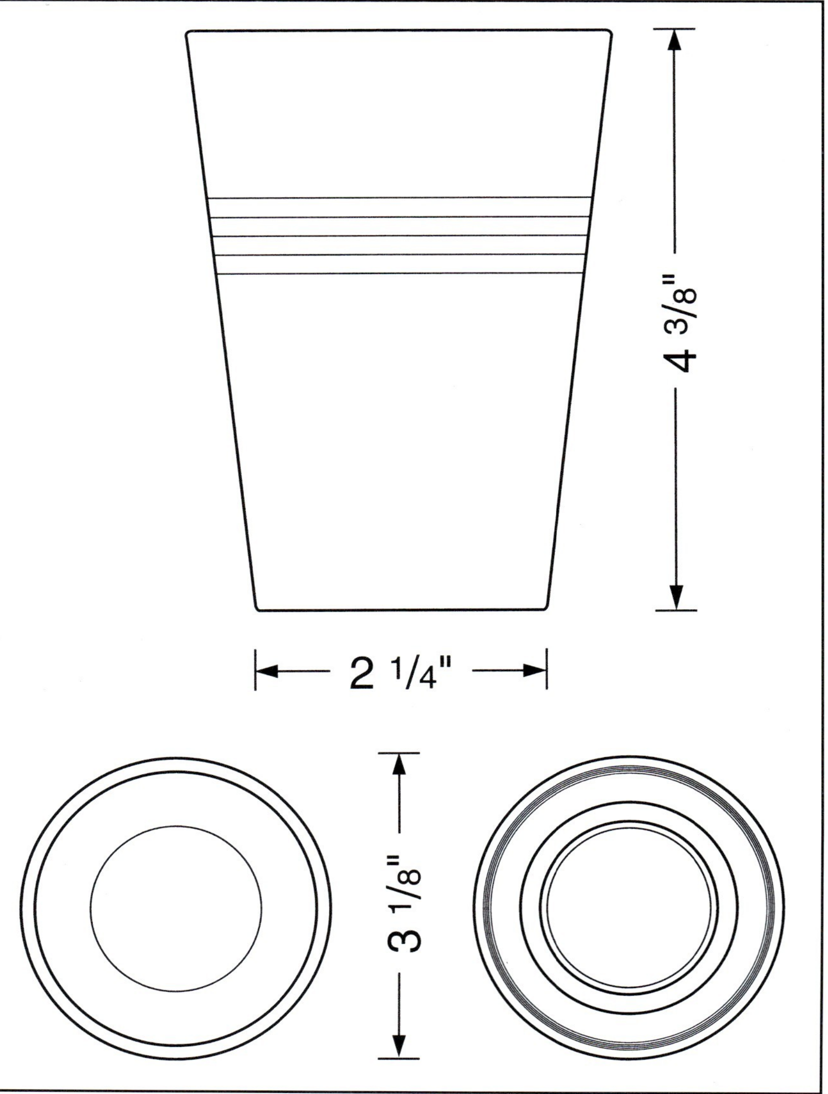

Animals

These miniature animals, glazed in Harlequin colors are perennial favorites with collectors. They also engender confusion and some controversy. It is probable that these were not designed to be marketed with Harlequin but rather as a novelty item exclusive to Woolworth. "Harlequin" is not mentioned in regard to the animals anywhere in the model log or Rhead's journal. Since they are dipped in Harlequin glazes Harlequin collectors seek them out.

In the late 1930s through the mid-1940s miniatures were very popular. In August 1939 Rhead designed a series of miniatures for Woolworth. Rhead noted in his journal on August 15, 1939 that "Samples sent to HHL; 1334 Novelty Duck, 1333 Novelty Fish, 1325 Novelty Penguin, 1324 Novelty Lamb, 1331 Novelty Cat, 1336 Novelty Donkey." According to the model log the miniatures were modeled in September. Besides the duck, fish, penguin, lamb, and cat familiar to collectors, an Indian man, Indian woman, and turtle were also modeled. It appears that these last three were dropped even before samples were executed. Miller modeled all of these—he appears to have specialized in sculptural designs rather than the regular dishes. The entire menagerie went into production on October 25,1939.

It appears the animals were only in production for a brief time. They were regularly produced only in the four original Harlequin colors.

At least two design varieties have been reported for the penguin and the lamb. The model log shows no revisions to these shapes, so these changes are unexplained. There are no hard data on whether one shape is more easily found, as most collectors are not aware there may be differences.

The animal shapes were popular novelty items. While in production, Homer Laughlin may have sold unglazed or bisque animals to various companies that glazed and decorated them. After production ended at Homer Laughlin, other small producers in the East Liverpool area may have made similar animals. It is not clear if they obtained molds from HLC or made copies. Some of these molds may still be used today.

HLC also sold finished glazed animals to decorators who added gold highlights or even an entire coat of gold over the original glaze.

The term "Maverick" has been used to describe animals that were obviously finished or decorated outside of Homer Laughlin. They can be found in solid ivory, ivory with gold trim, solid gold, or with a white pearlized finish. These are on rare occasions found in an original color under the ivory finish. In some cases they are slightly smaller than the original animals, indicating they may come from molds cast from the originals. Smaller versions, which are salt-and-pepper shakers, are known to exist.

Several animals in nonstandard colors have been found. A few light green, turquoise and red animals have turned up. It is likely bisque examples existed at HLC and outside the company for many years after production ended. Medium green animals that could have only been dipped in the late 1950s are on display at the outlet museum at Homer Laughlin.

As recently as the 1990s a barrel of bisque penguins was known to be in private hands. This may account for some of the penguins that have been found in post-1986 Fiesta glazes, possibly made as "favors" by HLC employees for outsiders that supplied the bisque figures for dipping in the new glazes.

From time to time, it is reported that Harlequin elephants have been found. An elephant with a similar glaze may exist but apparently was not modeled at Homer Laughlin. No mention of such a piece has been found in the model log or in Rhead's journals.

An assortment of unusual animals.

All Harlequin Animals

Modeling Date	September 1939
Model Number	Various
Revision	None
Production Began	October 1939
Discontinued	c.1940
Length of Production	1 Year

Colors: Maroon, Yellow, Spruce, and Blue

Turquoise duck with original mold. No established value.

Animals in the standard colors. See appendix E for pricing information.

Reissue of Harlequin Ironstone

With the approach of the 100th anniversary in 1979, Woolworth asked Homer Laughlin to reissue Harlequin to commemorate its all time best selling dinnerware line. Thus Harlequin Ironstone was born. The reissue was in stores from 1979 to about 1983.

The reissue pieces were developed between May and October 1978. This new Harlequin was very limited when compared to the original line. It was only available in four colors, yellow and turquoise (very close to the originals), and two new colors, coral (a pinker version of rose), and green (a milky version of medium green). This reissue green is not a match for the original medium green. It is more opaque and has a "milky" cast. Collectors should be aware of the difference, especially since the original medium green pieces command higher prices that those in reissue green.

The Ironstone assortment consisted of 10″ plate, 7″ plate, soup/cereal bowl (36s oatmeal shape in the original line), teacup and saucer, creamer, covered sugar, vegetable bowl (nappy in the original line) and a round platter.

The round platter was the only new shape; in the original line all the platters were oval. The sugar bowl was redesigned for more efficient production. The handles and the finial are closed triangles; in the original they are open. This allowed the sugar bottom and lid to be molded in one step. On the original, the handles and finials were molded separately and applied to the base or lid by hand.

This line was so limited that the serving pieces came only in a specific color: the vegetable bowl in reissue green, the creamer in turquoise, sugar bowl in yellow, the platter in coral. A very few of the platters and vegetable bowls were dipped in yellow. The Ironstone pieces are much heavier than the originals. Most of the plates and platters, and occasionally some of the saucers and bowls, are back stamped with "HLC" and a production date. The dates range from 1978 to 1983. Original Harlequin was never backstamped. The reissue Harlequin was not sold as open stock but rather in a 45-piece service for eight or a 20-piece service for four. This reissue of Harlequin preceded the re-introduction of Fiesta by several years. In retrospect, Homer Laughlin felt the re-introduced line never met its full potential, in part because of poor marketing by Woolworth.

The Harlequin Ironstone colors on the bowls.

Table Fair

In the early 1980s, Homer Laughlin introduced a new line called Table Fair. This line was intended for use as supermarket premiums. The production dates coincide with the production dates for reissue Harlequin, 1978 to 1983, and the line shared some of the Harlequin shapes. Table Fair used cream colored glazes that contained brown/tan speckles. Table fair was a good-sized line. According to the model log, the line consisted of teacup and saucer, 10″ plate, 7″ plate, mug, soup mug, cereal bowl, fruit bowl, creamer, covered sugar bowl, salt and pepper shakers, vegetable bowl, sauce boat with stand, covered butter and coffee server. Not all of these pieces have been accounted for but it is presumed that all went into production. Only the 10″ plate, 7″ plate, cereal bowl (the 36s oatmeal), fruit bowl, and vegetable bowl (the nappy) were based on the Harlequin shapes. The other pieces had new shapes that were not based on Harlequin. Table Fair appears to have done poorly and was short lived.

The Harlequin Ironstone teacups.

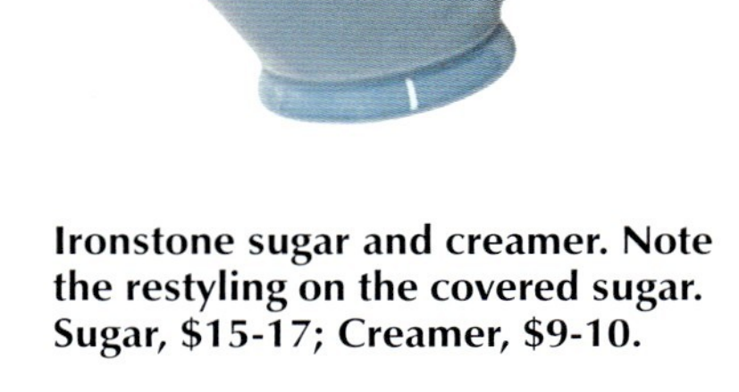

Ironstone sugar and creamer. Note the restyling on the covered sugar. Sugar, $15-17; Creamer, $9-10.

Ironstone 10" Plates in all colors.

Ironstone 7" Plates in all colors.

The round platter in both available colors.

Appendix A: Lead and Radiation in Vintage Ware

Vintage HLC pottery, like almost all pottery made in the U.S.A prior to 1972 contains, heavy metals, especially lead. In 1972, the FDA began monitoring dinnerware for lead. Coincidentally (or not) this is the time when Fiesta Ironstone ceased production. Post-86 Fiesta does not contain any lead and easily passes the Government safety tests. The question at hand is *Can I safely eat from my vintage HLC dishes?*

Lead is a naturally occurring element and is ingested in our food and drink. Lead is a neurotoxin that can cause physiological and neurological problems. This is particularly problematic for young children (under six years old). Chronic lead poisoning can cause learning disabilities, decreased IQ, behavioral problems, and stunted growth. These changes are frequently very subtle. There has never been a case of acute lead poisoning reported from eating off of lead glazed pottery made in the U.S.A. A more common and serious cause of lead poisoning in children is from eating leaded paint chips. Most homes built prior to 1978 contain leaded paint.

The FDA test for lead leaching in dinnerware is to place the scientific version of white vinegar in the dish and let it stand at room temperature for 24 hours. However, they only have performed this test on dishes made after 1972. Currently no flatware made in the U.S. or imported to the U.S. may leach lead levels greater then three micrograms per milliliter and the limits for hollowware are less. So, do not worry about any current HLC product. Dishes marked "For Decorative Purposes Only" often have failed the lead leaching test.

Can lead leach out of the glaze of vintage HLC? The answer is yes, although generally in extremely small concentrations. Heating the plate (including the use of a microwave oven) increases the leaching as does the use of acidic foods such as vinegar, coffee or sauerkraut. Heating a vintage plate with an acidic solution further increases the lead leaching. Dishes which are fired at a high temperature, like most vintage HLC dishes tend to leach less then those fired at lower temperature. While there is not danger of acute poisoning from vintage plate, chronic poisoning may be a concern. One meal heated in a microwave oven on a vintage plate can leach out more lead then the FDA recommended maximum. However, this is not true if the plate is just used for service. Remember; when vintage HLC dinnerware was made there were no microwave ovens. If you are concerned about specific pieces, test kits for lead in pottery are available at reasonable rates in many hardware stores.

The Fiesta red glaze and similar glazes used by Bauer, Vernon Kilns and other manufacturers contains Uranium in addition to the lead. A different firing technique was used to produce the mango red color that included the pottery being fired at a lower temperatures. The need for this separate firing was the reason why Fiesta red cost more then the other colors. This is significant since dishes this color leach more heavy metals then dishes fired at a higher temperature.

Uranium is a common colorant for many different purposes, including pottery, glass and enameling. For pottery, it is used for Fiesta red, and beige to red/brown colors. Uranium is found in much smaller quantities in HLC ivory glaze. The ivory glaze is fired at the same temperature as the other vintage colors, and has no increase in leaching. It has been used since the first century, long before the discovery of radiation and radioactivity or the specific metals. The incorporation of radioactive material in ancient pottery is used by archeologists to determine it's age.

The Uranium used in red Fiesta from 1936-1943 contained the natural relationship of isotopes of Uranium, while the red Fiesta made after 1959 contained Uranium that was depleted in the Uranium-235 isotope. Since the Uranium-235 isotope in natural Uranium is less then 1%, there is effectively no difference between the earlier and later red Fiesta, either in chemical or radiological properties.

Radiation, which is the energy emitted from radioactive materials, is measured in dose. A unit of dose equivalence (which is a unit of biological effect of radiation) is the mrem. If you are living at sea level, in a typical house your annual dose is about 360 mrem. This is from naturally occurring radioactive material. Your background is increased by 0.5 mrem/hr while flying at 39,000 feet. Working in Grand Central Station in New York can increase your background dose by 120 mrem/year do to the high concentration of Uranium in the granite. Individuals smoking 30 cigarettes per day for a year will get about 16,000 mrem to the lungs. The occupational whole body annual dose maximum is 5000 mrem. So what does this mean for our red fiesta? Measuring the penetrating radiation on a red chop plate, the dose rate is 2.4 mrem/hr on contact while at 3.5 inches away it was down to 0.55 mrem/hr. The ivory glaze is barely detectable with a Geiger Counter, and will not appreciably add to your natural background. If you strap a red chop plate to your chest for a day, while your skin will get 57 mrem your lungs will only get 13.2 mrem which is less then a typical chest x-ray. However, this is definitely not recommended, as you would have a lot of explaining to do, when you rolled over, broke the plate, and had to go to the emergency room to remove the splinters.

So back to our original question. Is it safe to use pottery glazed in Fiesta red? From a standpoint of radiation emissions, most people would say certainly. The dose that would be received under normal usage is significantly smaller your background dose. Large collections of red Fiesta will increase the radiation level around them, but again the dose is relatively small. However the leaching problem can be significant, particularly when using acidic foods and in the microwave. It can also be a serious problem for children under 6.

Another issue to consider with HLC pottery is decals placed on plates after glazing. These decals may or may not contain heavy metals, and these heavy metals can leach into the food. This is NOT true for under glaze decals, which leach lead exactly like other fired glazes. The decals placed over the glaze may also release other toxic metals such as Cadmium.

This again brings us back to the basic question, is it safe for me to eat off of my vintage HLC pottery? This is a decision that everyone must make for himself or herself.

Appendix B: Modeling Log Information

The concept of keeping a record of the plaster models made in the HLC art department was more than likely Frederick Rhead's idea. Until he became director of the department in 1927, outside artists and company officials had provided the ideas for new ware, which were then modeled by the skilled craftsmen of the art department. Apparently few records were kept of design changes. Even after his arrival, Rhead did not keep a separate list of models until January 1933, when the first entry was made in a ledger titled "Modeling Log Book."

Now in three volumes, the HLC modeling log is the single best source of information for collectors about HLC dinnerware. Volume One of the log covers 1933 to 1944. Volume Two lists models made between 1944 and 1997. Recollections of employees and personal journals cannot contain the amount of useful information found in these documents. They have been a profoundly important resource without which most of this book would not be possible. Our thanks must go to the current head of the HLC art department, Jonathan Parry, for allowing us to have access to the logs.

The art department has, to the best of its ability, kept many of the original models. The main workroom has shelves full of plaster models, some dating from the early 1960s. Drawers contain smaller models, such as those for teacup handles. Many of them are from the 1940s and earlier. Several storage rooms are for model storage only and many older items can still be found. All in all, the art department at Homer Laughlin is rich in the history of the company's wares and many of the resources there remain unexplored.

Log entries are numbered and dated, have an explanation of the item being modeled, and sometimes a size is given. Revisions often have a reference to a previous model, allowing the progression of design to be followed. A few entries contain references to other resources, such as Rhead's *Record of Sketches and Drawings*, which may provide additional information. Finally, the date the model was released to production was written, most of the time by Rhead himself, on many log entries. Taken together, these bits of information can clear up myths and mysteries about many HLC dinnerware lines and provide a clearer picture of how things developed.

The main focus of this section is to list log entries for the three lines under discussion: Fiesta, Harlequin, and Kitchen Kraft. Notes for most of the pieces will clarify what item was being modeled as several items had different names prior to full time production. We've also included examples of several log pages. Included are text pages and pages of drawings for each of the three lines covered in this book.

The first entry in the original modeling log was for a Virginia Rose oval baker. That was January 1933. Fiesta entries begin with number 324 in February 1935, those for Harlequin with number 613 in June 1936, and Kitchen Kraft models begin with number 781 in March 1937.

Harlequin Ironstone mold pieces.

Teacup handle models.

Fiesta

Date	Model	Description (actual log text)	Size	Notes
Feb 35	324	Ring plate for colored glazes	7"	9" plate
Feb 35	328*	Modern ribbed teacup and handles		Flat-bottom teacup
Feb 35	330*	Ringed tea saucer for colored glzs, old		Original saucer
Feb 35	336	Ringed tea saucer for col'd glaze, new		Teacup saucer
Feb 35	337	Handle for ring tea cup		Fiesta ring handle
Feb 35	338	Ringed plate for col'd glaze	8"	10" plate
Mar 35	341	A.D. ringed cup for col. glaze		Flat-bottom A.D. cup
Mar 35	342	A.D. ringed saucer		A.D. saucer
Mar 35	344	A.D. ringed cup handle		Handle for A.D. cup
Mar 35	348	Ringed fruit (now called dessert)	5"	6" dessert bowl
Mar 35	349*	Ringed sugar 36		Original sugar
Mar 35	350	Ringed plate	5"	7" plate
Mar 35	352	Ringed chop plate	14"	15" chop plate
Mar 35	354*	Ringed cream (first model)		Original cream
Mar 35	355*	Ringed onion soup (first model)		Original onion soup
Mar 35	356	Ringed nappie	7"	8.5" nappie

Date	Model	Description (actual log text)	Size	Notes
Apr 35	358*	Ringed flanged oatmeal (now called fruit)	6"	Original fruit bowl
Apr 35	361	Ringed nappie	8"	9.5" nappie
Apr 35	363*	Ringed comport	10" x 2 1/2"	Original comport
Apr 35	366	Ringed salad bowl	11" x 5 1/2"	Footed salad bowl
Apr 35	369*	Ringed shape casserole (one handle)	8 1/2" x 2 1/2"	Original casserole
May 35	370	Ringed shape eight cup A.D. coffee pot		Demitasse coffeepot
May 35	372	Ringed cream soup with lugs		Cream soup
May 35	374	Stem flower vase		Bud vase
May 35	377	Ringed comport	12" X 3 1/4"	12" comport
May 35	378	Ringed chop plate	12"	13" chop plate
May 35	379*	Candlestick (sketch 407)		Original tripod
May 35	380	Ringed footed relish (sweet comport)	5" x 3/4"	Sweets comport
Jun 35	383	Relish compartment dish	10 3/4" x 1 1/2"	Relish tray
Jun 35	385	Ringed mixing bowl 9 1/2" x 6 1/8"	12s	#6 mixing bowl
Jun 35	386*	Ringed teapot (sketch 381)		"2 cup" teapot
Jun 35	387	Ringed mixing bowl 8 1/2" x 5 3/8"	18s	#5 mixing bowl
Jun 35	388	Fiesta small sugar		Flat-bottom sugar
Jun 35	389	Fiesta small cream		Stick-handle cream
Jun 35	394	Fiesta 2 quart ice pitcher	2 quarts	Ice-lip pitcher
Jul 35	395	Fiesta grill (compartment) plate	11 1/4"	12" compartment plate
Jul 35	396	Fiesta mixing bowl 7 1/2" x 5"	24s	#4 mixing bowl
Jul 35	397	Fiesta salt and pepper		Salt and pepper shakers
Jul 35	398	Fiesta carafe (water bottle)	9 3/4" x 6"	Carafe
Jul 35	399	Candlestick (sketch 406)		Tripod candle holder
Jul 35	400	Fiesta eight cup coffee pot		Coffeepot
Jul 35	403	Fiesta mixing bowl 6 1/2" x 4 1/4"	30s	#3 mixing bowl
Jul 35	406	Fiesta mixing bowl 10 7/8" x 7 1/4"	9s	#7 mixing bowl
Jul 35	407	Mixing bowl, Fiesta 5 3/4" x 3 3/4"	36s	#2 mixing bowl
Jul 35	410	Mixing bowl 4 13/16" x 3 3/8"	42s	#1 mixing bowl
Jul 35	412*	Coffee cup, Fiesta		Coffee cup
Jul 35	413*	Coffee saucer, Fiesta		Coffee saucer
Jul 35	414*	Mixing bowl, Fiesta	48s	#0 mixing bowl
Aug 35	419	Casserole, Fiesta	7 3/4" x 3 1/2"	Casserole
Aug 35	422	Covered onion dish, Fiesta		Marked onion soup
Aug 35	423*	Cracked ice bowl		Footed mixing bowl
Sep 35	427*	Casserole, covered, Fiesta turned knob	8 1/2" outside	Trial casserole
Sep 35	429*	Casserole, Fiesta, inside cover, turned knob		Trial casserole
Sep 35	433*	Pie plate, Fiesta	9" x 1 1/2"	Trial pie plate
Sep 35	435*	Candlestick (sketch 401)		Trial candle holder
Sep 35	437*	Pie plate, Fiesta	10 1/2" x 2"	Trial pie plate
Sep 35	441*	Candlestick		Trial candle holder
Sep 35	443	Candlestick, square base		Bulb candle holder
Nov 35	468	4" plate, Fiesta shape	4"	6" plate
Nov 35	469*	Cream, regular, same as 389 but ring handle		Ring-handle cream
Nov 35	470	Large teapot, Fiesta	6 cup	Large teapot
Nov 35	492*	Fruit, Fiesta	4 1/2"	Original 5.5" fruit
Dec 35	495	Fruit, Fiesta	4 1/2"	5.5 fruit bowl
Dec 35	505*	Cover and knob for cream soup #372		Onion soup replacement
Dec 35	510	Fluted vase, Fiesta	10" high	10" vase
Dec 35	512	Ashtray, Fiesta	5 1/2"	Ashtray
Jan 36	519*	Beaker, Fiesta		Early tumbler
Jan 36	520*	Coaster saucer, Fiesta		Trial coaster
Jan 36	527	Vase, fluted, Fiesta	12"	12" vase
Jan 36	528	Vase, fluted, Fiesta	8"	8" vase
Feb 36	537	Onion soup (jiggered), Fiesta		Unmarked onion soup
Feb 36	538	Sugar, Fiesta		Round-bottom sugar
Feb 36	549*	Teapot stand, Fiesta		Flat disc shape
Feb 36	550	Covered mustard, Fiesta, renamed marmalade		Marmalade
Apr 36	582	Covered mustard, Fiesta, smaller than 550		Trial mustard
May 36	586*	Jug, small No. 1		1/2 cup jug
May 36	587*	Jug, small No. 2		1/2 pint jug
May 36	588*	Jug, small No. 3		1 pint jug
May 36	589*	Jug, small No. 4		1 1/2 pint jug
May 36	590	Jug, small No. 5	2 pints	2 pint jug
May 36	591	Tray, Fiesta	10" x 4 1/2"	Utility tray
May 36	597*	Cream soup (covered), Fiesta	4 3/4" x 2 1/2"	Onion soup replacement
May 36	598	Plate 6", deep, Fiesta		Deep plate
May 36	605*	S/S mustard, Fiesta (cancelled, too small)		Trial mustard
May 36	606	Egg cup, Fiesta, WW type		Egg cup
May 36	607*	Jug, Fiesta		Trial jug
May 36	610	Mustard (adjusts 605)		Mustard

Date	Model	Description (actual log text)	Size	Notes
May 36	612	Fiesta mug, Tom & Jerry with round handle		Tom & Jerry mug
Jun 36	629	Mixing bowl cover, Fiesta, No. 1		#1 mixing bowl lid
Jun 36	630	Mixing bowl cover, Fiesta, No. 2		#2 mixing bowl lid
Jun 36	631	Mixing bowl cover, Fiesta, No. 3		#3 mixing bowl lid
Jun 36	632	Mixing bowl cover, Fiesta, No. 4		#4 mixing bowl lid
Jun 36	633*	Mixing bowl cover, Fiesta, No. 5		#5 mixing bowl lid
Jun 36	634*	Mixing bowl cover, Fiesta, No. 6		#6 mixing bowl lid
Jun 36	635*	Mixing bowl cover, Fiesta, No. 7		#7 mixing bowl lid
Dec 36	735*	Mug, Fiesta, convex		Trial tumbler
Dec 36	736	Mug, Fiesta, concave		Water tumbler
Jan 37	741	Teapot, Fiesta, 20 ozs, 2 covers		Medium teapot
Feb 37	771	Plate 8" flat cake, Fiesta		Cake plate
Feb 37	775	Plate (divided), Fiesta compartment plate	10.5"	10.5" compartment plate
Mar 37	791*	Water jug, Fiesta	2 qts cap	Trial ball-shaped jug
Apr 37	800	Boat, Fiesta		Sauce boat
Apr 37	804*	Water jug, this is #791 with revised handle		Harlequin ball jug
May 37	836	Salad nappie [originally for KK]	11 1/4" x 3"	11 3/4" fruit bowl
Aug 37	897*	Divided plate, Fiesta	10 1/2"	One piece relish tray
Aug 37	899*	Divided plate, Fiesta, changed divisions	10 1/2"	One piece relish tray
Aug 37	902	Handle for Fiesta cup, sharpened lines		New ring handle
Aug 37	903	Salt, pepper, Fiesta, lines sharpened		Revised S&P shakers
Aug 37	904	Fiesta cup, lines sharpened		Round-bottom teacup
Aug 37	907*	Divided plate with center lowered 1/8"	10 1/2"	One piece relish tray
Aug 37	915*	Square jug, Fiesta B	2 quarts	Trial square jug
Aug 37	918*	Divided plate for casting, as 897		One piece relish tray
Sep 37	942	Sugar, Fiesta, lines deepened		"MADE IN USA" sugar
Sep 37	943	Cup, A.D., Fiesta, lines deepened		Round-bottom A.D. cup
Oct 37	962	Sugar cover, Fiesta, lines heavier		Revised sugar lid
Oct 37	964*	Fruit (Fiesta)	5" x 1 1/2"	Trial small fruit
Nov 37	986	Fruit, Fiesta, 1/4" smaller than 964		4 3/4" fruit bowl
Feb 38	1046	Dish 9", Fiesta shape	12 5/8" x 9 15/16"	Oval platter
Mar 38	1057*	Jug, Fiesta lines, flat sided	90 ozs. cap	Trial disc pitcher
Apr 38	1071*	Tray, Fiesta, for casting	9 15/16" x 4 5/8"	Revised utility tray
Apr 38	1075*	Jug, Fiesta, as 1057 spout changed	90 ozs.	Trial disc pitcher
Apr 38	1077	Tray utility, Fiesta, for casting	10 1/4" x 4 5/8"	Revised utility tray
Apr 38	1084*	Jug, Fiesta, small size, straight sided	30 ozs.	Trial disc pitcher
Apr 38	1088	Jug, Fiesta, 1/2" smaller dia. than 1075	71 ozs. cap	Disc water pitcher
May 38	1093	Jug, Fiesta, same as 1084 changed snip	30 ozs. cap	Disc juice pitcher
May 38	1095*	Jug, Fiesta, straight sided as 1057	53 ozs. cap	Trial disc pitcher
Jun 38	1098*	Nappie, Fiesta, 7 3/4" x 2 1/2"	34 ozs. cap	Trial 7" nappie
Jul 38	1104	Handle for Fiesta cream		Ring-handle cream
Jul 38	1107	Mug, Kraft cheese 2 1/2" x 3 1/4"	5.77 ozs. cap	Juice tumbler
Aug 38	1119	Drip Cut Server		Syrup
Mar 39	1210	Mug, Kraft cheese, 1107 made 1/4" lower		Juice tumbler
Sep 39	1323*	Bowl 7 1/2" x 2 1/8" lines inside, outside		Trial individual salad
Nov 39	1341*	Bowl, salad, Fiesta	8"	Trial large salad
Dec 39	1345	Bowl, salad, 1/2" deeper than 1341		Promotional salad
Dec 39	1349	Casserole, French, Fiesta	37.5 ozs.	French casserole
Dec 39	1350	Tray for Fiesta cream, sugar		"Figure-8" tray
Jan 40	1351	Sugar, Fiesta, to fit tray 1350		"Individual" sugar
Jan 40	1352	Cream, Fiesta, to fit tray 1350		"Individual" cream
Jan 47	2043	9" Fiesta dish		Revised oval platter
Jun 59	2552	Harlequin, Fiesta bowl		Individual salad bowl
Mar 67	2929	Fiesta fruit		Ironstone fruit bowl
Mar 67	2930	Fiesta sugar		
Mar 67	2931	Fiesta cereal/soup		Amb/Iron soup/cereal
Mar 67	2932*	Fiesta cup handle (no good, too small)		Trial teacup handle
Mar 67	2933	Fiesta cream handle for #386		Amb/Iron cream handle
Mar 67	2934	Fiesta 8 1/2" nappy		Amb/Iron vegetable bowl
Mar 67	2935	Fiesta casserole cover knob		Amb/Iron casserole lid
Mar 67	2936	Fiesta 5" dish/pickle		Amb/Ironsauceboat stand
Apr 67	2937*	Fiesta 7" nappy		Trial serving bowl
Apr 67	2938	Fiesta salad bowl		Amb/Iron 10" salad bowl
Apr 67	2939	Fiesta casserole		Amb/Iron casserole
Apr 67	2940	Fiesta cup handle		Amb/Iron teacup handle
Apr 67	2941	Fiesta coffeepot knob		Amb/Iron coffee server
May 67	2947	Fiesta-Amberstone teapot cover & knob		Amb/Iron teapot
May 67	2948	Fiesta-Amberstone mug		Amb/Iron coffee mug
Jun 68	3031	New Amberstone 8" plate	10 1/8"	Amb/Iron dinner plate
Jan 69	3047	Fiesta sugar (changed for casting)		Amb/Iron sugar revised

*Not produced

Fiesta Kitchen Kraft

Date	Model	**Description** (actual log text)	Size	Notes
Mar 37	781*	Bowl & cover for Jewel Tea Co.		Prototype for KK
Mar 37	799*	Casserole for new ovenware		Early model
Apr 37	803*	Cover for #799 casserole body		Early model
Apr 37	806	Mixing bowl, new OvenServe line	large size	KK 10" mixing bowl
Apr 37	809	Pie plate, same as Royal shape	9 5/8" x 1"	KK 9" pie plate
Apr 37	810*	Pie plate	9 5/8" x 1"	
Apr 37	811	Mixing bowl, new OvenServe line	2nd one	KK 8" mixing bowl
Apr 37	812	Mixing bowl, new OvenServe line	3rd one	KK 6" mixing bowl
Apr 37	813	Cookie jar (no handles)		KK large covered jar
Apr 37	815*	Casserole, new cooking ware line	2nd one	Early model
Apr 37	816*	Cookie jar, with handles		Flat tab handles
Apr 37	817*	Casserole, large, inside cover	9 11/16" x 3 3/4"	Early model
Apr 37	818	Water jug	2 quart	
Apr 37	819	Casserole, smaller than #817	9 3/16" x 3 1/2"	KK 8.5" casserole
Apr 37	820*	Small casserole	4 3/16" x 2 7/16"	Early model
May 37	821*	Cookie jar, with new handles		
May 37	822	Jug, same as #818, but with open top	2 quart	
May 37	823	Casserole, inside cover	7 7/8" x 3"	KK 7.5" casserole
May 37	824	Jug, with cover	2 qt.	KK covered jug (large)
May 37	826	Cookie jar, smaller than #816 & #821	second size	KK medium covered jar
May 37	827	Cookie jar, smallest	third size	KK small covered jar
May 37	828*	Refrigerator bowl	4 1/2" x 2 1/4"	Non-stacking
May 37	829*	Refrigerator bowl with lugs		Non-stacking
May 37	831	Bean pot, same as #820 but [size]	4 1/2" x 2 1/4"	KK small casserole
May 37	833*	Jug, covered, small		
May 37	836	Salad nappie	11 1/4" x 3"	Fiesta 11 3/4" fruit
May 37	837*	10" dish for jug tray	10"	
May 37	838	Flat plate, cake plate	10 3/4"	KK cake plate
Jun 37	842	Salt and Pepper; new ovenware		KK S&P shakers
Jun 37	843	Salad fork for old OvenServe		KK fork
Jun 37	844*	Onion soup		
Jun 37	846	New cover for bean pot #831		KK small casserole lid
Jun 37	848	Bowl and cover, as #781 but without lines		KK stacking refrig. set
Jun 37	853*	Salt & Pepper, same as O.S. without embossing		
Jun 37	854	Cover for water jug #824 with revised verge		
Jul 37	882	Jug, K.K., #824 made smaller	24s	Decaled KK only (?)
Dec 37	1015	KK casserole, Fiesta writing		Fiesta KK logo
Jan 38	1038*	Jug, covered, Kitchen Kraft	67.5 ozs. cap.	
Feb 38	1043	Jug, covered, Kitchen Kraft	61 ozs. cap.	KK covered jug (small)
Feb 39	1204	Pie Plate, KK, narrow rim, shallower		
Jul 39	1283	Casserole cover, Kitchen Kraft	7 1/2"	Flattened rim
Oct 40	1508	Bowl, Kitchen Kraft	8 1/2" x 3"	
Mar 42	1749	Bowl, salad, 2 qt ivory body, KK	2 quart	Decaled KK only
Apr 45	1951	Mixing bowl, K. Kraft	10 3/4"	
May 45	1955*	Mixing bowl, K. Kraft	8 1/2"	
May 45	1956	Mixing bowl, K. Kraft	6 1/2"	
Jul 45	1964	Mixing bowl, K. Kraft	8 1/2"	
Mar 51	2249	KK jug remodeled to 63 oz. cap.	63 ozs. cap.	
Apr 51	2254	Fiesta jug cover remodeled		

*Not produced

Harlequin

Date	Model	**Description** (actual log text)	Size	Notes
Jun 36	613*	Plate-embossed lines on ball 7"	7"	Three different initially
Jun 36	614*	Plate-embossed lines on ball w/8 panels 7"	7"	Plate
Jun 36	616*	Plate - similar decoration as Fiesta, but on ball - not edge	7"	
			7"	Plate
Jul 36	649*	Teacup - convex with line in center.		Two models made - handles designed separately
Jul 36	650	Saucer - for 649. Flat rim		Teacup/Saucer
Jul 36	651*	Teacup - straight side. Line in center.		Teacup/Saucer
Jul 36	651*	Handles - A, B, C		Teacup/Saucer

Date	Model	Description (actual log text)	Size	Notes
Jul 36	654*	Nappy - rolled top, mottled line inside 7"	7"	Nappy
Jul 36	655	Fruit Bowl - rolled top. Same as above 4"	4"	Fruit Bowl
Aug 36	657	Plate - same design as 613 - 8"	8"	Plate
Aug 36	658	Plate - Deep. Same design as 613. Woolworth 6"	6"	Plate
Aug 36	659*	Casserole		Three models; 1 convex; 1 straight side w/o foot
Aug 36	661*	Casserole - Straight sided. Woolworth		Casserole
Aug 36	662*	Sugar-modeled lines		Sugar Bowl - Convex w/rounded finials
Aug 36	663	Casserole - Straight sided but without foot		Casserole
Aug 36	665	Casserole - Curved side without foot		Casserole
Aug 36	668	Creamer - Straight sides with lines. Woolworth		Creamer
Sep 36	669	Sugar - Straight sides with lines. Woolworth		Sugar Bowl
Sep 36	671	HLD & BOW for 661		Handles and finial for casserole
Sep 36	672	Plate - Woolworth 5"	5"	Plate
Aug 36	674	Plate - Woolworth 4"	4"	Plate
Sep 36	675	Platter 8"	8"	Platter
Sep 36	679	Baker - Woolworth. Same design as Nappy # 654 - 7"	7"	Oval Baker
Sep 36	682*	Egg Cup - Double. Woolworth		Double Egg Cup
Sep 36	683*	Salt & Pepper - Woolworth		Shakers
Feb 37	773	Jug, 22 oz, Harlequin		Originally jug #48's - First time called Harlequin
Mar 37	776	Platter 8"	8"	Platter
Mar 37	795	Fruit - Harlequin 5 11/16"	5 11/16"	Fruit Bowl
Jul 37	880*	Jug, Ball as Hall China		Ball Jug
Sep 37	934*	Cup & Handle - Demitasse. Harlequin	3 1/16" x 2 3/8"	
			3 1/16" x 2 3/8"	Demitasse
Sep 37	935*	Saucer, Demitasse		Demitasse
Dec 37	1019*	Tumbler - Harlequin 11.5-oz		Tumbler Mug
Jan 38	1025*	Ashtray 5 9/16" x 1 3/16"	5 9/16"x 1 3/16"	Regular Ashtray
Jan 38	1029	Platter 13 3/8" x 10 1/2"	13 3/8"x 10-1/2"	Platter
Jan 38	1031	Tumbler - Harlequin. Smaller than 1019.	4 3/8" x 3 3/16"	
			4 3/8" x 3 3/16"	Tumbler
Jan 38	1032*	Egg Cup - Ivory body		Egg Cup
Feb 38	1039*	Ashtray - Copy of Japanese tray nut bowl		Basketweave Ashtray
Feb 38	1040*	Marmalade Jar 9 3/4-oz		Marmalade
Feb 38	1044*	Teapot - Harlequin 34.4-oz		Teapot
Feb 38	1045*	Cream Soup 11.15-oz		Cream Soup
Mar 38	1051	Platter - Harlequin for #5 jigger 8"	8"	Platter
Mar 38	1054	Platter - Harlequin for #5 jigger 10"	10"	Platter
Apr 38	1066*	Jug - 22 oz 22.5-oz		Jug
Apr 38	1067*	Sauce Boat 15.5-oz		Sauce Boat
Nov 38	1163	Cream Ball Oval		Two different designs. Novelty Creamer?
Nov 38	1164	Cream Ball Round 10.5-oz		Novelty
Jan 39	1181*	Creamer, Novelty (Jug Individual) Woolworths (Toy Creamer)		Individual Creamer
Aug 39	1291*	Perfume Bottle - Low & Wide		Perfume
Aug 39	1292*	Perfume Bottle - Tall & Narrow		Perfume
Aug 39	1309*	Ashtray - Basketweave		Basketweave Ashtray
Aug 39	1313*	Ashtray - Saucer		Saucer Ashtray
Sep 39	1319*	Salad Bowl 7 1/2" x 2 1/8"	7 1/2" x 2 1/8"	Salad
Sep 39	1320*	HLD Harlequin Demi Cup 934		Demitasse
Sep 39	1321*	Ashtray - Basketweave w/o flange		Basketweave Ashtray
Sep 39	1324	Lamb		Animals
Sep 39	1325	Penguin		Animals
Sep 39	1326	Salad, Individual		Salad
Sep 39	1327	Indian Man		(Animal series)
Sep 39	1330	Indian Woman		(Animal series)
Sep 39	1331	Cat		Animals
Sep 39	1333	Fish		Animals
Sep 39	1334	Duck		Animals
Sep 39	1335	Ashtray, Saucer		Saucer Ashtray
Sep 39	1336	Donkey		Animals
Sep 39	1337	Turtle		Animals
Jan 40	1353	Syrup Jar		Syrup
Mar 40	1380	Fruit Bowl 4 3/4" x 1 1/2"	4 3/4" x 1 1/2"	Fruit Bowl
Apr 40	1381*	Candle holder - 1a		One of three designs
Apr 40	1382*	Candle holder - 2a		Two of three designs
Apr 40	1383*	Candle holder - 3b		Three of three designs
Apr 40	1386	Relish Dish		Relish
Apr 40	1388	Oatmeal 6 3/8"	6 3/8"	Oatmeal

Date	Model	Description (actual log text)	Size	Notes
Nov 40	1516	Bowl, 36's Harlequin		This version has straight sides like the cream soup
Nov 40	1517	Bowl, 36's Harlequin		36s produced version
Oct 42	1845	Platter, for #4 jigger 13"	13"	Platter
Oct 42	1846	Platter, for #4 jigger 11"	11"	Platter
Nov 42	1847	Baker, for #4 jigger		Oval Baker
Nov 42	1849	Sugar, with straight foot and topping only		Sugar Bowl
Nov 42	1850	Cream with foot. Same as 1849		Creamer
Nov 42	1851	Sauce boat, with foot. Same as 1849		Sauce Boat
Jul 43	1890	Platter, same shape as Nautilus for plant #5 11"	11"	Platter
Jul- 3	1892	Platter, same shape as Nautilus for plant #4		Platter
Jun 44	1920	Plate, Harlequin for patent jigger 7"	7"	Plate
Aug 44	1922	Saucer for patent jigger		Teacup/Saucer
Aug 44	1923	Plate, Harlequin - for patent jigger 4"	4"	Plate
May 78	1925-1	5" plate	5"	use old mold
Sep 44	1926	Fruit - Harlequin - for patent jigger 4"	4"	Fruit Bowl
Jun 46	1988	10" Harlequin Baker	10"	Oval Baker
Jan 45	1943	7" plate /patent jigger	7"	9" plate
Jan 45	1944	8" plate patent jigger	8"	10" plate
May 50	2209	Harlequin Bowl		A small sketch looks like the Individual Salad
May 55	2411	Harlequin Handle for Epicure Cup		Large Cup
June 55	2412	Larger Harlequin Handle for Epicure Cup		Large Cup
June 59	2552	Harlequin, Fiesta Bowl -released July 8, #4		Individual Salad remodeled to be shared with Fiesta

Harlequin Re-Issue

Date	Model	Description	Size	Notes
May 78	1944-1	Harl 8" plate flat bottom	8"	10" dinner plate
May 78	3422	Harl 5" Plate flat bottom	5"	7" dessert plate
May 78	1920-1	Harl 7" Plate flat bottom		9" lunch plate
May 78	3424	Harl Sugar Bowl		Sugar bowl w/ handles
Jun 78	3426	Harl Chop Plate		Round platter
Jun 78	3431	Harl tea saucer		tea cup saucer
Jun 78	3432	Harl cereal		36's oatmeal
Jun 78	3433	Harl Sugar (with new model hld Att. To mold)		Re-issue w/closed finial
Jun 78	3434	Harl sugar cover with hld att.		
Jul 78	3436	Harl Chop Plate		13" Platter
Nov 78	3448	Harl cream (changed bottom & top of mould)		Design not changed
Oct 78	3449	Harl Creamer		regular creamer
Oct 78	3450	Harl Soup		soup/cereal

*Not produced

Record of Sketches and Drawings

The ledger that adds more details about HLC's early colored wares is the *Record of Sketches and Drawings* which covers the years 1933 to 1944. In it Frederick Rhead listed many drawings he made for the new lines. There are even some for items that never progressed to the stage of being made into plaster models. Following is a table of the relevant Fiesta, Harlequin, and Kitchen Kraft entries from 1935 to 1938.

Date	Number	Drawing	Purpose
02-01-35	342	Ringed plate	Colored glazes
02-01-35	343	Cup for above	Colored glazes
02-27-35	357	Handle cup	Colored glazes
03-08-35	361-362	Sugars	Colored glazes
03-10-35	363-364	Onion soup, cream soup	Colored glazes
03-12-35	365-366	Creams	Colored glazes
03-16-35	367	5" fruit	Colored glazes
03-19-35	370	French casserole	C.G. line
03-19-35	371	Salad bowl	C.G. line
03-19-35	372-374	Fruit bowl	C.G. line
03-21-35	379	14" platter	Colored glazes
03-25-35	380	8 cup chocolate pot	Colored glazes
03-25-35	381	6 cup A.D. coffee	Colored glazes
03-26-35	382-386	Round casseroles 5" to 9"	Colored glazes
03-29-35	387	Candlestick	Colored glazes
04-08-35	388	Round compartment plate	Colored glazes
04-08-35	389	Oval compartment plate	Colored glazes
04-16-35	394-398	Nappies	Colored glaze line

Date	Number	Drawing	Purpose
04-18-35	399	Compartment plate	Colored glaze line
04-20-35	400	Compartment plate	Colored glaze line
04-21-35	401	Candlestick, bulb	Colored glaze line
04-21-35	402	Small nut comport	Colored glaze line
04-26-35	403	Cream soup, lugs	Colored glaze line
04-30-35	405	Candlestick, 3 supports	"Flamingo"
04-30-35	406	Candlestick, 3 supports	"Flamingo"
04-30-35	407	Candlestick, 3 supports	"Flamingo"
05-03-35	408	Stem flower vase	"Flamingo"
05-19-35	411	Mark for molds	Fiesta line
05-19-35	412	Mark for clay stamp	Fiesta line
05-29-35	414	Relish dish	Colored glazes
06-28-35	445	Water bottle	"Fiesta"
04-24-36	722	Jug	Fiesta
05-12-36	736	New onion soup	Fiesta
05-24-36	757	Casserole "Fiesta"	Royal Metal
07-09-36	835	Fiesta display card	
07-13-36	836-843	Teas for Woolworth	new colored shape
07-21-36	845	Fiesta exhibit for [?] W. Va.	
08-10-36	864-867	Casseroles, sugars & creams	Woolworth
08-15-36	894-904	Sketches for new Woolworth shape	10 drawings
10-28-36	956-960	Colored photograph sketches [for ad]	Harlequin
11-16-36	969	Second folder for J.D.T.	Harlequin
02-03-37	1017	Flat cake plate 10"	Royal Metal
02-03-37	1018	Deep cake plate 10"	Royal Metal
02-03-37	1019	Lug cake plate 10"	Royal Metal
02-19-37	1033	Refrigerator jars	Jewel Tea Co.
03-09-37	1047	"Fiesta HLC USA" drawing	For patent office
03-25-37	1066	Chart	Modern Ovenserve (KK)
06-16-37	1227	Backstamp for new ovenware line	Kitchen Kraft
07-19-37	1241	[Paper] label for J.D.T.	Kitchen Kraft OvenServe
07-20-37	1242	Revised label for above	KK OS
09-02-37	1296-1298	A.D. coffee cup for Woolworth	Harlequin
11-08-37	1376	Drawing of Kitchen Kraft	Patent office
01-20-38	1402	Drawing for backstamp	Tricolator bowls
02-01-38	1412	Marmalade	Harlequin
04-01-38	1463-1464	1 1/2 pint	Harlequin
04-02-38	1465	Sauceboat	Harlequin
04-08-38	1466	Sketch for turners	Woolworth egg cup
10-18-38	1581	Harlequin sugar for C.L. Deeds	Drawing for turners

CLASS 30

Crockery, Earthenware, and Porcelain

Ser. No. 390,208. The Homer Laughlin China Company, Newell, W. Va. Filed Mar. 20, 1937.

The letters "U S A" are disclaimed.
For Earthenware for Table Service.
Claims use since Nov. 11, 1935.

Fiesta trademark.

Ser. No. 399,815. The Homer Laughlin China Company, Newell, W. Va. Filed Nov. 15, 1937.

The letters U. S. A. are disclaimed.
For Earthenware for Oven and Refrigerator Use and Table Service.
Claims use since June 16, 1937.

Kitchen Kraft trade

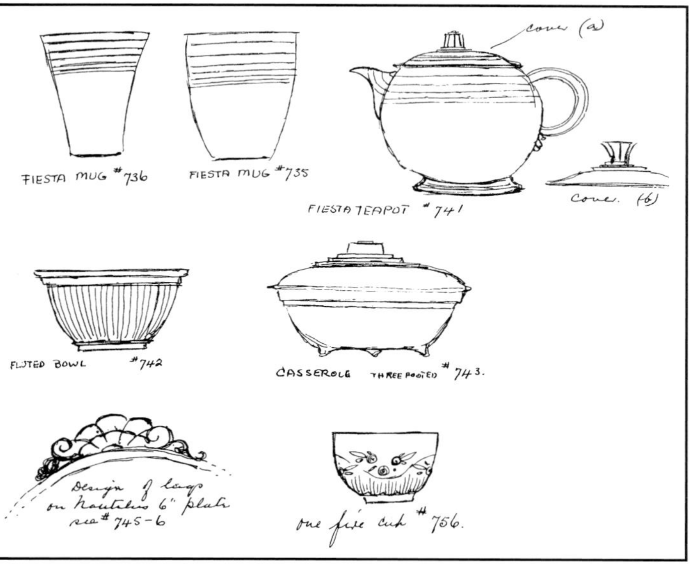

1936–37

ARTICLE	SIZE	MODEL Nº	DATE	MODELER.	
CREAM, TANGO	‖	725	1936 DECEMBER	BERRISFORD.	Released
TEACUP, NAUTILUS Revised for talc body.		726	"	KRAFT.	Released
NAPPIE, 7" " "	" "	727	"	BERRISFORD.	Released
CREAM SOUP STAND, NAUTILUS		728	,	"	Released
SUGAR, NAUTILUS, as #716 change in lower part of body		729	,	KRAFT.	Released
BAKER 7" " REVISED	7"	730	"	"	Released
DISH 6" " "	6"	731	"	"	Released
BOAT STAND, " "		732	"	BERRISFORD	Released
ONION SOUP, NAUTILUS		734	"	KRAFT	Released
MUG, FIESTA	Convex	735	"	"	
MUG. "	Concave. ×	736	"	BERRISFORD.	Released
SUGAR, TANGO, new handle & bow ‖	‖	737 ✓	"	KRAFT	Released
PLATE 10" BRITTANY to replace oval platter but with deeper ball. 11¾ diameter		738	"	"	Released
PLATE 11" BRITTANY to replace oval platter but deeper ball. 13" diameter		739	"	,	Released
SALT AND PEPPER, TANGO ‖	‖	740	"	BERRISFORD.	Released
‖ 222 MODELS MADE IN 1936. ‖					
TEAPOT. FIESTA 20 oz 2 covers		741	JANUARY. 1937	KRAFT.	Released
BOWL, FLUTED	General Mills.	742	" "	BERRISFORD	Released
CASSEROLE, THREE FEET		743	" "	"	
DEEP PLATE 6" TANGO ‖	‖	744	" "	KRAFT.	
PLATE 6" NAUTILUS with four lugs		745	" "	"	
" 6" 4½" fruit with two lugs		746	" "	"	
OATMEAL. ITALIAN DESIGN	Q.O.	747	" "	"	
FRUIT " "	Q.O.	748	" "	BERRISFORD.	
TEACUP, same as #708 but lower wider fluted.		749	" "	KRAFT	
TEACUP, same design as #640, but lower & wider		750	" "	KRAFT.	
TEACUP, same as #710, but lower, and without embossed crosses.		751	" "	"	
TEASAUCER, same as #711, but without small crosses.		752	" "	"	
TEACUP, same as #708 & #709 made lower.		753	" "	BERRISFORD	
CREAM SOUP, TANGO. ‖	‖	754	" "	KRAFT	
TEAPOT FOR LIPTON, SKETCH 1001, 6 CUP		755	" "	BERRISFORD.	
TEACUP, ONE FIRE,		756	" "	KRAFT & F.H.R.	
CASSEROLE, THREE FEET AS #743 but lower and two covers (A) inside cover (B) outside cover.		757	" "	BERRISFORD	
MUFFLE MODEL & MOULD for small kiln for lab		758	" "	KRAFT	
BAT MOULD for above for top of muffle		759	" "	"	
BAT "		760		"	

1936

ARTICLE	SIZE	MOD. Nº	SKE. Nº	DATE	MODELER
TEASAUCER, SHELL DESIGN, TO GO WITH CUP #641.		645		JULY, 1936	KRAFT.
TEASAUCER, to go with cup #643, illustrated opp. page		646		" "	BERRISFORD.
PLATE 7" DORIC		647		" "	KRAFT. Released 3 mos. Sept 24.36
TEASAUCER, for cup #644 illustrated opp. page.		648		" "	BERRISFORD.
TEACUP, conc., with line in center. illustrated opp. page.		649	836	" "	KRAFT.
SAUCER, for above. flat rim.		650	Released Sept 11.36.	" "	"
TEACUP, strait side, line in center, illustrated opp page.	Handles. A. B. & C.	651	Released Sept 11.36 836	Handle C. " "	KRAFT.
MIXING BOWL, for electric mixer,	9¾ × 4¾	652.		" "	BERRISFORD.
MIXING BOWL. same design as above.	6 × 4	653		" "	"
NAPPIE, rolled top, modeled line inside,	7"	654	Released Sept 11.36.	" "	"
FRUIT, rolled top, same design as above	4"	655	Released Sept 11.36.	" "	"
ELECTRIC SQUEEZER		656		AUG. 1936	KRAFT.
PLATE 8" same design as #613		657	Released Sept 11.36	" "	"
" 6" DEEP, same design as #613	woolworth.	658	Released Sept 11.36.	" "	"
CASSEROLE, illustration opposite		659		" "	BERRISFORD.
ELECTRIC BULB HOLDER		660		" "	KRAFT.
STRAIT SIDED CASSEROLE woolworth		661	Released Sept 11.36.	" "	BERRISFORD.
SUGAR. MODELED LINES, SEE OPP.		662		" "	KRAFT.
~~FOOT BATH FOR [illegible]~~				" "	
CASSEROLE, straight sides but without foot		663		" "	BERRISFORD
CUP, 5 oz. FOR ONE FIRE (illust. opp).		664		" "	KRAFT.
CASSEROLE, CURVED SIDE, ~~AS~~ without foot		665		" "	BERRISFORD
CUP 7 oz. for one fire. similar to #664		666		" "	KRAFT
CUP. 7 oz. one fire,		667		" "	"

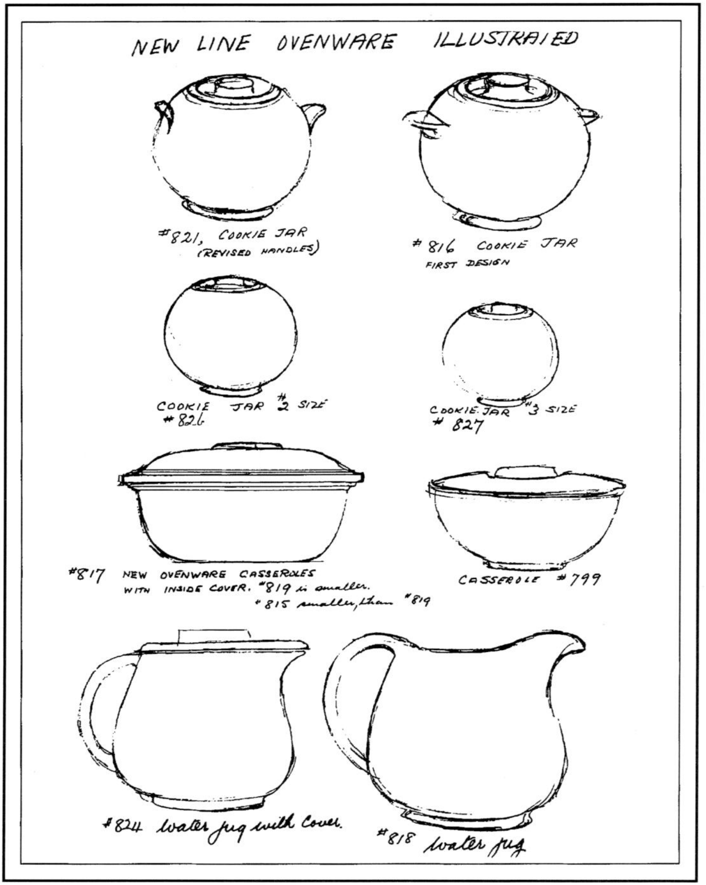

NEW OVENWARE LINE APRIL 1937
NOW CALLED "KITCHEN KRAFT."

	ITEM	SIZE	MOD. Nº	DATE MADE	SHAPE	REVISED	RELEASED
	CASSEROLE		799.	APRIL. 1937	1.		
	COVER for above:		803	" "	2.		
	MIXING BOWL.	Nº1 large [illegible]	806.	" "	3.		
same as Royal	PIE PLATE	9⅝" x 1"	✓809	" "	4		
	" "	" "	810.	" "	5		
	MIXING BOWL	(2nd one	✓811	" "	6		
	" "	3rd ")	✓812	" "	7		
	CASSEROLE Nº2	(INSIDE COVER	815	" "	8.		
✓	COOKIE JAR,	NO HANDLES	813	" "	9.	see #816.	May. 18.37
	~~CASSEROLE~~						
	COOKIE JAR,	with handles	816	" "	10.	see #821.	
	CASSEROLE,	large 9 1/16 x 3 3/4	817	" "	11.		
	WATER JUG	2 quart.	818	" "	12	see #822	
	CASSEROLE smaller than #817 inside cover	9 3/16 x 3 5/8"	819	" "	13	#817 revised	
	CASSEROLE, small (bean pot)	4 3/4 x 2 7/16	820	" "	14		
	COOKIE JAR	new handles	821	MAY 1937	15		~~May 18-37~~
	JUG. same as #818 but with open top.	(2 quart)	822	" "	16.	see 818	
	CASSEROLE inside cover	7⅞ x 3"	823 ✓	" "	17.		
	JUG with cover		824 ✓	" "	18.		
Nº2 ✓	COOKIE JAR smaller than #816 or #821)		826	" "	19.	#816 #821 revised	
Nº3 ✓	COOKIE JAR smallest.		827	" "	20.		
	REFRIGERATOR BOWL.	4½ x 2¼	828	" "	21.		
	— DITTO —	with lugs	829	" "	22.		
	BEAN POT same as #820 but	4½ x 2¼.	831	" "	23	#820 revised	6/16/37
	JUG, covered small		833.	" "	24		
	Salad Nappie,	11¼" x 3	836	" "	25		
	10" Dish for Jug Tray.		837	" "	26		
	Flat Plate	10¾"	838	" "	27		6/4/37
	Salt & Pepper		842	June. 1937	28		6/16/37
	S/s Onion Soup.		844	" "	29.		
	Salad Fork		843	" "	30		6/4/37.
	Revised Cover for 824 water jug		854	" "			

Appenxdix C: Frederick Hurten Rhead's Journal

The personal journals kept by Frederick Rhead during his tenure as art department director at HLC are both a blessing and a curse. The recording of his activities has provided an astounding amount of insight into his daily routine, how he worked with HLC management, his method of assigning tasks to the staff, and even how he dealt with the cancer that eventually killed him. However, the journal entries are often difficult to read. His handwriting could respectfully be called "messy." His notes appear hastily written and are full of abbreviations. Most of the time he used only initials for the names of many of the people he worked with. Still, without these volumes this book would never have been as accurate as it is.

Rhead wrote in his journal daily. He recorded his major activities including what he worked on, where he went, and whom he met. Visits from the retail buyers, whose opinion he held in high regard, are meticulously recorded. Glaze formulas, the stock number of decals examined, drawings made, which trial pieces were out of the kiln, and the meetings he attended are examples of the contents of these journals. Sometimes he pasted in clippings from newspapers or copies of memos from HLC management. There is even an example of his wife's personal stationery taped to a page, the engraved address perhaps designed by him.

The journals were given to the HLC art department by his family after his death in 1942 and they joined his large collection of books on pottery and art already there. The first journal was started in 1931 and the last in 1942. We are grateful to the HLC art department for allowing us to see them. With more than 4,000 pages to examine, it was a difficult task to find relevant entries. Our researchers spent the better part of three days marking pages to be photocopied. We searched for key words such as Fiesta, Harlequin, Royal Metal, colored glazes, OvenServe, Kitchen Kraft, etc. No doubt some things were missed. However, many collector questions were answered and the history of the development of Fiesta, Harlequin and Kitchen Kraft became much clearer.

The journal was created in separate volumes, one for each year. Unfortunately, the one for 1937 is missing. This had a significant impact on our coverage of Kitchen Kraft, and to a lesser degree Harlequin, since those lines were under development at that time. We attempted to make up for that by extracting what data we could from the modeling log and known price lists.

A detailed examination of the existing volumes was not made. There was too little time and too many pages. Many of the daily entries are extremely mundane or pertain to dinnerware lines not being examined in this book. We look forward to a future opportunity to view the journals again and update the contents of this book and future HLCCA books on HLC ware.

Two sample pages follow, one each for Fiesta and Harlequin. They serve to acquaint the reader with Mr. Rhead's method of record keeping and the style of his handwriting.

Thursday April 4 · 35

Red Kilns out. too much reduction and firing too quick for reds // Some red pieces and some nice mixtures but majority of ware brown and burnt out. Large red platter good except for brown reds. A.V. [illegible] exact temperature, etc. for reds while firing again with blue and turquoise //

Saturday August 22. 1936

J.M.W. up

saw Woolworth colored glaze line, liked cup handle. Spoke of green glaze. Told him that A.V. was working on new glazes.

J.M.W stated that he wanted other Pink –

Liked the [illegible] glazes, also [illegible] the new underglaze [illegible] [illegible]. Interested in new Woolworth [illegible] line //

We are to make Woolworth samples also in Yellow 2316

Appendix D:
The Homer Laughlin China Collectors Association

The Homer Laughlin China Collectors Association was formed in the summer of 1998 as an all volunteer, member run, non-profit organization dedicated to providing an educational forum for those interested in the important role the Homer Laughlin China Company has played in America from the late 1800s to present.

We are a non-profit, 501(c)(3) association with members all around the country (and in a few cases, the world). We meet annually for a conference which provides a forum for seminars, exhibits, and the sharing of knowledge. Also, we publish a quarterly magazine, *The Dish*, with a variety of informational topics relevant to anyone interested in HLC.

If you would like to join, simply make a copy of the membership form shown here and mail it back to us with your membership dues to: HLCCA, PO Box 26021, Crystal City VA 22215-6021

Membership Application

Homer Laughlin China Collectors Association

PO Box 26021, Crystal City, VA 22215-6021

Name: ______________________

Address: ______________________

City: ____________ State: ____________ Zip: ____________

Home Phone: (   )____________ Work Phone: (   ) ____________

Email Address: ______________________

Do you wish to be included on our email list? ❑ Yes ❑ No

I Collect/Have Interest In:

❑ Americana
❑ American Beauty
❑ Angelus
❑ Art Pottery
❑ Brittany
❑ Carnival
❑ Cavalier
❑ Century/Riviera
❑ Colonial
❑ Coronet
❑ Debutante
❑ Duraprint
❑ Eggshell Georgian
❑ Eggshell Nautilus
❑ Empress
❑ Epicure
❑ Fiestaware - Vintage
❑ Fiestaware - Contemporary
❑ Fiestaware 2000
❑ Genesee
❑ Golden Gate
❑ Harlequin
❑ Hudson
❑ Jade
❑ Jubilee
❑ Kitchen Kraft
❑ Kwaker
❑ Liberty
❑ Marigold
❑ Nautilus
❑ Newell
❑ Niagra
❑ Orange/Apple Tree Bowls
❑ Orleans
❑ Ovenserve
❑ Pastoral
❑ Picadilly
❑ Ravenna
❑ Republic
❑ Rhythm
❑ Serenade
❑ Skytone/Suntone
❑ Swing
❑ Tango
❑ Theme
❑ Virginia Rose
❑ Wells Art Glaze
❑ Yellowstone
Other: ____________

I am a: ❑ Collector ❑ Historian ❑ Dealer

May we print information about you in our membership roster? ❑ Yes ❑ No

(additional info) ______________________

What types of activities would you be interested in helping with:

❑ Seminar Classes ❑ Research ❑ Writing/Editing ❑ Conference Organizing ❑ Fundraising

Type of membership:

❑ Single ($25.00 US Funds)
❑ Couple ($40.00 US Funds)

Partner name: ____________

Send completed application along with dues payment to:

HLCCA
PO Box 26021
Crystal City, VA 22215-6021

Current issue of *The Dish* magazine will be mailed upon receipt of membership dues. Membership includes one year of *The Dish*, free classified ads, early information regarding the annual conference, and many other benefits.

The Homer Laughlin China Collectors Association is a Non-Profit 501(c)(3) Association

Appendix E: Price Guides

A note on prices

The prices given are for piece in mint (original) condition. Any damage detracts from the value. For pieces with chips, cracks, scratching or any other type of damage, expect the value to be 1/2 or less of the price given.

Price data was gathered primarily through a survey sent to all members of the HLCCA, although additional sources such as auctions (both live and on-line) were used. Many price guides simply average values for such surveys, but we felt that such a number might not be as useful to the reader, so we used some more sophisticated statistical functions. The result is a range of numbers that should provide a better representation of the value and the volatility of certain pieces. You will notice that some items have a much greater range between the high and the low values – these pieces show more volatility in the market and as such, prices will vary more. For items where we had a small sampling of values, we denote them in *italics* to indicate that the price may not be fully representative of the value. Very rare items are noted with *NEV* (No Established Value) if sufficient price data could be located, yet the piece is known to exist

The formula used to compute these prices is:

$$\bar{x} \pm \frac{s t_{\left(\frac{\alpha}{2}, n-1\right)}}{\sqrt{n}}$$

$\bar{x}$ is the mean.

s is the standard deviation.

$t_{\left(\frac{\alpha}{2}, n-1\right)}$ is the inverse T distribution.

n is the number of samples.

Additionally, for prices over $100, we have rounded to the nearest $5 increment for ease in use of this data.

Vintage Fiesta

	Red	Cobalt Blue	Ivory	Turquoise	Yellow	Light Green	Forest	Chartreuse	Rose	Gray	Medium Green
Ash Tray	$60-61	$56-58	$55-57	$50-52	$47-49	$51-53	$82-86	$86-88	$83-85	$85-88	$180-190
Covered Onion Soup	$670-715	$710-755	$710-735	*$6780-7970*	$515-570	$575-630					
Cream Soup Cup	$66-68	$62-64	$55-57	$47-48	$43-44	$46-48	$70-73	$64-66	$70-72	$66-70	$4580-4970
Dessert Bowl	$53-56	$47-51	$49-51	$39-41	$37-39	$42-43	$49-52	$51-55	$55-58	$51-54	$610-645
4 3/4" Fruit Bowl	$34-35	$34-35	$32-33	$26-27	$25-26	$26-27	$36-37	$33-35	$33-34	$33-35	$510-535
5 1/2" Fruit Bowl	$31-32	$31-32	$32-33	$25-26	$24-25	$28-29	$37-38	$37-38	$37-38	$35-36	$65-67
11 3/4" Fruit Bowl	$340-360	$330-365	$325-340	$305-325	$305-320	$315-330					
Mixing Bowl #1	$215-235	$265-285	$250-265	$240-260	$195-215	$210-225					
Mixing Bowl #2	$125-135	$120-130	$145-160	$135-145	$125-135	$125-135					
Mixing Bowl #3	$145-155	$155-165	$150-160	$145-155	$130-140	$120-125					
Mixing Bowl #4	$140-155	$150-165	$170-180	$145-155	$120-130	$135-145					
Mixing Bowl #5	$190-200	$200-210	$190-205	$170-180	$140-150	$160-165					
Mixing Bowl #6	$285-305	$295-320	$280-305	$280-310	$230-260	$235-260					
Mixing Bowl #7	$410-455	$380-420	$425-465	$335-370	$355-395	$395-430					
Mixing Cover #1	$1055-1170	$1070-1180	$995-1130		$955-1095	$880-1000					
Mixing Cover #2	$780-890	$785-890	$880-935		$820-905	$820-905					
Mixing Cover #3	$1010-1105	$1015-1110	$945-1055		$895-990	$895-990					
Mixing Cover #4	$1125-1200	$1140-1200	$1025-1135		$970-1080	$970-1080					

	Red	Cobalt Blue	Ivory	Turquoise	Yellow	Light Green	Forest	Chartreuse	Rose	Gray	Medium Green
8 1/2" Nappie	$54-56	$56-59	$53-56	$42-43	$43-44	$42-43	$57-61	$60-62	$57-60	$56-60	$155-165
9 1/2" Nappie	$70-76	$66-73	$66-70	$50-55	$54-59	$52-57					
Footed Salad Bowl	$350-375	$375-405	$360-385	$335-380	$350-385	$335-370					
Individual Salad Bowl	$97-100			$82-88	$78-85						$120-125
Unlisted Salad Bowl	NEV	$2620-3380	NEV		$99-105	NEV					
Bulb Candle Holders (Pair)	$115-120	$120-125	$115-120	$100-105	$100-105	$99-105					
Tripod Candle Holders (Pair)	$550-590	$585-630	$645-675	$620-670	$520-560	$520-545					
Carafe	$295-310	$325-340	$300-330	$280-295	$270-280	$300-310					
Covered Casserole	$195-205	$200-210	$195-205	$130-140	$155-160	$135-150	$285-305	$250-260	$285-300	$255-275	$1305-1405
French Casserole	NEV	$4295-4705	NEV		$295-310	NEV					
Promotional Casserole	$130-140	$170-180			$150-155	$150-155					
After Dinner Coffee Pot	$530-560	$475-505	$505-535	$620-665	$425-465	$465-505					
Regular Coffee Pot	$235-240	$235-245	$230-240	$200-205	$175-185	$175-185	$450-515	$435-485	$490-550	$600-645	
Sweets Comport	$98-105	$93-97	$83-88	$74-78	$77-81	$76-80					
12" Comport	$180-190	$170-180	$165-170	$150-160	$155-160	$135-140					
Cream (Stick Handle)	$62-65	$62-65	$62-65	$70-79	$43-46	$45-47					
Cream (Ring Handle)	$33-35	$34-36	$30-31	$23-25	$24-26	$25-27	$39-41	$40-43	$38-40	$40-42	$110-115
Individual Creamer	$305-325	NEV		NEV	$73-76						
After Dinner Coffee Cup	$78-80	$74-76	$74-79	$71-75	$57-60	$69-71	$380-400	$385-410	$385-420	$395-430	
Teacup	$28-30	$26-28	$28-30	$23-24	$22-23	$22-24	$31-33	$31-33	$30-32	$27-30	$43-45
Egg Cup	$78-82	$74-78	$72-75	$57-60	$61-64	$57-61	$145-155	$150-155	$155-160	$155-165	
Covered Marmalade Jar	$325-345	$320-345	$315-345	$310-340	$245-265	$285-300					
Tom & Jerry Mug	$78-80	$72-75	$75-79	$51-53	$56-57	$57-59	$79-82	$83-85	$79-82	$80-84	$105-110
Covered Mustard	$300-310	$290-305	$270-285	$230-250	$260-275	$240-260					
Disc Water Jug	$150-160	$155-160	$155-165	$115-120	$115-120	$110-115	$240-250	$245-255	$230-240	$230-240	$1515-1585
Disc Juice Jug[1]	$520-560			NEV	$45-46					$2550-2800	
Ice Pitcher	$150-160	$150-160	$155-165	$145-150	$130-135	$145-150					
Two Pint Jug	$110-115	$115-120	$105-110	$81-84	$80-85	$86-87	$130-135	$120-130	$140-145	$150-155	
Cake Plate	$1415-1575	$1360-1485	NEV		$1195-1330	$1080-1190					
13" Chop Plate	$48-51	$48-51	$43-47	$42-45	$37-39	$39-42	$89-92	$83-87	$93-100	$91-95	$390-420
15" Chop Plate	$72-78	$75-79	$64-67	$53-56	$46-48	$46-48	$105-110	$100-110	$95-100	$105-110	
12" Compartment	$69-78	$68-73	$63-67		$52-55	$54-57					
10 1/2" Compartment	$61-70	$44-45	$46-50	$40-43	$40-43	$40-44	$86-95	$77-79	$78-81	$79-84	
Deep Plate	$56-58	$56-57	$53-54	$38-39	$35-37	$37-38	$53-55	$49-52	$55-57	$54-56	$130-135
6" Plate	$6-7	$7-8	$7-8	$6-7	$6-7	$6-7	$8-9	$9-10	$9-10	$10-11	$22-23
7" Plate	$11-12	$10-11	$10-11	$8-9	$8-9	$9-10	$14-15	$13-14	$14-15	$14-15	$38-39
9" Plate	$17-18	$17-18	$15-16	$12-13	$12-13	$12-13	$20-21	$20-21	$20-21	$20-21	$51-54
10" Plate	$39-41	$41-42	$40-41	$28-29	$28-30	$29-31	$51-53	$49-52	$49-51	$45-47	$130-135
Oval Platter	$49-52	$45-48	$38-41	$37-40	$35-37	$36-38	$61-63	$56-58	$56-57	$58-60	$160-165
Relish Tray	$85-94	$91-100	$93-105	$84-88	$78-85	$84-94					
Relish Side	$52-57	$55-58	$57-61	$51-54	$50-53	$52-55					
Relish Center	$58-62	$46-52	$55-61	$57-62	$46-50	$52-58					
Sauce Boat	$76-84	$70-73	$69-71	$41-44	$43-45	$47-50	$77-80	$69-72	$78-81	$70-74	$185-195
After Dinner Saucer	$24-25	$19-21	$23-25	$20-21	$17-19	$20-22	$110-120	$110-115	$110-120	$115-120	
Teacup Saucer	$8-10	$7-9	$5-7	$7-8	$6-7	$6-7	$11-14	$7-8	$6-7	$7-8	$14-16
Shakers (pr)	$32-34	$30-32	$32-34	$24-26	$24-26	$24-26	$48-50	$48-50	$46-48	$46-48	$79-166
Covered Sugar	$54-57	$56-60	$56-58	$44-46	$41-43	$46-49	$67-70	$73-74	$73-74	$66-69	$155-165
Individual Sugar	NEV			NEV	$125-130						

	Red	Cobalt Blue	Ivory	Turquoise	Yellow	Light Green	Forest	Chartreuse	Rose	Gray	Medium Green
Dripcut® Syrup	$445-470	$440-465	$410-440	$380-425	$350-375	$350-375					
Large Tea Pot	$215-230	$220-230	$210-220	$185-195	$195-200	$180-190					
Medium Tea Pot	$195-200	$215-225	$200-205	$160-165	$155-160	$160-165	$330-350	$315-325	$310-330	$340-360	$1480-1645
Figure-8 Tray	$94-100		$365-395								
Utility Tray	$43-47	$45-48	$39-43	$39-41	$40-42	$38-40					
Juice Tumbler[2]	$45-47	$44-46	$43-45	$40-41	$39-41	$39-40	$825-980	$865-970	$78-87	$225-265	
Water Tumbler	$71-74	$73-75	$69-72	$60-62	$62-63	$60-62					
Bud Vase	$91-98	$100-105	$105-110	$93-97	$85-88	$84-89					
8" Flower Vase	$760-780	$720-740	$750-770	$550-600	$525-585	$485-580					
10" Flower Vase	$1045-1095	$940-980	$955-985	$855-905	$845-860	$785-820					
12" Flower Vase	$2140-2375	$1410-1470	$1220-1295	$1285-1365	$1230-1295	$1230-1295					

[1] Harlequin Yellow – $56-62, Celadon Green - $175-185
[2] Harlequin Yellow - $755-895, Shell Pink, Cream Beige, Mist Gray - $135-145

Fiesta Ironstone

Dessert Bowl	Any Color	$6-7
Soup/Cereal Bowl	Any Color	$7-8
Salad Bowl	Antique Gold	$27-35
Vegetable Bowl	Any Color	$21-23
Covered Casserole	Antique Gold	$29-39
Coffee Mug	Any Color	$28-33
Coffee Server	Antique Gold	$79-89
Cream	Any Color	$11-12
Cup	Any Color	$9-10
Saucer	Any Color	$3-4
Water Jug	Antique Gold	$62-67
Dinner Plate (10")	Any Color	$12-13
Salad Plate (7")	Any Color	$5-6
Oval Platter	Any Color	$25-28
Sauce Boat	Any Color	$32-35
Sauce Boat Stand	Mango Red	$165-205
	Green/Gold	$55-74
Shakers (Pair)	Any Color	$13-14
Covered Sugar	Any Color	$15-16
Tea Server	Antique Gold	$50-59

Fiesta Amberstone/Casualstone

Ashtray	$37-40
Dessert Bowl	$6-7
Soup/Cereal Bowl	$7-8
Salad Bowl	$39-43
Vegetable Bowl	$17-18
Covered Butter	$42-48
Covered Casserole	$65-73
Coffee Mug	$36-44
Coffee Server	$70-75
Creamer	$8-9
Cup	$5-6
Saucer	$3-4
Water Jug	$60-64
Marmalade Jar	$48-53
Dinner Plate (10")	$7-8
Salad Plate (7")	$5-6
Bread & Butter Plate (6")	$3-4
Pie plate	$29-32
Soup (Deep) Plate	$10-11
Oval Platter	$18-21
Round Platter	$20-22
Relish	$21-24
Sauce Boat	$19-22
Shakers (Pair)	$15-16
Covered Sugar	$10-12
Tea Server	$45-52

Fiesta Kitchen Kraft

	Cobalt Blue	Red	Yellow	Green
6" Mixing Bowl	$75-85	$76-87	$69-77	$68-75
8" Mixing Bowl	$89-97	$91-100	$82-86	$82-86
10" Mixing Bowl	$110-120	$110-120	$115-125	$97-100
Cake Plate	$63-67	$60-63	$49-52	$48-51
Individual Casserole	$155-170	$155-165	$145-150	$140-150
7 1/2" Casserole	$92-96	$90-95	$95-105	$95-105
8 1/2" Casserole	$90-98	$100-100	$98-100	$115-120
Small Covered Jar	$325-350	$320-340	$310-330	$305-325
Medium Covered Jar	$295-310	$280-315	$300-315	$300-320
Large Covered Jar	$320-350	$355-375	$310-330	$260-295
Small Covered Jug	$335-360	$325-355	$310-335	$285-310
Medium Covered Jug	$335-360	$295-320	$295-315	$295-315
Small Pie Plate	$44-46	$37-40	$31-34	$36-39
Large Pie Plate	$44-46	$43-45	$34-39	$41-44
Refrigerator Body	$46-51	$60-66	$45-49	$41-45
Refrigerator Cover	$94-110	$82-96	$88-105	$80-94
Shakers (pr)	$80-87	$76-83	$77-83	$69-76
Cake Server	$155-170	$175-190	$130-145	$140-155
Fork	$155-170	$145-160	$145-165	$115-125
Spoon	$140-150	$130-140	$130-145	$120-135
Platter, Oval	$64-74	$77-82	$67-70	$55-60

Harlequin Kitchen Kraft

	Yellow	Red	Blue	Green
6" Mixing Bowl		$91-94		$91-94
8" Mixing Bowl			$115-125	
10" Mixing Bowl	$130-135			

Contemporary Sapphire Fiesta

Soup Bowl (461)	$13-17
Serving Bowl (471)	$23-33
Carafe (448)	$31-41
Clock (473)	$34-52
60th Anniversary Clock	$15-120
Large Disk Pitcher (484)	$31-45
60th Anniversary Disk Pitcher	$45-59
60th Anniversary Beverage Set	$63-90
Teacup (452)	$11-16
Saucer (470)	$5-15
7" Plate (464)	$9-22
10" Plate (466)	$16-23
Large Oval Platter (458)	$23-33
Round Serving Tray with Fiesta Club of America logo	$37-61
Round Serving Tray (468)	$45-56
Tumbler (446)	$13-19
10" Vase (491)	$120-160

Contemporary Lilac Fiesta

Coffee Server (493)	$105-160
Teapot (496)	$68-110
Bouillon Cup (450)	$29-40
Soup Bowl (461)	$24-39
Serving Bowl (471)	$40-57
Small Bowl (460)	$20-35
Stacking Cereal Bowl (472)	$24-34
Fruit Bowl (459)	$26-37
9" Rim Soup Bowl (451)	$41-54
12" Rim Soup Bowl (462)	$50-85
Tripod Candle Holders (489)	$345-605
Covered Butter (494)	$55-74
Round Candle Stick Holders (488)	$82-125
Covered Casserole (495)	$120-225
Standard Creamer (492)	$31-46
A.D. Cup w/Saucer (478)	$82-125
Teacup (452)	$10-32
Saucer (470)	$10-15
Mug (453)	$21-35
Napkin Rings (469)	$61-94
Large Disk Pitcher (484)	$53-69
Mini Disk Pitcher (475)	$37-51
Small Disk Pitcher (485)	$59-95
6" Plate (463)	$15-24
7" Plate (464)	$20-32
9" Plate (465)	$29-46
10" Plate (466)	$31-42
Chop Plate(467)	$45-73
60th Anniversary Beverage Set	$60-95
Sugar/Creamer/Tray Set (821)	$63-93
Sauce Boat (486)	$46-61
Round Serving Tray (468)	$265-385
Standard Sugar Bowl (498)	$29-47
Shakers (Pair) (497)	$40-59
Large Oval Platter (458)	$35-51
Medium Oval Platter (457)	$37-53
Small Oval Platter (456)	$37-51
Pie Baker (487)	$66-110
Tumbler (446)	$21-32
Bud Vase (490)	$73-105
10" Vase (491)	$215-345

Harlequin

	Yellow	Spruce	Blue	Maroon	Red(Tangerine)	Rose	Turquoise	Light Green	Gray	Chartreuse	Forest	Medium Green
Ashtray, Basketweave	$36-39	$54-65	$41-45	$53-61	$49-56	$34-37	$44-48	$66-84	$62-71	$58-67	$65-78	$305-565
Ashtray, Regular	$38-46	$60-69	$48-54	$68-76	$63-71	$36-41	$39-45	$105-150				
Ashtray, Saucer	$62-68	$83-91	$72-80	$85-93	$83-90	$57-73	$65-72	NEV				
Bowl, 36s	$27-29	$82-105	$45-52	$105-130	$41-44	$35-38	$26-27	$42-44	$41-46	$42-46	$45-48	$165-185
Bowl, 36s Oatmeal	$16-18	$73-99	$21-22	$84-120	$18-20	$18-20	$16-17	$24-26	$25-29	$23-27	$29-31	$74-91
Bowl, Cream Soup	$23-26	$34-36	$29-31	$36-39	$33-35	$26-30	$23-24	$33-34	$34-36	$33-37	$34-37	$1465-1635
Bowl, Fruit	$9-10	$12-13	$10-12	$12-14	$13-16	$10-11	$9-10	$12-13	$10-12	$12-13	$12-14	$32-35
Bowl, Individual Salad	$29-32	$33-40	$31-33	$48-53	$40-45	$22-24	$18-20	$31-35	$42-47	$38-41	$43-48	$145-170
Bowl, Nappy	$30-31	$47-51	$34-37	$44-49	$33-37	$29-32	$29-31	$38-40	$41-45	$41-45	$42-46	$110-120
Bowl, Oval Baker	$27-29	$40-43	$31-33	$35-39	$35-37	$33-36	$30-33	$40-42				
Butter	$100-110	$140-145	$125-135	$150-160	$140-150	$160-175	$105-110	$165-195				
Candle Holders (Pair)	$265-285	$335-370	$315-360	$365-390	$300-310	$330-380	$290-320	NEV				
Covered Casserole	$105-115	$165-175	$125-140	$145-160	$120-130	$105-115	$100-110	$160-165	$140-155	$160-190	$250-320	NEV
Creamer, High-Lip	$175-195	$175-195	$200-225	$180-195								
Creamer, Regular	$12-13	$25-27	$19-21	$23-25	$22-23	$17-19	$13-14	$22-23	$19-22	$21-23	$26-28	$73-79
Creamer, Novelty	$29-31	$46-54	$39-42	$49-53	$38-41	$36-38	$29-31	$45-51	$62-72	$64-75	$63-73	$1880-3120
Creamer, Individual	$23-25	$24-28	$27-29	$34-35	$26-28	$44-54	$30-40	$88-98				
Cup, Demitasse	$45-48	$93-105	$71-76	$91-100	$87-97	$57-66	$43-46	$88-98	$145-185	$140-175	$165-195	$480-520
Cup, Large	$230-255					$240-265	$235-265			$240-265	$250-285	$680-785
Cup, Tea	$10-11	$12-13	$10-11	$13-13	$11-12	$10-11	$10-11	$11-12	$11-12	$12-13	$10-11	$18-19
Double Eggcup	$26-29	$29-33	$25-26	$33-35	$31-33	$25-28	$22-24	$27-29	$38-43	$39-46	$46-57	$1095-1255
Single Eggcup	$27-29	$33-37	$32-35	$37-38	$34-36	$35-42	$29-31	$220-380				
Marmalade	$210-230	$325-380	$265-300	$335-355	$285-300	$270-305	$235-255	$420-670				
Nut Dish	$16-17	$22-23	$18-20	$21-23	$19-21	$42-50	$12-13	$105-110				
Pitcher, 22 ounce Jug	$38-40	$80-89	$58-63	$76-84	$72-75	$58-65	$49-53	$76-78	$83-89	$75-85	$86-93	$1445-1555
Pitcher, Service Water	$68-70	$91-98	$67-73	$110-115	$86-89	$80-84	$68-70	$97-100	$115-125	$110-125	$145-150	*$2500-3200*
Plate, 10"	$25-28	$40-43	$29-30	$42-44	$38-40	$30-32	$22-25	$35-37	$33-36	$36-39	$39-41	$78-89
Plate, 9"	$10-11	$15-16	$13-14	$16-18	$14-15	$10-11	$10-11	$15-16	$14-15	$15-16	$16-17	$34-39
Plate, 7"	$7-8	$10-11	$9-10	$11-12	$9-10	$7-8	$7-8	$9-10	$10-11	$9-11	$10-11	$27-30
Plate, 6"	$4-5	$6-7	$6-7	$6-7	$6-7	$5-6	$5-6	$6-7	$6-7	$6-7	$6-7	$22-26
Plate, Deep	$18-20	$28-32	$26-28	$33-37	$30-32	$24-26	$16-18	$30-32	$29-33	$29-33	$39-41	$105-120
Platter, 11"	$20-22	$28-31	$24-26	$30-33	$26-28	$22-24	$18-19	$27-29	$27-30	$25-28	$32-34	$265-305
Platter, 13"	$26-29	$37-41	$31-35	$37-41	$38-41	$32-35	$22-25	$33-35	$36-42	$35-43	$43-49	$375-490
Relish Base							$100-105					
Relish Side Insert	$61-65		$59-64	$62-66	$59-64	$84-105	$79-95					
Sauce Boat	$23-25	$41-44	$30-33	$41-44	$30-32	$22-24	$21-22	$34-36	$43-51	$39-44	$45-50	$375-450
Saucer, Demitasse	$15-17	$22-27	$18-21	$27-32	$23-26	$18-22	$14-16	$24-27	$48-58	$53-70	$59-73	$205-260
Saucer, Tea	$4-5	$5-6	$3-4	$6-7	$5-6	$4-5	$4-5	$4-5	$4-5	$4-5	$5-6	$13-15
Shakers (Pair)	$17-19	$33-36	$24-28	$28-31	$31-33	$22-24	$16-19	$26-28	$31-36	$33-39	$35-40	$240-270
Sugar Bowl	$16-18	$41-44	$25-27	$36-39	$31-35	$22-24	$18-20	$36-39	$32-34	$32-38	$42-45	$115-135
Syrup	$335-350	$400-450	$400-450		$360-380							
Teapot	$95-105	$160-170	$125-135	$140-160	$135-145	$135-150	$96-105	$120-135	$155-170	$150-160	$170-185	$1365-1870
Tumbler	$47-51	$56-59	$52-56	$61-65	$55-58	$58-66	$41-42	$48-56				

	Yellow	Spruce	Blue	Maroon
Duck	$200-220	$215-235	$225-245	$225-240
Fish	$200-225	$235-255	$235-260	$230-250
Donkey	$200-215	$250-270	$225-240	$230-245
Penguin	$200-205	$245-270	$195-210	$250-275
Lamb	$235-260	$255-275	$225-240	$240-255
Cat	$200-215	$235-260	$225-250	$225-245

Harlequin Ironstone

	Yellow	Turquoise	Coral	Reissue Green
10" Plate	$11-14	$11-14	$11-14	$9-11
7" Plate	$5-6	$5-6	$5-6	$5-6
Soup/Cereal Bowl	$6-9	$10-13	$11-16	$13-16
Teacup	$4-5	$4-5	$4-5	$4-5
Saucer	$2-3	$2-3	$2-3	$2-3
Creamer		$9-10		
Sugar	$15-17			
Vegetable Bowl				$18-22
Round Platter	$60-65		$28-34	

Bibliography

Berkow, Nancy. *Wallace-Homestead Guide to Fiesta: The Complete History of America's Fastest Growing Collectible.* Des Moines, Iowa: Wallace-Homestead Book Co., 1978.

Clark, Garth. *American Ceramics 1867 to the Present.* New York: Abbeville Press, 1978.

Cunningham, Jo. *Homer Laughlin: A Giant Among Dishes, 1873-1939.* Atglen, Pa.: Schiffer Publishing, 1998.

Dale, Sharon. *Frederick Hurten Rhead: An English Potter in America.* Erie, Pa.: Erie Art Museum, 1986.

Duncan, Alastair. *Art Deco.* New York: Thames and Hudson, 1988.

Fournier, Robert. *Illustrated Dictionary of Practical Pottery.* 3d ed. Radnor, Pa.: Chilton Book Co., 1992.

"Frederick Hurten Rhead, China Company Art Director, Ceramics Artist, Dies." *China and Glass*, November 1942: 19.

Fridley, A. W. *Catalina Pottery: The Early Years, 1927-1937.* Costa Mesa, Ca.: Rainbow Publishing, 1977.

Gibbs, Carl Jr. *Collector's Encyclopedia of Metlox Potteries: Identification and Values.* Paducha, Ky.: Schroeder Publishing, Collector Books, 1995.

Hall, Eric, *Radiation and Life*, 2nd Edition, Pergamon Press, New York, 1984

Hillier, Bevis. *Art Deco.* New York: E. P. Dutton, 1968.

Homer Laughlin China Co. "Modeling Log Book, 1933-1944." Company records, Homer Laughlin China Co., 1944.

Homer Laughlin China Co. "Modeling Log Book, 1944-1997." Company records, Homer Laughlin China Co., 1997.

Huxford, Bob and Sharon Huxford. *The Story of Fiesta.* Paducha, Ky.: Schroeder Publishing, Collector Books, 1974.

Huxford, Bob and Sharon Huxford. *The Collectors Encyclopedia of Fiesta: Plus Harlequin, Riviera, and Kitchen Kraft.* 2d ed. Paducha, Ky.: Schroeder Publishing, Collector Books, 1976.

Huxford, Bob and Sharon Huxford. *The Collectors Encyclopedia of Fiesta: Plus Harlequin, Riviera, and Kitchen Kraft.* 3d ed. Paducha, Ky.: Schroeder Publishing, Collector Books, 1979.

Huxford, Bob and Sharon Huxford. *The Collectors Encyclopedia of Fiesta: Plus Harlequin, Riviera, and Kitchen Kraft.* 4th ed. Paducha, Ky.: Schroeder Publishing, Collector Books, 1981.

Huxford, Bob and Sharon Huxford. *The Collectors Encyclopedia of Fiesta: Plus Harlequin, Riviera, and Kitchen Kraft.* 5th ed. Paducha, Ky.: Schroeder Publishing, Collector Books, 1984.

Huxford, Bob and Sharon Huxford. *The Collectors Encyclopedia of Fiesta: Plus Harlequin, Riviera, and Kitchen Kraft.* 6th ed. Paducha, Ky.: Schroeder Publishing, Collector Books, 1987.

Huxford, Bob and Sharon Huxford. *The Collector's Encyclopedia of Fiesta: Plus Harlequin, Riviera, and Kitchen Kraft.* 7th ed. Paducha, Ky.: Schroeder Publishing, Collector Books, 1992.

Huxford, Bob and Sharon Huxford. *Collector's Encyclopedia of Fiesta: Plus Harlequin, Riviera, and Kitchen Kraft.* 8th ed. Paducha, Ky.: Schroeder Publishing, Collector Books, 1998.

Jasper, Joanne. *The Collector's Encyclopedia of Homer Laughlin China: Reference and Value Guide.* Paducha, Ky.: Schroeder Publishing, Collector Books, 1993.

Lehner, Lois. *Lehner's Encyclopedia of U.S. Marks on Pottery, Porcelain, and Clay.* Paducha, Ky.: Schroeder Publishing, Collector Books, 1988.

Lehner, Lois. *Complete Book of American Kitchen and Dinner Wares.* Des Moines, Iowa: Wallace-Homestead, 1980.

McCready, Karen. *Art Deco and Modernist Ceramics.* New York: Thames and Hudson, 1995.

Piña, Leslie. "Homer Laughlin's Fiesta". In *Pottery: Modern Wares, 1920-1960.* Atglen, Pa.: Schiffer Publishing, 1994.

Rhead, Frederick H. Typescript of autobiography. Museum of Ceramics, East Liverpool, Ohio.

Rhead, Frederick H. Personal journals, 1935-1941. Homer Laughlin China Co., Newell, W.V.

Rhead, Frederick Hurten. "Dinnerware Style and Decoration." *Crockery and Glass Journal* 118 (January 1936): 41, 70, 72.

Rhead, Frederick Hurten. "Color-A Designer Speaks." *Crockery and Glass Journal* 120 (May 1937): 13, 46.

Rhead, Frederick Hurten. "More About Color." *Crockery and Glass Journal* 120 (June 1937): 13, 38.

Rhead, Frederick H. "Record of Sketches and Drawings." Company records, Homer Laughlin China Co., 1938.

Riederer, LaHoma, Cynthia Bettinger, and Charles Bettinger. *A Collector's Guide to Fiesta Dinnerware.* Monroe, La.: privately printed, 1974.

Riederer, LaHoma, Cynthia Bettinger, and Charles Bettinger. *Fiesta II: A Collector's Guide to Fiesta, Harlequin, and Riviera Dinnerware.* Monroe, La.: privately printed, 1976.

Riederer, LaHoma, Cynthia Bettinger, and Charles Bettinger. *Fiesta III: A Collector's Guide to Fiesta, Harlequin, and Riviera Dinnerware.* Monroe, La.: privately printed, 1977.

Sasicki, Richard and Josie Fania. *The Collector's Encyclopedia of Van Briggle Art Pottery: An Identification and Value Guide.* Paducha, Ky.: Schroeder Publishing, Collector Books, 1993.

Siemsen, Barbara. "Fiesta Ware: Cheery Dinnerware of Recent Memory." In *The Encyclopedia of Collectibles: Dogs to Fishing Tackle.* Alexandria, Va.: Time-Life Books, 1978.

Shapiro, Jacob, *Radiation Protection, A guide for Scientists and Physicians, 3rd Edition*, Harvard University Press, Cambridge, 1990

Index